THE
UNTOLD
HISTORY
OF
ISRAEL

D0950057

"Some of the evil of my tale may have been inherent in our circumstances."
—T. E. Lawrence, *The Seven Pillars of Wisdom*

THE UNTOLD HISTORY OF ISRAEL

Jacques Derogy and Hesi Carmel

Grove Press, Inc.
New York

First Edition 1979
First Printing 1979
ISBN: 0-394-50622-7   Grove Press ISBN: 0-8021-0186-0
Library of Congress Catalog Card Number: 78-74552

Library of Congress Cataloging in Publication Data

Derogy, Jacques.
  The untold history of Israel.

  Translation of Histoire secrète d'Israel, 1917-1977.
  1. Israel—Foreign relations.   2. Intelligence service—Israel.   I. Carmel, Hesi, joint author.
  II. Title.
DS119.6.D4613   327'.12'095694   78-74552
ISBN 0-394-50622-7

Manufactured in the United States of America

Distributed by Random House, Inc., New York

GROVE PRESS, INC., 196 West Houston Street, New York, N.Y. 10014

CONTENTS

INTRODUCTION

For Jacques Derogy and myself this is not just another book. We have invested ten years of research, two years of writing, and a lifetime of experience in this book. Our lives are closely linked in deed and observation to the modern state of Israel.

As a child growing up in Israel, I saw my father imprisoned by the British in 1943 for assisting illegal emigration. Later, in 1948, in Jaffa, I witnessed the War of Independence and, in June of that year, the Altalena Ship tragedy on the beach at Tel Aviv. As a young man I studied political science and journalism in Paris. From 1957 to 1960 I served in the Israeli Army as a representative to the Mixed Armistice Commission meeting with ranking Arab officers who now occupy key positions in their respective countries. Having joined the Foreign Office in 1960, I represented Israel for ten years in over 30 countries, from Paris to Leopoldville, Singapore to Tokyo. My last diplomatic post was as Consul General of Israel in Los Angeles.

For most of the past decade I have worked as a foreign correspondent and resident Middle East expert for the French weekly news magazine *l'Express,* after having served on the editorial board of the largest Israeli daily newspaper *Maariv.* In this capacity I have covered all the conflicts from the Suez Canal to the Litani River. I was the only reporter to cross the canal into Egypt in a rubber dinghy on the night of October 15, 1973, with General Sharon's paratroopers, in the operation that reversed the tide of the Kippur War.

Since 1973 I have reported on all the events of the Egyptian-Israeli peace negotiations, beginning with the meeting between Israeli General Yariv and Egyptian General Gamassi at the tent at Kilometer 101, on the road from Suez to Cairo, through the Geneva Conference and Camp David. I accompanied President Sadat on his historic visit to Jerusalem and traveled with Prime Minister Begin to Isamilia and Cairo. I covered the meeting between President Carter and Begin at the White House and Carter's peace mission to Cairo and Jerusalem, and I was present at the historic meeting of the signing of the peace treaty in Washington on March 26, 1979.

Jacques Derogy, my colleague and co-author, is the senior investigative reporter for *l'Express*. He has been a respected and much-quoted journalist for thirty years. He first began covering the Middle East in 1948 when he wrote a series of influential articles on the Exodus. He has returned to Israel many times since then and reported extensively on both the Six Day and Yom Kippur Wars. His book, *The Law of Return,* describing the Exodus, is generally considered in France to be the most authoritative and best-documented account of that period of Jewish history. He is also the author of *Israel, Face to Face With Death,* a highly acclaimed study of the traumatic shock of the Yom Kippur War and its effect on Israeli society.

We have interviewed scores of political leaders, intelligence chiefs, and professional analysts in Israel, Egypt, the United States, and France. We have sorted through literally tons of documents in archives in Jerusalem, Paris, and London. Many of these documents have only recently been released by Israel and the other nations involved in its recent past. Yet, in spite of the voluminous material on Israel that has been published or available, the fact remains that much of the material that is germane, indeed essential, to our understanding of that country's recent past has remained, up to this point, undisclosed.

A nation's history carries with it the power to illuminate or to confuse, to reward and to condemn; to condition the very way in which we perceive and understand the present. Nowhere is the historical interpretation of the past of more consequence than it is for Israel; yet nowhere has that historical interpretation been more obscured by incomplete or biased information. Her history is a story that has been told and retold, but the telling has been almost exclusively the prerogative of those who have a special interest in how the personalities and events will be judged. Because of this, vital slices of Israel's past have been conveniently forgotten. Our book deals with several elements of that hidden past.

To understand the history of Israel one must first understand the role that secrecy has played in the shaping of Israel's life and character. As early as the 19th century, Zionism, the Jewish national liberation movement, was born and developed in essentially clandestine conditions. This early-felt need for secrecy as a means to survival has only been compounded by the fact that, since its independence in 1948, Israel has been in an almost continuous state of war. This has added to the Israeli national mentality an element of external distrust, an emphasis on self-reliance, and an abiding fear that history could repeat itself. As a result, an overwhelming emphasis on the twin goals of security and national survival have dominated Israeli international politics, and to a great extent, its domestic concerns. Secrecy has become the mode of operation in its foreign policy and within its diplomatic agencies. The justification, of course, is that the stakes are too high and that the vital interests of the state require selective disclosure, false unanimity, and private agreements. Israel today presents a posture of close national unity to the rest of the world that masks internal divisions and disputes. In reality, the Israelis present far less of a monolithic block than is currently supposed.

Security and survival have also contributed to the unprecedented importance of the Israeli intelligence agencies. Israeli intelligence is reputed to be one of the best in the world, and in several areas it may well be the best. In the early years it played an important role in the exercise of power and the conduct of foreign affairs. At all times in Israel's struggle for peace, the Israeli intelligence has had a unique, policy-making role in the attempt to establish clandestine contact in the Arab world, in an effort to open new avenues for a peace-making process. Much of Israel's secret diplomacy has been carried out by intelligence agencies rather than regular foreign office channels.

Secrecy has also been an important factor in Israel's internal policies. A single political movement and a single political party—the Labor Party—has dominated the political scene for 44 years. While Israel is a working democracy, this control by one party has created a certain stagnation in the democratic process. The very people who made history were the guardians of their own secrets. This has obviously influenced what has been published and much of that has been seen through the eyes of the governing party itself.

To cover 60 years of Israel's history, we selected and re-examined 30 key episodes, each of which served to determine the growth and shape the character of the state of Israel. We followed certain pivotal events to their conclusion, to close, as it were, the cycles of history. We traced the course of events that took place in Israel 40 to 50 years ago and which continue to be of importance in current affairs; indeed, they often have a greater influence than events of the recent past. This is especially true when they are linked, as they must be, with that relatively small group of political leaders who continually reappear and reassert themselves and dominate to this day the course of events.

On the eve of a new era, following the historic signing of the peace treaty with Egypt, the long journey into Israel's history, the open and honest confrontation with the errors of the past, should increase our chances and hopes for a better future.

— Hesi Carmel

Book One

BEFORE

NILI 17:
THE FIRST NETWORK

Caesarea's Turkish *mudir* (governor) Ahmed Bek was feeding his pigeons in the courtyard of his residence when he first noticed the banded bird which had just alighted on the edge of the pigeon coop. He removed the band from the bird's foot. Although the coded message inside was indecipherable, the representative of the Ottoman administration had no doubt as to its destination: the British Expeditionary Corps intelligence center in Egypt. At last, on September 3, 1917, he had solid proof that an espionage network was operating in Palestine. Furthermore, it was, in all probability, being masterminded by the Jews. Ever since the Ottoman Empire had entered the war on the side of the Central Powers (Germany and Austria-Hungary) against the alliance formed by England, France, and Russia, the Jews were suspected of disloyalty toward the Turkish authorities in this backwater southern province.

Only too delighted with a discovery that confirmed his suspicions, the *mudir* relayed the intercepted information to the *kaimakam* (prefect) of Haifa. He, in turn, forwarded it for decoding to the German experts who worked under General Kress von Kressenstein, Jamal Pasha's chief of staff. Commander of the Turkish Army's IVth Corps, Jamal Pasha controlled Syria, Lebanon, and Palestine from his general headquarters in Damascus.

The investigations centered very quickly on the region of Zikhron Yaakov, where the first wave of Jewish immigration had come from Eastern Europe early in the 1880s to establish an agricultural colony whose survival and viability had been made possible through Baron Edmond de Rothschild's philanthropic assistance.

On September 5, by way of warning, the pigeon was brought to the entrance of the Hotel Graff. The old terror of pogroms, which the Jewish colonists believed they had left behind forever upon their departure from the czarist empire, resurfaced. And it did so all the more suddenly because they had since lost the habit of thinking about them despite the baitings, the requisitions, and the expulsion measures with which they had been periodically threatened ever since the Allies had blocked the Mediterranean.

A week later, a young Jew named Naaman Belkind was arrested. He had been betrayed by his Bedouin guide while trying to make his way to the British lines in the Sinai, thereby confirming the Turkish suspicions. The suspect belonged to a family from Zikhron Yaakov known for its Anglophilia and was caught carrying compromising documents at the time of his arrest. Curfew, house searches, and the taking of hostages followed in short order. Helped in their task by the German experts, the Turks worked feverishly to dismantle the spy ring and to get their hands on one of its agents, Joseph Lichansky, who had slipped through the meshes of their net.

Sukkot was approaching. Commemorating the time the Hebrews dwelled in tabernacles during their forty years of desert-wandering after the exodus from Egypt, the holiday is both a celebration of this time and a feast of the harvests; a time of joy, as opposed to the "Days of Awe" which preceded Yom Kippur. Using strips of cloth and branches of the local trees, the first settlers improvised huts in the courtyards of their dwellings and decorated them with flowers, lemons, citrons, and oranges from Jaffa: all symbols of the burgeoning new life in a setting suffused with the remembrances of ancient prophecies.

The young colonists of Zikhron Yaakov were dancing under the foliage when suddenly the fiddles fell silent. Someone had just come to warn that, on this first day of October, the *kaimakam*, at the head of a mounted troop, was about to descend upon the scene of their festivities. The young colonists immediately scattered to hide in the surrounding orchards. Only one of them, a gracious and gentle twenty-seven-year-old woman, standing at the door of her parents' home, seemed to have kept calm. Although she knew why the mounted troop was coming, she did her best to reassure her frightened companions. Sara Aaronsohn had been informed of the incident involving the carrier pigeon from the very first day. She had put its band on herself. Ever since then, she had been pinning her hopes on a miracle: the offensive of the Allied forces which had been stymied on the approaches to Gaza since spring, and which had, in the meantime, been put under the orders of a new commander-in-chief, General Edmund Allenby.

The village was surrounded in a matter of minutes. The *kaimakam* dismounted in front of the Aaronsohn home. He demanded to know Lichansky's whereabouts. Rumor had it that the spy was this young woman's lover. Sara said she knew nothing. The soldiers proceeded to search the house. Enraged at finding no trace of the fugitive, they grabbed Sara's old father, forced him to lie face down on the floor, tied him to two rifles and began to beat him on the soles of his feet with a club.

Sara tried to intercede in his favor. In instant retaliation, the Turkish horsemen grabbed her and dragged her off to a previously requisitioned house. Once there, when she repeatedly refused to divulge Lichansky's hiding place, they tied her to a door, whipped her, crushed her fingernails, and applied red-hot bricks to the soles of her feet and breasts. When this ordeal was over, they took her back to her house along the deserted street. They returned the next day and subjected her once more to their brutal torture.

It was a pattern that was to be continued every day for the next five days. During the course of her renewed ordeals, Sara learned from her torturers that the *kaimakam* had ordered her transfer to Nazareth along with the other members of the spy ring. She was, in fact, the guiding spirit. On the morning of October 5, before the horsemen returned to take her away, she found time to leave a note addressed to one of her companions:

> Tell my brothers to avenge me. Have no pity for these bandits—they have had none for me. I no longer have the strength to endure the suffering they are inflicting upon me. I prefer to put an end to it rather than have them torture me with their filthy hands. They want to send me to Damascus. There they will certainly hang me. Fortunately, I have a small revolver hidden away. I don't want them to violate my body. My suffering is unbearable when I see the beating they gave to Papa. But all their cruelties to us are in vain. We will not talk. Remember that we will have died as honorable people and that we will have confessed to nothing. Pay no attention to humiliation and slander. I have wanted only one thing: to better the fate of my people. Try to hide in the hills once the soldiers have left. Here they come . . . I can write no further . . .

The tormentors were back. Taking advantage of the fact that she was a woman, she asked to be allowed to go into the washroom to cleanse the blood from her body. She took this brief opportunity to remove the revolver from its hiding place and fired it into her mouth. For the next three days, Sara lay dying, completely paralyzed but with her consciousness intact. She died on the very last day of Sukkot—Simhat Torah, the day of Rejoicing in the Law.

Three weeks later, British troops broke through the Germano-Turkish lines on the Beersheba front and made their entry into Rishon-le-Zion, south of Tel Aviv. They occupied Gaza on November 7 and captured Jerusalem by December 9. Their victorious

advance had been made possible because of the information relayed to them by the intelligence network Sara's older brother,
Aaron Aaronsohn, had set up. It was identified by the British as
the "A Group." Aaron and Sara called their clandestine undertaking—the first Jewish spy ring in two thousand years—by the code
name *Nili*. It stood for the first letters in the Hebrew verse *"Neẓah
Yisrael lo Yeshakker"* ("The strength of Israel will not lie" 1 Samuel 15:29); thus rooting a very modern political and military act in
the centuries-old tradition of the Bible. This code name also served
as a password for the group's first agent, Lova Schneorsohn who,
along with Lichansky, had disembarked from the British cutter on
February 19, 1917, which was about to carry out a clandestine
shuttle between Atlit and Port Said.

Aaron Aaronsohn, founder and head of the Nili network, had
nothing of the adventurer in him. He was six years old when he
came to Zikhron Yaakov with his parents in 1882 from Rumania
to join the colonists already settled on the slopes of Mount Carmel
above the narrow coastal plain. Passionately fond of botany and
geology since childhood, he became an internationally known
agronomist. Very early on, young Aaron learned to recognize every stone, every flower, every blade of grass in the region. He
dreamed of restoring to it the fertility of biblical times. But not
once had it occurred to his father to make farmers out of his children Aaron, Alexander, Sara, and Rebecca. His father was typical
of the early settlers who had been supported by the Rothschild
foundations. The agricultural school near Jaffa, which opened in
1870, still another philanthropic work sponsored by Western Jews,
proved to be too rudimentary for Aaron, who, at the age of sixteen,
was already remarkably well self-taught. For this reason, the Baron Edmond—(May he live long! as his protégés at Zikhron Yaakov were wont to say)—saw to it that he was granted a scholarship
to study at the Institute of Montpellier and at the agricultural
college of Grignon in France, which was one of the best in the
world at that time.

Thus Aaron found himself in Paris in 1895 at the same time as
the Austrian-Jewish journalist Theodor Herzl and when the
French army captain, Alfred Dreyfus, was undergoing public deg-
radation, unjustly condemned for treason. The shock of this event
upset Herzl's high-society life and prompted him to formulate the
doctrine of Zionism. It also confirmed Aaronsohn in his goal: to
restore the fertility of Israel's soil while waiting for the day when
the Jewish people could reclaim their sovereignty in their ancient
homeland. Although they had never met, the dreams of these radi-

cally different Jews superimposed themselves: each of them, in his own way, was to play a predominant role in the transformation of this dream into a reality. Aaron did not need to join Herzl's Zionist organization to share its ideals. Upon his return to Palestine with his degree in agronomy, he wandered up and down this belt of desert land, studying its rarefied vegetation, its meager resources, and the means available to Jews to revive the country in the event that it be restored to them one day.

Without a doubt, only the imagination of half-starved nomadic tribes could have pictured it as a land flowing with milk and honey. But, after all, a caprice of history could conceivably become part of the series of improbabilities that left their imprint on this corridor where West meets East, where the density of historical happenings per square mile beats all records. Moses, King Solomon, the Queen of Sheba, Nebuchadnezzar, Titus, Saint Louis, Suleiman, Mohammed, Napoleon: all the trails intermingle here in a jumble of gods and myths, dreams and mirages, fallen empires and future accomplishments. For three millennia, this land of Canaan—called "Palestine" by the Romans, from the name of the Philistines who inhabited the coastal plain (Philistia)—has never ceased to resound with the clash of arms and the murmur of prayers. But it had ceased to have a national existence from the day when the Hebrews were reduced to the point of such powerlessness that they were no longer able to lead a life of an independent people.

Work, experiments, articles in specialized journals soon gave this young Palestinian Jew an audience in scientific circles. He had come across a plant which he baptized wild wheat. The promising aspects of this discovery prompted James Wilson, the American Secretary of Agriculture, to invite Aaron to the United States in 1909. At thirty-two, Aaron resembled a force of nature: he was blocky and broad-faced, clean-shaven, suntanned, thick-lipped and firm of jaw. The luxuriant growth of hair which dangled over his forehead and his blazing look gave him the appearance of a small red bull. Overnight, he became the darling of the leaders of the Jewish community in New York: Julian Mack, Henrietta Szold, Julius Rosenwald, Judah L. Magnes, and their colleagues. They were so taken by his charm that they agreed to finance an experimental agricultural station which he had dreamed of establishing in the Atlit gap, slightly north of Zikhron Yaakov, facing the rocky spur on which rise the remnants of the old Frankish castle built by the crusaders to protect their vessels.

In 1924 the brothers Jérôme and Jean Tharaud wrote in their

travelogue titled *Next Year in Jerusalem:* "From here, after one hundred years of struggle, the last of the Frankish knights embarked." (Zikhron Yaakov is described as a comfortable "tiny Switzerland" for "emigrants, ensconced in the bourgeois life" of Baron Rothschild's colonies.) "That was seven centuries ago and since then nothing had happened in this ruin save the fall of stones, the silent crumbling of things, the slow suffocation of the past under parasitic vegetation, and the minuscule events which from birth to death (birth and death included) fill the existence of some Bedouin families camped amid these rich remembrances with their goats and asses. Nothing until Sara's story." But the brothers Tharaud were greatly mistaken! Thanks to its position, Atlit was to make a decisive contribution to the region's development and to the first Jewish war of liberation since the revolt of Bar Kochba in A.D. 70.

Henrietta Szold became the secretary of the committee set up to support the experimental agricultural station. A rather touching bond of friendship developed between Atlit and New York while they exchanged accounting and activity reports. This station, placed under the protection of the American consulate in Palestine, was to play a role—albeit obscure—in Israel's contemporary history as important as that of Herzl's "Jewish State" on the political plane. Aaronsohn, however, was not a party man or a "joiner" of any official organization. He always considered himself an outsider in those organizations whose activities provided the framework within which the Palestinian Jews' social life took place, and whose developing community formed the Yishuv (the Jewish community of Palestine).

Out of a total population of 700,000 inhabitants in 1914, the Yishuv already numbered 100,000. There were 70,000 Orthodox Jews rooted in the holy towns, deeply immersed in the study of the Torah and the Talmud, keeping body and soul together thanks to the collections taken up for them in Europe and the United States and who, for that reason, were called the Jews of the Halukah (distribution); 30,000 colonists, descendants of the two immigration waves *(Aliyot):* the *Bilu* (the first settlers came from Russia. The name is an acronym of Isaiah 2:5: "O, house of Jacob, come ye, and let us walk in the light of the Lord.") of 1882, financed by the Rothschild bank's administrators, and the altogether different immigration of the Hehalutz, a Zionist Socialist pioneer movement, whose people were still loyal to the goals of the abortive 1905 revolution. Among them was a certain David Gryn, soon to be Ben-Gurion, as well as a few young pioneers who had come from Russia, in order to participate in the dual regeneration of their ancestral soil and of mankind. One-third of these Jewish newcomers lived in Jaffa. Two thousand of them built Tel Aviv.

Although it had no official representation, the Yishuv was already solidly organized within a triple frame: the political parties which essentially reflected the two main currents of the Labor movement—Marxist and reformist—rooted in Poland and Russia; the colonial cadres of the dozens of villages financed by Baron de Rothschild; and, finally, the local bureau of the World Zionist Organization established in Jaffa. Short-lived and precisely defined alliances alternated with relations marked by conflict among these three factions. In particular, the politicized workers were opposed to the individualistic views of those Jewish farmers and landed proprietors who employed Arab labor. They had established the first kibbutzim, highly original achievements halfway between the free commune and the agricultural cooperative; they had formed the first self-defense militia with a guard unit, *Hachomer,* whose volunteer members kept watch over the tranquillity of the lands under cultivation; they had also furnished the first mayors for urban areas. Their rivalry with the notables of other less organized and more liberal social categories was the root of the divergence that subsequently was to divide the Zionist movement into the laborite worker and the revisionist bourgeois currents.

Within the liaison committee that was formed among all of these organizations to resolve certain practical problems that cropped up in the Yishuv, Aaron Aaronsohn represented an element that was itself very heterogeneous: American Jewry. Because of his family background, he belonged to the aristocracy of the first immigrants whose bourgeois life-style exasperated the collectivists of the second generation. But his main disagreement with the directors of the new establishment lay in his assessment of the international situation.

When war broke out in 1914, Zionism, already divided, split up still further into several factions. The majority of the Jewish population lived exposed to the persecution running rampant within the immense territory of czarist Russia, allied with France and Britain; the Yishuv developed within the framework of the Ottoman Empire, and the majority of its population retained its nationality of origin. The Zionist International directorate was located in Berlin under the presidency of a German Jew, Otto Warburg, but its financial institutions were based in London. Of the six directors of the movement's World Executive, two were German, three were

Russians, and one was Austro-Hungarian. Of the twenty-six members of the permanent council, thirteen were German.

The division of feelings and loyalties among these various elements was just as pronounced as it was among the citizenries of the belligerent countries. Most of the leading American Jews, German in origin and culture, hoped for the defeat of a dishonored czarism. Furthermore, most of the Jews who fled the Russian Empire and its pogroms so abhorred the regime that they fervently wished for a Central Powers victory and awaited the first signs of the approaching revolution. They also feared that if the Zionist organization took a position in favor of the Allies, it would endanger the Yishuv and deliver it up, defenseless, to the Turkish authorities who soon rallied to the cause of the Central Powers. Then the Jews would risk undergoing the fate of the recently massacred Armenians.

Accordingly, in December 1914, the World Zionist Organization decided to observe a strict neutrality between the warring camps. In order to cope with these new circumstances, the Executive divided its seat among three offices: the Berlin office headed by Warburg; the London office headed by Nahum Sokolov (soon to be replaced by Chaim Weizmann, who enjoyed a great deal of prestige with the British authorities); and last, the office in Constantinople headed by Victor Jacobson. In addition, a delegation was established in Copenhagen, a neutral territory; and a provisional committee was installed in New York headed by the jurist Louis Brandeis, whose friend, President Woodrow Wilson, was to appoint him to the United States Supreme Court in 1916.

Even the leaders of the Palestinian Jewish Labor movement, Ben-Gurion and Ben-Zvi, who were able to escape Turkish reprisals against Russian nationals and find a haven in America, shared the sentiments of the majority of world Jewry. Only a handful of the Zionist leaders dared to stake everything on an Allied victory in order to achieve their goal: a liberating charter for the Yishuv. Chaim Weizmann was among this group. Born in Byelorussia but educated in German and Swiss universities with a doctorate from the University of Fribourg, he settled down in 1904 in Manchester after having taught chemistry in Geneva. Weizmann, an opponent of Herzl's at the first Zionist congresses, sharply protested against any consideration given to the British proposal that Uganda be designated as a country for settlement by the Jewish refugees. When, at the age of thirty, beginning his new career in Manchester under very trying circumstances (he could barely speak English), he could not have imagined the important political role that he would be called upon to play. Weizmann's research in acetone production helped the British army produce explosives. When war broke out, Weizmann had no idea that in Palestine another Jewish scientist also deemed it the duty of all Jewish scientists to support the Allied cause. On January 15, 1915, Aaron Aaronsohn was the first prominent member of the Yishuv to express this bold position to the Zionist Organization's delegate in Jaffa, Dr. Arthur Ruppin. Later Ruppin refused to sit next to "so dangerous a man," even after his own expulsion by the Turkish authorities.

From the time that Turkey sided with the Central Powers, Aaron, a true visionary, had the presentiment that a page in Jewish history was about to turn. His extended sojourns in the heart of the Ottoman Empire had revealed the inherent weakness of its structure to him: the war would accelerate and complete its ultimate collapse. An opportunity was being offered to the Jews: to liberate Palestine with the help of the conflict. This opportunity should be seized upon and fate given a helping hand.

Aaron had been strongly influenced in the choice of his pro-Allied sympathies by Absalom Feinberg, the fiancé of his younger sister, Rebecca. In 1913, Absalom became Aaron's assistant at the Atlit station. Born in October 1889, in Hedera, one of the Rothschild colonies, this Palestinian Jew descended from a family that formed part of the Israeli "Mayflower" legend. His maternal grandfather had been the principal founder of the Bilu group in the Ukraine. His paternal uncle, Joseph, had been one of the first ten immigrants to establish an agricultural colony, Rishon-le-Zion. All that he brought with him in the way of riches were the family jewels and the piano his wife had transported all the way from Odessa. The jewels served to finance Uncle Joseph's journey to Paris for the purpose of soliciting Baron Edmond's generous assistance. The banker's first reaction was to promptly show to the door this infidel who, though coming from the Holy Land, had shown up in his office without a yarmulke (skullcap). At the insistence of the Grand Rabbi of Paris, however, Rothschild consented to listen to the grievances of this odd Jew who had learned French while studying chemistry in Zurich. By the time Uncle Joseph was through with his recital, he managed to draw tears and a check of 1,000 gold francs from the baron. This gift enabled the Rishon colonists to sink their first wells in 1883.

The Feinbergs had taken into their home (the only stone house on the sole and dusty road in the village) a Bohemian poet, Naphtali Herz Imber, a kind of hippie before his time, who became enamored of the mistress of the house. One night, while she sat at the piano playing Smetana's *Moldau,* Imber began to improvise words to the Czech composer's majestically slow, sad and solemn music. After orchestration in 1890, it was to become the *Hatikvah,* Israel's future national anthem. Uncle Joseph's wife also gave birth to a daughter who was eventually to become a grande dame of Palestine: Dora Bloch.

Thus Dora's cousin, Absalom Feinberg, was following in the footsteps of distinguished antecedents when, in 1904—the year of Herzl's succession to the leadership of the Zionist Congress—he too went to Paris to complete his studies with a scholarship bequeathed to him by Baron Rothschild. But it is here that the similarities between Aaron Aaronsohn and Absalom Feinberg cease. A poet, Feinberg preferred to frequent literary salons rather than scientific laboratories. He earned the friendship of Charles Péguy and Jacques Maritain, both Catholic writers who saw in him an author full of promise.

The brothers Tharaud were later to write about him: "He was a restless soul, wholly oriented toward literature and philosophy, suffused with an undirected ardor."

Upon Feinberg's return to Palestine in 1909, after having dreamed of making his fortune in America, he became friends with the Aaronsohn family, whose eldest son had just returned from a fruitful trip to the United States. He captivated the two daughters in the family, Sara and Rebecca. The following year, he became Rebecca's fiancé and broke Sara's heart. In a fit of pique, she agreed to marry the first man who came along: Chaim Abraham, a crude Bulgarian Jew, who had come to look for a wife. In April 1914, he took her off to Constantinople where they settled down.

Meanwhile, little by little Absalom (now his future brother-in-law's assistant at the Atlit station) won Aaron over to his politics, inciting him to revolt against the Turkish yoke. In the manner of a Gabriele D'Annunzio, he tells him of the dream he has had ever since 1912: that a Jewish army would again find the ten tribes of Israel lost in the Arabian desert. He further convinced him that when war broke out, their future in Palestine would be dependent upon the victory of the Allied powers, regardless of the perils and threats it might entail.

Information gathered during the course of his agronomic missions make him sure of something else as well: Palestine was the weak spot in the Turkish military apparatus which could be quickly outflanked by a British landing on the coastline. Having taken over the region's military command since November 10, 1914, Jamal Pasha had launched his offensive across the Sinai in the direction of the Suez Canal. He commissioned Aaron, as an expert, to coordinate the struggle against the invasion of grasshoppers threatening to destroy his troops' provisions. On March 27 Jamal Pasha appointed him inspector-general of an antigrasshopper project in Syria, Lebanon, and Palestine; an assignment which gave Aaron great freedom of movement throughout the three countries. In order to accomplish this mission which also afforded him the best possible cover for his intelligence gathering, Aaronsohn arranged to have Absalom Feinberg (who had remained behind at the Atlit station) officially appointed as his assistant. The two friends met again at the beginning of April at the Palace Hotel in Jerusalem.

It was here, for the first time, that they pondered the means for breaking the stranglehold blockade of the Mediterranean which threatened to isolate Palestine. They also discussed ways of making the British understand that their landing was imperative and could be carried out under highly favorable conditions. But while they were poring over the maps of the Atlit region, elaborating a plan of logistical support to ensure the success of such an operation, the British decided to attack the Turks not in Palestine—they had been content to remain on the defensive on that front since February 3 around the approaches to the Suez Canal—but at the very gates of Constantinople. The Franco-British expeditionary troops that had landed at Gallipoli suffered a stinging defeat in the battle for the conquest of the Dardanelles.

All the more reason for Aaron and Absalom to cling stubbornly to their plan. This time they gave it a concrete dimension: the relay of enough hard and exact intelligence to the British to persuade them of their strategic error. Thus it happened that they involved their families and friends in the formation of an intelligence network. From June 1915 to November 1917, a real spy novel, mingling love and adventure, unfolded around the windmill of the Atlit agricultural station. It became the center of the Nili network which came to a tragic end at the time of the death and, later, the oblivion of its heroes.

On July 8, 1915, provided with false papers, Aaronsohn's younger brother Alexander left Haifa for Cairo aboard an American passenger ship bound for New York. He was accompanied by his sister Rebecca, Absalom's fiancée, whom Aaron had decided to send to the United States for safety. Alexander himself remained in the Egyptian port of call, Cairo, and tried to establish the first contact with the British secret services, but the officer who received him did not take him seriously.

On September 6, Absalom took advantage of the last American

ship to land in Haifa in order to stow away and disembark in Alexandria. Once there, he managed to convince Lieutenant Leonard Woolley, an archaeologist occupying a high post in the general staff's intelligence service and a close friend of T. E. Lawrence. Together they worked out a code for the establishment of a spy network. On November 8, a British warship, the *Saint-Anne,* cruising at night 50 meters off the promontory of Atlit, brought back Absalom, who was dropped ashore by a launch. He now had his code and the messages. The *Saint-Anne* would return in a few weeks to pick up the answers.

On December 16, the network received a reinforcement: Sara had jilted her boorish husband and her unhappy home in Constantinople and returned to the family warmth in Zikhron Yaakov. She fell in love all over again with Absalom.

The launch of the *Saint-Anne* made only one fugitive appearance on the strand, on March 13, 1916. But because no signals had been agreed upon, its sailor found nobody there. He left a laconic message on the sands: "We'll be back."

But no one came back. Woolley was taken prisoner by the Turks in Alexandretta (now Iskenderun, Turkey) during the month of May. The information gathered by the network during the entire year of 1916 concerning train timetables, troop concentrations, the names and profile sketches of each unit's officers, coastal surveillance, the location of arms depots and fortifications could not be relayed.

Aaron decided to act on his own to reestablish the connection. Time was pressing. The year 1916 was turning catastrophic for the Yishuv: famine, abusive treatment, persecutions. The rescue of the 80,000 Jews in Palestine became a matter of great urgency.

Aaron's success in stemming the grasshopper invasion won him Jamal Pasha's authorization to go to Berlin to do research. He arrived there on August 21, 1916, after entrusting Sara and Absalom with the responsibility for running the spy ring and the Atlit station. From Berlin he succeeded in getting to Copenhagen where, with the help of the British Embassy, he arranged for his departure for London aboard a passenger ship of the Copenhagen-New York line. He traveled with the American judge, Louis Brandeis, through whom he submitted an appeal to the American Jewish community to rally to the British cause. Off the English coast, the harbor police boarded the ship and made a big show of arresting him as a stowaway. Thus Aaronsohn found himself in London on October 24. Weizmann was beginning to personally participate in the British war effort by exchanging explosives technology for promises about the future status of Palestine. Upon being offered a decoration and a check in reward for his services, Weizmann replied to Lloyd George, the new Minister of War: "I desire nothing for myself. But I would like you to do something for my people."

Aaronsohn, newly arrived in London, literally fascinated the deputy head of Scotland Yard, Sir Basil Thomson. He also managed to obtain a hearing with the Middle East Department of the Ministry. Here he met the future High Commissioner, Sir Mark Sykes.

Aaron obtained a safe-conduct for Egypt. En route, on December 7, he learned of the auspicious nomination of Lloyd George to the head of the British government. The new prime minister immediately gave the necessary orders for the preparation of an offensive in Palestine and of an Arab revolt against the Turks in Hedjaz, instigated by Lieutenant T. E. Lawrence.

Aaron disembarked at Port Said on December 12, but lost a month's time finding the head of the clandestine services of the Cairo general headquarters. Meanwhile, Absalom champed at the bit. After six months without news from Aaron, he decided to cross the Sinai and try to resume contact with Woolley who he thought was in Egypt. He paid no attention to Sara's entreaties but asked another of the network's pillars, Joseph Lichansky, to accompany him in his attempt. Lichansky was a member of the Hachomer but was not highly thought of by the "guardian" elite because he was a farmer's son, a dandy, and a womanizer, a quality to which Sara did not seem to be altogether insensitive.

On January 13, 1917, they set out by camel, disguised as Bedouins, and made their way to the Rafah gap, south of the Gaza strip, without arousing suspicion. But Lichansky arrived alone, wounded, at the approaches to El Arish, where he was picked up with three bullets in his body by an Australian patrol and transported to the Port Said hospital on January 25. According to his story, a brawl had pitted their guide against the Bedouins of another tribe who had fired upon them. Absalom, mortally wounded, had been thrown from his mount, but Lichansky managed to stay in the saddle and escape. There were allegedly no witnesses to these events, and later attempts to find traces of Absalom were in vain. There was even a rumor that Lichansky supposedly took advantage of an exchange of gunfire to rid himself of his rival for Sara's affections. Not until July 1967, after the Six-Day War, were Absalom's remains found and identified thanks to an amputated forefinger. A date tree had sprouted from a pit of one of the dried dates he had taken along with him, its roots allegedly entwined around his bones. The Bedouins had even given it a name: The Jew's Date Tree.

Learning that one of the network's members had been brought in wounded from the desert, Aaron Aaronsohn rushed to the Port Said hospital. Contact with the British services was at last reestablished as a result of Absalom's sacrifice. As early as January 27, Aaron obtained permission to proceed to the waters directly off Atlit aboard a French torpedo boat, the *Arbalète*. At midnight, five Jewish and Arab messengers were lowered into a rowboat which took them within swimming distance of the shore. They had money and messages for Sara.

It was agreed that from then on liaison would be maintained by sea: a small boat would assure a clandestine shuttle service between Port Said, Atlit, and Beirut on behalf of the British secret services. It would take advantage of moonless nights to let off agents and messengers and to take on endangered network members.

On February 19, the *Managem* which the Jews have dubbed the *Menachem* (the Consoler) arrived in view of the Atlit station where Sara was on the lookout, setting laundry out to dry. Lova Schneorsohn, the liaison agent, was aboard the dinghy launched by the *Managem*, escorting Lichansky to the coast to replace Absalom at Sara's side. Lova had invented the password "Nili," and from then on it was through him that the hopeful messages were passed announcing future British operations and the intelligence that the 200 network members gathered as they traveled across the region from Damascus to Beersheba under the cover of a war against the grasshoppers. These intelligence reports were decisive for the success of the offensive launched in March 1917 against the Germano-Turkish lines on the north coast of the Sinai. British troops seized Khan Yunis, but on March 26, their attack broke down before reaching Gaza. Aaronsohn was furious since he himself had relayed to the general staff the information that the enemy's most vulnerable point was located on the road to Beersheba, in the center of the Negev—and not the Gaza coastline which was more easily defended. He had discussed the matter at great length with Colonel Graves of the I.B. (Intelligence Branch-Army) for whom he had worked out a detailed tactical evaluation. At the Arab Bureau (political intelligence), he had made the acquaintance, the month before, of Lieutenant T. E. Lawrence, charged with recruiting agents from among the Bedouin tribes.

In his personal diary, Aaronsohn wrote: "A new apparition at the Arab Bureau. A young lieutenant by the name of Lawrence, permeated with knowledge about Palestine but a terrible snob."

As the head of the A Group, Aaronsohn was assigned the job of compiling a *Palestine Handbook:* a manual for the use of those in charge of military operations in the region. He also alerted international public opinion—above all, American—about renewed Turkish acts of violence perpetrated against the Yishuv since the beginning of the British offensive, despite the manifestations of loyalty on the part of its institutions.

On March 28, Jamal Pasha ordered the evacuation of all Jews living in Jaffa and Tel Aviv under the pretext of protecting them from the dangers of combat operations. Tel Aviv's mayor, Meir Dizengoff, protested on the grounds that non-Jews were being allowed to remain; he barely managed to obtain the maintenance of a Jewish guard to protect homes against looting and to irrigate the gardens. But 9,000 civilians were forced to take the road of exodus to the north, from Petah Tikva to Haifa. Dizengoff formed a committee to provide assistance to the refugees and did not hesitate to take advantage of the clandestine shuttle service of the *Managem* and the Nili courier for the delivery of provisions and gold collected in the United States in response to Aaronsohn's appeal.

The historian Renée Neher-Bernheim wrote later: "The Nili is no longer simply an intelligence network. It has become a channel through which provisions, medicine and funds are brought to a population in distress and to which the survivors will be greatly indebted without always being aware of their indebtedness." On the contrary, the Yishuv's institutions blamed the Nili for the misfortunes descending upon the Jews of Palestine. Sara was quite aware of the mounting hostility surrounding her house and the Atlit station. "You must know," she wrote to Aaron, "that we are endangering many heads, not just our own, but those of the entire population." And as her brother had sent her a few bars of soap and other toiletries via the launch from the *Managem,* she added: "It is not for such frivolities that our people risk their lives. Rather send me a revolver."

On April 15, Sara boarded the launch along with Lichansky in order to give Aaron a better understanding of the situation. She left the network in the hands of one of Absalom's cousins, Naaman Belkind. The British army in effect stood before Gaza, despite her messages which portrayed the Turkish army as demoralized and incapable of bearing the brunt of an attack.

In April and May, 1917, the Hachomer's central committee which had been officially dissolved as an auxiliary police unit since the beginning of the hostilities, met secretly to decide to put an end to Nili's spying activities—even if on this occasion it entailed giving assistance to the Ottoman authorities.

On June 15, when Lichansky returned to Atlit aboard the *Managem*, Sara was with him; she had refused to remain in Cairo with Aaron although the two men implored her to do so. General Allenby had just taken over the command of the expeditionary corps and had decided to follow Aaron's advice concerning the preparation of his autumn offensive. Sara and Lichansky brought back several carrier pigeons with them in order to ensure a faster and more regular liaison. On July 6, they released the pigeons for the first time; only one of the five birds arrived safely. On August 2, Allenby gave the *Managem* authorization to take aboard, in the waters off Atlit, two delegates from the Yishuv entrusted with resuming contact with the World Zionist Organization whose leaders had swung over to the Allied side since America's entry into the war on April 6, 1917.

On August 14, Sara and Lichansky transmitted an intelligence item of capital importance: the Turks had only 35,000 men available in Palestine. Two days before, Aaron had talked once more with Lawrence, who was fanning the flames of the Hedjaz revolt. His diary notes: "A conversation devoid of feeling with Captain Lawrence. He has the nature of a missionary and detests us cordially. I had the impression of listening to a Prussian anti-Semite speaking English."

According to the sole—and unconfirmed—testimony from the Aaronsohn family's Arab driver, Abu Farid, Lawrence allegedly came to Atlit on one of the *Managem*'s shuttle trips in order to make Sara's acquaintance.

On August 30, a carrier pigeon brought the first operational message from the Nili: "A deserter whom we are hiding at the station is in possession of intelligence of the highest importance. Send the *Managem* for September 10th." The boat did not arrive until September 21. It took aboard both the deserter and a real SOS from Sara to her brother: "The British must get here before the 27th. Who knows whether they will still find me? Our own Jews are causing us terrible anxieties. They are all angry and frightened by our activities. It is even possible that they are ready to hand us over to Jamal. For pity's sake, hurry, come, don't abandon us."

Sara knew that one of her pigeons had landed in the *mudir* of Caesarea's courtyard on September 3. She also knew that on September 13, Naaman Belkind had been caught with documents compromising to the network. Having no confidence in Joseph Lichansky of whose flashy display, conspicuous elegance, retinue, and life-style at the Hotel Fast in Jerusalem he did not approve, Belkind had decided to make his way to the British lines to discuss the situation with Aaron and his cousin Absalom whom he believed still alive since Sara and Joseph had hidden the news of his death from him. He took a Bedouin guide who had rallied to Lawrence of Arabia's call to revolt. But the guide betrayed him, and he was arrested en route by a Turkish patrol.

Aaron was ignorant of all of these details because he did not receive his sister's last message. After an interview on September 2 with the High Commissioner, Sir Reginald Wingate, who informed him of his government's decision "to support the national aspirations of the Jewish People," he left for London on September 13. He wanted to convince Weizmann to support the activities of the Nili network. In the meantime, since July, Weizmann had been engaged in negotiating a plan for a charter for Palestine between the British Minister of Foreign Affairs, Lord Arthur James Balfour, and the head of the English branch of the Rothschild family, Lord Lionel. Aaron had left the responsibility of his post in Cairo to his younger brother, Alexander, who was directly under the orders of Colonel Meinerzhagen, head of the intelligence section of Allenby's general staff.

Later, this high-ranking officer acknowledged in his memoirs: "I have employed some fifteen blond and blue-eyed Palestinians. These agents are as modest as they are bold." And, on a parallel with Lawrence's long march across the Arabian desert, they were to facilitate the Allied conquest of Palestine, Syria, and Lebanon.

On October 2, Aaronsohn finally met with Weizmann in London and, on October 6, he persuaded the Zionist leader to send a telegram of support addressed to the network's leaders. But it was too late. The next day, on October 7, as Sara lay dying, the Hachomer decided to deliver the final blow to the decimated spy ring by commissioning one of its members, Shabtai Ehrlich, to liquidate Joseph Lichansky and deliver his body to the Turks. Together with another Hachomer guard, Ehrlich won over the fugitive's confidence and offered to help him get safely to Metulla, his native village in Upper Galilee. On the way there, they shot Lichansky in the back. Wounded, he managed to escape, but no one would agree to offer him shelter. There was a price on his head. The Hachomer guard even went so far as to offer a reward for his capture. The fleeing spy hid in an orange grove belonging to a woman farmer, Mme Pascal, also a member of the Nili, but he was at the end of his rope. Near exhaustion, he surrendered to the Turks who were retreating before the British advance. Taken to the prison in Damascus, he again met Naaman Belkind and Belkind's younger brother, Eytan, sixteen, who were confined in the jail's death row.

The Turks abandoned the holy city of Jerusalem to General Allenby on the first night of Hannukah, the feast commemorating the conquest of Jerusalem by the Maccabees. General Clayton, one of Lawrence's patrons, confided later that "We owe the lives of 30,000 soldiers to the Nili." On December 16, the seventh day of Hannukah, Naaman Belkind and Joseph Lichansky were hanged in a public square in Damascus. Before his execution, Naaman had asked his younger brother, who had been pardoned, to bring his remains back to Rishon-le-Zion. As for Joseph, he cried out twice before his death: "Nili! Nili!"

"The Nili," wrote Renée Neher-Bernheim, "this fearless enterprise accomplished by a handful of novices exclusively driven by love for their people, is one of the most amazing and most moving wonders in the Jewish history of the day."

In the meantime, a letter dated November 2, from Lord Balfour to Lord Rothschild, made the Weizmann-inspired declaration public:

> His Majesty's Government views with favor the establishment in Palestine of a national home for the Jewish people, and will use their best endeavours to facilitate the achievement of this object, it being clearly understood that nothing shall be done which may prejudice the civil and religious rights of existing non-Jewish communities in Palestine, or the rights and political status enjoyed by Jews in any other country.

Aaron Aaronsohn was sent to the United States on the double recommendation of Mark Sykes and Weizmann to incite the Americans to intensify their war efforts. He remained there until the end of the hostilities in November 1918, while his brother Alexander occupied his place in Allenby's triumphal march on Aleppo. Upon his return, Weizmann appointed him adviser to the Zionist delegation incorporated within the British delegation to the Paris Peace Conference at the beginning of 1919. Aaronsohn hadn't been a docile agent in Cairo any more than he was an accommodating partner at the negotiations that were just beginning over the division of what was left of the Ottoman Empire. Nevertheless, he made friends in the British Parliament and government as well as with all the members of the delegation: Colonel House, President

Wilson's adviser; William Bullitt, head of the American delegation; Jan Masaryk, head of the Czech delegation; and even Colonel Lawrence, with whom he organized the second Weizmann-Faisal meeting from which was to issue, on January 3, 1919, an agreement of mutual recognition.

History moves swiftly. The first quarter of the twentieth century seems as remote as the era of the Napoleonic campaigns. Nevertheless, it is not too long ago that, in the palaces of London and Paris, wing-collared diplomats haggled in the name of king or republic over a piece of Africa in exchange for a piece of Asia; these diligent subordinates divided the world with ruler and square; while, over there, at the threshold of the Empire, functionaries in white helmets nailed under the bougainvillaeas the regulations in force in the metropolis. As remote as it seems to us now, these yesterdays carried the seeds of our today.

On behalf of his decimated network, Aaronsohn intervened in all these debates with a view to a Judeo-Arab arrangement that would have undoubtedly changed the face of Palestine. He agreed to serve as an intermediary for the Italian delegation, transmitting a secret memorandum on the question of Trieste to the Americans. He applied pressure on the Poles to put an end to the pogroms through the mediation of his friend Louis Strauss, secretary to Herbert Hoover upon whom American assistance to Europe depended. He shuttled between London and Paris in order to wrest from the imperial powers the price of the Nili's sacrifice and of the services rendered to the victorious cause.

On May 15, 1919, Aaronsohn boarded a mail plane, a DH-4 piloted by Commander A. B. Jefferson to join the delegation in Paris. Before his departure, Weizmann had given him a carton of cigarettes and jokingly said, "Be careful, don't get them wet." Vera, the Zionist leader's wife, had accompanied Aaronsohn to the airfield in the hope of getting on the plane with him, but the English did not permit women aboard. Several minutes later, the plane crashed and sank in the English Channel off the coast of France. The Boulogne fisherman who recovered the mailbags reported hearing an explosion. The wreckage disappeared forever.

Planned or not, Aaronsohn's disappearance has not been without consequences. The head of the Nili network had roots in Palestine and was one of the rare Jewish notables to enjoy good relations with the Arabs whose language he spoke. He had recruited the agents for his network in both communities. His proposals for an entente between the two nationalisms—symbolized by the Faisal-Weizmann agreement—were more realistic than those of the revolutionary settlers who had come from Poland and Russia and whose customs and ideology shocked their Arab neighbors.

Aaronsohn threatened the leadership of the Anglophile Weizmann, and Britain risked being deprived of its role of arbiter between the two Palestinian communities.His death thus halted the process of settlement which would have rendered the British role unnecessary. It also facilitated Churchill's unilateral decision to artificially sever Trans-Jordan from mandated territory in order to offer it to the Emir Abdullah, thus inaugurating a policy of alternately and proportionally playing up both the Jews and Arabs of Palestine. This divisiveness was to maintain the rule of a mandatory power at the gates of the Orient.

It also left the field free to the Zionist Socialists and their mystique of "Hebrew labor" by depriving of their leadership the independent, liberal-thinking Jewish farmers who were opposed to the pioneer theories of the new immigrants.

Two years after Aaronsohn's disappearance, Ben-Gurion established the Histadrut—the General Federation of Labor—the base of laborite power confronting the revisionist trend's rise to power. This rise was to be shattered twelve years later by a crime that has remained as enigmatic as Aaron Aaronsohn's accidental disappearance: the assassination of the political leader of the Jewish Agency, established in 1929 to officially represent the Yishuv.

2

MURDER ON THE BEACH

In the days of the British Mandate in Palestine, the terrace of the Kete Dan Hotel was a favored meeting place for the elite of Tel Aviv—for officers of the administration, newspaper correspondents, important members of the Jewish Agency, the occasional businessman or adventurer dazzled by visions of the Near East. But on the eves of the Sabbath there were as few diners there as there were moving vehicles in the streets of the Jewish city.

On the evening of Friday, June 16, 1933, a man and a woman were sitting on the practically deserted restaurant terrace, just finishing dinner. The man, well-groomed, in his thirties, wore thick eyeglasses and looked like a sensitive ascetic. The woman, a slim, languid-looking brunette, seemed to be totally fascinated by his conversation. It seemed obvious that these two had not been together for some time. They were not unfamiliar to the personnel of the restaurant which was Tel Aviv's most select at the time. "Doctor" Chaim Arlosoroff was in charge of the political department of the Jewish Agency, the organization designed to represent the Jewish community (the Yishuv) in Palestine. In a way, he was the Foreign Minister of the unborn State of Israel.

Having returned three days before from a two-month stay in Germany where the leader of the National Socialist Party, Adolf Hitler, had just assumed the office of Chancellor, Arlosoroff was telling his wife Sima about his reunions in Berlin with friends from school and university days, and also about his attempts to meet with a childhood friend, Magda Friedlander, now Magda Goebbels, the wife of the new regime's Propaganda Minister, Dr. Joseph Goebbels.

With the approach of summer, the weather was already a little humid. After dinner the couple left the restaurant terrace for the esplanade running along the seaside, to take a walk on the already shadowed beach. They walked toward the Islamic cemetery, a site presently occupied by the Tel Aviv Hilton. After a half hour or so, Sima said that she had noticed two men—one tall, one short—who seemed to be following them. Ever since her husband's political rise, Sima had expressed fear of being followed and spied upon;

her apprehension had not been relieved by the guard placed in front of their home in Jerusalem by the Haganah, the Jewish self-defense militia. Arlosoroff had done his best to reassure her: "With the Jews, there's nothing to fear."

The two men walking behind them had passed them at one point, and were now retracing their steps. It will never be known why Sima was walking a few meters ahead of Chaim, as if the couple had had one of their quarrels—quarrels which were frequent since the very beginning of their marriage in 1926. When Chaim caught up with his wife, one of the two men, now abreast of him, shone a flashlight directly into his face and asked, in Hebrew: "What time is it?"

Arlosoroff, a little taken aback, moved his hand toward his watch pocket. The stranger was faster on the draw. He pulled out a handgun. A single shot rang out, fired at very close range. Chaim collapsed on the sand. Sima started screaming. Two passersby, Moshe Weiser and Yaakov Zlibanski, hurried to her aid:

"They've shot Dr. Arlosoroff," she told them. "I'm his wife. Help me carry him to the road."

"Let us carry him," Weiser replied. "You hurry and alert the police."

Sima ran back to the Kete Dan, arriving there, totally out of breath, at about 10:30 P.M.

"Man hat den Chaim erschossen (They've shot Chaim!)" she shouted in German—her native language.

The two helpers carried Arlosoroff back to the road across the dunes and then had to wait twenty minutes for an automobile to drive by—few drivers broke the Sabbath laws. They had trouble convincing its driver to take the wounded man.

"What happened to you here?"

"Hurry, drive us to the Hadassah Hospital."

"But what happened?"

"Not now, not now," Arlosoroff kept repeating in a muffled voice.

The car sped to the Hadassah Hospital. But more than an hour had passed before the four physicians hastily called in performed surgery on the wounded man. The news of an attempt on the young Jewish leader's life spread rapidly through the city. Half a dozen close associates, among them his sister, his brother-in-law, the Mayor of Tel Aviv, Meir Dizengoff, and one of the members of the executive branch of the Jewish Agency, Eliezer Kaplan, hurried to his bedside.

"Look what they've done to me," Arlosoroff said to Dizengoff before being wheeled into the operating room.

"Do you know who shot you?" he was asked by a Palestinian police inspector, Zelig Kampf, later police chief of Tel Aviv.

"No," Arlosoroff whispered. "Someone blinded me with a flashlight, and then they shot me."

A few minutes later, the wounded man lost consciousness. Surgical efforts proved too late. At 12:45 A.M., the surgeons admitted defeat.

Sima Arlosoroff arrived at the hospital only after her husband's death. She had been detained at the Kete Dan since 10:30 P.M. by two police officers, Shmuel Shermeister and David Priman, who, although not on duty, had offered to take down her deposition in the presence of two witnesses, Shamai Kuperstein and the hotel's owner, Kete Dan. Instead of asking them to take her to the hospital as quickly as possible to find out about her wounded husband, she graciously agreed to answer their questions and even to participate in a reconstruction of the shooting on the beach. Sima gave them a vague description of the two attackers—a tall man and a short one—and specified that they were Eastern types.

"What do you mean by Eastern types?" Shermeister asked her. "Yemenite? Spanish?"

"No, no, they were Arabs," she replied.

The detective called Officer Stafford of the British criminal police and told him that Arlosoroff had been wounded by Arabs on the beach at Tel Aviv. His message, delivered in front of Sima and other people in the hotel lobby, was entered in the logbook of the commissariat at Jaffa. Mysteriously, the page containing Shermeister's deposition disappeared later when Sima Arlosoroff completely retracted her initial statements.

That same evening, after the improvised reconstruction of the crime, Sima Arlosoroff repeated her statements to the two men who took her on the belated trip to the hospital: Yehoshua Gordon, liaison officer for the Jewish Agency and the British police in security matters, and Bendy Gutt, a motorist parked in front of the Kete Dan: "I'm one hundred percent sure that the attackers were Arabs."

According to the log kept by the Jaffa police, five Arab suspects were apprehended the next morning, Saturday, June 17. On that same morning, several leaders of the Haganah gathered at the home of one of them, Eliahu Golomb, on the Boulevard Rothschild in Tel Aviv. During the night, Golomb had asked David

Tidhar, the only private detective operating at that time, to use his Arab contacts to come up with leads on the identity of the assassins, still thought to have been Arabs. No new factors had entered the situation when Golomb called him back at noon, in the middle of that meeting, to modify that point of view. It thus seems that it was this meeting that generated the notion of an eventual politicization of Arlosoroff's death: the possibility of exploiting the assassination of the Jewish Agency's political leader to eliminate the opponents of the Zionist World Federation's labor faction . . .

Chaim Arlosoroff had become the principal target of the ultranationalist Jews. He was the incarnation of the majority of moderate Zionists, both mystical and practical, who envisaged a progressive colonization of Palestinian soil, acre by acre, "*dunam* by *dunam*," performed while submitting to the tutelage of the mandatory authorities. This tendency, shared by liberals like Chaim Weizmann and socialists like Ben-Gurion, was opposed, after Theodor Herzl's death in 1905, by the "politicals" who, like Vladimir Ze'ev Jabotinsky, gave priority to the creation of structures leading to statehood—even in opposition to the British administration—"by steel and by fire."

Born in 1880 in Odessa to a bourgeois family, Jabotinsky, the child prodigy of Russian Zionism, conformed no more than Herzl to the traditional prototype of the East European Jew. Infatuated with poetry and literature, nourished by the works of Pushkin, Turgenev, and Tolstoy rather than by Holy Writ, fluent in six languages in addition to Yiddish and Hebrew, he had made Italy, where he finished graduate studies begun in Switzerland, his second homeland. His discovery of pogroms, upon his return to Odessa, was a rude awakening; he took an active part in the organization of Jewish self-defense and was elected a delegate to Zionist conferences, where his oratorical eloquence, his gifts as a professional agitator, and his great cultural erudition rapidly made him one of the leaders of the movement.

World War I uprooted Jabotinsky, his family, his friends, and it created a split in Zionism. The brilliant cosmopolitan intellectual soon assumed a role like Trotsky's: learning that Turkey had entered the war as an ally of Germany and Austia-Hungary, he immediately envisaged the creation of a Jewish army that would fight on the Allied side, with its own insignia and flag, to put an end to Turkish suzerainty in Palestine and to assert the rights of the Jewish people after the dismemberment of the Ottoman Empire.

While the great majority of Jews lived under the rule of the Czar, and the Yishuv was under Turkish domination, the Zionist

Federation had its headquarters in Berlin and a German president, and the movement's financial institutions were located in London . . .

Jabotinsky hurried to Alexandria, where the British authorized him to create a transportation unit—the Zion Mule Corps—which saw action at Gallipoli during the diversionary Dardanelles offensive, under the command of the Russian army's only Jewish officer, Joseph Trumpeldor, the old hero of the Russo-Japanese War. "Jabo" kept on pressing London to raise a regiment of Jewish volunteers, and after the Balfour Declaration, he succeeded.

On February 2, 1918, the first armed Jewish battalion since A.D. 135 marched through the City of London and Whitechapel under the emblem of the Star of David. On February 4, the 39th regiment of Royal Fusiliers embarked for Palestine, via France, Italy, and Egypt; Jabotinsky served as second lieutenant. The "Jewish Legion" saw action on the Shechem front, in the Jordan valley, and at Jericho with such bravery that it amazed General Allenby, who had been skeptical of the military worth of "small tailors from Whitechapel." At the end of the war, these Jewish units consisted of three battalions of over 5,000 men, roughly a third of these from Palestine, one-third from Great Britain, and the rest from the United States and Canada. "Jabo" hoped that they would form the nucleus for a defense force for the Jewish National Home.

He had seen himself as a Jewish Garibaldi, liberating Palestine at the head of Jews bearing arms, in an adventurous, Romantic fashion. He ended up believing in the value of military training and discipline; to his mind, these were absolutely necessary for the redemption of a people who had been unable to defend itself for so many centuries. Despite his own disappointments and hardships, he had found a certain personal satisfaction: "If this is militarism," he wrote, "we should be proud of it. No need to be afraid of that fine Latin word."

But the British authorities however did not listen to him. They decided to disband all the Jewish units incorporated in their forces after their demobilization in 1920. Appointed political commissioner to the Zionist commission that served as a liaison unit with the military authorities between the armistice and the beginning of the British Mandate in Palestine, from the very beginning "Jabo" was frustrated by the reluctances of the mandatory power and accused Weizmann of being too accommodating in his negotiations concerning the management of the National Home. When the first Arab attacks against the Jewish population of Jerusalem occurred in April 1920, he took command of the clandestinely founded self-defense militia of the city, the Haganah. He was arrested and sentenced to fifteen years in prison, but was released the following year in the context of the amnesty granted to the Arab rioters.

Admitted to the Zionist executive arm, in March 1921, "Jabo" distanced himself from the Zionist Labor faction, whose members were not sure that the establishment of an official Jewish defense force would not seem like a provocation directed against the Arabs. In January 1923, he resigned in protest against Weizmann's acceptance of the first White Book published by the British government that recommended a limitation of Jewish immigration to Palestine "to the country's capacity of absorption." He accused the executive leaders of reverting, to the point of compromise, to the prewar "practical Zionism," and did not hesitate to proclaim himself a total supporter of the ideals of "political Zionism" as set forth in Herzl's doctrine.

During a propaganda tour that took him to Riga, Latvia, Jabotinsky created the Betar, a youth movement to prepare for a Zionist revival under the label of "revisionism." It was not a question of revising Zionism itself, but rather the politics of its leaders. In April 1925, he rallied his supporters to the Taverne du Panthéon in Paris to found the Union of Revisionist Zionists, a party whose efforts would be directed toward the establishment of a state with a Jewish majority on both banks of the Jordan. Within the worldwide organization, the new party represented a faction opposed to three other competitors for the leadership of the movement: the "general Zionists," led by Chaim Weizmann; the Labor faction; and the "Mizrahi," the religious faction.

The Jewish Agency provided for in Article 4 of the Mandate was not actually established until August 1929, when a constituent assembly met in Zurich. The preceding year, the Palestinian revisionists had come out in favor of secession. Their principal theorist, Abba Achimeir, made no bones about the politics of his group: he wanted to break away from the spirit of liberalism and democracy which, according to him, had stripped Zionism of its original ideology. An admirer of Mussolini, in whom he saw the century's greatest political genius, Achimeir hailed the development of fascism as "the great national movement that will save Europe from its impotent parliaments and from the abominable dictatorship of the Soviets." He assumed the leadership of a small group of activists calling themselves the Biryonim, after an extremist sect of antiquity, and exhorted Jabotinsky upon his return to Palestine to become a "Duce"—not merely a party leader. Greatly embarrassed by these eccentric demonstrations and by a personality cult he disapproved of, "Jabo" rebuked the idea in no uncertain terms and at first did not side with the secessionists. But his attitude toward Great Britain hardened considerably. "The Balfour Declaration," he stated, "has degenerated into an anti-Zionist document." In 1930, Whitehall issued a second White Book to restrain Jewish immigration and to pacify Arab agitators who had generated a new wave of unrest.

Considering all these developments, it was obvious that the presidency of the Anglophile Weizmann became jeopardized at the Seventeenth Zionist Congress, held in Basel in August 1931. Britain's Labour Prime Minister, Ramsay MacDonald, was anxious to support him, and to that end had received the leader of the Zionist Labor movement, David Ben-Gurion, in London. He informed Ben-Gurion, the secretary general of the Histadrut, of some last-minute concessions designed to reduce the tension caused by the new White Book. These included the change of Palestine's high commissioner and the placing of Jews and Arabs on equal footing in all the local commissions. He also offered Ben-Gurion a military plane to take him to Basel just before the opening of the congress. Not wanting to risk the impression that he was an open supporter of the British, Ben-Gurion declined the offer.

Although the Labor delegates voted for him, Weizmann was unable to regain his majority. His successor as president of the world organization was Nahum Sokolow, whom Jabotinsky had supported, also hoping to slip in a resolution in favor of the national objectives of Zionism. Jabotinsky's proposal had not even been put to the vote when he climbed onto a chair, demonstratively tore up his delegate's card, and shouted: "This is no longer a Zionist congress. I'm leaving."

A telegram from the head of the Haganah, Eliahu Golomb, had effectively turned around the majority of those delegates who were inclined to remember that the ultimate goal of Zionism was an independent state, not merely a lobby. Golomb told them that the Arabs would start rioting again as soon as such a resolution was accepted. "Jabo" immediately left the hall with 52 other revisionist delegates, representing 21 percent of the votes. He knew that he could count on the proliferation of the Betar youth movement in the great Jewish centers of Europe, notably Poland, and also on the local Jewish lower middle class, in order to impose his views on the next congress. The Zionist Congress had 250 delegates: the Betar's representation had grown from 4 in 1925, to 9 in 1927, 21 in 1929, to 52 in 1931, thus becoming almost equal in strength to the Socialists. For the Eighteenth Congress, due to be held in Prague in July 1933, "Jabo" had already set the election campaign's tone by a simple slogan: "Give me a majority in the congress, and I'll give you a Jewish majority in Palestine."

Reflecting the Zionist executive's wishes, the Jewish Agency had been charged with the apportionment of immigration certificates, provided by the British in accordance with the limits established by the quotas given in their White Book, among the four main political component groups of the Zionist organization, based on their respective degrees of influence. The representatives of the Labor movement feared nothing more than to see the Betar gain control of this distribution and to see its brown-shirted militants prosper in Palestine.

To "Jabo"'s slogan, Ben-Gurion answered with his own: "From a class to a nation." It was his intention to turn the Zionist Labor movement into a national movement which would dominate the Zionist World Federation. Ben-Gurion persuaded his party to give him a mandate to campaign against Jabotinsky on his opponent's own turf. On March 31, 1933, he started his campaign among the Jewish population of Poland. His objective was to beat his adversary by 150,000 votes. He visited 800 Polish and Baltic cities and villages, directing his entire effort against those he called "Hitlero-Zionists," the brown-shirts of the Betar, who, if they won, would monopolize the certificates of admission to Palestine and impose their militaristic ideas on the Yishuv. He described them as an ignorant mob with connections to thieves, white slavers, and other dubious underworld elements. The revisionists, on the other hand, no longer restricted themselves to accusing Ben-Gurion of being a hired agent of the British. On April 21, they stink-bombed a theater in Warsaw where Ben-Gurion had intended to make a speech.

Two weeks before his departure for Poland, the Labor leader had had a disagreement with Arlosoroff, in the Central Committee of his party, regarding the strategy of this election campaign. A rising star in the Jewish Agency, now the head of its political department, Arlosoroff was an old supporter of Weizmann's; the Basel Congress of 1931 elected him one of the two Socialist members of the five-man directorate at the top of the Zionist World Federation. To him, the struggle against revisionism seemed too negative an issue. He felt it was more important to organize the immigration to Palestine of the German Jews, now threatened by Hitler's triumph in February, than to merely push for power in the July Zionist Congress. Arlosoroff himself traveled to Berlin in April for this purpose.

While in Poland, Ben-Gurion still tried to persuade Arlosoroff to come and join him in the final stages of his campaign. He did not conceal his irritation over Arlosoroff's dedication to the priority of saving Germany's Jews. At the time, Arlosoroff was still the only one to speak of the threat of extermination, even though the Nazi regime had not yet taken any serious action. Furthermore, Ben-Gurion was jealous of Arlosoroff's great popularity; he was a future rival for power. "Arlosoroff's activity in Germany is complicated by personal reasons . . ." he noted in his private journal on May 17, 1933.

Arlosoroff's assassination upon his return from Berlin fit right in with Ben-Gurion's plans and helped Ben-Gurion curb the development of the revisionist movement.

Who, then, was this young leader, whom his peers had regarded as destined for the greatest heights? Berl Katzenelson, the conscience of the Zionist-Socialist movement, said that Arlosoroff was its genius.

Born in the Ukraine in 1899 to a comfortable bourgeois family, the "new Foreign Minister of the Yishuv" got all his schooling in Berlin, where at the age of eighteen he founded the first Zionist-Socialist party, Hapoel Hatza'ir, precursor of the Israeli Labor party, Mapai. Two years later, he published his first work, *The Socialism of the Jews.* He emigrated to Palestine in January 1921 and immediately joined the clandestine Haganah. He returned to Berlin to complete his doctorate of letters, and became a delegate for the first time to the Thirteenth Zionist Congress at Karlovy Vary in 1923.

At the congress he met a young pretty Zionist student from Latvia: Sima. He traveled to Riga to lecture to her group and was invited to dinner by her father that very same evening. After dinner, Chaim and Sima took a romantic walk along the shore of the Baltic Sea. He had shifted the topic of conversation from Zionism and Socialism to his own situation as a young husband in the process of getting a divorce. Sima was taken by his romantic charm, and after his return to Palestine in 1924, they wrote to each other regularly.

Sima finally joined him, in 1925, after the birth of her daughter Nava, the child of a former relationship with another man. After his divorce Chaim promised to adopt Nava, but the couple had its first fight in 1926. During another visit to Europe, Chaim wrote to Sima that he had bought her a book by Anatole France, *The Red Rose,* whose title had inspired him to write a poem in German, dedicated to her as a sign of reconciliation. He married Sima the following year and then was sent to the United States by the Histadrut on a mission to the influential Jewish-American community. His most notable convert to Zionism was a student, Arthur Goldberg, who much later became the permanent representative of the United States at the United Nations, after being appointed a Justice of the Supreme Court.

In Palestine Arlosoroff became the pride of the leaders of the socialist elite with whom he associated during a few months in the kibbutz Deganyah. His sartorial elegance particularly impressed his comrades. After his participation in the Fourteenth Zionist Congress, he was regarded as the best socialist ideologist of his generation: he was nicknamed "Chaim the Second," as a worthy successor, one day, to Chaim Weizmann. In 1931 he was promoted to the political department of the Jewish Agency. Ben-Gurion appreciated the qualities of this newcomer who was only thirteen years younger than himself, but did not like his spectacular rise within the party's leadership and within the World Federation. He accused Arlosoroff of being too intellectual, out of touch with reality. On two or three occasions, the two even had arguments about the role and the influence of Jabotinsky, his Betar, and his "revisos." The leader of the Histadrut did not look kindly upon possible competition or rivalry.

Arlosoroff, for his part, had established good relations with the representatives of the British administration of Palestine, and with the new high commissioner, Lieutenant General Sir Arthur G. Wauchope in particular. He had gained his friendship in the hope, shared by President Weizmann, that this new man would at least honor the promises made in the Balfour Declaration.

Nevertheless, on June 30, 1932, Arlosoroff wrote a disillusioned letter to Weizmann (which the Labor party took care to bury in its secret archives for forty years). In it he expressed for the first time his recognition of the two-faced game the British were playing and came close to espousing Jabotinsky's theses: if the British have decided to no longer favor the realization of the Jewish National Home, then it is time to decide to impose it by force. Since the colonization of and immigration to Palestine under British control will never by itself lead to the desired solution, they will have to establish a transitory dictatorship by the actual Jewish minority of the Yishuv.

Despite this change of heart that remained unknown to the public, Arlosoroff found himself increasingly under attack by the revisionists for his mission to Germany. After Hitler's rise to power, even the Biryonim, who had been flirting with Italian fascism, had demonstrated against Nazism, and tore down the swastika flag flying over the German Consulate in Jerusalem. Jabotinsky himself had clearly separated himself from his extremist supporters who had considered Hitlerism as a movement of national liberation: "We have to fight to the death against Hitlerism, in every sense of the word."

In this new context, Arlosoroff's departure to Berlin in April 1933, caused a wave of public protest. The "Foreign Minister of the Yishuv" was accused of seeking to establish contact with the Nazi leaders who were proclaiming their willingness to rid the Third Reich of its Jewish communities. It is true that, as one of the few Jewish leaders of his time to recognize the approaching catastrophe, Arlosoroff intended to use all his old connections in Berlin to transfer money and assets necessary to pay for the dues demanded by the British authorities for certificates of immigration to Palestine exceeding the quotas fixed in the White Book. Once he had established contacts with the Reich's authorities, he planned another trip for the organized evacuation of the Jews, a prospect in which the German leaders appeared interested at first; in fact, they declared their readiness to facilitate the departure of the Jews, even permitting them to sell or transfer a part of their assets.

After a detour to London where he discussed his project with Weizmann, Arlosoroff went to Berlin to meet the leaders of the Jewish community and those of the local Zionist organization. He told the editor Robert Weltch, publisher of the journal *Jüdische Rundschau,* of his intention to request an audience with Magda Goebbels, the Propaganda Minister's wife, whom he himself had courted at one time. She had been the closest childhood friend of his sister Lisa. He wrote a letter to this effect to Sima. This letter, mailed in Berlin, never arrived in Tel Aviv, so he related its contents to Sima, and his two sisters, Dora and Lisa, after his return on June 13.

By way of a "welcome home" to Tel Aviv, the organ of the Biryonim, *The People's Front,* with which Jabotinsky had broken off relations, heaped abuse on the "criminal Arlosoroff": "The Jewish people will not forget your visit to Nazi Germany, and it will know how to react appropriately to this crime."

At the same time, Ben-Gurion thundered on in Poland against the man he now called "Vladimir Hitler." When he arrived in Vilna on June 17, he was informed of Arlosoroff's assassination by one of the members of the party's local committee who had come to meet him at the train and to take him to the hotel. Ben-Gurion fainted and was taken to his room, unconscious. When he revived, he drafted the text of a telegram to the Histadrut in Tel Aviv: "Send details immediately."

An hour later, he drafted two more telegrams: "Millions of pioneers weep for the death of Chaim Arlosoroff, assassinated by the bloodthirsty Biryonim." "Biryonim" has two connotations: it can be used to mean "ruffians" as well as the biblical sectarians whose name the extremist revisionists of Palestine had adopted. Before he had received any other information, Ben-Gurion had immediately recognized the advantage he could gain from the assassination in his relentless campaign against the revisionists that would culminate at the Zionist Congress in July. Nevertheless, he wrote in his journal on June 18: "The first [telegram received] said that Arlosoroff had been killed by Communists; the second, that his killer was an Arab. That seemed to be the more exact hypothesis."

The leaders of the Haganah, gathered on that day in the home of their chief, Eliahu Golomb, did not have to have wait for the arrival of Ben-Gurion's telegram on Sunday, June 18, to decide to deflect the criminal inquiry into channels indicated by that telegram, and thus to engage in the first plot of the secret history of Israel.

The version involving Arab killers did not last another day. One of the Haganah leaders, Dov Hoz, who had been present at the Tel Aviv police headquarters on Saturday while Sima Arlosoroff was shown photographs of suspects, reported his impression that the killers certainly were Arabs. That version, which conforms to the first spontaneous testimony given by the only witness—Sima Arlosoroff—was presented for the last time that evening at the meeting of the National Council, the Yishuv's supreme organ. Eliahu Golomb and Shaul Meyerov had already started a parallel investigation oriented toward a political exploitation of the crime.

On Saturday afternoon, a young Jew from Jerusalem, Itzhak Halutz, working in the British government's immigration department, had told a member of the local command of the Haganah, Dr. Abraham Izmojik, of his suspicions regarding Abraham Stavsky, a laborer who was a member of the Biryonim, whose physical characteristics resembled one of the descriptions of the two assassins broadcast by the police. On the afternoon of the assassination, Stavsky had presented himself at the immigration office to demand a refund of the sum he had deposited to extend his visa for residency in Palestine, saying that he had urgent reasons for going abroad. Halutz said that he recognized Stavsky as one of the men described in the police appeal and asked Dr. Izmojik to transmit this important information to Haganah headquarters.

On Sunday the two heads of the Haganah, Eliahu Golomb and Dov Hoz, went to Jerusalem to see Dr. Izmojik, who found them very excited. He heard them say on several separate occasions: "We have to blame it all on them." Izmojik got the impression that there was a plot afoot to accuse the revisionists of the murder of Arlosoroff. The next morning, he was surprised to find a stack of photographs of Stavsky in his apartment, which harbored the local command of the Haganah. All of them had been reproduced from a print the suspected laborer had submitted to the visa department—Itzhak Halutz's place of employment. Izmojik confided in no one . . . until 1973, when he told an Israeli journalist of his horror upon the discovery: "I kept quiet, out of loyalty and out of respect for the secrets of the Haganah."

On the afternoon of Sunday, June 18, a Haganah leader showed Stavsky's picture to Sima Arlosoroff, saying, "This is the man who used the flashlight in order to recognize Chaim and to point him out to his accomplice whose task it was to kill your husband."

Sima replied that the photograph strongly reminded her of attacker Number One. She was then taken to the Jaffa police, where she was shown a series of ten photographs of different individuals, including one of Stavsky; without hesitation, she chose it. Small wonder—it was the one she has been shown at the Haganah meeting a little while before. The police, however, were unaware of this detail which would warp the course of their inquiry. From that moment on, everything was set in motion to incriminate Stavsky, the Biryonim group, and beyond them, the entire revisionist ideology.

Sima Arlosoroff then proceeded to furnish a statement that differed from the spontaneous account she gave on the evening of the crime and the day after. She claimed to have cried as she saw her husband crumple, struck by the bullet: "Help! Some Jews have shot Arlosoroff!" Now she was quite positive: "Yes, the men who killed my husband were Jews."

On Monday, June 19, the British police arrested Stavsky at the home of the leader of the Biryonim, Abba Achimeir, who was also arrested and charged as the instigator of the crime. Sima declared that she could identify Stavsky as the attacker who held the flashlight. As evidence against Achimeir, the investigators, briefed by Haganah agents, presented an article published at the beginning of the year that can be interpreted as an apology for political crime. It was an ideological pamphlet known in the annals of revisionist Zionism as the *Manifesto of the Hired Assassins*. In it, Achimeir discussed the actions of the Sicari, a sect in antiquity whose members carried a dagger—the *sica*—concealed under their garments during the war against the Romans. They used the weapon to kill their political enemies at mass meetings from which they managed to escape, as often as not, during the commotion the stabbings caused. Achimeir wrote that every new order came into being only by means of the physical destruction of its adversaries. For him, the Sicari were unknown heroes who chose as their targets the most visible members of the established order. Strictly speaking, they were not assassins; they did not kill for material gain. The act itself was less important than its political motivation.

On Tuesday, June 20, the central committee of the Mapai (the Labor party) listened to Eliezer Kaplan's report on the Arlosoroff assassination: "It is necessary to shed light on the spiritual connection between the assassination and the ideology of its planners, and to create a propitious climate for the elimination of the revisionists from the political scene." One of the party's leaders, Itzhak Ben-Zvi, reinforced the point: "This has to be a war of destruction." Ben-Zvi, later to become President of the State of Israel, was ready to go far in the war against revisionism.

On July 4, the Histadrut's executive council met to discuss the inquiry. There Ben-Zvi made an unbelievable statement:

"In case it is impossible to judicially establish any link between the assassin Stavsky and Ze'ev Jabotinsky, if Stavsky's guilt is proven, I am willing to declare—under oath, if necessary—that Stavsky could have acted only under Jabotinsky's orders . . ."

At the same meeting, one of the Haganah leaders congratulated himself in his report on the close cooperation between his services and the British police authorities:

"The investigation is in the very best hands of superior police officers. This has not always been the case, as the revisionists still enjoy considerable influence at the heart of the police administration [which employs numerous Jews]."

Mandate authorities profited from this occasion to stifle the Jabotinsky sympathizers, who were the most hostile to their policy of a balance of power between Jews and Arabs. While preelection passions ran high, the police continued to manipulate, exert pressure, create false testimony, falsify admissions, prefabricate proof—all in an incredible witch-hunt atmosphere compliantly accepted by the Laborite and trade-unionist leaders of the Yishuv. Determined to prove the revisionists' guilt in Arlosoroff's murder, the Labor leadership kept on finding suspects and presenting crushing testimonials to confound them with: starting with the testimony of Sima Arlosoroff, who was always ready to listen to "advice."

In order to identify the second attacker, the CID (Criminal Investigation Division) had contacted one of its agents who had infiltrated the revisionist cell at Kfar Saba, a village on the outskirts of Tel Aviv. Rivka Feigin was a woman of dubious moral standards. The secretary of the cell, Zvi Rosenblatt, expelled her from the organization a few weeks before the event, for provocative behavior. Soon after Stavsky's arrest, anonymous letters were delivered to police officer Yehuda Tannenbaum-Arazi, the man in charge of Dossier No. A 37, first opened by Captain Reiss, of the British police in Palestine. According to these letters, Rivka Feigin had known the second suspect: her former husband, a certain Moshe Mendel. Arazi made inquiries and decided that the accusation had no foundation in fact. He also categorically refused to interrogate Rivka Feigin, although urged to do so, a couple of days later, by a prominent member of the Histadrut, Ephraim Kresner (later chief of the Haganah's first intelligence service, under the name Ephraim Deckel).

At that point, the Haganah ordered Inspector Bekhor Shitritt, one of its undercover agents in the police force, to Kinneret to question Rivka Feigin, who had been lodged there at the Haganah's expense. She gave Shitritt the name of Arlosoroff's assassin: Zvi Rosenblatt, her former superior in the Kfar Saba cell.

Rosenblatt was arrested on July 23, at the time of the opening of the Eighteenth Zionist Congress in Prague. Received with shouts of "Assassins! Assassins!", Jabotinsky and his supporters could hardly make themselves heard. Every time one of them mounted the speakers' platform, the Labor party's delegation left the hall in protest. With 44 percent of the votes, it was by far the strongest faction. The revisionists now had only 16 percent instead of 21 percent. Thus isolated and violently ostracized during the debates, they clashed against the Laborites' categorical refusal to deal with them on the executive level. The "Prague Coup" legitimized the ban imposed on them by the Zionist establishment: their exclusion from all institutions regulating the life of the Yishuv in Palestine. This suited the British, who had been unable to save Weizmann's presidency at the preceding congress by their last-minute concessions.

But the true victor of the trial of strength in Prague was Ben-Gurion, who would assert the absolute power of his party over the Zionist movement for forty-four years. Ben-Gurion actually took Arlosoroff's place in the directorate, where the Laborites now had four seats out of five, instead of two. His name received prolonged acclamation from the delegates who had literally expelled Jabotinsky and his "clique of assassins" from their organization.

The accused assassins, Rosenblatt and Stavsky, put up a brave fight against the witch-hunt. Both of them had been formally identified by Sima Arlosoroff, although neither one was the Eastern type that she had indicated at the beginning of the investigation. This identification was actually the only basis for the charges filed against them by the police.

Toward the end of July, Rivka Feigin, whom the Haganah had been moving from one hiding place to another, from Givat Brenner to Kfar Giladi, in order to protect her from possible reprisals, visited Rosenblatt in prison, pretending to have a message for him from his superior, Achimeir. She gave him a note: "Stavsky has confessed. You confess, too. Signed: Achimeir." Rosenblatt sent her packing and persisted in his protestations of innocence.

Intrigued, police officer Shitritt, who first interrogated Rivka Feigin, the witness rejected by Arazi, the official director of the investigation, decided to get to the bottom of the matter. He knew that Rivka had connections with the British CID. At the beginning of August, he conducted a discreet search of her apartment and found a number of scratchpads on which she had practiced forging Achimeir's signature. He immediately requested that she be barred from testifying in court. His discovery embarrassed his Haganah colleagues, and they decided to let their cumbersome witness disappear from public view. Shitritt, who later became the first Minister of Police of Israel, waited until the eve of his death before he revealed the truth about that dirty trick: "I knew that there had been foul play in that shady affair. I showed them the counterfeit signatures produced by Rivka Feigin. They told me that those were totally unimportant, but agreed that she had to be prevented from testifying. It was just a question of finding a way of sending her out of the country before the trial."

Berl Repetor, one of the leaders of the Histadrut, undertook that task, sending her on a mission to Rumania. She remained there until her disappearance in the smoke of some extermination camp, some ten years later.

Rivka Feigin was no longer needed for the case against Rosenblatt, if only because another false witness had been produced out of the very same prison where he was being held. A habitual criminal answering to the name of Moshe Cohen, among others, was serving a sentence there for the theft of a watch. He was locked up in the same cell with Rosenblatt. At the beginning of August, he claimed to have confidential information: "Rosenblatt told me: 'Look at these hands. They killed Arlosoroff.' "

That piece of false information would miscarry, but would nevertheless play a part—an essentially psychological one—in the overall plot based on Arlosoroff's murder, intended to permanently discredit the supporters of revisionism. And, for a long time, it would remain a taboo item in the Haganah's secret archives.

On Yom Kippur, 1936, Moshe Cohen, imprisoned at Acre for fraud this time, wanted to ease his conscience. He told fellow prisoner Itzhak Hankin, the son of one of the founders of the Hachomer movement and a Haganah militant himself, how his testimony against Rosenblatt had been fabricated. It had not been necessary for him to steal a watch in order to find himself in Rosenblatt's cell. In July 1933, he had been visited at home by a British officer accompanied by one of the top men of the Haganah, Dov Hoz. Knowing his criminal background, his two visitors offered him the sum of £70 for being the stool pigeon in Rosenblatt's cell to "extract" that false confession.

Stavsky had less luck than Rosenblatt, whose alibi proved unassailable in the end. To prove his innocence, he requested the testimony of a hotelkeeper in Jerusalem, Y. Turjeman, who had registered his arrival on June 16 at 4:00 P.M. and had seen him fast asleep at the time of the crime in Tel Aviv. This hotelkeeper soon became the target of a smear campaign, to which he succumbed before the end of the preliminary investigation. According to rumors spread in Laborite circles, he was about to undergo a secret conversion to Islam, and his hotel was not just seedy, it was an outright establishment of prostitution. Thus his testimony was discredited in favor of the countertestimony of Stavsky's landlady in Tel Aviv, Rivka Hazan. She affirmed that she had indeed seen Stavsky on the evening of June 16. Some six months later, she ended up admitting to Michael Rabinovitch, a police officer, that her deposition had been extorted from her with the explanation that "these people are worse than the Communists, so it's a good deed to smash them by whatever means."

In mid-August 1933, Inspector Yehuda Tannenbaum-Arazi hit the jackpot: the very investigation he had been appointed to conduct suddenly appeared prefabricated. On August 28, he wrote a nineteen-page report to the joint chief of the CID, Captain Reiss, pointing out all the anomalies and incongruities of the investigation that resulted in the indictment of Stavsky and Rosenblatt: "It is my impression that all the witnesses, beginning with Mme Arlosoroff, have wanted to incriminate the suspects at any cost." As if to justify their identification of those suspects, Arazi recommended a supplementary inquiry into the strange behavior of Arlosoroff's widow between the night of the crime and the third day of investigation, in order to determine:

• the veracity of her statements;

• whether her accusations were not designed to conceal her knowledge of her husband's real assassins;

• why, if she did not know them, she persisted in charging two suspects who did not correspond to the initial description she had given of them.

Inspector Arazi suspected that Sima Arlosoroff's contradictions resulted in part from exterior pressures and in part from a wish to conceal what had taken place when her husband was attacked on the beach.

As for the anonymous letters regarding the suspicions of the CID's agent, Rivka Feigin, these were only a bait that he had refused to take; they seemed intended to cause the dubious testimony of that young woman to be included in the dossier.

After this report to Captain Reiss, Arazi was discharged from his duties on Dossier No. A 37 concerning the assassination of Arlosoroff. When he gave his superiors in the Haganah, of which he was a clandestine member, a copy of his report, they ordered him to keep his nose out of the affair from then on. After World War II, Arazi became one of the prime movers in the organization of secret arms purchases for the Haganah, and the head of the illegal immigration network in Italy. His report was buried forty years, until after his death.

The investigation of Arlosoroff's murder took a spectacular turn at the beginning of the following year, when Stavsky was the sole remaining suspect. After the Zionist Congress in Prague, Achimeir had been quickly cleared of all suspicion, and Rosenblatt had been released, thanks to the verification of his alibi.

On January 10, 1934, an Arab detainee in Acre Prison, awaiting his sentence in a vendetta case, confided in his warders. Abd el-Majid el-Bukhari, nineteen, a plumber from Jaffa, he described the murder of Arlosoroff. It was an accidental murder, which he got involved in through a friend, Issa Darwish. On January 12, he repeated his story to police officer Bekhor Shitritt, who took his testimony in the company of Sima Arlosoroff's lawyer, Dov Joseph. Confronted on January 14 by two women, he easily recognized one of them as Sima Arlosoroff, whom he had run into on the beach on the night of the crime.

That evening he was returning with Darwish from an athletic demonstration given by Egyptian champion Mukhtar Hussein in Jaffa. The two young men strolled along the beach of Tel Aviv in the direction of the Islamic cemetery, hoping to pick up some girls. They noticed a young woman walking by herself by the water's edge and decided to accost her. A man who had been walking thirty or so meters behind them then moved up to them, and in order to save face, they asked him for the time. The man reached into his pocket, and Issa pulled his gun, discharging it by accident. "I just wanted to scare him so I could have some fun with the young woman," Issa had told Abd el-Majid as they were running away.

Two days after these revelations, a delegation of Arab lawyers visited Abd el-Majid in Acre Prison. It included Ouni Abd el-Hadi, a member of the Supreme Arab Committee, who represented the Arabs of Palestine. The members of the delegation told Abd el-Majid that Arlosoroff's death was a serious political matter, and that he risked hanging if he stuck to his deposition.

To make him even more aware of that risk, the young prisoner underwent medical examinations to determine his age. In the absence of a civil registry for Arabs at that period, the outcome of those examinations would determine whether he was a candidate for capital punishment, since British law did not permit the execution of anyone under eighteen. In fact, this was a way of preparing the prisoner psychologically for the consequences of his confession.

The dissuasive effect was almost instantaneous. On January 22, Abd el-Majid demanded a hearing before a judge to rescind his deposition of January 12. Although the request did not receive much publicity, Stavsky's lawyer, Horace Samuel, got wind of it by mere chance—perhaps through the prison grapevine—and asked that the young Arab be put under oath. Abd el-Majid swore that his deposition was made only to comply with a bribe from Stavsky and that it was not true. This accusation was even accompanied by the testimony of another Arab prisoner who claimed to have been present at Stavsky's attempt to corrupt his compatriot. According to him, Stavsky had told Abd el-Majid that since he was already imprisoned for murder, he would not stand to lose anything if he also admitted the murder of Arlosoroff.

The tribunal called upon to judge Stavsky did not admit the Arab's deposition as evidence. In the course of the trial, Sima Arlosoroff involuntarily confirmed a detail of the rejected testimony by telling that one of the two assailants on the beach had directed lewd gestures at her. In Judge Moshe Valero's dissenting opinion, that point was clarified: "It seems that one of the attackers exhibited himself in front of the Arlosoroff woman . . . Thus it could well have been a sexual assault, and in that case, neither Stavsky nor Rosenblatt had anything to do with this murder."

On June 8, 1934, by a vote of two against one (Judge Valero dissenting), the district tribunal of Tel Aviv declared Stavsky guilty of Arlosoroff's assassination and sentenced him to death. However, on July 20, the Supreme Court acquitted him, stating that no proof had been presented to confirm Sima Arlosoroff's accusation. The Court also revealed that the testimony of two experts in tracking footprints, who claimed to have detected traces of Stavsky and Rosenblatt in the sand in the vicinity of the attack, had been solicited by some police officers who had "warmed them up" beforehand.

After Stavsky's release, the British police authorities decided not to reopen the investigation.

In 1936 Itzhak Hankin, a hero of the Haganah imprisoned in Acre by the British, became friendly with Abd el-Majid, who was still detained with his brother, Abd el-Hamid, in connection with a vendetta in which an Arab barber, Lufti el-Halabi, had been murdered. The little plumber from Jaffa confirmed that, contrary to what he had been made to tell the presiding judge two years before, he was indeed present at Arlosoroff's assassination: his friend Issa Darwish fired that shot after having tried to abuse Sima, whom he had surprised in the dark, at some distance away from her husband. Abd el-Majid had merely been tagging along, scouting for girls on the beach after a few drinks in the cafés of Tel Aviv. Why had he decided to tell this two years earlier, before he was forced to retract the confession for fear of the death sentence? Because, he says, Issa Darwish had left him in the lurch in the matter of the vendetta against the barber, contrary to his promise to help in exchange for Abd el-Majid's silence on the murder of Arlosoroff. When his brother Abd el-Hamid had been arrested in the meantime, as an accomplice to that vendetta murder of which he was innocent, Abd el-Majid had decided to break his pact with Issa Darwish. But no one had wanted to believe him.

After his release from prison in 1941, Hankin informed Golomb and Meyerov, the two chiefs of the Haganah, of the Arab's new confessions.

"The revisionists must have brainwashed you," Golomb told him and showed him Inspector Shitritt's dossier of investigation. "Please refrain from spreading that apocryphal story in the future. It is a matter of the main interests of our organization."

Hankin agreed to keep silent "to avoid possible civil strife." But he was not at all convinced. What interest would Abd el-Majid have had in reverting to his original story unless there was some truth in it? And why had he repeated that version to a Jewish lawyer, Max Seligman, in 1939? Tormented by his conscience, Hankin later used his position as an officer in the military administration of the Rafiah, right after the victory of the Six-Day War, to send an inhabitant of that territory to Amman, Jordan, to track down the Palestinian Abd el-Majid el-Bukhari. In 1968 the messenger found the fifty-four-year-old former prisoner of Acre running a small repair shop for bicycles and stoves. Hankin tried to get the Israeli authorities interested in his initiative. Since the affair had been officially closed, the testimony of the aging Arab might shed some light on the mystery of Arlosoroff's murder. Several details of the story repeated many times by Majid el-Bukhari to different interlocutors have been found to be truthful: as an example, the Egyptian athlete Mukhtar Hussein did indeed give an exhibition at Jaffa on the evening of June 16, 1933.

So it was only a question of finding out whether it was truly by accident that Issa Darwish shot Arlosoroff while trying to importune his wife, or whether someone had handed him that gun with definite instructions.

When Hankin tried to get an official response, he met with total silence from his old comrades-in-arms, and with the authorities' refusal to reopen an old wound in the side of Zionist history. The affair had already surfaced once during the election campaign of 1965 for the renewal of the Israeli parliament, the Knesset. The old Haganah leader Shaul Meyerov, later known as Shaul Avigur, broke his silence by publishing an article in which he expressed his conviction that Stavsky and Rosenblatt were indeed guilty of Arlosoroff's assassination, thus discrediting the right-wing opposition led by Menachem Begin, the heirs of the revisionist tradition. Although declared innocent by the Supreme Court, Stavsky was no longer there to reply. He was killed on June 23, 1948, fifteen years after Arlosoroff, on that same beach at Tel Aviv—by bullets fired by a unit of the Palmach (strike force of the Haganah) commanded by Itzhak Rabin during the tragic incident of the *Altalena,* a gun-running vessel chartered by the Irgun for its besieged garrison in Jerusalem (see Chapter VI: Birth of a Nation).

Rosenblatt brought a defamation suit, demanding that the Israeli judiciary formally acknowledge his innocence. In 1966 Judge Joseph Lam awarded him £2,000 (Israeli) damages with interest, while refraining from any pronouncement on the background of the case. The question "Who killed Arlosoroff?" remained unanswered.

The affair made another comeback in June 1973, forty years after the murder, when Tamar Meroz, a journalist working for the daily newspaper *Haaretz,* reopened the dossier and turned it into a bone of contention in the new election campaign that was brutally interrupted by the Yom Kippur War. Three months before the surprise attack by Syria and Egypt, the question still inflamed Israeli public opinion, because for the first time, the coalition of the Right threatened the hegemony of the Laborites. For four decades, this assemblage of the heirs of the Betar, of the Biryonim, of the revisionist organization, the Irgun, and a faction of the Stern Group had been excluded from all participation in public and parliamentary affairs, in part because of the repercussions of the Arlosoroff affair. Now they prepared for revenge. They triumphed four years later, under the banner of the Likud, in the elections for the Ninth Knesset.

It was, however, no revelation of the truth of the matter that put an end to almost half a century of Laborite rule over the Jews of Israel. That truth still remains to be established, after the passions have died down. The majority of the protagonists have now taken their secrets to the grave: Eliahu Golomb and Dov Hoz, two members of the Haganah triumvirate who warped the judicial inquiry by preparing their parallel dossier, are dead, and the third member, Shaul Avigur, recently died in a home for the aged in Galilee.

Their hireling, police officer Bekhor Shitritt, and Sima Arlosoroff, the prime witness, are dead.

Former police officer Yehuda Tannenbaum-Arazi died after leaving his report to molder in the vaults of the Haganah; but that report, of prime importance for an understanding of the workings of the plot devised by its clandestine leaders, was exhumed for the first time in June 1973, after some other witnesses had timidly come forward to relieve their conscience of weighty secrets of state—after four decades of silence due to reasons of unconditional loyalty to the party, to the system, or due to fear of reprisals by a machinery as mysterious as it was totalitarian.

Thus Shamai Kuperstein, one of the witnesses present on the terrace of the Kete Dan that evening of June 16, 1933, waited until June, 1973, before relating Sima Arlosoroff's spontaneous reaction on her return to the hotel: "I clearly heard her tell the people: 'Some Arabs shot at us.' She said *Arabs*—I'm sure of that. I said so in my statement at the time, but they tried to pressure me into changing it."

Sima Arlosoroff herself told the journalist Tamar Meroz that Shaul Meyerov-Avigur had worked behind the scenes conducting a parallel inquiry, while Dov Hoz had been uncertain at first as to what course of action should be pursued. At this time, there no longer is any doubt that the British tried by all possible means to exploit the case to their own advantage, in order to eliminate the "revisionist threat." On page 235 of his memoirs, Joseph M. Broadhearst, the former commander of the British police in Tel Aviv, lets the cat out of the bag: "We did not have any incriminating evidence, not one real clue, but since the victim was a politically symbolic figure, we had to do something. Thus we decided to arrest a number of militant extremists whose ideas were opposed to those held by the victim. We knew for a fact that none of the accused had been involved in the murder. We were forced to pervert justice for reasons of state."

Nor is there any doubt that Captain Reiss, joint chief of the CID, knew the truth about the testimony fabricated or falsified by his services. In 1970 Tuvia Arazi, the brother of the deceased former police officer, wrote a letter to Israel Galili, perennial minister without portfolio in all the Labor governments, a kind of *éminence grise* of the regime, keeper of the secrets, expert in compromise. Arazi offered to travel to South Africa, where Captain Reiss had retired, to question him on what he knew about the inquiry. Galili's reply was terse: "I do not see any need for that kind of testimony. As far as I can see, it would be quite useless." Today it would be too late: Reiss is dead.

Shmuel Tamir, present Minister of Justice in the Begin government, was only ten years old at the time of the Stavsky trial. It was that very premeditated miscarriage of justice that inspired him to embark on a career in law. In 1966 he acted for Rosenblatt in his defamation suit against Shaul Avigur and demonstrated how the Mandate's administration had succeeded in turning the Stavsky case into a perfectly typical political trial, along the lines of the show trials in Moscow. Stavsky's death sentence handed down by the regional tribunal, and its subsequent reversal by the Supreme Court, served only one purpose: to leave the wound open and foment dissension among the various Zionist factions and in the heart of the Yishuv itself.

It was a successful operation. After the Prague coup which excluded them from power, the revisionists, still going strong in the great Jewish centers of Europe, founded in the spring of 1934, in Palestine, a confederation of trade unions to combat the Histadrut hegemony. The clashes between the 60,000 members of the Histadrut and the 7,000 militants of the new confederation became an almost everyday affair.

Having secured power, Ben-Gurion continued to try to maintain contact with Jabotinsky in order to arrive at a *modus vivendi*. The two men's feelings toward each other proved complicated and contradictory, blending animosity with esteem, hatred with fascination. They were not able to forget that they had both worn the uniform of the Jewish Legion.

On July 3, 1934, "Jabo" sent a letter to the Mapai proposing negotiations to put an end to acts of violence between Jews. On

August 9, the Laborites rejected the offer in their party organ, *Davar*. Ben-Gurion still favored a meeting with the revisionist leader who had installed himself in London. Unable to get his party to agree, Ben-Gurion himself went to London on October 8, where a mutual friend, Pinhas Rottenberg, founder and director of the Palestinian Electric Company, organized a meeting in a small hotel room. After two days of discussion, the two leaders drafted the terms of an agreement to prohibit the exchange of insults, acts of violence, and defamatory campaigns between their respective supporters, but the agreement was rejected by both sides' rank and file in February and March, 1935. If their personal relationship remained relatively cordial, public secession had become inevitable. In September 1935, the constitutive conference of the new Zionist Organization was held in Vienna.

When the British finally declassified the documents relating to their colonial administration of Palestine from 1917 to 1947, one single dossier was kept from the curiosity of historians, because it was protected by the laws governing the security of the United Kingdom. Its title has never been revealed, but it contains a list of the names of Jewish agents working for the special intelligence services. The publication of this list might embarrass several people who have occupied important posts in the Israeli administration since the end of the Mandate. Does it, as some people in Jerusalem seem to believe, contain the keys to a half-dozen political mysteries that remain unsolved—including the truth behind the Arlosoroff affair?

Were we to trust—at least in part—the repeated confession of Abd el-Majid, the thesis that the crime was committed by a pair of sexual prowlers runs into certain incongruities that make it seem less than plausible. First, that kind of crime was rare in Palestine during an epoch of unprecedented peace between the two communities. Furthermore, if the two young Arabs wanted merely to molest Sima Arlosoroff, why did one of them shine a flashlight into her husband's face, pretending to ask him for the time? The gunman fired only after seeing Arlosoroff's face—after identifying him. He fired only one point-blank shot before disappearing into the night with his gun. Mission accomplished.

Two hypotheses have been suggested to make sense of a murder which, if it was committed by the two Arabs, cannot have been as accidental as Abd el-Majid claimed.

The first interpretation proposes the British Secret Service as the *deus ex machina* pulling the two Arab puppets' strings. The British knew of the recent and carefully camouflaged evolution of Arlosoroff who had, by 1932, arrived at conclusions close to those of Jabotinsky regarding to the role of the Mandate's power, while still maintaining the best of relations with Lieutenant General Sir Arthur G. Wauchope, the new High Commissioner of Palestine. Around the middle of that year, Arlosoroff had written a private series of letters to Chaim Weizmann in which he expressed an extremist point of view: the need for armed revolt to establish a temporary dictatorship of the Jewish minority over the territory of Palestine.

The Laborite leadership has always taken care to suppress those explosive letters of the summer of 1932; they do not appear in the collections of Arlosoroff's writings published by the party, nor do they occur in the complete published correspondence of Weizmann. Indeed, they would be singularly detrimental to the thesis that Arlosoroff was the implacable enemy of all revisionist ideology! Nevertheless, it is possible that the British had the means to find out about Arlosoroff's political evolution, and that they saw in it a dangerous threat to their own interests. In the history of the British secret services, particularly in matters of colonial policy, political crimes have never appeared illegitimate.

There is, however, another hypothesis,—a far more credible one—on the true powers behind the assassins of Arlosoroff: a hypothesis that in the light of newly discovered evidence gives the crime quite particular historical dimensions and effects. There is every reason to believe that Arlosoroff's death was decided upon and ordered by the Nazi regime's second-in-command, Dr. Joseph Goebbels, Propaganda Minister of the Third Reich.

In 1930 Goebbels, then the Berlin Gauleiter of the Nazi party, met a pretty young divorcée named Magda Quandt. She was the result of a love affair between a house servant, Augustina Bernhardt, and her employer, wealthy engineer Oscar Ritschell, who then married her. Magda's parents were divorced when she was three years old, and her mother remarried a Jew, Max Friedlander, who adopted her. Magda Friedlander received an excellent education in the best boarding schools of Germany and Belgium and made friends with one of the most brilliant students of the *lycée* she went to in Berlin, Lisa Arlosoroff. She also became intimate with members of her family, particularly her sister Dora and her brother Victor, who later took the name Chaim. At the Arlosoroffs, Magda frequently heard conversations about Palestine and about plans to move the entire family to a kibbutz. Feeling half-Jewish herself, she thought of moving to join them there. But, at age eighteen, pretty Magda fell in love with a wealthy German industrialist, Günter Quandt. She married him, and Victor Chaim Arlosoroff emigrated to Palestine. A few years later, Magda divorced

Quandt and found a "steady" job with Hitler's party. In 1931 she became Frau Joseph Goebbels. The future Führer was a witness at that wedding. Later, Hitler had to intervene several times in order to straighten out the couple's marital differences. Soon after Hitler became Chancellor, on January 31, 1933, Magda had a violent quarrel with her husband, in the course of which she revealed to him her family background and, above all, her relationships with Jews. She told him that her first friend from the days of her youth was now the Minister in Charge of Foreign Affairs for the Jewish Agency in Palestine.

Goebbels proceeded to research and to liquidate all evidence of his wife's "Jew-tainted" past, and also to impregnate her with no less than six children in rapid succession. In March 1933 Magda's stepfather Max Friedlander was arrested by the Gestapo. No one ever saw him again. Other old friends of Magda's also disappeared from Berlin. Then, at the end of April 1933, came the announcement of the imminent arrival of Dr. Arlosoroff, traveling from Tel Aviv to Berlin via London. He even had the audacity to ask for an audience with Magda Goebbels. He told this to his wife in a letter that was intercepted by the German censors, as were all the letters he wrote her during his stay. Not one of them reached her. She probably expressed her vexation to him when he returned on June 13, and perhaps was still sulking that fatal evening of June 16, on the beach of Tel Aviv.

Informed of Arlosoroff's moves by the censors and, no doubt, by some agents actually shadowing him, the propaganda minister of the new regime could not see his way to liquidate a person on official business, protected by a British passport, on German soil. This would mean risking diplomatic complications as well as irksome revelations about Magda's past. On the other hand, Arlosoroff's plan to institute a shuttle between Tel Aviv and Berlin and to establish contacts with the authorities of the Reich might prove inestimably dangerous to Goebbels's career in the Nazi hierarchy.

Goebbels must have known that two Gestapo agents were in Jerusalem, where they had arrived on April 5, three weeks before Arlosoroff's departure for Europe. They had checked in with the German consul, Dr. Friedrich Wolf, and told him that they were looking for the place where German soldiers under Field Marshal von Sanders had hidden some spoils of war, in the Jenin mountains in Samaria, during their retreat in 1918. On May 2, the strange treasure hunters came to say good-bye to the consul. Their mission terminated without apparent results, and they informed him of their imminent return to Germany. The consul remembered the bizarre interlude, whose dates coincided with the preparations and the departure of Arlosoroff to Berlin: preparations and departure both vociferously lambasted by the activists of the Betar and the Biryonim.

There are indications that the two Nazi emissaries of April 1933 contacted members of the German community then living in the village of Sarona on the outskirts of Tel Aviv, presently the headquarters of the Israeli Defense Forces in the Kyria. At that time, the Sarona cell of the National Socialist party was very influential and active and engaged in cordial relations with the Arab nationalist leaders gathered around the Grand Mufti of Jerusalem.

It seems quite probable that after consultations with the two messengers from Berlin, the leaders of the Nazi group in Sarona started looking for a hired killer to liquidate Arlosoroff upon his return from Berlin. That killer may very well have been Issa Darwish, Abd el-Majid's companion on the evening of June 16. Concealing the true objective of the night's outing, Issa took Abd el-Majid on a ramble along the beach. The young plumber from Jaffa probably did believe that it was just a matter of cruising for girls.

There are three factors that support this theory of a camouflaged assassination executed by remote control by the master of Nazi propaganda:

• —In their flight, the two attackers did not retrace their steps toward Jaffa, following the shore, deserted and frequently covered with dunes at the time; this would have seemed the most natural reaction in the case of accidental murder. They headed toward the interior, toward the German quarter of Sarona.

• —between the time when they left the showcase exhibition of the Egyptian champion in Jaffa and the time when they came upon the Arlosoroffs taking the air after dinner at the Kete Dan, the two men visited several cafés in Tel Aviv; these stops could have been prearranged with the organizers of the assassination. According to certain witnesses, they seemed to be waiting for orders or passwords while stopping for drinks.

• —Abd el-Majid's turning his flashlight onto Arlosoroff's face—known from the wounded man's final statements in the hospital—after having been asked to do so by his companion, who then opened fire, indicates both the wish to identify the victim and a premeditated intention to commit murder.

Thus, according to this hypothesis, Chaim Arlosoroff, one of the few Jewish leaders of his time to have predicted the Nazi Holocaust, can be seen as its first martyr.

3

THE COMMANDO SPIRIT

In the early months of 1942, Field Marshal Rommel's Afrika Korps, had driven back Marshal Montgomery's British troops on the Egyptian front in a seemingly irresistible rout toward the Suez Canal, and once more stood at the gates of Palestine. This time, however, Rommel's advance was coordinated with the entry of the Wehrmacht into the Caucasus, where it had just penetrated deep into the Soviet lines. This enormous pincer movement threatened to crush the whole of the Near East like a ripe fruit, which would cause Palestine and its Jews to fall into the hands of the executioners of European Jewry.

The strategic plans of the English high command maintained, in fact, that the region was incapable of being defended. Should Rommel reach Suez, the only option was withdrawing from Palestine and a widespread retreat of British forces into Mesopotamia. Current rumors were so convincing that the Yishuv expected an invasion. Some Jews, who had escaped from Europe, rushed to pharmacies to buy poison to kill themselves rather than fall into Nazi hands. The Arabs, on the other hand, awaited the arrival of the Germans with an apparent apathy which barely concealed their inner jubilation. Not content with ignoring the blackout, the Arabs covered Jewish dwellings with mysterious chalk markings.

When Palestinians of all origins were allowed to enlist in the British Army in September 1940, no more than 9,000 out of the 1,200,000 Palestinian Arabs volunteered at the recruiting offices. In comparison, from September 1939, nearly 90,000 men and more than 50,000 women out of the 650,000 Yishuv Jews had spontaneously joined the ranks of the national service, entrusted with turning out munitions, weapons, and fighting personnel, and had contributed to the Mandate power's war effort despite administrative obstacles.

At the same time, nationalist Arab leaders did not wait patiently on the outcome of the battle before choosing sides, so certain did an Axis victory appear to them. As early as September 1940, el-Hadj Amine el-Husseini, Grand Mufti of Jerusalem, had sent his private secretary to Berlin to urge Germany and Italy to publicly recognize the independence of all the Arab states and of their right to "settle the Jewish question in the national and popular interest, along the lines of Germany and Italy." In the spring of 1941, in conjunction with Prince Rashid Ali—who had attempted a pro-Nazi coup in Iraq—and Azziz-el-Misri in Egypt, the Grand Mufti had launched an appeal for a true jihad (holy war) against England, at that time without allies, before proceeding himself to Germany and raising a division of Muslim S.S. in occupied Yugoslavia. The Syrians and Lebanese, who were under French mandate, allowed the Vichy government to place those territories at the Wehrmacht's disposal to support the Iraqi rebellion and threaten the army of Marshal Wavell—Montgomery's predecessor—from the rear when it was first forced out of Libya toward Alexandria by Rommel's tank force.

In the beginning of 1942, Rommel's new offensive, centering on El Alamein, brought with it the prospect of widespread massacre for the Jewish population of Palestine. Faced with this threat, the British high command went over the head of the Mandate's administration and acceded to the repeated requests of the Yishuv's leaders that they be allowed to play a more direct and more active role in the region's defense and to ally themselves with the two Jewish self-defense organizations: the Haganah, a semiofficial workers' militia, and the Irgun, which was made up of dissenting revisionists. This agreement was purely military and operational in nature and had no political ramifications. The setting up of special units and their training in secret reconnaissance and sabotage missions behind enemy lines had been authorized earlier. Within the Haganah, elite commando units (Palmach) had been formed to defend the kibbutzim. The Irgun took advantage of the high level of the recruits to establish units of Jews speaking perfect German or Arabic who were, if necessary, to remain in Axis-occupied Palestine to carry out guerrilla warfare.

At Palmach headquarters on Mount Carmel, two men were drawing up a plan known to insiders as "Masada II," in memory of the fortress on the shores of the Dead Sea where, in A.D. 73, Jewish Zealot defenders had chosen collective suicide over a return to slavery. These men were Itzhak Sadeh, organizer of the first prewar mobile commando unit against the Arab uprisings and chief of the Palmach, and Yohanan Ratner, a member of the Haganah general staff. Their plan provided for the evacuation and regrouping of the entire Jewish population of Palestine in the northern part of the country should Germany invade Egypt. In contrast to Masada itself, however, Masada II—known officially as the Haifa Plan—was not an end in itself, but the beginning of long-term resistance. It entailed establishing an enormous armed camp from which trained and equipped shock troops could make raids and sorties into enemy-occupied Palestine, supported by local underground resistance forces. "For the English, Palestine is only a backwater," Sadeh stated, "but for us, it is everything."

The plan provided for the placement of munitions dumps, for setting up transmitting and clandestine broadcasting facilities, and for mining all bridges connecting Palestine with neighboring regions. The preparation of these defense projects under the plan would later assist in the War of Independence: a few hours prior to the proclamation of the State of Israel on May 14, 1948, all the mined bridges were blown up, thereby slowing down the invasion of the country by the five Arab armies.

In the spring of 1942, the Office of Special Operations in the War Ministry in London decided to finance—for the first time—the creation of a Jewish Task Force in Palestine under the command of Major T. B. Wilson. A special branch of Mideast Headquarters reached agreement with the Haganah to establish a framework of small autonomous units capable of engaging in terrorist activities behind the German-Italian lines. Under the terms of this agreement, a top-secret training camp was set up at Mishmar Haemek, a kibbutz near Haifa, where British military instructors trained Palmach teams in the techniques of sabotage and commando actions, and in the handling of explosives. The local British authorities were carefully kept ignorant of these preparations, which contravened their policy of keeping the Palestinian communities neutral, and their policy of appeasing Arab nationalism.

Consequently when the police caught members of the Palmach in the Mishmar Haemek camp in the act of bearing arms and engaging in military exercises, special intervention was sought to obtain their release. Aubrey Eban, a young South African captain in the British Army's intelligence service in Cairo, was assigned as liaison officer between the Special Operations section and Haganah headquarters to iron out these problems. Later on, he would be better known as Abba Eban, when he became Israel's Minister for Foreign Affairs. With his very British sense of humor, Eban was later to recall this episode: "I was supposed to obtain my posting from the commander of the Special Operations Section in Cairo, Colonel Dumwill, known both for his courage and for his enormous capacity for alcohol. I therefore requested an appointment at ten in the morning, in order to be sure of finding him sober. Despite a large bottle of whiskey on the table, everything went well. I left his office with the impressive title of liaison officer between Special Operations and the Jewish Agency for Palestine."

In fact, from the end of 1939, London was interested in the possibility of relying on the cooperation of the Yishuv's self-defense forces which had, since the large-scale outbreaks of Arab unrest fomented in 1921, 1929, and 1936, been alternately banned and repressed, or tolerated—if not abetted—by the Mandate's administration. Unbeknownst to the administration, contact had been established during this period between the leaders of Special Operations and representatives of the Jewish Agency, led by David Ben-Gurion. A preliminary secret meeting had been held in Rumania between David Hacohen and some agents of the Intelligence Service, who wanted to explore the capabilities of the Jewish Agency for recruiting candidates who spoke the Balkan languages, with an eye to possible future operations in Central Europe.

Toward the end of 1940, after the fall of France, in face of the new threat created by the access of the Axis forces to important bases in the Levant turned over to them by the Vichy government, the British services decided to assign secret missions to Jewish volunteers from Palestine. In April 1941, London decided to intervene in Lebanon and Syria before it was too late. The code name for this operation was "Exporter." The general staff, fearing the imminent arrival of German-Italian squadrons in Syria, considered it urgent to begin by blowing up the oil refineries at Tripoli in Lebanon in order to cut off the supply of oil to the Vichy forces and to the enemy air force. To accomplish this, the general staff turned to the Haganah, some of whose most active members were already in the British Army, and others of whom were in prison for having engaged in the clandestine activity so actively repressed by the Mandate's administration. Because of these conflicts, the Haganah was in the throes of an internal reorganization.

On May 15, 1941, the Haganah national committee met to decide in effect on the creation of special groups to be henceforth at its own disposal: shock troops—*Plougot Hamachatz* in Hebrew—and known by the abbreviation Palmach. The Palmach thus became the striking force of the Haganah. Nine companies of thirty volunteers each were recruited, primarily in the kibbutzim. Stationed throughout the country, these operational units were under the direct control of Haganah headquarters and under the command of a coordinating officer: the already legendary Itzhak Sadeh, the first "veteran" ("Old Man") in the history of the Jewish defense forces.

Because of their semiclandestine status, and owing to the policy of moderation then being followed by the leaders of the Jewish Agency, up until 1937 these defense forces were limited to purely static defensive operations. Faced with the scope of the new wave of Arab outbreaks in protest against what nationalist leaders in the pay of the Axis called the "preferential treatment of the Jews in Palestine," Sadeh had just created a Jerusalem mobile unit aimed at more than conventional defensive strategy and with offensive capability, in spite of its tiny supply of weapons. Sadeh taught what he called a "sense of irresponsibility"—knowing how to break rules, guessing what could and should be done, initiating actions. He had then taken command of field units of the rural police—known as POSH—which had been authorized by the British administration of Palestine to operate against the bands of Arab irregulars who since 1938 had begun to terrorize the countryside and to transform the so-called nationalist revolt into total anarchy. Bandits and mercenaries from Syria, more or less under the command of a Lebanese known as the "Scarlet Pimpernel," attacked cars on the roads, sacked Jewish and Arab villages, massacred prominent figures in the moderate Arab faction, stepped up extortion in areas colonized by the Jews, and even set fire to British installations. As long as these pillagers confined themselves to burning nineteen Jews alive in Tiberias in one night—ten of whom were children—the British Army stood idle. However, when they began attacking the pipeline transporting oil from Iraq to Haifa at more or less regular intervals, High Commissioner Sir Arthur Wauchope authorized the still-quasi-legal Haganah to form a rural militia of 16,000 men and to furnish guards for a newly formed military group, the Special Night Squad, created by an intelligence officer, Captain Orde Charles Wingate.

Wingate, a thirty-three-year-old Scot, never without his Bible, his revolver and his whiskey flask, had been assigned to Palestine in the latter part of 1936 as an Arab affairs expert. He could read the Koran in the original. He arrived with all the Colonial Office prejudices against the Zionist colonization of Palestine, but in his room in the Savoy Hotel in Haifa, where he established his headquarters, he set out to reread the Bible and, in less than three months of contact with the existing situation, he was totally converted to the cause of the kibbutzim. Appointed "intelligence officer" to Jerusalem headquarters, he wrote to Weizmann on May 31, 1937: "I wish to offer my services to you, the leader of the Zionist movement."

Greeted at first with suspicion by the Haganah leaders, Wingate's services eventually earned him a place in Zionist history as the "Lawrence of Judea."

In light of the futility of the actions taken by the authorities to combat Arab bands with regular troops, whose rigid training was ill-adapted to this form of savage guerrilla warfare, Wingate suggested to his superiors the organization of night patrols, the SNS (Special Night Squadrons), recruited from the ranks of the Jewish auxiliary police and led by British officers, which would operate out of the kibbutzim with the stated objective of protecting the Galilee pipeline. Once he had gotten the green light, Wingate set up the headquarters of the new force, which consisted of three Jewish companies and one British company, at Kibbutz Ein Harod. He instructed an entire generation of Jewish combatants in the art of carrying out small-scale but vigorous attacks with small mobile units; taking advantage of nighttime conditions and employing any kind of trick and diversionary tactic to make daring surprise raids on the enemy.

The Haganah sent him its best men—the members of Itzhak Sadeh's rural militia—and Wingate personally led many attacks against the Arab villages in Upper Galilee, where bands of the Grand Mufti's or the Scarlet Pimpernel's men had taken refuge. Looked up to by his men—his nickname in Hebrew means "The Friend"—Wingate himself trained the future leaders of the Palmach. His name was to be given to many streets in Israeli cities, and his influence lasted far longer than his short stay in Ein Harod.

On January 23, 1939, a conference of intelligence service officers at the headquarters in Jerusalem decided that the use of Jewish elements from the Yishuv in the SNS was undesirable: "We must not provoke the Arabs by employing Jews in our offensive actions against their rebellion." Wingate was recalled to England in May 1939, first to serve in an antiaircraft battery, and then to glory in Burma.

"I am forced to leave the country I love," he said in his farewell message in Hebrew to the night commandos. "I imagine you know why. I am being transferred because we have become too friendly. I promise you I will return; if not by regular means, I shall return as a refugee."

A senseless fatal airplane crash in Burma prevented Wingate—then a general—from keeping his promise. But his example was a profound inspiration to the six principal commanders of the Palmach who were appointed in the days following its creation on May 15, 1941.

Even before the Palmach had fully organized, Special Operations requested a contingent of saboteurs needed for an expedition against the Tripoli refineries. The operation was planned so quickly that the British were unable to have weapons delivered from their Egyptian headquarters—there was no question of using local arsenals for this kind of secret mission. The Haganah thus had to draw upon its own stockpiles of illegal arms in supplying the twenty-three volunteers who had been hastily picked from among the best elements of the nascent Palmach. David Hacohen protested to Sadeh: "We could be sending them to death senselessly." Sadeh's answer was: "It's urgent. The offensive is imminent, and we must deprive the enemy of fuel."

On May 18, 1939, the group embarked aboard a coast guard cutter, the *Sea Lion,* under the command of Major Anthony Palmer. Its radio fell silent an hour later, after announcing its arrival in Lebanese waters. After the capture of Syria and Lebanon in 1941, traces of the *Sea Lion* were sought in vain.

"They were for us the best of the best," said Joseph Fein, the Haganah investigator, father of the future chief of the Israeli Air Force in 1967, Motti Hod, to a high French official who expressed surprise at the persistence of the later search for some indication of the fate of the twenty-three men who had been lost. "It's as though your army had lost all its twenty-three top generals at once."

All Fein could come up with was a pair of trousers with the initials of one of the men, Aryeh Gelbard. Members of a German radio post captured at the end of June 1941 were said to have mentioned an Italian submarine's interception of a boatload of Jews and Englishmen. According to a witness, a certain Commander Sollages was said to have buried seven bodies found on a Lebanese beach at the end of May 1941.

Another witness said that he had heard from a Vichy judge posted in Tripoli that a group of Palestinian prisoners had been transferred to Aleppo on May 22, 1939. Apparently the *Sea Lion* was destroyed by the explosives she was carrying on board, after being attacked by a Vichy patrol boat. Those who escaped were transferred to Aleppo and summarily executed. No file on this matter can be found in the French archives.

On the eve of its offensive against the Vichy forces in the Levant, Special Operations dispatched the first two companies of the Palmach in scouting vessels with a mission to cut telephone lines, open routes for Australian reconnaissance units, and take several bridges: A Company, under the command of Yigal Allon from Kibbutz Guinossar, and B Company, under the command of a young working-class soldier from Nahalal who had just been freed from the prison in Acre, where he was serving ten years for illegally forming a clandestine guerrilla group. His name was Moshe Dayan. At the Iskandrun Bridge, 20 kilometers from Rosh Hanikra, B Company went into action against the Fort Gouraud garrison. During this engagement, a French bullet struck Dayan's field glasses and took out his left eye.

At the same time, David Raziel, one of the founders of the Irgun, formed in 1935—who had broken with the Haganah's policy of temporizing and who had also just been released from the Latrun internment camp, was killed in Bagdad in an attempt set up by the British intelligence service to kidnap the Grand Mufti.

During the next year, 600 Palmach troops were given sabotage training in the Mishmar Haemek camp, which was equipped for training only 100 agents. The troops trained in shifts, using the same false identity papers.

At the beginning of 1943, 250 volunteers—some of them women—were sent to a camp in Egypt to learn parachute and radio techniques. Those with German backgrounds were formed into a commando unit which was to be parachuted into Libya behind Rommel's lines, wearing Wehrmacht uniforms. Those who were Judeo-Arab made up the Arab section.

The German section of the Palmach never got the chance to see action, so rapid was the Afrika Korps' retreat into Tunisia. Thirty-two of its members were parachuted into Yugoslavia and Italy in an attempt to organize a Jewish resistance and information network in the Balkans. Most of them were captured by the Germans, among them the heroic Hannah Senesh, who was tortured and shot in Budapest, her birthplace, in 1944.

Since the German threat no longer hung over the Near East, that same year, the British broke off relations with the Palmach, which was forced to go back underground overnight. Toughened by its commando spirit, however, it was to play a prime role in the struggle against the British blockade of the Palestine coastline in a renewed attempt to prevent Jewish immigration. In November 1947, its two thousand members were in effect the only permanent mobilized force at the service of the future Jewish state. "With three thousand more men," said Itzhak Rabin, who was one of them, "the war of independence would have been won at a lower price."

Because of its lack of funds, the Palmach put its men on half-time work in order to be able to continue maintaining its units, sending them for fifteen days a month into the kibbutzim and thus gradually transforming them into the shock troops of the socialist left. Overshadowed by the seeds of dissent on both left and right, Ben-Gurion took quick steps to dissolve the Palmach—the elite of his combat army—after having eliminated the Irgun, under cover of the war.

But the Palmach had left its mark and its style on an entire generation—the generation of 1948. Without insignia or salute, its distinctive sign of command was the rallying cry "Follow me," given by the leader of the operation at the head of his unit. Neither the wounded nor the dead were ever left on the field to fall into enemy hands. "A fighter who knows that his comrades are prepared to sacrifice themselves to save him will never know fear," Arik Sharon commented, having himself been saved in the nick of time during the Battle of Latrun. "First to be strong, and only afterward to be right," would remain one of the slogans chanted in chorus around the campfires by "comrades" who call themselves by their nicknames to this day.

The commando spirit passed down from the Palmach to Tsahal (Tsva Haganah Le-Israel: Israel Defense Forces) was to prevail throughout Israel's military history: the reprisal raid of Unit 101, obligatory parachute training for all officers and navy commandos, the crossing of the Suez Canal in October 1973 that Sharon called a "commando operation on the division level," the raid on Beirut, the raid on Entebbe.

The political activities of the Palmach's most radical elements were in fact more indicative of *esprit de corps* than of party spirit. This spirit is encountered later on among the super-doves as well as among the hawks of Greater Israel. Ben-Gurion's groundless fears and their being pushed into the background left nothing but bitterness and resentment among these heroes of Israeli independence. Personal quarrels thus became more important than political or ideological differences, as demonstrated by Itzhak Sadeh's two favorite disciples: the one-eyed Moshe Dayan and the timid Yigal Allon, a general at age thirty who captured a prisoner named Gamal Abdel Nasser in 1948 in the Falouja pocket. Rivals in politics as they were rivals in the army, in 1969 Dayan and Allon vied with each other for the seat of Prime Minister Levi Eshkol—which fell to Golda Meir. In June 1977, they were to meet face-to-face during the course of a brief ceremony when they handed power one to the other, succeeding each other at the head of the Ministry of Foreign Affairs.

Like all the Israeli leaders, Dayan and Allon were opposed to each other not only out of personal ambition, but also because of the childish quarrels prevalent in another leadership nursery, the Shay (from *Sherut Yediot*), the Haganah's principal intelligence service, which Ben-Gurion turned into his secret police.

"The Shay is everywhere," wrote Isser Harel, one of its former chiefs, longtime Number One in the Israeli services. "No one knows when, how, or where this phantom service was born." But its name was never spoken without fear.

One need only go back to the guard corps—the Hachomer—created in 1907 by the activists of Ben-Gurion's and Ben-Zvi's Labor Party to find its genesis. After the British conquest of Palestine, the Hachomer was broken up—it never had more than about a hundred members, but they were extremely influential on the ideological level—and gave rise to the Haganah, founded by Jabotinsky on the model of Trotsky's Red Army, but subject to the civil authorities of the Yishuv. The Haganah was led by a national six-member committee—three representatives from the Histadrut founded in 1921 by Ben-Gurion, and three from the private sector—with an operational headquarters. Little by little, the Histadrut took over supreme direction of this headquarters, entrusted to a bureaucrat who was chosen in turn from among three brothers-in-law: Eliahu Golomb, a Hachomer veteran; Dov Hoz, and Shaul Meyerov-Avigur, a former companion of Joseph Trumpeldor, the one-armed captain. In 1935 Avigur succeeded Dov Hoz and set up the first permanent office of the Haganah in Room 33 of the Histadrut Building in Tel Aviv, where he centralized all intelligence derived from local commanders into one single information service: the Shay. He appointed Reuven Shiloakh to a half-pay post as editor of a confidential bulletin which contained information consisting of intelligence, propaganda, and counterespionage. Soon there were thousands of agents of this top-secret bureau, from which sprang most of the future Israeli services: almost all of the Jewish inspectors and officers in the Palestinian police, unbeknownst to their English superiors and their Arab colleagues; post office employees; telephone operators; employees in the large hotels; journalists; secretaries; café waiters; highly placed Jews in the British administration. Clandestine listening devices were hooked into the telephone lines of the military and civilian officials of the Mandate's government.

Israel Amir, the first all-powerful boss of this shadow army, appointed Isser Harel as secretary of the Jewish department of the Shay. His task: hunting down dissidents and liquidating traitors. Since it was impossible to employ legal procedures, there were summary executions. Members of the Shay even delivered over to their British adversaries wanted dissidents who were members of the Irgun and the extremist group Lechi (*Lochamei Herut Israel: Fighters for the Freedom of Israel*) organized in June 1940 after a schism in the Irgun, when its chief, Abraham Stern, accused the Irgun of giving priority to the anti-Nazi struggle.

Never having read a manual of secret warfare, Isser Harel discovered the principle of clandestine action—compartmentalization—all on his own. This practice enabled the Haganah leaders to escape the widespread raids and arrests made by the British Army in its attempt to liquidate the Zionist adventure by military means on Saturday, June 19, 1946, a date which is known in the history of Jewish resistance in Palestine as "Black Sabbath." This action was countered by Begin's Irgun, which blew up the King David Hotel in Jerusalem, the headquarters of the British forces, on July 22. From Paris, Moshe Sneh, the Haganah commander-in-chief had given the go-ahead for the action.

This was the moment at which the Haganah entered the death struggle against the Mandate's administration, joining with the Stern Group after having fought against them; two years before, the Stern Group had assassinated the British Resident Minister in Cairo.

4

"KILL THE MINISTER!"

Abraham Stern—known as Yair—had been thinking about it ever since the appointment of a minister of state to the post of Resident Minister for the Near East in the spring of 1941. Barely a year earlier, Stern had resigned from the Irgun Zvai Leumi (IZL or Etsel for short), the national military organization that had grown out of the Haganah B, a group that had rallied to Jabotinsky between 1931 and 1937. Following the policy established by the Haganah at the beginning of the war, the Irgun had made the decision to subordinate everything to the struggle against Hitler. Stern had disagreed with this truce, which allied the revisionist nationalists with the international socialist members of the Haganah and the Jewish Agency. He maintained that the Jews must not abandon their activities against British imperialism, which was occupying Palestine and forbidding entrance to the persecuted Jews of Europe. Stern formed a small group of "ultras," attracting many followers of high quality and character, which came to be known as the Lochamei Herut Israel (Lechi).

While the Irgun leader David Raziel went to work for the British who had interned him in the camp at Latrun, and while Menachem Begin (who had been freed from a Soviet camp along with the Poles from Anders's army with the help of Marshal Sikorski, head of the Polish government-in-exile in London) took over from Raziel when Raziel was killed on a mission to Bagdad, Stern and his handful of supporters were pursued from hideout to hideout, isolated and cut off from the majority of the Yishuv. Caught in his hideout in Tel Aviv, Stern was killed by the police in February 1942.

His companions, who had been interned in Acre and later transferred to the camp at Latrun, staged a spectacular escape on November 1, 1943, at the moment when the Most Honorable Walter Edward Guinness, Lord Moyne, then sixty-five years of age, his fortune built on beer ("Guinness is Good for You"), was preparing to assume his functions as Resident Minister for His Majesty's Government in the Near East, appointed to the post by Winston Churchill, the British Prime Minister. Soon after his appointment,

in January 1944, the escaped members of the Lechi central committee held a clandestine meeting to condemn Lord Moyne to
death. They had decided to go into action against the British—no
longer merely against buildings and installations in Palestine, but,
in line with Stern's basic tenet, against personnel, and in particular
against those persons throughout the United Kingdom who symbolized and supported imperial policy.

According to the indictment set forth in the Lechi's internal
bulletin of February 1942, the newly appointed Resident Minister
in Cairo was both a symbol and a supporter of that policy. As
director of the Colonial Office in 1941, Lord Moyne had been
regarded as being responsible for the strict application of the terms
of the White Book that closed the doors of Palestine to the Jews
fleeing Europe. In particular, he was held responsible for the decision to forbid the debarcation into Turkey of the refugees on the
Struma, a Danubian cattle boat that had arrived at the port of
Istanbul on December 16, 1941, with 769 Jews on board, including
250 women and 70 children. After a two-month wait, the *Struma*
had been forced into the Black Sea, where it sank with cargo and
passengers without ever having received any assistance. Only one
passenger had survived to tell the tragic tale. Finally, Lord Moyne
was accused of having directed the official whitewash of the British
police implicated in the Stern assassination.

Nathan Yalin-Mor, one of the Lechi leaders, added to these
counts in the indictment the point that in a speech before the
House of Lords, Lord Moyne had denied the very existence of the
Jewish people.

Itzhak Shamir, who had organized the Latrun escape disguised
as an Orthodox rabbi, called for the sentence to be executed in
these words: "One does not crush the dragon's tail, but its head.
Who is the dragon's head? Lord Moyne. He is a minister of state,
the representative of the London Government in Cairo for the
whole of the Near East. Even more than the High Commissioner
for Palestine, he is the incarnation of England's anti-Zionist policy.
He is the one we must destroy. Kill the minister!"

The two men picked for this mission shared the same first name:
Eliahu. The elder, Eliahu Ben-Zuri, known as Zebulon, was
twenty-two years old, and as blond as Eliahu Hakim, who was
known as Benny, seventeen years of age, was swarthy. Zubulon
was an intellectual, born in Tel Aviv. Benny had left Beirut with
his family at the age of six, and he looked like an Arab. Both of
them had been deeply shocked by the 1938 hanging of the first Jew
executed by the British in Palestine for an act of reprisal during the

Arab uprisings. Above all, however, Eliahu Hakim had retained the memory of the tragic shipwreck of the *Patria* on November 25, 1940, in the port of Haifa. The ship had been preparing to set out for Mauritius with 1,800 refugees aboard: Jews intercepted upon their arrival in Palestine who were being deported by the British to the Indian Ocean in an attempt to cut off the clandestine immigration movement. The Haganah had planned to sabotage the ship's engines, but an error in calculation by Shaul Meyerov-Avigur, who headed the mission, had turned sabotage into catastrophe. Blown apart by the explosion, the *Patria* sank in twelve minutes; 252 passengers had perished, blown to bits or drowned barely 100 meters from the dock. On the slope of Mount Carmel, Eliahu Hakim, a child of fourteen, had watched the spectacle through field glasses: bodies of armless or headless women floated in the water or were hauled onto boats with poles and grappling hooks.

Determined to avenge the martyrs, Hakim joined the British Army to learn how to handle weapons. Having become an expert marksman, he had deserted his post in Egypt in December and offered his services to the Lechi. In British uniform and with his weapon, he returned to Cairo under an assumed identity at the end of the summer of 1944. He had carefully studied the habits, movements, and schedule of the Resident Minister. On October 20, he was joined by the other Eliahu, who was posing as a soldier on leave: the uniform and identity papers had been appropriated earlier. . . .

On November 6, 1944, at 12:45 on the dot, Lord Moyne's limousine drew up at the entrance to the minister's residence, concealed behind huge masses of bougainvillaea and set a short distance back from the road. It was terrifically hot—nearly 113°. The aide-de-camp came out to open the villa's gates. From the recess where they were concealed, two men carrying revolvers leaped toward the car. One was blond and looked like an Englishman, the other dark as an Egyptian. The dark man pulled open the rear door and fired three times at the passenger, who was killed instantly. The blond man fired at the driver, who was attempting to get out of the car. Their mission accomplished, Benny and Zebulon leaped onto their bicycles, but the shouts of the aide-de-camp attracted the attention of a motorcycle policeman in the Egyptian police, who was passing on the road. The policeman caught up with the two fugitives at the Nile Bridge, ordered them to halt, and, when they did not obey, opened fire and hit the blond. His companion turned, but since he had been given strict orders not to fire on an Arab, he got off his bicycle and rushed to the aid of his wounded friend rather than returning fire. Surrounded by a crowd of people, both the Eliahus were disarmed without resistance.

The news of the assassination exploded like a bomb, pushing the fourth-term reelection of Franklin D. Roosevelt into the background. "Throughout the world," Yalin-Mor wrote in his memoirs, "everyone was asking the same question: Why? Why was this done? Why had two young Palestinian Jews killed a British state minister? Pertinent questions indeed, questions of capital importance, the answers to which had been withheld for far too long."

As for the two Eliahus, they held out for three days before revealing their true identities, before relating the motive for their act, before admitting their allegiance to the Lechi—and this delay was long enough to allow those members of the group whom they had contacted in Cairo to take the necessary steps to protect themselves. They evinced only one concern: that they be tried in Egypt, respecting Egyptian sovereignty, and not sent before a British military tribunal. This contrasting of the sense of fairness of Egyptian judges to the partiality of the British magistrates was designed to flatter the egos of the Egyptian nationalists and to infuriate the English, who were shown up as imperialist occupiers of Egypt. It was too much for Churchill. In the course of the House of Commons funeral eulogy for Lord Moyne—who had been his friend for thirty years—the British Prime Minister gave vent to threats:

"If our dreams in favor of Zionism are to end in the smoke of assassins' guns, and if our efforts are to result only in producing a new world of gangsters worthy of Nazi Germany, then many among us will revise our positions."

The Yishuv Jewish press had not waited for Churchill's threat to condemn this "monstrous crime" unanimously. Led by Ben-Gurion, the Jewish Agency exhorted the population to hunt down the terrorists and deliver them over to the authorities. Chaim Weizmann, president of the International Zionist Organization, wrote a personal letter to Churchill in which he expressed his sorrow and begged him not to hold the Jews of Palestine collectively responsible for the faults of a few black sheep who were rejected with horror by every member of his organization. He went so far as to add publicly that he was more saddened by Lord Moyne's death than by the death of his own son, who had been killed two years earlier in battle while serving in the Royal Air Force. Begin, too, who barely three weeks before had signed an agreement of cooperation between the Irgun and the Lechi designed to revitalize the struggle against the British, openly disavowed the terrorist act as being contrary to the spirit of this agreement, since the intention was to confine the struggle to Palestinian territory.

Far removed from these tensions, which seemed to be bringing the Yishuv to the brink of civil war—the Mandate administration's appeal for collaboration against subversive elements went against the conscience of many militant members of the Histadrut, the Palmach fighters, and even part of the Haganah—Lord Moyne's assassins planned to make their trial into a political forum and into an appeal for Judeo-Arab friendship against British imperialism!

Separated from their families and from their organization, the two began by refusing to let Asher Levitsky, the lawyer assigned them—who was being secretly directed by the Haganah from Jerusalem—enter a plea of "temporary insanity brought on by the suffering of the Jews of Europe," and to rely upon the court's mercy. At the opening of the trial on January 10, 1945, before an Egyptian military tribunal, Levitsky announced that he was withdrawing from the case because of his clients' refusal to adopt the defense he had outlined. Nothing made it more evident that his real principles were not concerned with the fate of the accused. The men chose three Arab lawyers to defend them, and these succeeded in moving the Egyptian dignitaries admitted to the courtroom to tears. Representatives of the press were not allowed to take notes of the statements made by the accused, and British military censorship took control of the courtroom records.

Both men were sentenced to death on January 18, 1945, in accordance with the Koran's precept, "He who kills shall be killed." As soon as the verdict was announced, a wave of petitions began to flow across the desks of King Farouk, King George VI, President Roosevelt, and Pope Pius XII, all calling for clemency. Egyptian students marched through Cairo shouting, "Free the innocent!" Then, on February 24, 1945, one of the demonstrators killed Farouk's prime minister.

Immediately after sentence had been passed on the Eliahus, Churchill had sent a telegram to Lord Killern, the British minister in Cairo, calling for the sentence to be executed:"I hope the sentence will be carried out, or else we shall proceed straight into a conflict between Egypt and ourselves." On February 26, 1945, in tendering the condolences of his government to King Farouk, Churchill stated: "There can be little doubt that measures of security must be reinforced and, above all, that the execution of sentences meted out to men shown to be guilty of political crimes must be rapid and exemplary."

On March 2, 1945, Farouk signed the Eliahus' death sentence to be carried out on March 22. Eliahu Hakim was the first to mount the scaffold. He paused at the foot of the stairs and sang the "Hatikvah"; then he turned himself over to the hangman. Eliahu Ben-Zuri's turn came three-quarters of an hour later; he refused the succor of a rabbi.

Their exemplary conduct at their execution made a deep impression in Egypt. The British, however, saw to it that their last wishes were denied them: burial in Eretz Israel, in the Holy Land. They posted guards in the Jewish cemetery in Cairo to forestall any attempt to transfer the bodies to Palestine. They were afraid that the graves would become sites for pilgrimages and sources of inspiration to the freedom fighters.

And yet their sacrifice was to serve as model for other sons of the Yishuv, overriding any and all ideological disputes. Fifteen years later, it inspired Eli Cohen, the Cairo-born Israeli master-spy hanged in a public square in Damascus, on his march to the scaffold.

More than thirty years later, President Sadat acceded to the request of the aged Pauline Hakim, presented through Dr. Henry Kissinger on March 18, 1975, to see her son reinterred at the foot of Mount Carmel. The remains of both the Eliahus were repatriated in June 1975 within the framework of an exchange of prisoners resulting from the negotiation of the final provisional accord between Israel and Egypt. The Hakim family was plunged into mourning again by a further sacrifice on March 18, 1978, with the death of Sergeant Major Yaron Hakim, Eliahu's nephew, during an Israeli military operation in South Lebanon.

Contrary to Ben-Gurion's initial predictions, however, Lord Moyne's assassination was, above all, the signal for a revolt that gradually drew the Irgun and the Haganah into active resistance against the Mandate's policy. The Lechi, a restricted and ultraclandestine organization whose chiefs were continually being sent to prison up until the day of independence, furnished the Israeli political class with very strong personalities: men who were outstanding not for any precise common ideology, but for extremism in all things. On the far left, Nathan Yalin-Mor, a militant for the left-wing peace movement, and the novelist Amos Kenan of the "Peace Now" movement. On the far right, Geula Cohen, former announcer for the Lechi's clandestine radio station, a spokeswoman for the hard-line Likud group in the Knesset, and Itzhak Shamir, president of the current Knesset.

And yet, perhaps Lord Moyne was the wrong choice of target

for Shamir and Yalin-Mor. Before his posting to Cairo on November 1, 1943, Moyne had submitted to the British cabinet a memorandum calling for recognition of a Jewish State on the Palestinian coast, to be balanced by independence for a Greater Syria extending from Lebanon to both banks of the Jordan. The philosopher, Sir Isaiah Berlin, was to note in 1973 that the assassination had, in fact, had an effect contrary to Yalin-Mor's thesis, according to which the act would have "succeeded in breaking the wall of silence built around Palestine, as it was around the Nazi extermination camps." Instead, it had caused Churchill to draw back from a partition solution envisaged in 1945: one that might have avoided the war for independence, since at that point the Arabs had been without the means to oppose it by force. Far from changing direction, the succeeding British Labour government had closed Palestine to the survivors of the Holocaust, thereby forcing the active forces in the Yishuv to organize mass clandestine immigration.

5

EXODUS 47-EXODUS FROM EUROPE 5707

Of the 1,000,000 European Jews remaining at the end of the war, only 300,000 were able to find a home in their countries of origin; 700,000 homeless people dragged their uncertain nationality along the roads of Europe, human flotsam on the surface of the wave of liberation. Among these were 100,000 who had survived death. This homeless residue of the Holocaust of six million of their fellows found themselves in "displaced persons" camps set up by the Allies at the very sites of their martyrdom.

Out of all the havens cruel experience had shown them to be so fragile, one—the imagined memory of the far-off homeland of their prayers or thoughts—was ineradicable. Now that the entire world seemed closed to them, this image of their lost country was made more intense by the arrival among them of former Jewish partisans, militant members of the Zionist movements, rabbis in the American Army, Jewish Brigade fighters who had been part of the British Army, the early emissaries of the Yishuv from Eretz Israel—the Holy Land—all of whom followed in the footsteps of the liberators.

On June 18, 1945, two months after the horrible discovery of the death camps, and one month and ten days after the surrender of the Third Reich, the Jewish Agency for Palestine asked the Mandate authorities for 100,000 immigration permits for the 100,000 who had escaped the mass killings. Three weeks later, the British electorate voted into power the leaders of the Labour party, traditionally favorable to the Zionist calls for a Jewish National Home. At its most recent congress, the Labour party had called for the immediate lifting of the restrictions set up by successive White Books on Jewish immigration to Palestine.

However, Clement Attlee, the new Prime Minister, delayed his reply even when, two months later, he received a letter from American President Harry Truman, supporting the Jewish Agency's request. As though the Holocaust had never happened, on September 24, the Colonial Office called in Chaim Weizmann, president of the World Zionist Organization, to inform him of its generous offer of the last 1,500 entry permits for Palestine provided under the terms of the regulations in effect since the 1939 White Book. Not until November 13 was the Labour government's official position made known by the ex-union leader Ernest Bevin, now foreign minister. Britain was willing to renew this monthly 1,500 quota of immigration permits—but no more. This time the reason given was the possible danger of Soviet penetration into the Middle East. The real reason was support for the course of conduct backed by the so-called experts in Arab affairs, haunted by the T. E. Lawrence mythos and anti-Semitic attitude.

Instead, Bevin proposed the establishment of an Anglo-American investigating committee to study both the status of the Jewish refugees and the Palestine question. He did so because he was anxious not to alienate the United States, whose aid was indispensable to the economic recovery of Great Britain. His refusal of the Jewish request was to be a fatal blow to the future of the temporary cooperation that had prevailed in Palestine between the Jewish Agency and the Palestine Mandate in the common battle against Nazism, and also to the episodic collaboration between the Haganah and British police in the fight against Jewish terrorism following the assassination of Lord Moyne. On December 30, 1945, Ben-Gurion, the president of the Jewish Agency, and Moshe Shertok-Sharett, head of its political department, informed the British High Commissioner that this policy of procrastination was at an end. And, in any event, their followers had not waited for this decision: as early as October 10, 1945, the Haganah had carried out a raid on the Atlit internment camp, aimed at liberating 210 "illegal" immigrants who had been intercepted on arrival. For the first time, an English officer was killed. Since that date, the Haganah had blown up patrol boats belonging to the maritime police in the port of Haifa. At last the Haganah was able to turn all its activities to battle on one single front: against the *de facto* maintenance of the blockade of the Palestinian coast by the successors of Chamberlain and Churchill.

On May 2, 1946, Prime Minister Attlee announced his government's *de facto* refusal to follow the conclusions reached by the joint investigating committee without the prior dissolution and disarmament of Jewish resistance organizations in Palestine. On the one hand, the Anglo-American commissioners had recommended an increase in immigration permits for 100,000 Jews in displaced persons camps and, on the other, a formula of progressive self-determination for Palestine. And they had explicitly rejected the prior conditions now demanded by Whitehall.

The long, bitter battle that ensued to save the 100,000 Jews from their despair was to become the front line in the struggle for national liberation waged by the Yishuv activists, up until the day of Israel's independence. By refusing to grant 100,000 visas, the British were forced to send 100,000 troops to Palestine. Nevertheless, they were unable to set up a bulwark against the tidal wave of clandestine immigrants.

In the footsteps of the Allied armies making their way through the ruins of Europe, came mysterious emissaries who were already at work organizing escape over frontiers and an exodus across the forbidden Mediterranean. They formed a virtual supply network, receiving its wares at a "central office" that had been established before the war, and which was now hastily reconstituted as the war drew to a close. This was the Mossad Aliyah Bet—the "Organization for Aliyah B"—i.e., the unauthorized immigration.

The creation of this very special service had been ordered in 1937 at a secret meeting held in Tel Aviv among the worker movement leaders and leaders of the kibbutzim and the Haganah, in order to prevent the organization and control of the "wild" immigration of persecuted Jews from Germany and Poland from falling into the hands of unscrupulous "slave traders" and "revisionist adventurers." Ben-Gurion, who on several occasions had gone to London to negotiate increases in the annual quotas, had taken three years to come round to this point of view: one that had been supported by a minority of the pioneer movement since 1934.

The Mossad set up its headquarters in Paris and had links throughout Europe sending agents into the heart of Nazi Germany and annexed Austria to organize a network for clandestine immigration. However, the war soon forced it to limit its activities to the Near East. Now there was only one link, in Geneva. The Mossad moved its headquarters to Istanbul, the last bridgehead through which Jews fleeing the invasion of the Balkans could pass.

As of March 1945, Mossad headquarters were again established in Paris, a stone's throw from General Eisenhower's headquarters, with at its head the former watchman from the Galilee, Shaul Meyerov-Avigur, one of the three brothers-in-law on the Haganah staff. He was a taciturn, aging, and somewhat spectral man, whose huge eyes seemed to devour his face. As a rule, he was to be found ensconced in his simple hotel room near the Place de l'Étoile, on the telephone to the four corners of the globe, receiving the infrequent visitor while lying on his bed with a cup of tea—his sole luxury—which he liked to prepare and serve with a certain amount of ceremony. "Treating myself to a good time," he would say. He had had many altercations with Ben-Gurion, his "master," who had, before the war, been little concerned with the problem of "illegal" immigration and had threatened to eject him from the Histadrut for having smuggled in a boatload of refugees on his own initiative. It was not to be the last disagreement. Most quarrels were over questions of defense, which he accused Ben-Gurion of misunderstanding, and to which stand he owed his downfall following the war of independence.

During this period the Mossad divided its activities between two branches: the Brikha, entrusted with the transporting of refugees from displaced persons camps to the shores of the Mediterranean; and the Ha'apala, which had the difficult job of getting them across the sea and into Palestine.

The Brikha stationed its agents in trouble spots to organize the spontaneous exodus of uprooted populations, people who set out with no other purpose than to flee the theatre of their nightmares. It set up headquarters in Prague's synagogue—nearly a thousand years old—which stood at the crossroads of the currents of western and southern migration. Soon the Brikha had 300 agents in 11 countries, and 1,000 locally recruited guides and convoy leaders. It made use of all kinds of subterfuge in making frontiers "penetrable" and in procuring transit visas.

Meanwhile, the Ha'apala put to sea 12 schooners of under 250 tons between July and December 1945; with these it succeeded in landing 4,500 of the first immigrants, out of two Greek and six Italian ports. In the next six months, it transported twice that number. The 20,000 men of the Jewish Brigade who were being demobilized procured British Army trucks and American surplus materiel for the Mossad. But it soon grew impossible for the Ha'apala to keep up with immigration since it relied solely on summary embarkations of from 10 to 100 passengers and was dependent upon the sympathetic cooperation of the U.S. Army in Germany and on diversionary actions to circumvent the British authorities in Italy. An emissary was sent to the United States to collect funds for the operations and for the purchase, repair, renovation, and equipping of a fleet of blockade runners with a higher tonnage than the fishing boats and tramp steamers chartered from small Greek shipowners then being used. Crews, ready to meet any eventuality, were to be led by sailors and former Palmach fighters and would be able to put up, along with the passengers, active resistance to boarding-and-search missions at sea, and passive resistance to being transferred to deportation vessels bound for Cyprus. This step was taken by the Haganah leadership in response to the August 13, 1946, decision adopted by Mandate authorities to intern on that island all clandestine immigrants intercepted in Palestinian waters.

At the beginning of the year, the Mossad had set up an operational base in Marseille and had established transit camps and obtained rail and other facilities, all with the assistance of high officials in the Socialist party and in the Communist labor unions. The Minister of the Interior agreed to furnish collective entry visas in duplicate that could be used simultaneously at various frontier crossings. As for the DST (Défense et Sécurité du Territoire—roughly the French FBI), its director, Roger Wybot, was eager to support the Mossad's clandestine activities on French territory, as much out of sympathy for the Zionists as in the hope of recapturing English documents in the Haganah's possession relating to the manipulations that had led to France's being evicted from its positions in the Levant. Wybot was encouraged in this by the successive government ministers to whom he reported: Adrien Tixier, Edouard Depreux, Jules Moch, all of them SFIO leaders (Section Française de l'Internationale Ouvrière—French Socialist party). Wybot knew that the Haganah's main broadcasting station had been set up in the villa of the ministers' former chief secretary, the lawyer André Blumel, not far from Rueil, on the outskirts of Paris. For its radio transmissions, according to an American source, the Mossad had at its disposal a "better network than the American army in Germany." In addition, the Mossad had a complete logistic backup: the forgery of papers, navigation companies, cover identities and operations—an impressive infrastructure which would form the kernel of Israel's future spy system, which was to retain the name Mossad. The Mossad's creation was indicative of the active complicity of the administration and services of countries like France which acted as forwarding areas for clandestine immigration. This complicity was to have interesting consequences: before Israel became a country, it existed as a state within a state in France.

The DST also took a hand in the secret war waged by the British services against this "traffic" by protecting the Mossad's network and misleading British Intelligence Service agents. It kept a tight surveillance on a particular Englishman residing in Cassis who had been assigned to spy on the setting up of clandestine receiving stations. The man was arrested on July 10, 1947, in the act of informing London of the departure of 4,550 self-styled immigrants to Colombia, who set out aboard the *President Warfield,* a strange ship anchored at Sète: it had been salvaged in Baltimore, fitted out in a Ligurian shipyard, and now flew the Honduran flag.

Notwithstanding the pressures brought to bear by the British embassy to prevent its sailing, the *President Warfield* slipped cable and fled to the open sea, in the face of many perils. Once on the high seas, the crew hoisted the blue and white flag with the Star of David and the true name: *Exodus 47*—in Hebrew, *Exodus from Europe 5707.* Seven days later, after a violent boarding that resulted in 3 dead and 146 wounded, its passengers were removed to three prison boats for deportation to Cyprus. Instead of heading toward the island, however, whose camps the Mossad had purposely planned to fill to bursting to call attention to the Jews' plight, the three floating jails headed for the French coast. Bevin had personally decided to take revenge for the *Exodus* survivors' insolent defiance by returning them to France, which was accused of having allowed them to leave in the first place.

Once having dropped anchor before Port-de-Bouc, the unfortunate passengers, clinging to their prison bars beneath a leaden sky, refused to disembark. Their amazing resistance to blackmail, and the stifling heat, lasted throughout the month of August. Bevin then took upon himself the terrible responsibility of having them returned to their original point of departure: Germany, where they were interned on September 10, 1947, after their tragic two-month voyage, in camps near Hamburg.

To quote Fouché, the father of modern intelligence, this was worse than a crime—it was a blunder. The fate of the thwarted passengers of the *Exodus* weighed heavily on the conclusions then being drawn up by the United Nations Special Commission, which had been considering the Palestinian question. In its conclusions, the commission called for the withdrawal of the mandate granted to Great Britain by the former League of Nations in 1920, and for the division of the territory into two sovereign states: one Jewish and one Arab. Less than two months after the *Exodus*'s odyssey, these conclusions were adopted by the United Nations General Assembly.

6

BIRTH OF A NATION

The "Old Man" was sleeping! On this Saturday evening, November 29, 1947, at the moment when, beneath the dome of a former skating rink in Flushing Meadows, New York, the great decision was being made, Ben-Gurion was dead to the world. He had chosen to spend the night in a hotel near the Dead Sea, in the midst of a lunar landscape of hills, the most desolate, austere, and sublime region of the country. He had turned in early while the Jews of Palestine, huddled over their radios or crowded around the loudspeakers that had been set up by the leading newspapers in public squares in Tel Aviv, Haifa, and Jerusalem, prepared to listen to the vote—an expectant, attentive population, nerves on edge, half-frenzied with excitement and anxiety—to hear, country by country, the United Nations General Assembly, which was scheduled to convene at ten o'clock local time.

Ten thousand kilometers away, the delegates from 56 countries were meeting to decide the fate of this narrow strip of land on the edge of the Eastern Mediterranean, a land half the size of Denmark, with one-fourth the population of Belgium: the land that was all that was left of Palestine under the British Mandate which was to expire thirty years to the day after the 117-word Balfour Declaration.

It was three in the afternoon in New York when Oswaldo Arahana, the Brazilian delegate who was president of the session, called the meeting to order. A two-thirds majority—32 votes—was required for adoption of the plan of partition jointly supported by the USSR and the United States. Following alphabetical order, Afghanistan was the first country called upon to vote yes or no.

In her modest home in one of the new Jewish quarters of Jerusalem, a forty-nine-year-old woman listened to the progress of the vote over an old radio, as she chain-smoked cigarette after cigarette, checking off each vote on a note pad. Although there was usually a crowd in her kitchen, this evening she had wanted to be alone with her cup of coffee, her perpetual cigarette, her notebook. For her, it was the culmination of her entire life's struggle.

Golda Mabovitch, daughter of a Kiev cabinetmaker, had been

eight years old when her family emigrated to the United States in 1906, fleeing the pogroms of the czarist counterrevolution. She had become a Zionist at the age of seventeen, collecting funds for refugees on the streets of Denver. At twenty-three, having become Mrs. Meyerson, a Milwaukee schoolteacher, she had persuaded her husband to follow her to Palestine to raise chickens on a kibbutz in Galilee. She had already separated from her husband when, at age thirty-eight, she had been elected head of the Histadrut's political section. She was later to take the name Golda Meir.

It was 12:30 A.M. when her trembling hand wrote the outcome of the vote being broadcast direct from the indescribable uproar of the New York skating rink: 33 yeses, 13 nos, 10 abstentions. One vote over the required majority: the unexpected vote of France, which had hesitated to set itself apart from Great Britain.

The harsh, primitive sound of the shofar—the ram's horn that traditionally calls Jews to pray and to assemble—suddenly split the soft night. A joyous crowd spilled into the streets of West Jerusalem to converge on the lighted building of the Jewish Agency.

In the camps on Cyprus where 16,000 clandestine immigrants were still interned, in camps in Germany where 250,000 displaced persons were still languishing—their ranks swollen by refugees from the East—flags and bottles miraculously appeared in tents and barracks. In kibbutzim and in Jewish villages, as well as in the city streets, tens of thousands of pioneers danced frenzied horas in the moonlight.

In the crowded courtyard of the Jewish Agency, where the assembled throng was chanting the names of well-known leaders, there was a silence when Golda appeared on the balcony, her face streaked with tears in the glare of the spotlights. Placing her strong, square hands on the balustrade, she took a deep breath and spoke:

"For two thousand years, we have awaited our deliverance. We have always known this day would come. And it has come . . . *Yehudim, mazel tov!*—Jews, good luck!"

Forty kilometers away, Ben-Gurion had just been awakened. His eyes puffy from sleep, his white hair standing on end, his habitual white shirt hanging out over his trousers, the "Old Lion" called for paper to write a draft declaration on behalf of the Jewish Agency. The only paper to be found was toilet paper. Workers from the salt flats arrived at his hotel and began to dance with guests and the hotel staff.

"I cannot be among the dancers," Ben-Gurion noted. "I am like someone in mourning at a wedding. I am filled with an awful fear at the sacrifice that awaits our people."

The dawn of November 30 had already begun to touch the smooth blue-green surface of the Dead Sea when Ben-Gurion returned to his office in Jerusalem. He, too, went up to caress the folds of the huge blue and white flag hung from the balcony. He could not keep from murmuring, "At last, we are a free people!"

The statement he read to the guiding committee approved the partition plan the United Nations had just adopted, notwithstanding the irregular shape and strategically indefensible position given the future Jewish State. The same day, Menachem Begin, on behalf of the Irgun, rejected the very notion of partition, maintaining that the whole of the region west of the Jordan must by right belong to the Jewish people. However, the Jewish Agency's guiding committee had made a secret decision: to mobilize all the Jews in the Yishuv between the ages of seventeen and thirty-five, under the Haganah. The Arabs had been quick to react to the U.N. vote.

On that same Sunday morning, the first 6 victims of the thirteen-month war, which was eventually to cost the lives of 6,070 of the 650,000 Israeli Jews, had been claimed. They were 5 passengers on a bus attacked by an Arab commando unit between Natanya and Jerusalem, and a Jewish passenger on another bus between Hedera and Jerusalem. In the afternoon, the body of a seventh Jew was discovered in Jaffa, headquarters of the armed bands who from that time on would foment hatred and carry out terrorist attacks against the Jewish population.

On December 2, 5 Jews were killed in broad daylight in the Arab city of Ramle. An Arab mob set fire to the Jewish business center of Jerusalem in plain sight of the impassive British police. Two days later, the Irgun launched reprisal attacks with grenades and bombs on an Arab café in Jaffa, on a district of Haifa, and on a bus station in Jerusalem. A Haganah unit attacked a bus station in Haifa: the toll was 8 dead, 40 wounded. Each succeeding day was to have its crop of bloody incidents.

On December 8 the leaders of the seven independent Arab states met in Cairo to contravene the United Nations plan, which they countered with a secret plan drawn up by their military heads: the "Bloudan Plan." No details of this military plan were released, but the Secretary-General of the Arab League announced: "When the world learns the secret decisions we have reached, it will know with certainty that the Arabs will be victorious." The communiqué issued by the conference affirmed the Arab countries' determination to "wage the struggle for independence and for the freedom of Palestine until victory is achieved."

For the moment, however, they merely supported "without reservation" the formation of a Palestine Liberation Army. Its sinister chieftain was Fawzi el-Kawkji, the infamous "Scarlet Pimpernel" of the bloody uprisings in the 1930s, who had been recruiting volunteers in the Syrian Golan Heights since October for the "Holy War" against Zionism. This Arab outlaw was a strange character, a Lebanese Muslim trained at the Ottoman military academy, an organizer of the Druze guerrilla warfare against the French in Syria, and of uprisings against the Palestinian Jews; he had fled to Berlin during World War II, and had only recently returned to Aleppo via the Russian-occupied zone of Germany. The increasing number of armed confrontations in these early days of December, however, were primarily the work of the mercenaries of the Grand Mufti, a war criminal who had escaped from France after having recruited SS troops for Hitler.

In the two weeks following the United Nations resolution, these confrontations resulted in 160 dead, 54 of them Jewish. By the end of the month, the Jews had lost more than 80 men. Beginning with the first week of January 1948, bands of Arab irregulars began to infiltrate from the north of the country, out of Syria and Lebanon; they unsuccessfully attacked the first two kibbutzim in Upper Galilee. Elsewhere the clashes became more intense each day, and the Yishuv militia was often forced to fight on two fronts, since the British had not abandoned the pretense of "keeping order" until the expiration of their mandate at midnight on May 15.

One of history's strangest wars was waged in the presence of the 100,000 elite troops of the British security force, who acted as though nothing were going on. It was a war without front lines: the battle raged around isolated outposts, in the suburbs of large cities, on highways, and in orange groves. It was a war without armies: irregulars against clandestines, mercenaries against illegal immigrants, PLA fanatics against Palmach and Haganah fighters, the Mufti's terrorists against the clandestines of the Irgun or the Lechi. Ambushes, surprise attacks, criminal acts, minarets turned into machine-gun nests, random raids by the Arabs, gradually took the form of a countrywide strategy: to sever the lines of communication, isolate the cities, segregate the zones of Jewish population, and conquer the besieged areas one by one.

Worse was to come. As early as December 11, 1947, the Arab Legion had attacked a motorized convoy bringing reinforcements from Jerusalem to the outpost of Gush Etzion which had been practically encircled, south of the Holy City. The convoy was forced to turn back after suffering heavy losses. On December 14 the Arab Legion went into action again, this time attacking an aid convoy on the way to a childrens' village near Ramle. And on January 14, 1948, it undertook the siege of the Jewish Quarter of the Old City, inhabited by a small community of religious Jews.

The Arab Legion, which was led by British officers and commanded by a disciple of Colonel Lawrence, Major John Bagot Glubb, known as Glubb Pasha, was in the service of the Hashemite kingdom of Jordan, and was the strongest, best trained, and best equipped army in the Near East. "Loaned" to the Mandate's authorities by King Abdullah for the occupation of strategic points in the Arab zone, and already giving support to the irregulars who had seized the Arab quarters of Jerusalem—despite the international status of the Holy City laid down by the United Nations—this troop was the Jews' most formidable threat.

In an attempt to mitigate this threat, Golda Meyerson (Meir) had had a clandestine rendezvous with King Abdullah on the banks of the Jordan on November 17, 1947, twelve days before the United Nations decision. At the time, she was filling in for the Jewish Agency's political director, Moshe Shertok (Sharett), who was detained at United Nations headquarters by preparations for the forthcoming debate. This first secret meeting between a Zionist leader and an Arab head of state had been arranged by the director of the Naharaym hydroelectric center, Abraham Daskel, known to his many Arab friends as Abu Youssef.

The interview took place at Daskel's villa near the bridge linking Palestine and Transjordan. Golda was accompanied by two Arab specialists—her adviser Ezra Danin, and Eliahu Sasson, who acted as interpreter since she spoke no Arabic. At the beginning of the meeting, King Abdullah had been unable to conceal his surprise at finding himself confronted by a woman. He had to be told that Golda held the second highest position in Jewish diplomacy. The king calmed down and attempted to put the interview on a friendly footing by assuring Golda of his admiration for the Jewish people and by inviting her to visit him "someday" in his palace in Amman.

In the course of the ensuing talk, he informed her of his intention to annex the territories attributed to the Arabs if Palestinian partition became a reality, and he proposed a compromise designed to allow him to save face with the other states of the Arab League: the establishment of a Jewish republic within the framework of a federation of which he would be king. He also told her that, far from desiring to attack the Jews, he was prepared to sign a treaty of entente with them, and that he would undertake to deal with the Grand Mufti of Jerusalem and to require the Arab nationalists to put themselves completely under his control, or else forgo being able to rely on his assistance.

In conclusion, Abdullah and Golda agreed to a new meeting after the vote in the United Nations. This meeting, however, was not destined to take place, despite the contacts maintained by Daskel, their intermediary, who saw the Hashemite king on two occasions after the first conflicts had occurred.

Sir Alec Kirkbride, British High Commissioner in Amman, wrote in his memoirs:

> "When I was told of this interview, I thought that the Israelis had made a mistake by being represented by a woman. Although he respected the opposite sex, King Abdullah was a conservative: in his eyes, women could not be the equal of men, particularly in politics. Arguing politics with a woman made him uncomfortable. In addition, Golda had had little experience in negotiating with the Arabs. It is regrettable that this mission was not entrusted to someone like Sharett, who knew the Arab language and the Arab mentality."

When Dayan was received by Abdullah at his palace at Sunna at the end of the war and informed the king that Golda Meyerson had been sent to Moscow as Israel's ambassador to the USSR, he reported that the king murmured: "Very good, very good. Keep her there."

At the outset of his disagreements with the Arab Legion, the Hashemite king, rightly or wrongly, had the impression that the Jewish leaders would not ultimately accept any of the concessions designed to enable him to appear before the Arab world as the one man able to make the United Nations proposal work. If conflict were to come, "they would take all they could get."

The flow of events brought an end to all exchanges of views, even through intermediaries, until Mohammed Zubeiti, Abdullah's private secretary, received from his friend Daskel, the head of the hydroelectric center, a request from the "National Council"—the body that had succeeded the Jewish Agency on March 30, 1948—to set up another secret meeting between the king and Golda. This meeting was held in the early days of May, at the time when rumors were growing of an intervention by the Arab Legion against Jewish positions—this time an overt and massive intervention—when the British Mandate expired.

Meanwhile, in an attempt to counter the widespread attacks of bands of Arab irregulars, Golda Meyerson had been sent to the United States to collect the funds needed to purchase weapons for survival—primarily from the newly formed People's Republic of Czechoslovakia. Her tour among the American Jews had brought in $50 million. In greeting her upon her return, Ben-Gurion exclaimed, "History will remember that it was a woman who enabled the Jewish State to be born."

Indeed, proclamation of the new state was the purpose of a meeting held on May 12 by the embryo provisional government, consisting of thirteen members of the Yishuv National Council, headed by Ben-Gurion.

At the end of March, when western Galilee was on the verge of being cut off from the rest of Palestine, few Zionist leaders were decided on proclaiming independence. Panic had reached a new high in influential Jewish circles. At the United Nations, pressures were being brought to bear from all sides to overturn the decision of November 29. On March 18 the American delegation had submitted a draft resolution abandoning the partition plan: it proposed replacing the British Mandate by an international trusteeship. On March 30 it submitted a draft armistice which it attempted to have passed in the Security Council. Since that time, Washington had threatened to block the transfer to Palestine of the funds that had been collected.

In the field, certainly, the military catastrophe had been avoided for the time being. In April the Haganah had victoriously counterattacked, reestablishing communications between the majority of the settlements that had been cut off. The Irgun and the Lechi had agreed to put their combined forces at the service of the Haganah in order to reopen the road to Jerusalem, and to wage an assault against Deir Yassin. The "Scarlet Pimpernel's" PLA had been cut to pieces on the Esdralon plain, and since their defeat on the hill of Kastel, the other bands had launched no more operations in force. Tiberias, Haifa, and Safed had been liberated.

The road to Jerusalem was once more being threatened, however, and it appeared that the Arab Legion was about to reenter the fray; an orchestrated invasion by the regular Arab armies would not be far behind. To resolve this problem, Golda received an order from Ben-Gurion on May 9 to renew contacts with King Abdullah. This time Abdullah refused to meet her by the Jordan. He would receive her in his palace in Amman, where she would have to come at her own risk. He was unable to guarantee her safety, nor even to keep her visit a secret. Daskel undertook to set up the journey.

In order to get past the border checkpoints, Golda disguised herself as a Bedouin woman and set out on the Naharaym road in a car driven by Danin, her adviser, who was dressed in a Bedouin keffieh. The king's private secretary came to meet them in his car and take them at night across the Jordan and on to the capital, where they went straight to meet Abdullah, not in the palace, but in a villa belonging to a close adviser. The welcome was still cordial, but the king's tone had changed, as had his proposals. He appeared depressed, preoccupied, nervous.

When Golda reminded him of his November promises, he said his hands were tied by other agreements with the British.

"I am not allowed to keep my promise. Last year, I was alone; I had complete freedom of action. Today, I am merely one head of state among five others."

He could offer only a temporary autonomy within the framework of a Jewish-Arab Palestine.

"Put off your declaration of independence, suspend immigration for a few years. Why are you in such a hurry? I have no choice: either you agree to my new proposal, or it will mean war, whatever the cost to me. However, I will always be glad to talk to you and to sit down with you around a table in order to achieve peace."

"Well," Golda replied, "we'll meet again after the war!"

As they were saying good-bye, the king leaned toward Danin. "After all, you're from the East, like I am," he said in a fatherly tone, "but this time, you haven't helped me."

During the long trip back, Golda and her adviser could see large convoys of tanks and field artillery in the distance: it was the Iraqi army on its way to Palestine.

After arriving back in Tel Aviv on May 11 and having changed back into Western dress, Golda went quickly to the Jewish National Fund headquarters where the Mapai central committee was debating the feasibility of proclaiming statehood, which Ben-Gurion was supporting with all his strength. The majority of the Labor party's leaders had been hostile up until a few days before. Now, however, to everyone's surprise, Moshe Shertok (Sharett) delivered a speech indicating he had changed his mind. He had been among those who had the most serious doubts about the stand to be taken, but now he reported the reply he had recently made to the American Secretary of State, General George C. Marshall, during his mission to Washington. Fearing the extension of the conflict and the outbreak of another world war, the American statesman had kept repeating the same warning: "Don't proclaim independence! Agree to our armistice formula. Otherwise, the Arabs will crush you. In the new international situation that has been created by the Soviet threat in Europe, you cannot count on any help from us."

"The only thing we ask of you," Shertok reported he had replied, "is that you abstain from any intervention."

Shertok no longer believed that rejection of the American plan, which entailed the postponement of the proclamation of independence to some indefinite date, would result in tension with the United States, for that country was too involved in its approaching presidential election to take any steps to cut off the collected funds.

At this juncture, Golda Meyerson passed a hastily scrawled note to Ben-Gurion in which she related the disappointing outcome of her mission to Amman. Ben-Gurion glanced through it and suddenly got up. Concealing his emotion, he left the meeting and leaped into his armored car. A few moments later, he was dashing up the stairway of the Red House on the beach where the Haganah had its headquarters. He called an urgent meeting of the general staff to inform them of what lay before them.

On the next day, May 12, events came thick and fast. Supported by tanks and by cannon, 1,500 of Glubb Pasha's legionaries made a final assault against the Jewish colonies in Gush Etzion in the Hebron hills, which had been isolated by the five-month siege. A few hours later, the General Secretariat of the Mandate's government announced the departure of the British High Commissioner at midnight on May 14, and the immediate withdrawal of the security forces.

The countdown had begun even as the Yishuv's supreme authority, the National Council, was meeting in the halls of the Jewish National Fund in Tel Aviv. Two of its thirteen directors were stuck in Jerusalem. A third was in the United States. The ten members present met without interruption from 10:00 A.M. to 11:00 P.M. trying to reach a decision. Before taking the most important step in the history of the Jewish people since the time an unknown warrior named David had returned the Ark of the Covenant to Jerusalem amid the sound of shouts and trumpets, they listened to reports on the diplomatic and military situation.

Ben-Gurion laid out the problem. "The question of time is vital for two reasons:

"One: the invasion of the country can begin at any minute. The Arab Legion's attack this morning is the first wave of this invasion. Faced with this threat, we must act, and action should not be left to the military leaders alone.

"Two: the date of May 14 unilaterally set by Bevin is fatal for us. It is obvious that serious outbreaks will occur during the night of Friday the 14. Whatever happens, we must face it."

Golda Meyerson then reported on the failure of her talks with King Abdullah of Transjordan; she believed him to be controlled by the British, who had promised him the crown of Palestine in return for a military base at Rafah. Moshe Shertok (Sharett) explained the relations between the great powers: after the rejection of their proposal for an international trusteeship, the United States mostly wanted a cease-fire and a lessening of tension in the Middle East brought about by an indefinite delay in setting up a Jewish State. England, hostile to the notion of international trusteeship, was only halfheartedly supporting the American proposal; hoping, in fact, that the ensuing conflict would weaken both the Jews and the Arabs. The French plan, which was even more unacceptable, was a combination of armistice and temporary trusteeship. The USSR was awaiting the outcome of events, but opposed the French plan.

Israel Galili, the Haganah commander-in-chief, and its interim chief of staff, the archaeologist Yigael Yadin, then took the floor to brief the group on the military situation, which was set forth with a clarity that left no room either for illusions or for undue apprehension. The successes of the preceding month had shown not only the very high morale of the combatants, but also the tactical and strategic superiority of the Jewish units. On the one hand, the directors of the Shay, the intelligence service, did not believe in widespread and immediate Arab aggression. But other speakers noted that a delay in declaring independence would not prevent invasion by the Arabs sooner or later. The world had come to expect a trial by force in Palestine; this was shown by the fall of Gush Etzion.

Ben-Gurion then entered the fray. This was to be his great historic moment.

"The disaster at Gush Etzion has not shaken me. I expected such reversals, and I fear we will have even greater trials to come. There can be no outcome but the destruction of the majority of the Arab Legion. . . . The problem must be resolved by arms."

Then came the vote. Either accept the American proposal and delay the declaration of independence to some distant future, or reject it, which would mean becoming a sovereign state in two days, with all the concomitant dangers.

By show of hands, four members of the council voted for, six against, the American plan. The decision to go forward was thus passed by only a two-vote majority. The motion not to set out the frontiers of the nascent state passed by only one vote.

During the night, two-thirds of the Mapai central committee approved the decision. And Menachem Begin, for his part, proclaimed the Irgun's allegiance to the Jewish State as it had just been defined. Ben-Gurion spent the entire morning hours in meetings with the general staff at the Red House.

It was at this juncture that he received his first visit from a short man with the expressionless, sphinxlike face of a secretive poker player—Isser Harel, the former director of the Shay's Jewish Department, who had been appointed chief of the Tel Aviv sector, where his principal task was to recruit informers for that sector's Arab section. Unlike all his colleagues, who were convinced that King Abdullah was still agreeable to the partition of Palestine with the Jews, and that at the last minute he would restrain his Arab Legion from attacking, Harel alone among the intelligence leaders foresaw an offensive by a coalition of all the Arab armies the minute the Jewish State was proclaimed.

Harel brought more than this conviction to Ben-Gurion; he brought him last-minute information he had just received from one of his agents whom he had, on his own initiative, sent to Amman in a convoy of refugees fleeing the danger zones. This envoy was an Arab from Jaffa named Hassan el-Batir, engaged to a Jewish girl, who had already carried out dangerous missions for the Haganah in its struggle against the British. He spoke flawless Hebrew, and he had a cousin who held a high post in King Abdullah's government.

The informer had returned at midnight on May 12 across the front lines at Hulda, not without having been fired upon by both sides. He handed his safe conduct, written by Isser Harel in invisible ink, to the Palmach commander who intercepted him, and was taken at dawn to Tel Aviv, where Isser came to see him at once.

"Abdullah is going to war—that's certain," reported el-Batir. "The tanks are ready to go. The Arab Legion will attack tomorrow."

Isser Harel immediately passed the message to Ben-Gurion, who dispatched several units during the night to confront the legion's tanks and to establish a defense line across from the hills of Judea and Samaria, ruining the invader's surprise. The "Old Man" was to remember this first meeting with the short man whose star was in the ascendant within the Shay despite attempts to keep him out of its directorship—then entrusted to another Isser, Isser Beeri, known as Big Isser, to distinguish him from the other.

Later, Ben-Gurion was to make Little Isser the chief of his secret police.

For the moment, however, Ben-Gurion's concern was with winning his victory for History. On Friday, May 14, at 4:00 P.M., an hour before the sunset marking the beginning of the Sabbath, the thirteen members of the National Council convened in a room in the Tel Aviv Museum of Art, beneath a portrait of Theodor Herzl flanked by two flags and a Chagall painting, *The Jew Holding the Tablets of the Law.* Dressed in black, and, for once, wearing a necktie around the collar of his white shirt, Ben-Gurion rose and unrolled a parchment, from which he read in his slightly nasal voice the declaration of independence which at that moment gave birth to the State of Israel.

Still, the "Old Man" had every intention of consolidating this victory by not only taking personal charge of the destiny of this State created from the "dregs of humanity," but by actively leading the war against the invader. For over a year he had been preparing himself to play not only the part of political leader and national unifier, but also of military leader, head of the army, of statesman, and strategist.

On March 26, 1947, Ben-Gurion invited the chief of the clandestine Haganah militia, Ze'ev Sheffer, to his Tel Aviv apartment. Following the failure of negotiations with Foreign Minister Bevin over the transformation of the Palestine Mandate, Ben-Gurion had realized that war was inevitable at some future date were the Yishuv ever to have a national existence and the freedom to admit the Jews of the Diaspora. The month before, the Zionist Congress had made him responsible for the defense department. He asked Sheffer to brief him on these latter problems; the seminar lasted several weeks and included the leaders of Sheffer's clandestine military organization.

Although Ben-Gurion's political authority was unquestioned, his competence in matters of defense and security was extremely limited. Those theretofore responsible for leading the army of resistance—Shaul Avigur, Itzak Sadeh, Moshe Sneh, Israel Galili— all doubted the "Old Man" 's ability, at sixty years of age, to turn himself into a military leader, especially since he had never spent much time in military circles. Ben-Gurion himself was somewhat wary of these "partisan leaders"; men who were fine at launching sabotage missions, overseeing illegal immigration or battling with bands of Arab irregulars, but whom he considered unfit to head up a regular army. As an elite unit, the Palmach had never had to prove itself in set battles along classic lines. Ben-Gurion preferred the young, newly demobilized officers of the Jewish Brigade who had fought in the ranks of the British Army during World War II—men with real military experience—to these undisciplined fighters who were accustomed to receiving orders only from their own leaders.

A more serious drawback, in his view, was the anarchy that prevailed within the higher ranks. Who was responsible for the security and defense of the Yishuv? he asked. At the time, the Haganah had a national command, headed by a commander-in-chief chosen by the guiding committee of the Jewish Agency; it had a general staff with its own commander; a political body—the defense committee, whose exact role no one knew—and which, for that matter, had no influence in decision making. The Palmach took orders from no one and behaved like the dissident members of the Irgun and Lechi, both excluded from this overall organization.

When he was made head of the National Council on March 30, 1948, to provide a supreme authority to the Yishuv that would be more governmental than the old Jewish Agency had been, Ben-Gurion believed that all these groupings must be merged into one single body, under a hierarchy directly subordinate to the future defense minister. But how was he to convince all these men, without hurting their feelings, that the romantic era had ended and must give way to the structures and principles of statehood? How was he to make them subordinate to such former Jewish Brigade professionals as Shlomo Shamir or Mordechai Makleff?

"I found the army in two parts," he was to write in his memoirs, "the Haganah and the military. And there was no trust between the two."

Ben-Gurion's decision was influenced by another misgiving. To the technical problem of transforming a resistance movement into a regular army was added a political problem which concerned him even more. The Palmach had been conceived, created, and led by members of the Kibbutz Unity faction who had left his party (the Mapai) in 1944 to found an extreme-left workers' party, the Mapam, whose pro-Soviet sympathies worried him. The Jewish Agency had entrusted the Haganah national leadership to Israel Galili, who was also one of the instigators of this schism and one of the leaders of the Mapam.

Such dangers—real or imaginary—of the "bolshevization" of his future army, and of a possible pro-Communist military putsch, haunted Ben-Gurion. He therefore decided to begin at the top and to attack the national command and its leader in March 1948 by refusing to subordinate the command on the Negev front, which he was establishing, to the Palmach's own general staff. To smooth the way for the transfer of the Jewish Agency's defense powers to the provisional executive of which he had been named head on March 30, he decided to disband the national command, which was no longer a necessary element between the civil authority and the military personnel of the general staff, since the supreme defense responsibilities would be held from then on by the provisional executive, also known as the Council of Thirteen. On April 26 Ben-Gurion informed Galili of this decision. The Haganah leader protested. Galili intended to maintain his position as intermediary between Ben-Gurion and the general staff, and he called on his party to support him.

On May 2 the "Old Man" fired Israel Galili. On the following day, a state of crisis existed: early in the afternoon, the four chiefs of staff, among them General Yigael Yadin—and with the exception of their commander-in-chief Jacob Dori, who was ill—reported to Ben-Gurion's office to demand Galili's immediate reinstatement. That same evening, there was a stormy meeting of the Council of Thirteen. Totally isolated, Ben-Gurion informed them that he would accept the defense ministry only on his own terms. Three days later, the Haganah leaders returned to the attack. Generals Zvi Ayalon, Yigael Yadin, Eliahu Ben-Hur, Moshe Zakok, and Joseph Avidar sent an ultimatum to Ben-Gurion: "If the matter is not settled within the next twelve hours, the department chiefs of the general staff will relinquish responsibility for the conduct of the war."

Ben-Gurion summoned the five generals. Their reception was glacial. The "Old Man" informed them that he would not countenance their inadmissible revolt in the midst of combat. His only compromise would be to reinstate Galili, but without any defined duties. Three days later, Galili agreed to accept the position of his personnel adviser. However, no orders were to pass through him.

When war broke out with the Arab League countries on May 15, dissension was still rife, and orders were poorly channeled when they were not openly contested. Relations between the Palmach's "Harel" brigade and Ben-Gurion's commander on the Jerusalem front, the american colonel David "Mickey" Marcus, were on the point of breaking down. When Marcus was accidentally killed by a sentry a few hours before the truce was to become effective, Ben-Gurion ordered an investigation to find out whether he had been assassinated by members of the Palmach.

Meanwhile, the Mapam leaders continued to press for Galili's reinstatement in his former posts. They particularly blamed Ben-Gurion for having launched the May 24 assault on the Latrun fort with a battalion that had been hastily assembled from immigrants from the *Exodus,* who had landed the evening before. This inexperienced battalion was decimated in two battles.

On June 24 when the front line was only five kilometers from Tel Aviv, General Yadin, interim chief of the general staff, demanded the appointment of the Palmach leader, Yigal Allon, to command the central front. His objective: to break the Arab vise in the Lod-Ramle-Latrun sector, which was blocking the road to Jerusalem, before the recommencement of fighting. However, Ben-Gurion planned to appoint his protégé, Mordechai Makleff, a former officer in the Jewish Brigade. Ten days before the termination of the United Nations truce, he announced a thorough shake-up in the general staff. On July 1 a week before the recommencement of hostilities, the rebel generals reissued their ultimatum of May 6 and threatened to resign.

This second revolt was more serious than the first. Since May 28 the members of the general staff were no longer under the Haganah of the Yishuv, but had been made a part of Tsahal, Israel's defense forces. Much later, Yadin was to admit that his mini-revolt in time of war had been morally questionable, but that events had proved him correct on the choice of Allon for the liberation of the central sector. When called in by Ben-Gurion, however, he had refused to budge.

This time, the "Old Man" was forced to call upon the government.

"We are dealing," he told them, "with a further attempt to transform the army as a whole into an army with allegiance to a particular party. Of our thirteen brigade commanders, eight are Mapam members and only two are loyal to the Mapai. The Palmach, which is already in a state of overt insubordination, is attempting to politicize the army. A Red army or a national army—Galili or Ben-Gurion. Take your pick!"

On July 3 the question was brought before a limited committee of five ministers. Having listened to the generals tell their tale of the military mistakes and unwise strategies of Ben-Gurion, the ministerial committee proposed to reinstate Galili under another title on July 6, two days before the expiration of the truce. The "Old Man" saw red, left the meeting, and wrote a letter of resignation from his posts as prime minister and minister of defense . . . if the matter was not settled as he wished.

On July 7 Ben-Gurion called in sick. Horrified, the ministers agreed to give him Galili's head and to entrust him with direction of all operations and with the complete reorganization of the army. On that evening, Galili returned to his kibbutz to begin what was to be a long political exile. Yadin, however, succeeded in obtaining Allon's transfer to the central front.

Hostilities recommenced on July 8. Allon took Lod and Ramle in three days, much to the satisfaction of the young Palmach chief of operations, Itzhak Rabin. Leading the column of jeeps that had taken Lod in a parade down its main street was a daring lieutenant-colonel with a black patch over his left eye: Moshe Dayan.

Before settling accounts with the Palmach, which had dared to defy his authority but which he still needed in order to win the war, Ben-Gurion first dealt with the threat from the right wing—so right as to be called "fascist"—by taking advantage of a dual set of circumstances and by first extirpating two other hot-beds of dissidence: the Irgun and the Lechi.

As a matter of fact, the Irgun had renounced its own independence of action at the time of the May 15 declaration and had incorporated itself into the newly formed national army—except in the Jerusalem sector, and especially where the defense of the Old City was concerned, because of the United Nations partition plan, which gave international status to the Holy City. As far as Ben-Gurion was concerned, however, there was still a danger that elements of the Irgun might form an army faction loyal to Menachem Begin, who had become his principal political rival.

The agreement signed by the Irgun high command on June 2 that provided for the integration of its 15,000 men into the 45,000 men of the Haganah within Tsahal, also provided that Begin's organization would stop stockpiling war materiel for its own use, and that it would put all of its contacts at the service of the national army. A temporary Irgun headquarters was to remain intact for one month in order to achieve this fusion. There were still 5,000 men in seven battalions left to be integrated when Begin brought to the attention of the defense ministry the matter of a freighter carrying weapons and troop reinforcements chartered by his organization well before the proclamation of statehood.

An old American Navy surplus vessel that had taken part in the Allied invasion, the ship had been purchased in 1947 in Brooklyn for $75,000 by two American sympathizers, the screenwriter Ben Hecht and the novelist Louis Bromfield. It had been rechristened the *Altalena,* in homage to the memory of the revisionist leader

Vladimir (Ze'ev) Jabotinsky, who had used the name as a nom de plume for his literary works. In April it had put in at Port-de-Bouc in France, and had requested arms for the Irgun through Jean Morin, a subordinate of Georges Bidault, the French Foreign Minister. The ship was expected to sail in time to reach Tel Aviv around the middle of May—upon the expiration of the mandate. Its precious cargo: an arsenal sufficient to equip a dozen battalions and a contingent of 900 trained volunteers. However, its loading had been delayed by lengthy negotiations with the French authorities.

Bidault had had to intervene personally with his colleague in the Ministry of the Interior, the socialist Jules Moch, in order that the convoy of military materiel, including 5 tanks, 150 antitank guns and antiaircraft guns, 300 machine guns, 5,000 rifles, 4 million rounds of ammunition, and thousands of bombs and grenades, some purchased elsewhere in Europe and the remainder provided by French arsenals, might be allowed to cross the country.

This was a surprising intervention, coming as it did from a politician who had attempted to prevent the clandestine departure of the *Exodus* the year before, and who had always seemed to be the mouthpiece of Bevin, his British counterpart, in the earlier Ramadier government, in which Moch had at the time been Minister of Transport. Now Bidault seemed to be supporting the extremist cause in Israel—which he had hardly done at the United Nations—and seemed to be speculating on the eventuality of a civil war among the Jews when the British Mandate expired. Jules Moch immediately expressed his concern to his party leader, Léon Blum, who thought it advisable to tell Ben-Gurion, through Zionist friends, what was going on in the French ministries.

Apparently the French government had agreed to supply weapons to the Irgun's emissaries in return for their promise that the Irgun would see to the protection of French Catholic institutions in Palestine.

However, the *Altalena* had been unable to begin loading cargo before May 28. Under the terms of the June 2 agreement, Begin offered to sell the ship's cargo to two of Ben-Gurion's adjutants, Israel Galili and Levi Eshkol. There had been a great deal of publicity in America and Europe concerning this 141st boatload of clandestine immigrants, and the two men rejected the offer. Furthermore, the affair was complicated by the four-week truce imposed by the United Nations and beginning on June 11. This prohibited the belligerents from bringing in reinforcements. And this was the very day on which the *Altalena* left its anchorage at

Port-de-Bouc for Tel Aviv. A telegram from Begin telling his emissaries to delay the sailing had arrived too late. And, for the time being, it was impossible to establish communication with the ship's radio.

Begin immediately contacted the ministry representatives. He gave them information concerning the passengers, the cargo, and the ship's precise itinerary: "It's up to you to decide whether to let it come or make it turn back."

On June 13 Galili arrived at Irgun provisional headquarters to give Begin the government's green light, and to pass on instructions for docking and discharge. This must be at night, and at a place more suitable than the beach at Tel Aviv: the tiny cove of Kfar Vitkin, a labor stronghold some 30 kilometers to the north. Above all, it must be out of sight of the prying eyes of the United Nations observers.

There remained the question of the discharge and transfer of the arms and munitions so badly needed on all fronts. Begin demanded one-fifth of the cargo for his units in Jerusalem, which were still autonomous and where, because of the international status theoretically in force, each Jewish defender was fighting under the flag of his own organization. He demanded two-fifths for the Irgun battalions in Tsahal, particularly those on the central front who, according to him, needed 300 rifles to liberate Ramle.

After much hesitation, Galili telephoned the ministry's agreement to send a fifth of the *Altalena*'s weapons to the Jerusalem contingent. However, he accepted only that provision. For the rest, the Tsahal general staff would be the sole judge of how the weapons were to be used. Begin protested and opened new talks—as the ship with its arsenal and its 900 volunteers came ever closer, slowing down during the day and changing course to avoid being discovered, taking advantage of darkness to make full speed toward its destination.

On June 17 there was a change of attitude. Without an agreement on the distribution of weapons, Galili informed Begin that the country's legal authorities would play no role in their discharge: "We wash our hands of it."

How could the Irgun alone carry out such a difficult task in such restricted circumstances? Begin accepted the challenge. Galili discerned another, more serious, drawback: should the *Altalena*'s arsenal fall into the hands of such an aggressive minority as the Irgun, an opposition party, it could be a dangerous tool against the institutions of the state itself.

Nevertheless, when the ship entered Israeli waters on June 20,

Begin telephoned army general headquarters to invite it to send a representative to oversee the operation on the spot and to keep track of its implementation. The officer with whom he spoke promised to come, and to send him some trucks "privately." This did not reckon with Ben-Gurion, who was under Galili's influence, and who requested authority from the Cabinet to use force if the Irgun went ahead with its plans: "Begin cannot do just what pleases him," he said. "If he doesn't obey, we will fire. If it be true that his men have 5,000 rifles and 300 machine guns, then what they are in the process of doing now is nothing in comparison to what they will do tomorrow. And then we will have two countries—and two armies."

The government unanimously approved the use of force if preliminary warnings proved to be ineffective. On the next day, at nightfall, the *Altalena,* which had been sailing aimlessly around throughout the day, dropped anchor off the beach at Kfar Vitkin, in accordance with government instructions. Having informed the ministry's liaison officer, Begin came to await its arrival dressed in civilian clothes and accompanied by some followers. The 900 immigrants disembarked first and were at once sent off to the Tsahal camp in Natanya. Volunteer longshoremen, with the help of the local population, of some of the military units stationed nearby, and of some Irgun troops who had deserted from their units, worked throughout the night to unload the cases onto the beach across an improvised pontoon bridge. Approximately one-third of the cargo was unloaded. At sunrise, they discovered, to their surprise, that they were completely surrounded by two regiments of tanks and artillery, which had taken up positions on the cliffs overlooking the beach, and under surveillance by a white United Nations plane. Three Israeli corvettes stood by on the horizon. It was a trap.

Colonel Dan Epstein, commander of the Alexandroni brigade, presented Begin with an ultimatum that gave him ten minutes to unconditionally surrender his equipment and his men to the authorities and to leave the cargo that had already been unloaded to the army's discretion. Begin replied that he needed more than ten minutes in order to make contact with the government, and he dispatched Yaakov Meridor, his adjutant, to the mayors of Kfar Vitkin and Natanya. Hours went by. Then, in the middle of the afternoon, without warning, the troops opened fire with automatic weapons and mortars, forcing the men on the beach to seek refuge in the neighboring orange groves.

Begin leaped into a small boat and set out for the *Altalena,* but was caught in the fire from one of the corvettes, which had zeroed in on his embarkation. The *Altalena*'s captain maneuvered her sideways to act as a shield for him to board. Then he raised anchor, gained the open sea, and headed south along the coast in the direction of Tel Aviv.

Meanwhile, the firing onto the beach had ceased. Meridor had come to an agreement with Colonel Dan Epstein to deliver over to him all the unloaded weapons, and to give him the names and addresses of the militants who had been caught in the trap, in exchange for their freedom.

Barely had this agreement been reached, however, than Epstein received the order from Galili to arrest four of the Irgun leaders, including Meridor. Tension rose further when the *Altalena* ran aground in shallow water during the night a few hundred meters from the Kete Dan Hotel in Tel Aviv.

During the early morning hours, a crowd of sympathizers arrived at the beach and cargo again began to flow from boat to shore. Ben-Gurion was at Tsahal Headquarters in Ramat Gan. He spoke breathlessly: "Where is Yadin? If he can't be here when he's needed, I'll put someone else in charge of the army!"

Ben-Gurion had come privately to a decision to put an end to the affair and to sink the *Altalena*. However, before calling the government into emergency session, he sought moral support for this action from his army chiefs. A rumor was rampant that the Irgun was to make an attempt to establish an independent force, and many desertions from Tsahal were being reported. The *Altalena*'s presence off the coast of Tel Aviv, the congregating of an excited crowd and hundreds of partially armed Irgun adherents face to face with the Palmach cordons that had been thrown up to block access to the beach—and the explosive situation that resulted—all seemed to be leading to imminent civil war.

The government ministers were divided. Jewish blood had been spilled by other Jews on the beach at Kfar Vitkin. Horrified at the prospect of fratricide, some ministers wanted to renege on their unanimous decision of the day before to employ force, and to negotiate some arrangement with Begin, at whatever cost. However, in the midst of the meeting, a breathless emissary brought news: the *Altalena* was unloading weapons onto the beach at Tel Aviv, and was refusing to submit to the authority of the state.

"You see," shouted Ben-Gurion, "there's no question of negotiating with such people!"

Finally he obtained the government's approval to seize the rebel boat. Indeed, he sent a further furious order to Yigal Allon, who had been appointed "commander of the beach front" at noon on June 23, 1948: "Arrest Begin! Arrest Begin!"

Ben-Gurion ordered Yadin to sink the ship. The interim chief of the general staff received the following order in writing, at his request: "You must take all measures. Assemble cannon, machine guns, flamethrowers, and all other means at your disposal. All these weapons will be used if the government so orders!"

In the center of Tel Aviv, under the stupefied gaze of foreign observers and journalists on the terrace of the Kete Dan, the battle was already raging. At 4:00 P.M., Allon brought up a cannon manned by a German Jew named Blücher. At that moment, Begin, who became a target each time he appeared on the *Altalena*'s bridge, reminded Allon that he had agreed to a cease-fire and that he had stopped trying to discharge cargo. He requested a launch to evacuate those wounded in the firing.

In reply, Blücher fired his first shell. The captain raised the white flag. A second shell hit the ship broadside, setting her afire and blowing her up. At the captain's side, Abraham Stavsky, the illegal immigration veteran who was accused of being the murderer of Chaim Arlosoroff, a man with thirteen clandestine crossings to his credit, was mortally wounded.

Fifteen other Irgun members were killed during the battle. Two hundred and fifty were arrested in the city by the newly formed security service, led by Isser Harel, and some hundred soldiers were put under close arrest for having refused to obey orders.

Two ministers resigned, but there were no longer any Irgun battalions in the army.

Begin had managed to reach his headquarter's clandestine broadcasting station. There—and not without some basis in fact—he accused Ben-Gurion of having fired on the *Altalena* with the intent to kill him. However, he adjured his troops by a solemn oath never to turn their weapons against their fellow Jews.

"Blessed be the cannon that set fire to that ship!" Ben-Gurion exclaimed. "It will have a place in Israel's war museum!"

Begin, for his part, refused to engage in civil war. However, he assumed leadership of a political opposition which was for many years to play the role of Cassandra vis-à-vis the overwhelming strength of the Labor regime, and which was to work untiringly toward its downfall.

When he became part of the government of national unity on June 1, 1967, in preparation for the Six-Day War, however, Begin showed that he harbored no ill-feeling: it was he who suggested recalling the "Old Man," who had been in retirement for four years. His was the only voice.

After having seized this opportunity to crush the Irgun, Ben-Gurion continued to exploit every situation and every event that occurred—without himself creating them—to feed his own obsessions and to satisfy his goal of totalitarian democracy. He eliminated all his rivals one by one as representing potential threats to Israeli unity, whose "Armed Prophet" he considered himself to be.

At the beginning of July 1948, Ben-Gurion asked Colonel Dan Epstein, whose brigade had encircled the Irgun at Kfar Vitkin, if he was prepared to prevent an attempted leftist putsch fomented by the Palmach. Ben-Gurion entrusted Epstein with defending the building housing the general staff and the prime minister's residence and put one of his battalions on the alert.

The Palmach, however, had no more intention of launching a coup d'état than had the Irgun. Ben-Gurion couldn't have cared less about real intentions. On September 14 he called a meeting at Galili's kibbutz—Galili had been superseded in July—with all the higher officers in the Palmach: out of 64 attending, 60 were Mapam members! Ben-Gurion brought up the question of the existence of their private general staff, which Allon was proposing to make the general staff of a division. Most of the participants were outraged and justified their command structure by the existence of a threat of "Jewish fascism." The Lechi should be liquidated first—that ultranationalist movement that had thrown off its cloak of secrecy but which was carrying out "dissidence" in Jerusalem by fighting against the internationalization of that city provided for in the United Nations resolution.

On September 17 the Swedish count Folke Bernadotte, who had been the United Nations mediator since May 20, was assassinated in his automobile in Jerusalem. He was accused of having been in league with the British and the Arabs. Isser Harel met with Ben-Gurion:

"I know for a certainty that the Irgun had nothing to do with it. It was a Lechi act. Jewish terrorism must be attacked at its head."

Harel made two hundred arrests throughout the country, and the Lechi was outlawed as a terrorist organization. As chief of the Shin Bet, the security service created out of the former Shay, he presented Ben-Gurion with the names of the three men suspected in the attack on Bernadotte. One of these would later be among the founders of the Sde Boker kibbutz in the Negev where the "Old Man" retired, and would be his last companion during his final days.

The merciless repression of the last Lechi elements, which had been infiltrated by Isser Harel's agents, extended to the Irgun as well. The fighters in Jerusalem were forced to turn over their weapons and to be integrated individually into regular units. Harel had drawn up lists in advance, had had telephones tapped and had listened in on conversations from abroad; he had checked into the financial dealings of all known "dissidents." This vast spy operation—the Shin Bet's first—enabled him to strike quickly and with great force, and to track down the Lechi's number-one man in Haifa, the uncapturable Yalin-Mor. Arrested on September 30, this terrorist chief was sentenced to eight years in prison for complicity in Bernadotte's assassination at the end of the War of Independence in January 1949.

This operation also made Little Isser one of Ben-Gurion's most trusted confidants and advisers for a long time to come. With the "Old Man" 's agreement, Harel freed the majority of the internees, some of whom agreed to become agents of the Shin Bet.

While the war was still going on, on October 28, the eve of the conquest of the Negev, Ben-Gurion turned against the Palmach, and despite Yadin's protests, he signed an ordinance putting an end to its independent structures and its private general staff. This dissolution created such discontent that at the war's end most of the Palmach commanders—who made up half Tsahal's superior-officer strength—retired. Except for the small group under Itzhak Rabin, one of the men who had fired on the *Altalena*. This group took its revenge after the "Old Man" 's fall in 1963. As of January 1, 1964, Rabin, Bar Lev, Elazar, Gur, and Eytan had succeeded each other as head of the general staff: all Palmach veterans!

After the Palmach's liquidation, Ben-Gurion looked for an opportunity to depose Big Isser, the last vestige of the extreme left to hold any position of power. In this attempt he received the support of Little Isser, who had been unable to stomach the promotion of Isser Beeri, Big Isser—the left-wing Mapam member—to head of the Shay in 1947. Beeri, the last all-powerful head of the Shay, had retained a great many of his powers upon becoming the first head of Aman, the army's intelligence service, on June 30, 1948. This was by far the most important post in the security hierarchy, since it was entrusted with both espionage and counterespionage, the areas later delegated to the Mossad and the Shin Bet, respectively.

Beeri's clandestine work had made him turn to practices not very compatible with legality and justice; particularly the use of summary proceedings, which made him feared as a kind of Jewish Beria. Beginning in December 1948, a dossier was opened on the summary trials and admitted executions in which he had had a hand. First was the July disappearance of Ali Kassem, a Jaffa

Arab whom the Haganah had employed as a double agent. His body was found riddled with bullets two months later at the bottom of a wadi. Big Isser admitted having had him killed because he suspected him of playing a double game. Ben-Gurion seized upon this as a pretext for relieving him of his functions. Brought before a tribunal of three colonels, Beeri was suspended. It was the beginning of the end.

On January 15, 1949, Shaul Avigur provided Ben-Gurion with proof that between May and August 1948, Beeri had had the chauffeur of Abba Houshi, one of the Mapai leaders, kidnapped and tortured, and that he had created forged papers to prove that Houshi had been a British police informer in 1946. Colonel Isser Beeri was demoted and forced to retire from the army.

On July 10, 1949, Beeri was arrested and accused of the murder of Captain Meir Tubianski, who had been sentenced to death by an improvised court-martial on June 30, 1948, without having been allowed to defend himself. The court-martial had consisted of Beeri's adjutant, Benjamin Gibli, and two of his Shay underlings, and Tubianski had been shot on the spot by a Palmach detachment. An engineer working for the electric company in Jerusalem, then directed by the British, Tubianski had been suspected of having given his Arab counterparts a list of Israeli weapons factories and military bases dependent on the company's lines—all prime targets for the Arab Legion's guns.

At the time, Beeri had informed the government of the traitor's capture and execution. On December 27 Ben-Gurion, at the behest of Tubianski's widow, ordered a review of her husband's "summary trial." The investigation revealed the procedure's illegality and concluded that judicial error had been committed.

"I plead not guilty," Isser Beeri stated to the tribunal at Rehovot that sentenced him to one symbolic day in prison on November 23, taking into account his "devoted service to the defense of Israel."

However, Beeri was definitely out of the running. Up until his death in 1958, the man whose "secrets could have blown the country apart"—in the words of one of his friends—refused to justify himself. He had agreed to bear the entire burden himself, and he remained silent to the end. Only his son Itay, a naval officer, holds the secrets of his journal, none of which has ever seen the light of day.

Tubianski's posthumous rehabilitation had done more than cost the career of the last leftist chief of the secret services, a victim of the young State of Israel's childhood disease: acute spy fever. It also enabled Ben-Gurion to make these services responsible to the prime minister, and to make them—through the rise of Isser Harel—an instrument of his own policies.

Six years later, another "Dreyfus case" enabled Little Isser to eliminate a second rival: Big Isser's successor as head of Aman, Benjamin Gibli. However, this would have implications and repercussions far more significant than a mere war among the secret services.

Book Two

AFTER

"Here it is
unrealistic not to
believe in miracles."
——David Ben-Gurion

7

AN ISRAELI DREYFUS AFFAIR

On December 24, 1977, Philippe Nathanson, a forty-three-year-old newspaper photographer, was seated before his television set in Tel Aviv watching the live coverage of the fabulous outcome of Sadat's visit to Jerusalem the previous month: the Ismailia meeting between Israel's Prime Minister Menachem Begin and the Egyptian president. He attentively watched the men shaking hands at the foot of the steps leading down from the El Al Boeing: Egypt's Prime Minister Mamdouh Salem, who had come to receive the delegation, and Israel's Minister for Foreign Affairs, Moshe Dayan, easily recognizable behind Begin because of his famous black eye-patch.

"Well, there are the two men who are responsible for my troubles," he might have exclaimed, remembering the somber days in July 1954 when he had first met Mamdouh Salem in the Atarin police station in Alexandria. At that time, Salem had been the police officer in charge of that city's aliens, assigned to watch over Zionist activities. After preliminaries had been taken care of, Nathanson had been subjected to his first interrogation about the handmade bomb that had burst into flame in his pocket in front of the Rio Cinema. The unfortunate young man, just turned nineteen, had been part of an Israeli spy ring and had been recruited by a special services agent to take part in a series of provocative actions. This deed was to lead to his spending fourteen years in Egyptian jails. More important, his capture precipitated the most serious incident in Israel's secret history, giving rise to a scandal whose many repercussions—in 1958, 1960, 1963, and even 1976—were to shake up its interior politics, its intelligence community, and its relationships with its Arab neighbors: the Lavon affair.

Pinchas Lavon was the defense minister who succeeded Ben-Gurion at the end of 1953, when the "Old Man," weary of opposition and of the intrigues undermining the government coalition and his own party, voluntarily withdrew from power "for two or three years," and retired to his kibbutz in the Negev.

The Father of his Country had found it hard to put up with the many partisan quarrels within the party's old guard, and between it and ambitious newcomers. In 1952 one of his close collaborators, Ehud Avriel or Katriel Salomon, had advised him to carry out a coup d'état so that he could govern without the "damn nuisances," and achieve the totalitarian democracy of which he dreamed. However, the "Old Man" had refused to become a dictator, and had preferred to disappear from the political arena for a while to demonstrate his position as a providential and indispensable leader. He was careful to leave command in the hands of his own men, like so many guideposts for his return: before his departure, he appointed Shimon Peres as director of the Defense Ministry, Moshe Dayan as chief of staff, and Isser Harel as head of the secret services.

Ben-Gurion had also picked Levi Eshkol to replace him as prime minister but the old guard had succeeded in substituting his rival, Foreign Minister Moshe Sharett. However, the old guard in turn had been forced to accept Ben-Gurion's choice of Lavon as defense minister.

Lavon, the brilliant leader of the Mapai left wing, known for his militant antiimperialism, had already been acting defense chief for six months. He was regarded by the army with no more sympathy than he was by the other leaders or future leaders of the party, all of whom disliked him for his arrogance, his aggressiveness, his taste for taking risks. Ben-Gurion himself had little esteem for him, except in regard to his isolated position and his touchy relationship with Sharett. Peres and Dayan both disliked Lavon for having denounced to the "Old Man" the year before their plan to eliminate the old guard from political life: the Young Turks had suggested that he head the plot in exchange for their support of his candidacy for the post of deputy prime minister. Lavon had refused and had told Ben-Gurion about the plan, which killed it.

Contrasting with the pacifist ideas he had always held, Lavon's sudden military activism had brought him into active opposition to Sharett, who remained faithful to his dovish image. In October 1953 Lavon had been responsible for a reprisal attack on the village of Kybia, in Jordan, in which 70 civilians had been killed. In that same month, Lavon had advised Mordechai Makleff, then chief of staff, to carry out Machiavellian activities involving British holdings in Amman aimed at undermining Jordanian-British relations. Lavon had also suggested occupying the east bank of the Jordan in the Gilead region, in order to blow up the canal that had been built by the Jordanians.

On February 27, 1954, during a general policy debate convened by Sharett in the wake of Nasser's accession to power in Egypt,

Lavon had called for the immediate occupation of the Golan Heights and the Gaza Strip. Apparently, no one had supported him. In later debates in the Foreign Affairs and Security Committee in the Knesset, Lavon was to advocate military reprisals against fedayeen infiltration; a position completely opposed by Sharett, who deemed such operations to be totally without any preventive value.

Nevertheless, Lavon pretended not to have changed his ideological orientation. His support for reprisal operations he felt was only a method for gaining favor with the general staff. Above all, he saw it as a means of weakening the reactionary Arab governments, of making their regimes unstable, of weakening their positions in the antiimperialist camp. He felt it was to Israel's advantage to reduce Western influence in the Middle East. And he reproached the Mapai leaders with having pushed Israel into the arms of the West.

This brief history makes us better able to understand how Lavon's name came to be implicated in the army's intelligence intrigues.

To this must be added the deterioration of Lavon's already shaky relationship with Peres and Dayan. Having indirectly learned from a general staff officer about Lavon's decision to delay purchase of the French AMX tank, Dayan resigned on June 15, 1954. He agreed to remain at his post only after a long talk with Ben-Gurion. Two days later, the "Old Man" had summoned Lavon to Tel Hashomer Hospital, where he was undergoing treatment, to discuss his relations with Dayan. Lavon complained about the chief of staff's unwillingness to share important decisions with him. The major portion of his complaints, however, had to do with Peres who, he said, was a "systematic liar."

Thus, in the course of Sharett's shaky reign, there had been a continual coming and going of rival ministers between Tel Aviv and Sde Boker—or Tel Hashomer—as each of the protagonists in the government's psychodrama came to consult the "Old Man." In this ceaseless ballet, Isser Harel, the head of the secret services, played his role of éminence grise to the hilt, proposing candidates for certain posts, opposing others.

This little man who prided himself on being no man's friend, whose habit of continually biting his nails irritated everybody, had risen phenomenally since the Shin Bet days. The downfall of Isser Beeri, his main rival, had led to a cutback in the powers of Aman (the military intelligence service) in favor of a central agency for intelligence (the Mossad), set up in 1951 and entrusted to one of the mystery men of the clandestine era: Reuven Shiloakh. The very next year, Shiloakh, accused of lacking common sense, had relinquished his post and had been assigned to maintain liaison between the intelligence services and the government. At the beginning of 1953, however, Isser had succeeded in getting him removed from that job, too, as well as the candidate who had been named to succeed him: Ehud Avriel, the former right-hand man of Shaul Avigur in the clandestine Mossad immigration operation. He had even succeeded in having the post abolished by making himself directly responsible to Ben-Gurion, who that year appointed Harel as "memouneh"; responsible for both the Mossad and the Shin Bet (internal security), and coordinator of all five of the intelligence agencies.

Now at the top of the ladder, Little Isser, who had had political police bugging telephones and creating dossiers on opponents on both the left and the right from 1948 to 1952—from army officers, including Dayan, to judges—held immense power, that no one either before or since in the history of the Jewish State has held.

However, one intelligence service partially escaped his control: Aman—the army's intelligence branch—which jealously guarded its administrative and operational independence. And Aman had a secret unit for special overseas operations: Unit 131, entrusted with spy missions in peacetime and with actions behind enemy lines in wartime, modeled on the OSS (Office of Special Services), the forerunner of the American CIA. It was staffed primarily by former members of the Palmach's special section, men such as Lieutenant Colonel Motkeh Ben-Zur, who headed it in 1954. The heads of this unit rejected any control other than Aman.

In 1953 the interim chief of Aman, Colonel Yehoshafat Harkabi, had, as an exception, informed Isser Harel of certain operations Unit 131 was preparing. Without any power over this unit, Harel had chosen to ignore these plans, some of which seemed to him "silly, adventurist, and monstrously irresponsible." However, in January 1954, Harel called for supervision of these activities by a coordinating committee. His demand was refused by Lavon, who had, in the course of his first interim appointment to the ministry, discovered the small building on the outskirts of Tel Aviv where the Unit 131 commanders had set up a psychological warfare network in the tradition of the Palmach, outside the Mossad's espionage network. And these plans—often notable for an extreme naïveté and for a total absence of political maturity—fascinated the left-wing intellectual just as they had fascinated the scholarly Colonel Harkabi.

In addition, however, Lavon had been inspired by a very particular political thesis: light the Middle East powder keg, accelerate the departure of the British and other imperialist powers, and encourage revolution to overthrow the feudal regimes of the Arab countries. In short, this was the opposite of Prime Minister Sharett's thesis, which was aimed at seeking grounds for détente with the Arab states by means of negotiation and through the absence of border tension. In April 1954 relations among Sharett, Lavon, and Dayan had become so exacerbated that no cooperation—and even no intelligence—was possible between the prime minister, the minister of defense, and the general staff. It was under such conditions that Lavon, bypassing Dayan, established direct communications with such officers as Colonel Gibli, head of Aman, who sent reports to him without going through the general staff and without the knowledge of the coordinator of the secret services, Isser Harel.

These contacts outside the chain of command that occurred between Lavon and Gibli suddenly gave the chief of military intelligence a privileged place within the secret service community. On Lavon's instructions, Gibli began to refuse to provide Harel with information on Unit 131 activities for which the Mossad could have provided technical or logistic assistance. Harel was dependent upon a weak prime minister, Moshe Sharett; he was fighting with Peres and Dayan for the role of Ben-Gurion's principal confidant; and he was up against competition from Colonel Benjamin Gibli, who was in sole charge of strategic evaluations of intelligence analyses. Such was the state of affairs when, in mid-spring of 1954, Harel left for a few months in America.

And this was the explosive background against which, in the late spring, Israel was informed of Britain's intention to withdraw its garrison on the Suez Canal.

Anglo-American policy in the Middle East had changed radically since the overthrow of the corrupt regime of King Farouk in Egypt on July 23, 1952, by a military coup led by General Neguib. Immediately after the coup, which had been abetted by the American CIA, State Department experts and "public relations specialists" took off for Cairo, where they were met by Kermit Roosevelt, grandson of former president Theodore Roosevelt, who had, since March, been establishing close ties with the strongman of the new regime, Colonel Nasser.

The ties had borne fruit. In 1953 the leaders of revolutionary Egypt had asked United States assistance in organizing their army and secret services. Paul Leinberger, a veteran of the OSS, was loaned to their government to produce propaganda against enemies of the regime. At first these changes did not unduly disturb Israel. Great Britain's military presence in the canal zone served to moderate the ardor of Egypt's new leaders and to calm the misgivings of some Israeli leaders.

During this period, there were two main political currents in Israel: that of Ben-Gurion and that of Moshe Sharett, his minister for foreign affairs. At the outset, the prime minister had sent a message of congratulations to the new masters of Egypt in Cairo. And he had not opposed the steps taken privately by Yigal Allon, now a private citizen, to establish contact with Nasser, his onetime prisoner in the Faluja pocket at the time of the conquest of the Negev in 1948.

Faced with terrorist activities against Israeli frontier villages by Palestinians infiltrated from Transjordan and Gaza, however, Ben-Gurion had backed a policy of military reprisals, to which Sharett had been opposed for two reasons: first, he believed in the feasibility of a policy of moderation, particularly vis-à-vis Egypt, which he regarded as being the key to the Israeli-Arab problem; second, he feared the West's disapproval.

In 1953 the mounting tension between the two men had affected the relations between the Ministry for Foreign Affairs and the Defense Ministry. The mixed Israeli-Arab armistice commissions established in 1949 became the arena for perpetual confrontation between the diplomats and the Israeli military. At the end of October 1953, after the reprisal attack on the Jordanian village of Kibya, Ben-Gurion had issued a kind of political testament for his successors. In it he foresaw a second round in the Israeli-Arab conflict for the year 1956. Sharett wrote in his journal at the time: "Even accepting Ben-Gurion's analysis as a possible eventuality, I believe that nonmilitary solutions must be sought." Among these solutions he envisaged the following: one, a daring plan for indemnifying Arab refugees from the 1948 war; two, the improvement of relations with the Great Powers, and principally with the United States, to counter the more European orientation of Shimon Peres; and last, a continuing search for an understanding with Egypt.

Upon becoming prime minister, Sharett had exchanged letters with Nasser, who had replaced General Neguib as head of the Revolutionary Council on February 25, 1954, before taking over officially as premier. Through his regular CIA contact, Nasser then asked the Americans to intervene with their British allies to produce results in the secret negotiations that had been started in 1953 with a view to their evacuation of the Suez zone. He let it be known that he would not join in the defense pact with Iraq and Turkey being planned by Secretary of State John Foster Dulles, within the framework of his plan for a *cordon sanitaire* around the USSR, as long as there were 80,000 British troops stationed on Egyptian soil.

The United States then began work on two initiatives: to put pressure on Great Britain to agree to withdraw its forces from the canal, and to attempt to bring an end to Israeli-Arab conflicts, beginning with an agreement between Egypt and Israel.

In April 1954, in fact, the State Department had assisted in the groundwork for a first meeting between the Egyptian Mahmoud Riad and the Israeli Yosef Tekoah, but the course of events prevented the meeting—as it did all the succeeding attempts made during the eighteen months of the Sharett government.

In London, on the other hand, American pressure produced the desired results. The Churchill government had been on the verge of agreeing to evacuate the canal zone, with guarantees regarding British property and bases, in spite of determined opposition from the "young Conservatives" in Parliament. Following a meeting between Churchill and Eisenhower on June 26, the English agreed in principle to an agreement to be negotiated in Cairo on July 27.

This news caused great consternation in Israel. Without the British presence, what would become of the status quo? How could the British be forced to remain? In April the general staff analyzed the situation in the light of information concerning the possible delivery of important quantities of American arms to Iraq and perhaps to Egypt. At the beginning of May, Colonel Benjamin Gibli, the head of Aman, along with his collaborators from military intelligence, had made an evaluation of the repercussions of the evacuation of the Suez Canal zone by the British forces. In his Kyria barracks in Tel Aviv, headquarters of the Tsahal general staff, Gibli examined a plan prepared by officers in Unit 131 which was designed to stir up unrest in Egypt in order to prove the fragility of Nasser's regime and thus of any agreement to be concluded with him. Chief of Staff, Moshe Dayan, who was consulted pro forma, showed little enthusiasm for such a plan, but he did not formally oppose it. On a trip to the United States on July 19, he would receive a report from Gibli mentioning that "the green light has been given for the Egyptian operation."

However, Gibli was not overly concerned with having Dayan's advice, since he was in direct contact with Defense Minister Pinchas Lavon, and he felt in a position to make such a decision on his own, without being obliged to refer it to anyone. It was, furthermore, a plan that was not incompatible with what he knew of Lavon's temperament and ideology. Had not Lavon in the beginning of the year entrusted Unit 131 with a sabotage mission against British advisers stationed in Jordan in the hope of creating Anglo-Jordanian tension?

In Egypt also, the agents the Aman officers had been recruiting for the past three years from among Jewish youth groups had been carefully following the course of events during this spring of 1954. Up to this point, they had been led by a former Palmach fighter who had become deputy chief of Unit 131 and who had been sent to Cairo in mid-1951 posing as the commercial representative of a large English electrical appliance company. His name was Avraham Dar, but his British passport was in the name of John Darling. He had turned up at the home of Dr. Victor Saadi, a Zionist Egyptian Jew, who was the leader of a small clandestine group known as the "The Group," whose objective was the emigration of Jews to Israel. Darling had asked for Saadi's help in setting up a network designed for special missions behind the Egyptian lines in case of war.

Over the next months, Dr. Saadi had provided him with a dozen trustworthy young Jews, whom Darling assigned to two cells: one in Cairo, led by Dr. Moussa Marzouk, a doctor in the capital's Jewish hospital, and the other in Alexandria, which was entrusted to a teacher named Sami Azzar. Communication between the two cells was maintained by a beautiful young Jewish girl named Victorine Ninio, known as Marcelle, the daughter of a prominent middle-class family in Cairo and a well-known member of a very select sporting club. Marcelle was also in contact with an Aman commander installed in Cairo under the name of Max Bennett; he also had a business cover, but for a completely different intelligence task: the German firm manufacturing prosthetic devices for war injuries which he was supposed to represent enabled him to maintain close ties with several high-ranking Egyptian officers, including General Neguib.

The other Israeli spy center—the Mossad—had a completely different and separate network in Egypt.

In 1952–1953 several members of the Darling network had gone to France on vacation; from there they had gone on to Israel, where they were to be trained in the handling of explosives and invisible inks, in the use of miniature sending-and-receiving sets, in coding and decoding, and in the art of undercover photography and topographic map reading. The course was held in a seemingly abandoned building in Jaffa. A young officer named Rachel taught them how to make homemade bombs from chemicals that could be openly purchased in pharmacies.

When a new commander arrived in June 1954 to head the network, its members were far from being seasoned, although a few of them had spent time in Unit 131's intelligence school. On the contrary, they were childishly careless. They often left papers, photographs and other compromising material lying around, and they were still ignorant of the rigid rules of conspiracy and isolated cells.

Stationed in Egypt since the preceding winter under the guise of Paul Frank, a representative of a German electrical appliance firm, their new chief was a familiar figure in Cairo's German colony. This handsome young Israeli, twenty-eight years old, blond with blue eyes, had succeeded in passing himself off as a former member of the SS. His first job had been to track down the escape routes of former Nazis who had taken refuge in Egypt. His real name was Avri Elad. He had been called to France by a secret message on May 26 to meet with Lieutenant Colonel Ben-Zur, the head of Unit 131, who was then on an inspection tour in Europe. Their meeting took place in a Paris café.

Ben-Zur instructed him to take over the Egyptian network and to engage in "material terrorism"—without aiming at human lives—against American and British targets to incriminate the Nasser regime for its inability to control the fanaticism of the Moslem Brotherhood or to contain Communist subversion. Such was the plan that had been drawn up in the little barracks on the outskirts of Tel Aviv. It was given the code name Operation Susanna.

The order to commence with Operation Susanna was to be sent to Elad's network either by radio message or by a recipe mentioned during the cooking program "For the Housewife" broadcast over the Voice of Israel (*Kol Israel*), the Israeli national radio. The date set for the initiation of action was July 23, the anniversary of the Egyptian revolution, just as negotiations for an agreement on the withdrawal of the British from the canal zone were about to begin.

Ben-Zur provided Elad-Frank with two names to use in contacting the network: Philippe Nathanson and Victor Levi, both in the Alexandria cell. Upon returning to Egypt on June 25, Elad contacted the first man on the same day, and on the following day met his comrade, the team's radio man. Two other agents in the Alexandria cell were needed to get Operation Susanna under way: Robert Dassa and his chief, Sami Azzar. Thus Elad met neither

Marcelle Ninio, the liaison agent, nor any of the members of the Cairo cell.

On Elad's own initiative, a first attempt was made on July 2, using rudimentary, homemade explosives: soap boxes and eyeglass cases stuffed with a chemical mixture were placed in a post office and in a public locker room. The effects of the explosions were insignificant: a little smoke, an abortive fire.

The next day, Victor Levi sent a radio message from the artist's studio Sami Azzar had rented at 18, rue de l'Hôpital, which served as meeting place for the Alexandria cell, announcing this first "experimental operation." On July 9 and 10 the Voice of Israel broadcast a recipe for English cake in its "For the Housewife" program.This was the prearranged signal to go into action. Later, Israeli radio received several letters of complaint from angry housewives who had tried the English cake "recipe" . . .

On July 14 taking advantage of Alexandria's joyous Bastille Day celebrations, a French symbol of the overthrowing of monarchist tyranny, the four agents split up into two teams and placed similar incendiary bombs in the American libraries and at the United States Information Center, as well as in United States consulates in Alexandria and in the capital. On the following day, Levi transmitted another message to Unit 131 announcing the success of these attacks: for the first time, the Middle East News Agency, quoted by the AFP (Agence France Presse), mentioned a wave of explosions that had been easily brought under control by firemen. On July 16 this dispatch was reprinted on the front page of the Israeli daily, *Haaretz.* Lavon circled the article and sent it to Colonel Gibli with a question scrawled in the margin: "What's this?"

On Friday, July 23, police and firemen patrolled the streets in both large cities, where the government appeared to be expecting trouble on the occasion of the celebration of the anniversary of the revolution, from the Moslem Brotherhood, the Communists, or from Neguib's supporters whom Nasser had thrown out. Avri Elad took advantage of this forty-hour festival to send his four men to place bombs in the baggage room of Cairo's main station and at the entrances to four movie houses: the Rivoli and the Radio in Cairo, and the Metro and the Rio in Alexandria. Azzar and Dassa carried out their mission in Cairo. In Alexandria, however, a catastrophe occurred: Nathanson's pocket suddenly burst into flame, and he fell to the ground in agony in front of the Rio Cinema, surrounded by bystanders. An officer of the city's special section of police, Captain Hassan el-Manadi, who was patrolling in front of the movie house, ran up, shouting, "We were expecting them!"

He tore off the jacket of the burning man, quickly smothered the fire, and drew a large, fire-blackened eyeglass case from the pocket. Inside were the burned remains of some chemical explosive. Victor Levi, who had been with his comrade, escaped unnoticed.

After brief questioning at the hospital, Philippe Nathanson was taken to the Atarin police station, where the police officer in charge of the foreign population, Mamdouh Salem, had already opened a file code-named "Atarin 10." A police raid on Nathanson's apartment had uncovered a photo lab, some hundreds of negatives—one of which contained instructions Nathanson had brought back from the spy school in Jaffa—and a message written in invisible ink that he had prepared for transmission to an address in Europe.

Meanwhile, Nathanson's parents had been brought to the Atarin police station for questioning. Nathanson's father is believed to have stated naïvely that his son had gone to see a film with a friend, a student named Victor Levi. In any case, Levi was arrested two hours later in front of his home, where Egyptian counterespionage agents had found a tiny transmitter concealed between the pages of a book.

When Philippe Nathanson passed his father later in the evening in the corridors of the police station, the father hissed at him with unconcealed rage: "Assassin!" For his part, Levi confessed to his role in fabricating and placing bombs.

In the five hours between the accident at the Rio Cinema and his arrest in front of his building on the rue Cléopâtre, however, Levi had successfully taken two steps to protect the network. He had run to the studio on the rue de l'Hôpital where the main transmitter was kept, and had thus been able to contact Unit 131 in Israel. He had had time to conceal the transmitter (it was not discovered until much later), to destroy all papers, and to leave a note for Sami Azzar: "Philippe is sick. Meet me at the café on the rue Mislah tomorrow, Saturday, at 10:00." This was the agreed meeting place with Avri Elad for the day after the operation.

Levi then returned home to burn compromising papers and to hide his tiny backup transmitter in a book. He forgot only one document: the message announcing Avri Elad's arrival from Paris on June 25. Levi then went to check Nathanson's house and was taken by the police awaiting him at his home when he returned around midnight.

When he returned from Cairo, Sami Azzar went by his studio and found Victor Levi's note. On Saturday at 10:00, he went to the café on the rue Mislah and handed the note to Elad, who was waiting for him. Since the newspapers had mentioned nothing about the successful bombings in Cairo, it seemed obvious to them that something had gone wrong with Operation Susanna. Levi's absence at the meeting worried them as much as had his note about Nathanson's being "sick."

When they met again at 9:00 that evening, Azzar told Elad about the arrest of the two youths. Elad told him to warn Dassa, the fourth member of the cell, and they set a meeting for the following day. An hour later, Elad was at the central post office in Alexandria to send a telegram to a telegraphic address in Geneva: "Peter and company have gone bankrupt. Staying here to attempt to save the situation. Send instructions."

On the following evening, Robert Dassa's parents were arrested in turn. Their son fell into the trap set at the entrance to his home when he returned from Cairo, where he had remained for one more day after he had placed his bomb in front of the Radio Cinema.

Out of the four, Azzar was the only one who was still free on Sunday, July 25. He had a final meeting with Elad on Saturday morning, July 31, a few hours before he himself was arrested. In his memoirs, Avri Elad maintains that Azzar arrived at this rendezvous flanked by agents of the Egyptian secret police, and that he barely escaped. He further maintains that he had urged Azzar to let him drive him across the Libyan frontier so that he could go safely to Europe, but that at the last moment Azzar had refused to leave because he had not wanted to leave his aged mother alone in Alexandria.

After their liberation, the captured cell members were to say later that Elad had himself canceled this escape trip on the pretext he was setting up their escape. They were to accuse him of having betrayed the network himself.

Actually, Azzar's arrest resulted from the police investigation. On the morning of July 31, the police found the keys to the studio on the rue de l'Hôpital in Victor Levi's apartment. There they learned that the studio had been rented by someone named Sami Azzar, whereupon they simply "collected" him at noon at his home.

Step by step, the network was unraveling. On August 5 a man named Meir Meyouhas, with vague connections to the network, was arrested in Alexandria; in Cairo, Dr. Moussa Marzouk was arrested, even though he had played no part in Operation Susanna and had had no contact with Avri Elad. But his owning four apartments in the capital made him suspect. Then a transmitter was found in an oil can in his car. Dozens of Egyptian Jews were picked up for identity checks. On August 8 the lovely Marcelle Ninio, who had had no contact whatever with the four members of the bomb squad, was arrested as she returned from a weekend at the beach. On the following day it was the turn of Max Bennett, the lone spy, who had had nothing to do with the network.

Learning of Bennett's connection with General Neguib through his business cover, Nasser took advantage of this opportunity to finish off his rival, whom he placed under house arrest at the beginning of October.

Avri Elad, alias Paul Frank, succeeded in closing out his affairs, in selling his celebrated convertible, and in booking a seat on the regular August 6 flight to Frankfurt, Germany. He was accompanied by Melki Klaudian, the wife of a rich Armenian living in Cairo, who unknowingly carried in her luggage the transmitter from the studio in the rue de l'Hôpital he had dismantled. He also carried with him, in a matchbox, the plans for a tiny rocket developed in Egypt by German and Austrian technicians. Elad spent a week in Germany and returned to Israel on August 13 to report to Ben-Zur on the dissolution of the network.

Meanwhile, Israeli public opinion had been shaken by the July 28 announcement in the international press of the ongoing destruction of a Zionist spy network in Egypt, where the final phase in the negotiations for British withdrawal was just getting under way; the worst was feared for the young Egyptian Jews who had been arrested.

Avri Elad's telegram, which he had sent to a post-office box in Geneva belonging to Unit 131 on July 24, in which he had reported the "bankruptcy [arrest] of Peter [Levi]," had reached Colonel Gibli's office at the Tsahal intelligence service on July 26. The head of Aman had sent, at once, a note to his minister, Pinchas Lavon, informing him of the arrest of "two of our men in Egypt." This was, in effect, a reply to the question Lavon had scribbled on the clipping from *Haaretz* of July 16 mentioning the series of explosions on the 14th. On receiving the note, Lavon merely initialed it, P.L., without asking any further questions.

A communiqué from the Egyptian Ministry of the Interior on July 27 contained the reply, and it was carried without comment by the Israeli newspapers the following day. The next day Prime Minister Moshe Sharett, who still knew nothing of what was going on, asked Isser Harel, the Mossad chief who had just returned from his lengthy studies in the United States, whether it involved any of his men.

"Negative," Isser replied. "I'll look into it with Colonel Gibli."

Gibli, the Aman head—who knew what to make of it—told his colleague in the secret intelligence community that he was engaged in an investigation, but that he was "unaware of the existence of any operational order of this nature." As soon as Isser left, he picked up the telephone and called Lavon to inform him that Isser Harel was taking an interest in the affair. Given the state of the relations between the two ministerial offices, in return Lavon told Gibli to give the Mossad chief no information whatsoever.

"If the prime minister wants to know more about it, he can contact the defense minister directly," Gibli then informed Harel, by telephone.

Pale as a ghost, Little Isser dashed to Sharett and pressed him to order an investigation, but the prime minister was not eager to press Lavon for explanations. He had a difficult enough time holding his government coalition together, without running the risk of an additional confrontation with his defense minister.

On August 1 Motkeh Ben-Zur, the head of Unit 131, prepared his first report on the destruction of the Egyptian network. In it he described the three operations of July 2, 14, and 23, in the framework of Operation Susanna.

On August 8 Ben-Zur's superior, Colonel Gibli, presented Lavon with an expurgated version of this report which contained none of the dates of the operations. The affair might have been buried following Avri Elad's return to Israel on August 13, had public opinion not been aroused by the forthcoming trial of the twelve Jews arrested in Egypt, which was scheduled to begin on December 11. The Israeli press called this trial a "political anti-Semitic farce."

In the Knesset on December 12, Premier Sharett, still unaware of the truth, made a violent statement against "this fake trial, these calumnies designed solely to strike at the Jews of Egypt." An international campaign of intervention and petition was being waged to save the accused—particularly since Marcelle Ninio, broken down by torture, had jumped twice from the windows of the central police station and had had to be dragged wounded into the courtroom. In the midst of the trial, on December 21, Max Bennett, whom the indictment singled out as having been the chief of the network, committed suicide by opening his veins with a rusty nail he had pried out of the door of his cell.

Richard Crossman, the British Labour M.P., went to Cairo to see Nasser. Edgar Faure, the French foreign minister, sent a personal letter to the Egyptian president. In Paris, a director of the

Israeli Foreign Ministry, Gideon Rafael, met with the Egyptian Colonel Saroit Okasha, transmitting to him a message from Prime Minister Sharett to the Egyptian.

In Israel, however, among those who knew that the "calumnies" were based on fact, the first of the three series of questions that distinguished the three phases in the development of what was rapidly to become an Affair, with a capital A, were already being asked:

1. Who had given the order for the disastrous Operation Susanna? Who had given the green light?
2. How could the destruction of an entire network be explained? Had it been betrayed?
3. Why had nothing been done in the fourteen years since 1954 to free those who had been arrested? And what had Dayan's role been in the Affair? Did the one-eyed general have something to hide?

Among the Israeli leaders, therefore, the search was already in progress to find a guilty party—if not a scapegoat—to banish to the desert. Who had been responsible for such an operation; one that—aside from the threat to human lives—ran the risk of poisoning Israel's relations with the United States?

General Moshe Dayan, who was Colonel Gibli's direct superior on the Tsahal general staff, had returned from a long survey trip to the United States on August 19. He had left on July 7 under rather curious circumstances. He claimed to have been invited by the Pentagon, but the American military leaders had apparently forgotten this invitation, since in the end the State of Israel was forced to pay a large portion of his travel expenses from one American base to another.

During this expensive visit, he had received Gibli's letter dated July 19 by diplomatic pouch; the letter that had informed him that the green light had been given for Operation Susanna. Dayan had destroyed this letter. However, a copy had been retained in the Aman's files.

Upon his return the following month, Dayan scented a trap once the network's destruction became known. Having been consulted during Unit 131's planning, he knew that the Egyptian operation was a risky one, and that its widely publicized failure threatened to snowball. He explained to Gibli that he required proof that the green light had been given by the minister of defense. Without this formal authorization by his superior, the responsibility would fall upon his own shoulders, in fact, as chief of staff.

On August 24 Dayan made the required pilgrimage to Sde Boker to call on the "Old Man." Relating this visit in his private journal on that day, Ben-Gurion wrote: "It's about some criminal stupidity of Lavon's." Dayan returned to Tel Aviv more concerned than ever. He urged Colonel Gibli to furnish a written report on the circumstances in which he had received the green light from Lavon. He was fully aware that such a document could bring the minister's career to an end, but this eventuality hardly displeased him. The problem was that the chief of the intelligence service did not want to commit himself in writing. He immediately left for Europe on the pretext of hiring lawyers to send to Cairo for the defense of the indicted members of his network. He was not to return until September 19.

Gibli then prepared his own defense system: Lavon was to have given him the green light verbally in the course of a July 15 meeting at headquarters; two or three generals would actually testify to having seen the minister and the colonel chatting together on that day. The Egyptian network was to have engaged in only one operation; the disastrous one of July 23. Finally, the green light had become a formal order—also verbal—confirmed by Lavon in a meeting with Gibli at his home on the evening of July 16.

When it became known on December 21 that Max Bennett had committed suicide in his cell while the Zionist network trial was going on in Cairo, Israeli indignation reached its climax. Summoned to explain himself by his government colleagues, Lavon denied having given the order. Having heard from the trial proceedings that the attacks had actually begun on July 2, he demanded that Prime Minister Sharett appoint an investigating committee to get at the truth of this unfortunate affair, in which he sensed he was being implicated. On December 29 Sharett appointed the president of the Supreme Court, Itzhak Olshan, and the former chief of staff, Reserve General Yaakov Dori, to head a committee entrusted with finding the answer to a single question: "Who had given the order to act in Egypt?"

It was of prime importance for Colonel Gibli, who had protected himself behind a supposed verbal order from Lavon on July 16, to erase all trace of the operations that had been carried out on July 2 and 14 by the Alexandria network. This erasure necessitated some corrections of documents in the Unit 131 files. Gibli first had his secretary, Dalia Carmel, destroy the telegraphic and written reports that dealt with the "experimental" attacks of July 2 and 14. Next, on his instructions Colonel Ben-Zur ordered the young woman to alter the copy of the July 19 letter from his boss to

Dayan announcing that the "order had been given to begin Operation Susanna." Three words were added: "with Lavon's agreement." And she was to alter two pages of the document register sent to the minister, so that it would prove he had been kept abreast of the network's destruction before the news was made public.

It was now essential that Gibli secure the cooperation of the sole witness to the network's activities: its chief, Avri Elad. Still undercover as Paul Frank, he had left for Germany, where he was setting up a company designed to serve as a new cover for him in special operations in Arab countries. He maintained that his cover credibility had not been damaged, despite the fact that the name Paul Frank had figured on the list of those being tried in absentia at the Cairo trial. As far as the Egyptians were concerned, he stated, Paul Frank was really an ex-Nazi refugee in Cairo who had sold his services to the Israelis as he would have to the highest bidder, and who was thus still a valid and employable agent if he were paid the right money.

The investigating committee appointed by the government on December 29, 1954, began by summoning Avri Elad to Israel to take his testimony on the Alexandria network's activities. Before he left Europe, Aman sent an officer, Lieutenant Colonel Mordechai Almog, to Paris to rendezvous secretly with him on January 2 at 2:00 P.M., at the corner of Avenue Wagram and the Place de l'Étoile. During this clandestine meeting, he was given a letter from Lieutenant Colonel Ben-Zur, chief of Unit 131. The latter very simply ordered Elad to forget all the activities of his network prior to the July 23 operation and to "correct" all papers and documents relating to the actions of July 2 and 14. Loyal to the man who had made his career in the special services, Elad agreed to play a part in this manipulation of documents.

Ben-Zur met Elad upon his arrival on January 4, 1955, at Lod Airport. He verified the preparation of the scenario and brought him to a private meeting with Colonel Gibli so that they could go over, together, the testimony Elad was to give to the committee. Elad handed him the original of the logbook in which he had recorded, in code, all the instructions he had received from headquarters, and kept only a duly altered copy for the committee's examination.

Olshan and Dori, the committee members who took Elad's deposition, felt, however, that something was being concealed from them. In the greatest secrecy, they had collected between January 2 and January 10, 1955, a dozen or so statements which contained a whole gamut of accusations and counteraccusations revealing the tension existing in relations between the principal defense chiefs. Dayan and Peres even urged Lavon's secretary, Ephraim Evron, to testify against his boss, but he refused. In public, however, Israel was continuing to deny all responsibility in the affair of the Zionist network in Egypt.

Owing to the overwhelming mass of documents and questionable testimony, the authenticity of which they had no way of judging, the select committee members reported to Sharett on January 13 that they were unable to determine whether or not Gibli had acted on orders from Lavon.

On January 27, the Cairo tribunal delivered its verdict on the ten survivors of the Zionist network: Dr. Moussa Marzouk, chief of the Cairo cell, and Samuel Azzar, chief of the Alexandria cell, were sentenced to death; six of the remaining accused were given sentences of from three years to life imprisonment; two were released for lack of proof. At Sharett's request, Maurice Averbach, a British Member of Parliament, met with Nasser and Ali Sabri, but the Egyptian president, who, six weeks before, had rejected a plea for clemency on behalf of six members of the Moslem Brotherhood who had been sentenced to death, was unable to spare the two Zionist cell leaders from the gallows. On January 30 despite pleas for clemency from political, cultural, and religious leaders of all persuasions, Marzouk and Azzar were hanged in the courtyard of Cairo's Central Prison.

There was a great hue and cry in Israel. On February 2 Sharett, at Isser Harel's urging, forced Lavon to hand in his resignation. On February 17 Ben-Gurion returned from Sde Boker—earlier than expected—to take over the Defense Ministry in the government of his rival Moshe Sharett, whom he would soon replace as prime minister.

The "Old Man" summoned Colonel Gibli and told him that he was unable to keep him on as head of Aman. He assigned him to command the Golani Brigade on the northern frontier and brought Colonel Harkabi back from Paris, where he was pursuing his studies, to replace him.

Sudden border tension with Jordan, infiltrations of fedayeen in Gaza and Samaria—such things would have gradually caused the "ugly affair" ("Haessek Habish", as it was called in the Hebrew press) to be forgotten, had it not been for two men who had no intention of forgetting it: Pinchas Lavon and Isser Harel.

Lavon had consolidated his position in the Labor party by getting himself elected to the key post of secretary-general of the

Histadrut, the all-powerful labor union. There he bided his time to take revenge.

Upon Ben-Gurion's return to the corridors of power, Harel returned as supreme boss of the secret services. He then took the opportunity to examine the file on Avri Elad and was astounded to discover that he was being allowed to continue with his military espionage activity under the name Paul Frank, a cover that had been been blown apart by the Cairo trial. This he took to be a clear sign that Aman, the military intelligence service, was badly run and had to be brought under control.

Little Isser soon found out the truth surrounding Elad's false deposition before the investigating committee and figured out the workings of the plot that the forgers had constructed against Lavon. He had no liking for Lavon, but he liked Peres and Dayan even less, since they were his closest rivals with the "Old Man." Avri Elad's file therefore provided him with a decisive means of forestalling any attempt by Gibli to come back as Aman chief—and it could also prove to be highly useful in his struggle with Dayan.

Little Isser got Harkabi to call off Avri Elad's mission in Germany and to cross his name off the army intelligence roster. Without a cover and without a job—all his business fronts had been closed down—the former mastermind of Operation Susanna vegetated in Israel for a while and then went to Vienna, where his father was dying. From there, in March 1957, Elad made a trip to Dusseldorf, where one of his former German friends from Cairo, Bob Jantzen, was running a gasoline station. He asked Jantzen to put him in contact with the Egyptian military attaché in Bonn, Colonel Osman Noury, formerly the assistant head of the Egyptian military intelligence at the time of the December 1954 trial.

Noury still knew Elad as Paul Frank, a former SS man for hire to the highest bidder. In 1956 he had tried to hire him for his own service, at least according to a report Elad had submitted at the time to his Aman bosses, which told of this attempt. Aman had forbidden him to risk following through with this recruitment.

After contacting Jantzen, Elad returned to Vienna to his father's home and got a job in the Austrian office of El Al, the Israeli airline. Bob Jantzen was on the Mossad's list of potential recruits. In July 1957 he was actually contacted by an emissary from the Israeli center who offered him a tidy sum to return to Egypt. Jantzen allowed himself to be persuaded. However, one can imagine the Mossad emissary's stupefaction at hearing him say:

"I've already transmitted the request of Paul Frank, your man in Vienna, to Osman Noury, the Egyptian military attaché."

"He's not our man," the emissary replied, thinking to himself that here was a typical case of lack of coordination between the services.

He at once cabled to Isser Harel: "The competition has already gotten to Jantzen, whom Paul Frank has asked to contact Osman Noury."

The Mossad boss was startled. He knew that Avri Elad was no longer active in Aman and that he had been expressly forbidden to set foot in Germany. He summoned Ben-Zur's successor at Unit 131, Yossi Hamburger, the former Haganah commander aboard the *Exodus 47*. He asked him to verify whether Elad had been given any new assignments in Germany, and especially whether he had been assigned to contact the Egyptian military attaché. Hamburger returned with a totally negative response.

The red lights on the Mossad switchboard all began flashing. Hamburger was ordered to get Elad discreetly back to Israel without awakening his suspicions in order to get to the bottom of things. When his father died in October 1957, the erstwhile Paul Frank returned to Tel Aviv, where he intended to pursue a legitimate business career.

On December 16 Colonel Yaakov Hefetz, the chief of military security whom Elad had known in earlier days in the Palmach, invited him to drop by his office in the Kyria for a chat. In the middle of their conversation, Hefetz suddenly threw out a blunt question:

"Can you swear to me that you have never betrayed your country?"

Elad was totally taken aback. Before he had had time to recover himself, two Shin Bet officers entered the room. One of them, Zvi Aharoni, was the security service's senior interrogator:

"Admit you are a traitor!" he shouted brutally.

The "friendly chat" lasted for an entire week. Elad, accompanied by a military security officer, was allowed to go to Haifa to collect some things in his apartment there. He took this opportunity to ask a girlfriend to convey a message to Benjamin Gibli, the former Aman chief: "Help! the Little One has me in his clutches." He also managed to deliver to a friend, Peter Landesman, a former police sergeant, a briefcase stuffed with documents, some of which may have contained evidence of the plot against Lavon in which he had participated, notably a compromising letter from Gibli.

Aharoni, the Shin Bet's chief interrogator, learned that this briefcase had been transmitted to Landesman, and he immediately ordered a secret search of his apartment. In vain. The counterespionage team went at once to Landesman's father's house in Pardes Hanna. There it found the briefcase half-burned in a field behind the house. All the contents had been destroyed, with the exception of a few negatives, some of which belonged to Elad. Another group consisted of photographs of the most secret Unit 131 file, the "mauve file."

Under questioning by Aharoni, Elad maintained that he had never seen the photographs of this file, that he had never had access to it, that he was totally ignorant even of where it was kept. The Unit 131 archivists confirmed that Elad had never had an opportunity to get near it. No one had any idea of how the photographs of an ultrasecret file had come to be in the briefcase. The fact that they had, however, was enough for Aharoni, who suspected that Elad had long been in contact with the Egyptian services.

Elad was unable to give any satisfactory explanations concerning his time in Egypt—December 1953 to August 1954—because he was following Ben-Zur's and Gibli's orders of silence with regard to the planning of Operation Susanna. In the face of so many falsehoods, omissions, and unbelievable contradictions, Aharoni reasoned as follows: during the Cairo trial, the Egyptians had on several occasions let it be known that they had a "secret source of information" on the activities of the unmasked Zionist network. Must not this source be one of the members of the network? Was it not its final leader Avri Elad, alias Paul Frank?

The disappointing results of Aharoni's interrogation made Isser Harel decide to set up a military investigating committee to examine the question of who had been responsible for the network's destruction. This was the second major question in the Lavon Affair: "Had there been treason?"

Confronted with this committee—which consisted of the military prosecutor, Schlomo Shamgar, later appointed a judge of the Supreme Court, Colonel Ariel Amiad, later on director of the National Electricity Company, and Aharoni himself—Elad at last agreed to talk.

Violating the orders from his former chiefs in the army's intelligence bureau, Elad went into detail concerning the plot of the Gibli-Ben-Zur-Dayan trio against Lavon. Shocked by these revelations, Colonel Amiad realized that they could well bring the entire military hierarchy into disrepute. As of that moment, he did all he could to delay the committee's work. And the committee reached no conclusions concerning Elad's possible treason. Of course, there were suspicions, sufficient enough as far as Isser Harel was concerned, but there was no proof, no direct testimony to confirm them.

Such proof, such perpetually elusive testimony, the Mossad chief was to attempt to ferret out for ten years, pursuing it unflaggingly across three continents. His service managed to get hold of a copy of the files and complete records of the Cairo trial and to contact an Egyptian officer who had testified at that trial. It subjected the German, Bob Jantzen, and half a dozen foreigners who had known Paul Frank in Egypt to exhaustive interrogations. It even attempted to get something out of Osman Noury, the military attaché who had always thought Elad to be a former SS man. It all came to naught.

Nor could the first prisoners returning to Israel in 1968 provide any additional proof of supposed treason. The files of the Mukhabarat (the Egyptian secret service) kept their secret. The prisoners who had been released only made Zvi Aharoni's and Isser Harel's suspicions more acute:

1. Paul Frank had remained in Egypt from July 23 to August 5, 1954, a time when he ran the risk of being denounced by one of the agents then undergoing interrogation by Egyptian security police during this lengthy period.
2. Before his departure, Frank had been able to sell his Plymouth convertible—so well known to the network members—without difficulty.
3. The first four agents who had been arrested were the ones Frank had contacted for Operation Susanna.
4. Frank ran the risk of taking the network's main transmitter with him when he left, rather than getting rid of it by tossing it into the Nile.
5. Frank had attempted to contact in Germany the former assistant chief of the Egyptian military intelligence.
6. Azzar had told his fellow prisoners that Frank had not shown up at their final rendezvous to take him out of Egypt by car. Instead, the police had shown up on July 31 to arrest him.
7. The officer on duty in front of the Rio Cinema in Alexandria had shouted, "We were expecting them!" when he had run to Philippe Nathanson, who was on fire from the bomb burning in the pocket of his canvas jacket.
8. At the trial, the prosecutor had several times mentioned a "sensitive source" behind the network's destruction.

On the other hand, other facts tended to favor Elad's innocence:

1. Victor Levi had had five hours to take security measures before he was arrested. He would not have had all this time if Elad had given his name as well as Nathanson's.
2. From clues left by Levi, the Egyptian investigators had taken eight days to find the artist's studio which had served as the network's meeting place.
3. Azzar had been found only because he had rented the studio under his own name.
4. Had they been told of the network's existence, the Egyptian police would hardly have allowed it to carry out the attacks of July 23, given the political tension then prevailing in Egypt. They could have taken preventive action at the time of the first failed attempts without having had to worry about protecting their hypothetical informer.
5. Had he been Osman Noury's source in 1954, Elad would not have had to resort to subterfuge with Bob Jantzen in Germany in 1957 in order to reestablish contact with him.
6. Elad had never had any information concerning Max Bennett, the military spy, and yet the police had arrested Bennett less than twelve hours after they had arrested Marcelle Ninio, who was the only member of the network to have had contact with him.

The Egyptians could have had sources of information other than a supposed inside traitor—for example, from among the Egyptian Communists, who were not happy to see a rival group engaging in anti-American provocation. This was an unlikely hypothesis. Or from the CIA network in Cairo, whose chiefs, such as Kermit Roosevelt, were powerful enough to have withheld a letter from John Foster Dulles to Nasser because they felt it contained items that might displease the Egyptian president. CIA agents must have investigated the attacks of July 14, 1954, against American institutions in Egypt, and they could have communicated the results of their investigations to their Egyptian counterparts.

The most likely answer to the question "Who is the traitor?" however, was that there was no need for any treason for its first misstep to have destroyed this amateurish network, which was without false papers, without any warning system, without any real compartmentalization, without any regular radio contact with Israel during the brief period of the operation that Elad had devised between June 25 and July 2. And Elad had certainly not been the best choice for such a mission, stupid as well as special, dreamed up by an action service with dubious recruiting policies: at this time Unit 131 was full of adventurers and unbalanced people attempting to rehabilitate themselves.

Such was the case with Avri Elad, former fighter in the Jewish Brigade in Italy, an Israeli immigrant at fourteen, following a harsh childhood in Austria. A captain in Rabin's Palmach brigade during the War of Independence, Elad had been demoted and discharged from the army for arbitrary confiscation of Arab property. Unstable, divorced, and out of work, he had joined Unit 131 in November 1952 and had been sent to Cairo in December 1953.

"I accepted this risk," he wrote in his memoirs in 1974, "because I owed it to myself to regain my lost pride."

Arrested by the Shin Bet in 1958 and sentenced to ten years in prison in 1960—not for having betrayed the network, but for detention of secret documents with the intent to sell them to the enemy—Elad served out his sentence in the wing of Ramle Prison reserved for dangerous prisoners, the X's. Another X prisoner made his acquaintance by tapping out Morse code on his cell wall—he may have been a murderer.

His name was Mottaleh Kedar. Rejected by his parents and raised by his grandmother in Hadera, he had taken his revenge on life by becoming a gang leader at an early age. Suspected—without proof—of having taken part in several robberies, in 1952 he had agreed to place himself under the care of a psychotherapist who had been suggested to him by a doctor in Ramle Prison. A hanger-on in artists' cafés in Tel Aviv and Jerusalem, Kedar next attempted to enroll in Hebrew University by feigning that he had received the necessary degree. When this trickery was discovered, the door to higher education was closed to him.

Later, Kedar was sent abroad, where he was suspected of having committed a crime. Repatriated to Israel, he was arrested on arrival by four officials armed with machine guns. Now regarded as a hardened criminal, he spent two years in solitary confinement under an emergency law inherited from the British Mandate. After four and a half years of judicial maneuverings, he was sentenced to twenty years, which landed him in the cells of section X in Ramle Prison. He was released in 1974, at which time he left the country. Meanwhile, he played chess in Morse code on an imaginary board with his neighbor, Avri Elad.

When Elad was released from prison in 1968, he discovered that the main prosecution witness at his trial had disappeared: Peter Landesman, the man who had received the briefcase of compromising documents, had been found dead a short time before, burned alive in his bed by a cigarette he had been smoking before he fell asleep!

Meanwhile, Elad's trial in 1960 had opened the third phase of the Lavon Affair. Now it was for real, a fight to the finish between Ben-Gurion, who had brought down all his rivals and his opponents, with Isser Harel's assistance, and had taken upon himself the posts of prime minister and minister of defense since 1955; and Pinchas Lavon, the man who, pursued by Ben-Gurion's pitiless vindictiveness, soon came to seem like an Israeli Captain Dreyfus. For ten years the affair had been poisoning the Israeli political scene, culminating in the cashiering of Lavon, in Ben-Gurion's final retirement, in a split in the Mapai party, and—a long-delayed aftershock—the ultimate downfall of the Labor regime!

At the beginning of 1960 having entered into a business relationship in Ethiopia, Yossi Hamburger, who had at one time succeeded Ben-Zur as head of Unit 131, had good working relations with Pinchas Sapir, the minister for industry and a strong man in the Labor party apparatus. In February he told him all he knew about Elad's confessions with regard to the plot against Lavon in 1954. Sapir, who already foresaw the coming struggle to succeed the "Old Man," was determined to prevent the rise of the candidates of the 1948 generation, men like Dayan and Peres. In April he sent Hamburger to Lavon to tell him everything, in the presence of his former secretary, Ephraim Evron.

Always on the alert, Isser Harel, got wind of this meeting and informed Ben-Gurion, who called in Lavon on May 5, 1960—Lavon was then secretary-general of the Histadrut—on the pretext of discussing teachers' salaries. However, he very soon came to the point:

"I hear that you are still interested in the 1954 affair, that you still have hard feelings against me, and that you are preparing to take revenge."

"Yes, I now have proof that forgeries were used against me then. I'm prepared to ask for public rehabilitation."

It was a crisis. Ben-Gurion rejected Lavon's demand. He had no intention of permitting him to seek political redress. However, the party apparatus decided to set up a ministerial commission of seven members, under the chairmanship of a member of the old guard, Levi Eshkol. At the end of Elad's trial in August, the three large daily newspapers in the country had taken up Lavon's cause. Then, in December, the commission totally cleared him of the Aman debacle in 1954.

Furious, Ben-Gurion tendered his resignation on January 31, 1961, since Lavon's reentry into political life threatened to sound the knell for his protégés. Blackmail by resignation was the only weapon left him in his fight against destruction. The Mapai central committee met on February 4 in the Ohel ("Tent") Theater in Tel Aviv to reach a decision.

"There's a very sad play being put on here today," said one of the participants. It was the breakup of the party.

In a moving appeal, Sharett, who was ill, excoriated the "voice of fear that is outshouting the voice of justice." The central committee voted to remove Lavon as secretary-general of the Histadrut. Such was the price the "Old Man" was demanding to return to the saddle, but the public now saw him as a dictator who was on his last legs. He held the reins for two more years, years full of sorrow and pity. On June 16, 1963, he returned to his kibbutz in the Negev and to his books. With his departure, the third chapter in the Lavon Affair was closed.

When Dalia Carmel, Colonel Gibli's former secretary, went to see him in 1967 to ease her own conscience—Shaul Avigur was present—Ben-Gurion refused to listen to her confession that the Aman documents had been falsified in 1954.

However, a fourth phase began in February 1968 with the liberation of the last prisoners of the Susanna network, under the prisoner exchange agreed upon after the June 1967 Six-Day War: Nathanson, Levi, Dassa, and Marcelle Ninio. Their arrival in Israel was kept secret by military censorship until 1970. It was then learned, however, that Meir Amit, the chief of the Mossad who had succeeded Isser Harel in 1963, had threatened to resign on three occasions if these four detainees were not on the list of prisoners to be exchanged against 5,000 Egyptian soldiers. Dayan, now minister of defense, had not insisted on their inclusion during the exchange negotiations. Amit offered to free one of the Egyptian generals captured in the Sinai if he would carry a message to Nasser telling him that he would keep the return of the four prisoners a secret. A few weeks later, the Egyptian president agreed to this bargain.

Every previous attempt to free them had failed: one had been made through the American lawyer William Donovan (whose mediation had led to the exchange of Francis Gary Powers, the U-2 pilot, for Rudolf Ivanovich Abel, the Soviet superspy); one had been made through General Franco and Greek and Austrian leaders, all of whom had refused to intervene. Only Ben Bella, the first president of an independent Algeria, had agreed to intervene with

Nasser at the request of Henri Curiel, one of the founders of the Egyptian Communist party, who had set up a network to assist the FLN (the Algerian liberation army), and who had supported the actions of an Israeli-Algerian committee set up in Tel Aviv. But in vain.

The question then being asked in Israel, however, was why no attempt had been made to exchange the Cairo prisoners for General Fuad el-Digwi in October 1956, after he had been taken prisoner in Gaza. This general had presided at their trial! Not only had no pressure been put on Egypt, but no one had taken advantage of the occasion even to make the general talk about the facts underlying the network's destruction.

When Lavon had been fired in 1961, Dayan had indulged in a pun: "This is the happy end—and the end of Eppi." He was referring to Lavon's assistant, Ephraim Evron, nicknamed Eppi, who had remained faithful to his boss. Since that day, like Peres before him, Dayan continually made use of this official, who was appointed successively by one or the other as director of the Foreign Affairs Department, and who ended up occupying the highest post in Israeli diplomacy: ambassador to Washington. Was all this in payment for his silence? Evron was the last remaining witness to the plot cooked up by his boss's former foes at the outset of the Affair, the last person to know the secrets told to Yossi Hamburger, of Unit 131, by Avri Elad.

And this is not the only bizarre element in the Lavon Affair—the affair that, after having enabled Isser Harel to settle personal accounts, brought about his disgrace; the affair that led directly to Ben-Gurion's downfall and to a fifty-year-old "establishment's" later going down the drain. An affair, above all, that destroyed Israel's attempts to make secret contacts with Egypt.

In January 1955 an emissary from Sharett met in Paris with an emissary from Nasser to make plans for a summit meeting between the two men. At the same time, in Washington, Reuven Shiloakh, the former chief of the Mossad and now a minister plenipotentiary, was discussing with Allen Dulles, the head of the CIA, and with his collaborator James Angleton, a plan created by the American intelligence center for a Cairo meeting between Nasser and another of Sharett's emissaries. And in London, Yigael Yadin (former chief of staff and future leader of the Dash party [Democratic Party for Change] which was to assist in overthrowing the Labor party in 1977) awaited the green light from Israel to make a secret trip to Cairo to set up a Sharett-Nasser meeting; on January 27 he received a telegram from Isser Harel canceling his mission. Sharett had changed his mind because of the death sentence just passed on the two members of the Zionist network in Egypt. "We will not negotiate in the shadow of the gallows," he told Harel.

And several months later, the shadow of the Affair was to fall upon the final attempt at a meeting in New York between Joseph Tekoah, the Israeli diplomat, and the Egyptian representative of the joint commission, Salah Gohar.

Ben-Gurion's resumption of the post of the Ministry of Defense and his return as prime minister had dealt a final blow to the Sharett government's moderate policy. It was immediately followed by an escalation of reprisal raids and an increase in frontier tensions. Fifteen months later came the Suez war, and with it, the first successful Soviet penetration into the Middle East.

8

1956: THE RUSSIANS ARE COMING!

On July 13, 1956, a filler item on page three of the Cairo newspaper *Al Ahram* reported the accidental death of an Egyptian superior army officer stationed in Gaza, Colonel Mustafa Hafez, whose car had driven over a mine.

The real facts were quite different. On the previous evening, "Bikbachi" (colonel) Hafez had been enjoying the cool shade in the garden attached to the stark military intelligence building in the center of the white city isolated between the Sinai Desert and the blue Mediterranean. A sentry on guard duty had respectfully approached him to inform him that one of his agents was asking to see him on an urgent matter. The man was waiting for him in the small room set aside for agents returning from missions, next to the entrance to the building. He was a Bedouin named Mohamed Soliman el-Talaka, a regular member of the military intelligence service. Talaka snapped to attention as his superior entered and informed him that he had just arrived from Israel where, a few hours earlier, he had met with three Israeli intelligence officers whom he knew only by their pseudonyms, Sadek, Abu Nissaf, and Abu Salim.

He said that they had entrusted him with a top-secret mission: to deliver a book containing coded instructions to a very important Israeli agent who was none other than—the Gaza police chief.

The Bedouin drew the book from a fold of his baggy trousers where he had concealed it while crossing the border to deliver it into the hands of Colonel Hafez. The colonel's face grew pale as he took the book. The Gaza chief of police, Lufti el-Akawi, who the Bedouin, Talaka, was telling him was an agent of the Israeli services, was not only a loyal colleague—he was also a friend, with whom Hafez often shared a nargileh and played shesh-besh (backgammon). And yet there could be no doubt: Talaka handed him a calling card belonging to el-Akawi which the Israelis had given him along with the book.

Intrigued, Hafez opened the package to examine the messages before returning it to Talaka, so that Talaka might continue playing his game. The room was rocked by a terrible deflagration. Both men were thrown to the ground by the force of the loaded book's explosion. Only Colonel Hafez, who had been holding the bomb, succumbed to his injuries.

El-Akawi had an easy time proving his innocence. The police chief's name had been used as bait by Aman, the Israeli military intelligence service, to strike at the man who had been in charge of fedayeen activity in the Gaza Strip since the first of the year.

The first Palestinian terrorists had actually begun to infiltrate into Israel by way of the Gaza Strip around 1953-1954. In 1948 this Egyptian Army-occupied zone had been a vast refugee camp left over from the first Israeli-Arab war. The terrorist raids across the cease-fire line that had served as a frontier since that time resulted in many victims in the Israeli villages in the area, and had reached as far as the nearby southern suburbs of Tel Aviv. Most of these terrorists were subsidized by the Egyptian Army intelligence service and were also used as informers. Even those who were assigned to act merely as agents, however, took advantage of their missions to pillage and to murder on the side.

In April 1955 Nasser decided to officially organize the fedayeen units ("Death Volunteers") in Gaza. Their infiltrations, which occurred daily throughout the next year, created a situation that quickly became untenable for the population living near the border. At Aman headquarters, kept on constant alert against the tensions persistently occurring along the Jewish State's fragile borders, the files grew ever larger. All the information collected revealed the prime role played by one man controlling the fedayeen: Colonel Mustafa Hafez, chief of Egyptian intelligence in the Gaza Strip. He had personally sent some 200 fedayeen across the "green line," and thus had been responsible for dozens of dead and wounded among the civilian Israeli population.

Around the end of June, the Aman drew up a plan to liquidate Mustafa Hafez. This was not an easy task to accomplish, since six years of intelligence service in Gaza, where he was in charge of all Egyptian espionage in Israel, had made this brilliant officer exceedingly prudent. A colonel at the age of thirty-four, his success in recruiting fedayeen, in training them, and in sending them on sabotage operations, had earned him the honor of having been personally cited by the Egyptian president. In 1956 he felt secure enough and sure enough of his position to begin engaging in that most dangerous aspect of the intelligence game: the manipulation of double agents.

Soliman el-Talaka had been one of the best of these. A Bedouin able to roam easily across the frontier, he had managed to approach Israeli intelligence officers whom he encountered in his wanderings in the Negev, and had passed them sufficient information to lead them to accept his offers of service. In fact, of course, he was acting on Colonel Hafez's instructions to engage in this double game in order to penetrate the Israeli services. However, the Israelis soon became wise to the game. In June, when various plans were being examined for the liquidation of Colonel Hafez, one of the officers in the Aman special unit that had been linked to the group behind the Lavon Affair proposed to make use of this double agent. He saw this deed as a way of taking revenge for the men who had been executed in Cairo.

The murder of the head of Egyptian intelligence's Gaza bureau was in effect an indication of the imminence of a new armed conflict between the two countries. A preliminary clash had already occurred sixteen months before, on February 25, 1955, when a group of Gaza Palestinians had infiltrated into Israel and killed a Jewish cyclist near Rehovot, in the center of the country. In the pocket of one of the terrorists, who was killed by a patrol, the Israelis had found a report on vehicle movement in the southern part of the country intended for Egyptian military intelligence.

Two days later, Ben-Gurion, who had recently returned as minister of defense, and General Dayan, chief of staff, had paid a visit to Prime Minister Moshe Sharett to seek his authorization for launching a reprisal raid against an Egyptian military base in Gaza. Dayan estimated the possible losses on the Egyptian side as ten dead. Sharett, the soft-liner, gave way before the exigencies of the action. He wrote in his journal: "I regret that the credit for this operation will surely fall to Ben-Gurion."

Although the two men were divided by deep differences of opinion as to the inevitability of a renewal of armed conflict with Egypt, both Sharett and Ben-Gurion were at the time equally avid to avenge, by means of a military response to the infiltrations of Egyptian intelligence, the deaths of the two leaders of the network involved in the Lavon Affair, Samuel Azzar and Moussa Marzouk, who had been hanged in Cairo on January 31. Sharett went so far as to admit this to Edward Lawson, the American ambassador to Israel.

In Dayan's thinking, however, the operation would also serve as the beginning of a widespread offensive designed to chase the Egyptians out of the Gaza Strip—that salient that had been driven into Israel's southwest flank. He even asked his general staff to draw up a plan for the conquest of Gaza, which he was to have his minister, Ben-Gurion, submit to the government two months later.

"This region must be transformed into a steel fist to counter the threat of Egypt," the Old Lion had said to his secretary, Elhanan Ishai, when, at the time a common citizen, he had visited the then desert region of Lachish in mid-July of 1954. His companion had expressed surprise:

"Don't Jordan and Syria pose greater threats to us?"

"When a fly is buzzing around your head," Ben-Gurion had replied, "and a snake is at your feet, the snake is the more dangerous. Egypt is the snake."

Ben-Gurion did not doubt for an instant that the Egyptians were planning revenge. He looked on the imminent departure of British troops from the Suez Canal zone as marking the beginning of a period that would be fraught with strange perils of which the new regime created by the officers' revolt in Egypt would be tempted to take advantage. The Zionist leader had no liking for the young and dynamic Bikbachi Gamal Abdel Nasser, who was then taking over the destiny of Egypt. Nasser's book, *The Philosophy of Revolution,* first published in pamphlet form the preceding year, revealed an ambition that could not be confined within the geographical and political boundaries of Egypt.

Nasser's triumph during the first conference of nonaligned countries in Bandung, Indonesia, in April 1955 provided Ben-Gurion with the final item for the historical indictment he was mentally preparing against the Egyptian president. He saw the war with Egypt as a real danger. Unlike Dayan, however, who believed in its inevitability and in the need to prepare for it at the expense of everything else, Ben-Gurion thought it might be possible to stave off this threat of war by a policy of widespread reprisals aimed at keeping the Egyptians quiet—at least on the Israeli frontiers.

On February 21, 1955, Ben-Gurion came out of his retreat at Sde Boker and took over from the unfortunate Pinchas Lavon as head of the Ministry of Defense. His notions quickly came into conflict with those of Moshe Sharett, who was still the prime minister. Cooperation between the two quickly became extremely difficult. Ben-Gurion did not believe in the possibility of a true peace with the Arabs in the foreseeable future. But Sharett was not prevented by events from pursuing a policy of contacts with the Arabs, and particularly with the Egyptians. He even attempted to maintain an indirect and discreet liaison with Nasser, and he opposed the policy of reprisal supported by Dayan and Ben-Gurion.

For his part, Dayan continually pressed Ben-Gurion, from the moment the latter returned to the government, to accelerate the movement toward armed confrontation before Egypt got modern weapons, thereby allowing Israel to choose the time . . . and the terrain.

Three days after Ben-Gurion's return, the Middle East experienced one of the most dramatic of the crises that have periodically shaken the region. On that day, in Baghdad, Turkish Prime Minister Adnan Menderes signed a defense pact with Iraqi Premier Nouri Said aimed against the Soviet Union, urged on by the Americans, who had at the last minute decided against officially joining in the treaty as a sop to both Nasser and Ben-Gurion. For different reasons, both Egypt and Israel were vehemently opposed to the signing of a regional pact. Nasser regarded it as a concealed return to British imperialism and as a success for Nouri Said, who was his rival for leadership in the Arab world; Said, the West's protégé, had gone so far as to say to Eden in London, when Nasser had nationalized the Suez Company, "Strike him; strike the bastard!" Ben-Gurion, feared for Israel if a treaty linked the West to a group of Arab states.

In this context, on February 27, with Sharett's agreement, a decision was made on the first reprisal operations against the Egyptian Army in the Gaza Strip.

The following night, a young colonel, Arik Sharon, whom Tsahal had recently appointed commander of the paratroops, gave an order to 150 of his men to infiltrate the Gaza Strip under Operation Black Arrow, the code name given to the operation by the poet of the general staff. The two commanders working with him on this plan were Aharon Davidi, who was later to succeed him as commander of the parachutists, and Danny Matt, who on October 15, 1973, would be the leader of the first unit to cross the Suez Canal under his orders in a decisive thrust.

In the course of this nocturnal raid against an Egyptian military base in Gaza, Sharon's parachutists knocked 38 of Nasser's soldiers out of combat. The announcement of the raid shocked the world. In Israel, it raised the army's and the population's morale, badly shaken by the implications of the Lavon Affair. Sharett, however, did not hide his concern. The goal set for the reprisal raid had been greatly exceeded.

In Egypt, Nasser was later to tell Robert Anderson, President Eisenhower's special envoy, that the Gaza raid had literally "caught him with his pants down." It had led him, on the one hand, to form the fedayeen Palestinian volunteers into combat units in Gaza and, on the other, to turn to the Soviet Union for weapons. What, in reality, as well as the Baghdad Pact, had played a determinant factor in Nasser's decision to seek Soviet aid, linking as it did his main rival at the time to the West, was his dream of nationalizing the Suez Canal; while playing a very careful game in this regard, he felt it would be a good thing to have the Russians on his side if the French and British hardened their position.

To one of the senior CIA officials in Cairo, Kermit Roosevelt, with whom he enjoyed a mutual trust, Nasser simply said that he needed Soviet arms to defend himself against Israel's expansionist aims. When setting up the first fedayeen units, Nasser gave strict instructions to the Gaza commander to limit Palestinian infiltration into Israel to intelligence operations.

In Tel Aviv, Sharett's government had no intention of exacerbating the situation. It rejected the plan for conquest of the Gaza Strip proposed by Ben-Gurion on March 25, 1955. Yet tension continued to mount along the border. On August 28, a group of fedayeen massacred 6 Israelis 18 kilometers from Tel Aviv.

Dayan called for an immediate reprisal. Sharett opposed him firmly. The one-eyed general then submitted his resignation as chief of staff. Ben-Gurion, the defense minister, announced that he was taking a vacation and actually did leave, as a sign of protest. Sharett caved in.

Three days later, Colonels Motta Gur and Rafael Eytan, known as Rafoul, send their commandos into action against the Khan Yunis police station in southern Gaza: 37 Egyptian soldiers were killed.

War seemed increasingly inevitable. Sharett's moderate policy was set aside to make way for Ben-Gurion's hard-line plans when he returned as prime minister after the July Knesset elections.

On September 27, 1955, Israel was shocked to learn that an agreement had been signed between Czechoslovakia and Egypt for the delivery of 200 Soviet MIG fighter-bombers. Against this, the Israeli Air Force had only 30 jets.

"Nasser will go to war in six months," Ben-Gurion predicted, and he consulted with his closest advisers on the stance to adopt: either start a defensive war before the Egyptian air strength became operational, or counterbalance the Soviet supplies coming into Egypt by a massive purchase of armaments.

Dayan was for immediate confrontation. Isser Harel, head of the Mossad, preferred—as did Sharett—to temporize and to seek arms from the United States. Shimon Peres, the head of the Defense Ministry, who had already established very close personal relations with Maurice Bourgès-Maunoury, Defense Minister in Edgar Faure's government, and with Abel Thomas, his personal assistant, tended toward a treaty of alliance with France, which was already engaged in a difficult test of strength with Arab nationalism in Algeria.

At first Ben-Gurion went along with Dayan's theory, calling him in on October 23, 1955, for a meeting at the President Hotel in Jerusalem. He asked him for an operational plan aimed at a rapid conquest of the Straits of Tiran at the entrance to the Gulf of Eilat. The attack, given the code name Omer—the name of the son of the commander appointed to lead it, Colonel Chaim Bar-Lev—was set for the end of December.

On November 13, however, Ben-Gurion changed his mind and canceled the order for the operation. He decided to send Isser Harel to Washington in the hopes of persuading the Americans to send modern weapons to Israel.

The Eisenhower administration, which had supported the Bagdad Pact—though it had abstained from taking part, and which was later to refuse to help Nasser build the Aswan Dam—had ambiguous relations with Egypt. While it was trying to maintain good relations with the Egyptian president, it was also making many mistakes that would lead to Soviet penetration into the Middle East by forcing Nasser to appeal to Moscow.

From the earliest days of the Egyptian revolution of July 1952, the CIA had been in contact with Nasser through two of its agents: first Miles Copeland, who—on his own admission—had turned $3 million over to the colonel, and then Kermit Roosevelt, through whom Nasser was able to allay State Department fears at the time of the Egyptian-Czech agreement of September 1955. This friendship reached its high point in the years 1954-1955. Copeland and Roosevelt often dined informally with Nasser and his colleagues, all in shirtsleeves, calling each other by their first names and trading off-color stories in the American way. They were Nasser's best advocates in Washington, and obtained for his army $20 million worth of parade equipment: helmets, boots, revolver holsters . . .

When Nasser met with Chou En-lai, prime minister of the People's Republic of China, in Bandung, and told him of his need for weapons, and when Chou transmitted the request to Moscow, which regarded it as an unexpected opportunity to gain a foothold in the Middle East—which had up to that point been the West's exclusive preserve—the two CIA guardian angels tried to explain their protégé's position: an arms contract with the East could only strengthen Egypt's power and independence. And they advised Nasser to forestall Western criticism by announcing that the contract had been signed with Czechoslovakia, not the USSR. After

all, hadn't Czechoslovakia provided arms to Israel in 1948 during
its war of independence?

When Isser Harel arrived in Washington, he was unaware of the
secret link between Nasser and the CIA. He was dismayed to discover that the Republican administration regarded the Egyptian-
Czech agreement as an innocent business deal rather than as an
attempt by the Soviets to infiltrate the region. Harel asked his hosts
to assist Israel in redressing the balance in order to prevent an
eventual war. In reply, Ike sent Robert Anderson, a Republican
businessman with influence in oil circles who had been made undersecretary of defense, on a secret mission to the Middle East to
make another attempt at Israeli-Egyptian reconciliation.

In January 1956 Nasser welcomed the visitor, who was traveling
incognito, to the presidential palace in Kubbeh and informed him
that he was prepared to engage in talks with Israel through him.
Following this secret interview, Anderson left for Athens, changed
planes, and landed in Tel Aviv.

"Tell Nasser I'm ready to meet with him anytime, anyplace,
even in Cairo, to negotiate a peaceful settlement with him," said
Ben-Gurion.

Upon his return to Cairo, Anderson got a rude awakening: "I
would be prepared to meet with Ben-Gurion, as you know. But I'd
be assassinated an hour afterward. What's the point of taking such
a risk?"

Disappointed, Anderson returned to Jerusalem—still in the
greatest secrecy—to inform Ben-Gurion of the failure of his mission. Nasser then continued to arm himself with the help of his
new protectors. As for Israel's request for arms, it was formally
rejected by the United States on April 3. The State Department
now seemed interested only in Israeli plans against Nasser personally. Reuven Shiloakh, Israel's number two man in Washington,
had a talk on this subject with the American officials involved.
Allen Dulles, the head of the CIA, would be prepared to hear any
future proposals from Israel in this regard, particularly after the
nationalization of the Suez Canal, which had taken his service by
surprise on July 23, 1956. In the State Department, in fact, the
plans were for a Mossadegh solution; that is, long-term action that
would lead to Nasser's being overthrown by opposition from
within.

Livid with rage at such procrastination, Ben-Gurion decided to
give Shimon Peres *carte blanche* to strengthen ties with France.

For the past two years, in fact, France had been almost the only
country selling arms to Israel: a few Ouragan planes and AMX

tanks. It was waging its own war in Algeria against the FLN, which was being backed by Nasser. Peres traveled regularly between Tel Aviv and Paris—fifty round trips in 1956 alone—and his personal relations greatly improved with the installation of the Mollet government in January 1956 and with the appointment of Bourgès-Maunoury to the Ministry of Defense.

On April 11, 1956, France delivered to Israel the first dozen Mystère IV jets, and on April 23 Peres and Bourgès signed an agreement for delivery of a second dozen. In May the two men reached a secret military cooperation agreement against Egypt. To discuss the details of its implementation, an Israeli delegation left discreetly for France on June 22. It consisted of three men: Peres; the chief of staff, Dayan; and the chief of Army intelligence (Aman), Colonel Yehoshafat Harkabi. Minister of Foreign Affairs Sharett, opposed to such combined military preparations, had been relieved of his functions four days earlier by Ben-Gurion.

The secret Paris meeting culminated in the delivery to Israel of 72 Mystère IV jets and 200 AMX tanks over the next two months. At the beginning of July, Operation Fog went into effect; this covered the ultrasecret shipment of French weapons to Israel. Colonel Yaakov Hefets, the head of military security, was on the spot to oversee it, in coordination with the heads of the French secret service. The weapons were loaded at Toulon on cargo vessels bound for Algiers, but on the high seas, the ships changed course for Haifa. Only the commanders and officers of the fleet were aware of the true destination of these first deliveries. The sailors were not told of the change of course. It was one of the most secret operations in Israel's history. During the night of July 24, the first shipload of French weapons arrived in sight of the port of Kishon, near Haifa.

The world was still echoing with Nasser's glee as he had announced the nationalization of the Suez Canal the night before.

The number of tank drivers and carriers brought to Kishon had been kept minimal. In one hour, 30 tanks and 60 tons of materiel had been brought onshore. The food and drink prepared for the French sailors on the transport ship had no Hebrew lettering on it, no indication of Israeli origin. A soldier was assigned to collect the empty bottles so that in the morning the port would look as usual. Deliveries such as this occurred throughout the month at the rate of one ship per night. It was a real bridge across the sea. Dayan oversaw nearly every unloading in person.

With the exception of Peres, who had created Operation Fog, Ben-Gurion did not inform his ministers of the arrival of the

:h materiel before August 19. On September 18 Peres left for
to make an official request for Franco-Israeli military coop-
～.aいっn, even without British participation. On September 22 Premier Guy Mollet and Bourgès-Maunoury agreed. On September
25 Peres returned to Israel to report to Ben-Gurion. On September
28 he set off again for Paris with a delegation headed by Golda
Meir, who had taken over from Moshe Sharett at the Ministry of
Foreign Affairs, for the purpose of completing preparations for a
tripartite intervention, with the English, who were determined—
despite American opposition—to confront the Russians in the
United Nations Security Council, which was scheduled to meet on
October 13 and 14. The first clandestine meeting since the Liber-
ation was held at the home of Louis Mangin, one of Bourgès's and
Chaban's earliest companions in the Resistance.

Beginning October 1, Operation Fog went into its second phase;
it was no longer possible to camouflage the status of military preparations. Colonel Hefets and his team now resorted to a strategic
ruse to conceal the true nature of these battle preparations by
suddenly increasing tension on the Jordanian border.

Circumstances at the time favored this ploy. Fedayeen infiltrations from Jordan had caused several deaths in Israel since the
beginning of the year. Furthermore, the Egyptian military attaché
in Amman, Colonel Salah Mustafah, had taken over control of the
fedayeen based on Israel's eastern flank, in liaison with the Gaza
intelligence section. On July 13 two days after the attack that had
cost Colonel Hafez his life, a package arrived at the Egyptian embassy in Amman. Posted in East Jerusalem, it bore the stamp of
UN Headquarters in that city and contained a book by Field Marshal von Rundstedt titled *The Red Commander*. The mined book
exploded in the hands of the man to whom it was addressed: Colonel Mustafah was killed on the spot.

Ten days later, the bluster accompanying the nationalization of
the Suez Canal had silenced the sound of these two explosions.
Since mid-July, Palestinian infiltrations in the Gaza area had
stopped, though they continued across the Jordanian frontier.

An agreement was finally reached between Amman and Bagdad
for the entry into Jordan of an Iraqi brigade; this increased the
threat from the east, and Israel vehemently denounced the action.

Colonel Hefets's ruse in October succeeded in fooling a large
part of the officers on the general staff, who were not privy to the
secret operation, the Israeli press, which had heard rumors of military preparations, and the Arab intelligence services. Even the
United States was to be kept in the dark.

The latter decision had been reached during a secret meeting in Sèvres, held from October 22 to October 25, in a villa belonging to the Bonnier de La Chapelle family—parents of the perpetrator of the assassination of Admiral Darlan in Algiers in 1942—between the leaders of the French and Israeli governments and the British foreign minister. Arriving with his face half-hidden beneath an enormous hat, Ben-Gurion had proposed to his French and English partners that they keep the Americans informed concerning their plans against Egypt, but he had met with categorical opposition. The British especially feared the United States, whose opposition to any action by the West in response to the nationalization of the Suez Canal had been made clear in July and August, and they believed that the U. S. would put pressure on them to stop any tripartite intervention.

Colonel Hefets, who was in charge of Operation Fog, and his team were thus ordered to mislead the Americans as well.

A week before D-Day, a dozen officers of the general staff had been let in on the plan. In the government, some dozen ministers and their assistants were also in the know. In order to perfect the ruse, officers in command of the central region were ordered to prepare an offensive plan against Jordan "in the greatest secrecy."

On October 22 a group of these officers were ordered to test the terrain by occupying positions on a hill overlooking the Jordan valley south of Lake Tiberias. Several tons of fortifying materiel and bridge-making equipment were delivered and stockpiled near the Hussein Bridge in the Beit Shean valley. The officer in charge of military security in the central region gave strict orders to close all civilian routes into the Jordan valley.

Anxious to verify for himself whether the rumors of an impending operation against Jordan were true, the assistant military attaché of the American embassy was met by a roadblock denying him access to the Beit Shean valley and was forced to turn back. Upon his return to Tel Aviv, he alerted the Pentagon and the State Department in Washington.

A few hours later, CIA chief Allen Dulles contacted Mossad leader Isser Harel through his agent Jim Angleton, and asked him a direct question: "Are you preparing for war?"

The head of Israeli espionage did not want to lie to Dulles. In response, he sent Dulles the speech Ben-Gurion had delivered the week before to the army's high-command school. It implied that Israel intended to teach Jordan a lesson and force it to put a stop to the fedayeen's murderous activities, but that there was no question of starting a war.

Thus, when a dispatch from Tel Aviv to Allen Dulles arrived in his Washington office with the information that Israel had launched a military operation against Egypt at noon on October 29, the CIA chief gave vent to his fury in the presence of his close collaborators: "They fooled me!"

The secrecy of the Suez campaign and tripartite intervention had almost been blown some forty-eight hours earlier by the odd behavior of a French diplomat stationed in Tel Aviv.

Mr. X, a practicing Catholic, maintains that he was only following the dictates of conscience—even if those dictates contravened those of his superiors. Disagreeing with his superior, Ambassador Pierre-Etienne Gilbert, a militant pro-Zionist, he decided to make public the tripartite operational plan and to clear the fog created by his government and its two partners.

On Friday morning, October 26, Mr. X picked up the telephone and called two journalists at their homes, inviting them to lunch. Donald Wise, was a correspondent for the London *Daily Telegraph.* Teddy Leviteh was on the staff of *Maariv,* a large daily paper, as well as representing an English newspaper. Meeting them at the Yarden Restaurant, he informed them of the plan for tripartite intervention against Nasser and advised them to send the scoop to their London publications.

At the conclusion of lunch, Leviteh wrote up his story at the table and went to turn it in to the office of military censorship, which prechecked all correspondents' articles dealing with security, defense, or the military. As an active element in Colonel Hefets's Operation Fog, the censor had instructions to put a lid on all news concerning preparations against Jordan.

Leviteh's article, however, dealing as it did with a Suez operation, seemed to the censor no more than a harmless fantasy, a diversionary tactic, which he felt could go through . . .

On the same afternoon, the Israeli journalist relayed his scoop to the *Maariv* editor-in-chief, Aryeh Dissentchik, who telephoned Shimon Peres for confirmation of the astonishing news.

"Don't do anything," the minister replied. "And see me tomorrow in my office at five o'clock."

Since the next day was the Sabbath, Peres's presence at his ministry told Dissentchik that something was up. On his arrival the next day, Peres was on the telephone to Josef Almogui, the party secretary in Haifa: "The Ata factory must work day and night. We need 20,000 uniforms before Monday. Sapir will fill you in on the details."

He hung up. Dissentchik looked him in the face and let several minutes pass before he spoke. "Okay, I understand. You don't need to say a thing." Peres smiled sadly and, as a matter of course, asked for his silence about what he had found out. There was no question of publishing Leviteh's story. Mum was the word until Tuesday.

That same day, Peres attempted to persuade Hubert Beuve-Méry, editor of the French daily, *Le Monde,* in another way. The editor, on a visit to Israel, was urged to postpone his departure for twenty-four hours. The journalist was to return to Paris the following day, Sunday. Peres told him he had arranged an exclusive meeting for him with General Dayan on Monday. This was to ensure that he not miss being in on things, even though obviously he could not tell him in advance.

"Too late," Beuve-Méry replied. "I have a very important editorial meeting the day after tomorrow, and I can't put off my departure."

In the meantime, the director general of the Defense Ministry was trying to get in touch with his British counterpart to stop publication of Leviteh's article. On Sunday, October 28, the correspondent received a Telex from his paper: "The news from Korea prevents us from printing your article because of lack of space."

Thus was the secret Suez operation, set for October 29, almost let out of the bag. It will never be known just how the French diplomat had got wind of a decision that had not yet been told to Ambassador Gilbert, who was not informed until the very last minute on Monday morning. Did his subordinate have an informer at the Quai d'Orsay who was eager to sabotage an action he opposed? Did he learn of it in Israel? Mr. X spoke Hebrew fairly well and was a close friend of a French-Jewish investor who owned a large villa on the Côte d'Azur which he had often lent to Ben-Gurion.

It is still a puzzle. There has never been an investigation, either in France or in Israel. Mr. X remained at his post for nearly two years after the Suez campaign. And neither Pierre-Etienne Gilbert—nor Shimon Peres—has any memory of the leak for which he was responsible. In any event, his career has not suffered because of this mysterious affair. On the contrary—Mr. X would later be awarded the Legion of Honor, and was to be made a commander in the National Order of Merit.

Despite the exceptional security measures and the subterfuge of the Israeli secret services, there were other leaks with regard to the

Suez operation that also indicate organized and systematic espionage.

When Dayan sent his tanks onto the sands of the Sinai on Monday, October 29, 1956, the Soviets were the only ones who were not taken by surprise. They were fully aware of the tripartite intervention, but they had not shared their knowledge with the Egyptians—nor would they in 1967. In each instance, they were hoping for an explosion of the Middle East powder keg. In 1956 they had even hoped for an Arab defeat, which would have enabled them to step up their penetration into the region. Eleven years later, their calculations would be different, and would reveal a momentary miscalculation.

By and large, Soviet penetration into the Middle East had followed the broad outlines of Russian policy since the days of the czars. On November 29, 1947, the USSR had made its first move by supporting, in the United Nations, the partition plan for Palestine and for an independent Jewish state. The famous text of the speech Gromyko delivered, in which he recognized the martyred Jewish people's historic ties with this land, had been written by Stalin and sent to New York by a special courier a few hours before the meeting.

In fact, the Soviets had been concerned about the fate of Palestine since 1920, even before Great Britain had received its mandate. The Palestine Communist party had been the first created in the region to assist in the formation of other Communist parties throughout the area, and in 1929 the Russians had begun to install intelligence networks. Among the Jewish militants in the PCP, for example, was Leopold Trepper, secretary of the Haifa section, whom the British would later expel to Switzerland, and who would direct the Soviet spy network known as the "Red Orchestra" ten years later, in Paris. As head of the Comintern for the Middle East, Moscow installed a former PCP member, Berger Barzilai, who held this position until the Stalinist purges of 1936–1939 wiped out most of the Jewish professionals in this spy network. After twenty years in the Gulag, Barzilai returned to Israel in 1958 and to his place in the Zionist movement he had left in 1921. He became special adviser to the former head of clandestine immigration, Shaul Avigur, for the Soviet Jewish problem.

After World War II the Soviet intelligence services had increased their activities in the region, aimed at the outset particularly against the young State of Israel. The threat of a Communist takeover was discerned at the time by more than one observer, even without knowledge of two important agents who had been infiltrated into high posts in the Israeli government in 1950. The ambassador of the United States in Tel Aviv had even sent a report to the State Department concerning the "Red Menace" in Israel.

When Stalin changed course the following year and turned to the Arabs, the Soviet services stepped up their efforts: first the KGB, the political intelligence center; then, from 1955, the GRU, the military intelligence service, which moved in following the Egyptian-Czech arms deal. Both services were from then on to find themselves in frequent competition with one another, and with a third service, the political commissariat directly responsible to the Communist Party Central Committee. The Soviet embassy was the base for their activity in Israel. In February 1953, Stalin had closed it down and had severed relations with the Jewish State: a group of Israeli extremists had bombed the Soviet legation to protest the wave of Soviet anti-Semitism created by the discovery of the purported Jewish doctors' plot against the Kremlin leadership.

Shortly after Stalin's death the next month, the Soviet intelligence services urged his successors to reestablish relations with Israel and to reopen the embassy at the end of the year.

In 1956 there were three sources that, because of their knowledge of the combined Franco-Anglo-Israeli intervention against Egypt, enabled the Soviet Union to make a decisive entry into the Middle East: there was a source within the French government and two teams of superagents in Tel Aviv, Beirut, and Cairo.

On the French side, at least one leak had been discovered by the Israeli services in August, during the ultrasecret arms deliveries to Israel. On leaving Toulon, only a small handful of those in charge had been aware of the true destination of the transport ships which were being loaded in relays. One day, the Israelis were astounded to see a group of gendarmes arrive at the port; their commander announced that he had been assigned to oversee the implementation of a confidential mission. The Israeli officers called off the loading and asked for the immediate withdrawal of the incongruous police detachment.

In the Middle East, the Soviet services had at least four key men: the *Observer* correspondent in Beirut, Kim Philby, an agent of the British espionage group MI 6, who had been its man in Washington for many years. Sami Sharaf, Nasser's *chef de cabinet* in Cairo was another; there were also army reserve Colonel Israel Beer, the special advisor to Ben-Gurion, and Ze'ev Goldstein, a high official in the Israel ministry for foreign affairs in Jerusalem.

On September 28, 1956, Beer met with the Soviet embassy's

press attaché for a chat, what he was to call an "insignificant conversation." This diplomat was a KGB agent, one of the many with which that agency had filled the embassy since its reopening. The date of this meeting, which he knew might well be discovered by the surveillance that was being maintained on his companion, is significant. Since at the time he was working under his orders, Beer was aware of the mysterious comings and goings of Shimon Peres, the defense chief, between Paris and Tel Aviv: on September 25 he had noted his return from the French capital and had observed his discreet second departure on September 28. It took no great effort of imagination for him to deduce from these mysterious trips that there was some secret joint mission afoot with the French military authorities. So it was no fluke that he had called a meeting with the Soviet attaché on that day. Aware of the working methods of the Shin Bet, the Israeli security service, he was also well aware that this meeting would most likely be watched.

Beer attempted to cover himself against this risk by informing Colonel Meir Argov, Ben-Gurion's military aide, of this "academic exchange of views" that he had just had—in all innocence—with the Soviet attaché. Argov strongly advised him to get in touch with the head of the Shin Bet, Amos Manor. Far from trying to conceal the interview, Beer faithfully reported it to Manor, who was furious.

"What imprudence! We have identified your companion as a KGB agent. In the future, avoid all contact with him."

Beer replied that he would obey the order.

A week later, Isser Harel, the Mossad chief, called in for a private interview a number of people whose names he had privately noted down on his personal list of suspects to be watched. He intended to make a discreet investigation as part of the preventive measures being taken in light of the coming Sinai campaign. Israel Beer was among this group. In order to conceal his true purpose, Harel told him that he had called him in to find out whether, to his knowledge, the militant members of his former party, the Mapam (left-wing socialist), were maintaining any kind of contact with the Soviets. Sensing a trap, Beer referred to his own chance meeting on September 28 with the embassy press attaché, taking pains to add that he had reported it to Manor, a fact that Harel was able to check on the spot. Harel confirmed that the man was a KGB agent, and he ordered Beer not to see him again.

Beer humbly agreed. He knew that the Mossad chief had not yet caught on to the operational nature of this meeting, which had, of course, been a meeting between agent and control.

When he had first assumed responsibility for the Shin Bet (internal security) in 1948, Isser Harel had paid suspicious attention to Mapam activity in line with a reduction of dissidence and a dissolution of the armed militias left over from the days of Zionist resistance. Until the internal Mapam schism in 1954, this Zionist Marxist party had counted among its members some of the outstanding heroes of the Palmach and the Haganah, men who had distinguished themselves during the War of Independence: from Yigal Allon to Israel Galili, from Itzhak Sadeh to Itzhak Rabin. It would be politically delicate to suspect them. However, Harel had not hesitated to install listening devices in party headquarters and in the party leaders' homes and offices. Very little was gained: his attempt to prove that defense matters discussed among the Mapam members often ended up in the hands of the Soviets had provided him with only two minor examples: his clandestine eavesdropping had picked up a scientific exchange between one of the party leaders, Aharon "Aharontchik" Cohen, and a Soviet diplomat, for one.

The discovery of a Shin Bet microphone on Mapam premises in June of 1953 had created a miniature Watergate in Israel before that term became famous. However, Ben-Gurion used his authority to protect Isser Harel, and the agitation created by this espionage witch hunt soon died down.

Harel also had a network of informers within the party, which he considered too far left not to be a front for Moscow. He was the only person—even within the Shin Bet—who knew the names of these informers, for whom he had private code names. Even after leaving the Shin Bet and becoming head of the Mossad, he had continued to maintain such contacts on a personal level.

Although Harel often made his most outstanding coups out of instinct, in 1953 he had turned things over to a professional who was better versed in scientific espionage methods, his adjutant Amos Manor, a Rumanian who had emigrated in 1947 and who was acquainted with the Soviet mind and its methods. Under his rule, which lasted until 1963, a dozen or more Soviet spy aces would be uncovered in Israel. And among them—outstanding owing to his position rather than his activities—was Dr. Israel Beer, the admitted traitor of the 1956 war: a special adviser to Ben-Gurion and Shimon Peres in the Ministry of Defense.

Twenty years later, the Beer affair is still the number-one puzzle in the secret files of Israel. Its importance stems from the role played at the summit of state power by this man who had been a former lieutenant colonel in the War of Independence, the assistant to the chief of operations, and who, in the 1950s, was one of the most widely respected military specialists in the country, maintaining, up until his arrest in 1961, both his close ties with the Ministry of Defense and his role in the Soviet Union's nefarious international game. Ten years after his death, his identity is still in doubt.

Long-boned, his skull shaped like an egg, his features Mongoloid, his teeth long and equine, with a tiny moustache above his sensual mouth, was he really, as he maintains in his autobiography, "Israel Georg Beer, born October 9, 1912 in Vienna" to an assimilated Jewish family that had emigrated from Central Europe to America and then, having made a fortune, returned to Austria? Or was he an NKVD agent dispatched during the unrest in 1936; had he taken his identity from a friendless and orphaned Jewish student who had disappeared without a trace?

Was it an identity that had been used by a Communist refugee in Berlin, and that he took over in turn when he came back from the Spanish civil war upon the dissolution of the International Brigade, in which he may have served as a lieutenant colonel. Was he already a sleeper agent sent by the Soviets to infiltrate the Near East when he disembarked at Haifa in November 1938 with authority to emigrate to Palestine as a "university research assistant," the author of a purported doctoral thesis on the bourgeois novel which has remained undiscovered in the archives of the University of Vienna? Or had vanity caused him to listen to the siren voice of the Soviet secret service only at the time of the Suez affair, as Isser Harel persisted in believing, having regarded him up to then as merely a rival for Ben-Gurion's favors?

It seems likely, in any case, that this man—actually born in Vienna in the same year as the Englishman Kim Philby—had been recruited by Moscow by the time of his participation in the worker uprising of February 12, 1934, against the dictatorship of the Christian-Democratic Chancellor Engelbert Dollfuss; he was then a member of the Schutzbund, the private militia of the powerful Socialist party in opposition to the regime. The national guard had opened fire on the Schutzbund militants in the two working-class centers of the period, Karl Marx Hof and Goethe Hof. Israel Beer appears to have been greatly affected by this armed confrontation. Also present, as an onlooker, was a brilliant young Cambridge student who had come to complete his studies at the university in Vienna—Kim Philby. Brought into Austrian Socialist party activities by his girlfriend, Litzi Friedmann, he had helped six wounded Schutzbund members escape through the city's sewers.

Philby's presence on the scene—reminiscent of Graham Greene's *The Third Man* even then—is undoubtedly a key to the Beer mystery. According to a special CIA-MI 6 study, Vienna, before the Anschluss, was the Soviet intelligence center for the recruitment of sleeper agents.

Philby was recruited there in 1934 by Peter Gabor, a Hungarian refugee who had fled the repression of Admiral Horty's regime. Gabor had been a high official in the Hungarian Communist party and had gone underground after the revolution was crushed. After the Soviet victory in 1945, he took over direction of the new regime's secret police. In 1934, however, his role was to discover and enlist in the Comintern's service young militants in Communist or Socialist refugee circles in Vienna who could later function as agents upon their return to their respective countries.

Gabor met Philby, the English student, through Litzi Friedmann, an Austrian Jewish divorcée, whose parents had rented a room to the young man. Litzi's ex-husband, Karl Friedmann, was a leader in the Zionist-Socialist *Blau Weiss* movement, and was later to emigrate to Moshe Dayan's kibbutz, Degania, on the shore of Lake Tiberias. In spite of his ugliness, Gabor had great success with the ladies, and he had no trouble persuading Litzi to work for the Soviets after her divorce. After the repression of the 1934 uprising, she married Philby and left with him for England.

Forty years later, Litzi could be found living in East Berlin on the Wildensteinstrasse, with a maid and a private car, the outward signs of bureaucratic success in a people's democracy.

When Philby left Vienna, Gabor assigned him to penetrate the British intelligence service, taking all the time he needed. He did not go into action until 1945, when he helped the Soviets to recapture one of their "defectors," the Hungarian professor Rado, who had headed their espionage network in Switzerland during the war. Regarded with suspicion by his bosses because of his overly close relations with the British and thought to have informed them of his activities in Switzerland, Rado was recalled to Moscow at the time of the Allied victory. The plane on which he was traveling touched down in Cairo and he took advantage of this to get off and seek asylum from the British authorities in Egypt. No one was told of his defection, but in less than twenty-four hours the Russians had heard of it through their agent, Philby, and had obtained Rado's extradition from their British "allies."

Through a strange twist of fate, one of the rising young men in Rado's Swiss network, Wolf Goldstein, was to become the "third man" in Soviet espionage in the Middle East in 1956, along with

Philby in Beirut and Israel Beer in Tel Aviv, under the Hebraized name Ze'ev Goldstein.

Some inexplicable leaks having made him suspect in the eyes of his CIA colleagues and the leaders of MI 6, Philby was recalled from his confidential post in Washington and in 1956 was sent to Beirut with a valid correspondent's job for the *Observer* as a cover. He had extremely friendly relations with his bureau chief, who was unaware of the suspicions about him from his days in Washington. He met him regularly at the Saint-Georges bar, where he spent the greater part of his time drinking.

A few weeks before the Suez operation, MI 6 alerted its posts in the Middle East: British forces, concentrated on Cyprus, were being put on a war footing. Philby got wind of what was going on from a friend on the spot, and he kept his Soviet directors informed. Peter Gabor, who had first recruited him, had been in a cell in Budapest's central prison for three years, a victim of the anti-Stalinist purges of those days. While Philby was hobnobbing in Israel with his former Schutzbund comrades from Vienna, in the final days of October Gabor was listening to Russian tanks stifling the shouts of the Hungarian revolution beneath their grinding treads.

On his nostalgic pilgrimage, Philby may have met another of Peter Gabor's choice recruits from among the former Schutzbund members, that ideal hatching ground for Comintern agents. There is no indication that Beer had followed the same path as Philby, but there are grounds for believing that their experiences had been parallel.

In order to lay down a false scent after the Viennese unrest of February 1934, Beer had enlisted in the government militia and, according to him, had been admitted to the officers' school in Wiener Neustadt for weapons training. The destruction of relevant files during the war makes his story impossible to verify. When Beer arrived in Israel in 1938 with this romantic tale of adventure and combat in his baggage, and, on the recommendation of the legendary Itzhak Sadeh, presented himself as a former Schutzbund officer at the agricultural school at Mount Tabor, which was a clandestine training center for Haganah special forces, he was not very good with weapons. He was put into a unit undergoing training at the foot of Mount Gilboa. At the end of the day, the unit commander had the impression that the new recruit had never touched a rifle before in his life. Having had enough, Israel Beer disappeared after the exercise. He returned to the center a year later, this time to deliver lectures on military strategy.

In fact, Beer must have had an opportunity to study a complete file on the combat activities of the International Brigade in Spain—probably during a stay at the Soviet intelligence school in Moscow from 1936 to 1938. It would be from there that he came to Palestine on his long-term mission with a falsified background as a lieutenant colonel in the brigade. In furthering this purpose, he may have got himself hired as an employee at the Jewish National Fund in Vienna, where he could well have inserted his own name on a list of 200 Jewish university students being issued British-authorized visas under the quota set up for Jewish immigration to Palestine.

Beer played his role as veteran of the Spanish civil war so well that twenty years later, when he met a former Czech volunteer named Jean Mikcha, a military historian in exile in Paris, he talked for more than an hour, in the presence of the military attaché at the Israeli embassy there, about past battles and "their" participation in them. When an Israeli diplomat later questioned him about it, Mikcha admitted that he had no memory of ever having met Beer in Spain: "However," he added, "he was so knowledgeable about certain details of my stay in Spain that I ended up convinced that we had really met there."

Beer advanced rapidly through the Haganah ranks, until he became one of the six Israeli Army (Tsahal) colonels at the time of the War of Independence, stationed on the northern front under the orders of the chief of operations, General Yadin. He became assistant chief of planning and military operations at general staff headquarters at the end of 1948. He left the army when the Palmach was dissolved in 1949 and followed other leftist officers into the Mapam party. After the 1953 schism, however, he returned to the Labor party and provided military reportage for *Davar,* the Histadrut publication.

"He had read a lot, but had learned nothing," General Dayan was to remark; Dayan had never liked the skull-like doctor's Viennese ways.

Acting more out of jealousy than distrust, Isser Harel had also opposed his reintegration into the army. That, however, was no obstacle. Ben-Gurion, head of Israeli defense, and Shimon Peres, his adjutant, hired him to write the official history of the War of Independence, on the recommendation of Shaul Avigur, the founder of the Mossad. And Beer observed the policy of reprisals against Arab villages.

"Israel is a wonderful country," Beer cynically remarked in private. "You only have to shout 'Long Live Ben-Gurion!' and you can do anything you want."

Beer was also a special adviser to the Ministry and professor of military history at the University of Tel Aviv.

In March 1956 in the course of a long discussion on the role of the USSR in the Middle East, Beer managed to persuade Ben-Gurion that Moscow was prepared to protect its interests in the region by force. This argument weighed heavily in Ben-Gurion's decision to abandon the Sinai after the victorious Suez campaign. In fact, the Old Lion took the Soviet threat to send volunteers and bombers to assist Egypt very seriously.

It was at his meeting with the Soviet press attaché on September 28, 1956, that Beer once again came into contact with a working member of the KGB and transmitted a report on the preparations for this campaign.

In fact, Beer made use of his office at the Ministry of Defense to chat in the hallways with his former army companions who were still in high positions in Tsahal, and with the higher-ranking officers to whom he lectured at the war college. He was unique in being able always to seem better informed than others; telling one group what he had just learned from another group, and vice versa. On the eve of the Suez war, Dayan discovered that Beer was present at a secret general staff meeting, and had to ask him to leave.

Although Beer may not have known the date of the beginning of the tripartite intervention, he knew enough to alert his contacts in the Soviet embassy, one of whom held the rank of third secretary in charge of press relations.

Later, Beer would have occasion to meet with top KGB officials in East Berlin because of his increasingly frequent trips through Germany made with the cooperation of Peres and Franz Josef Strauss, then the German Federal Republic's defense minister. The most important Soviet agents were controlled in this way, preferably outside the countries in which they were stationed.

As a result of Beer's visits to the German Federal Republic, a Munich publisher issued his book, titled *The Middle East: Decisive Arena between West and East*. That having been accomplished, Beer was invited to inspect German bases forming part of the NATO European general staff. From West Berlin, it was an easy matter for him to cross over to East Berlin, flouting the formal orders of the Israeli services. There, he could have his real contacts with the Soviets.

In the middle of May 1960, Beer became even more daring: on

a visit to München-Gladbach, he managed to ingratiate himself with General Reinhard Gehlen, chief of the German Federal Republic's special intelligence service, a former Abwehr member, and the major source of the intelligence information on the USSR then available to the West. When the "Gray General" met him in his headquarters for an exchange of views on Soviet activities in the Middle East, he was obviously aware of Beer's frequent trips between the two Berlins. Far from making him suspicious, however, these trips by Shimon Peres's special adviser into the German Democratic Republic seemed to intrigue the West German spy chief, who thus let himself be taken in by a Soviet masterspy.

And it was for this reason that Isser Harel, the Mossad chief, took a certain sly pleasure in informing Gehlen less than a year later, by personal message, that Beer had been arrested in Tel Aviv. Harel equally relished a top-secret telegram he sent to Peres, who had stopped over in Paris on the way to Africa, where he was to represent the Israeli government in various independence celebrations in the former French colonies. "Oh, *Oi weh!* no!" Peres muttered as he decoded the telegram in the embassy on the Avenue Wagram.

According to official reports, Beer had been arrested on the night before the Passover seder, March 31, 1961, at 2:30 A.M. However, as he himself was to relate in his autobiography which he wrote while in prison, the arrest had actually taken place on March 28; the Shin Bet had kept it quiet for two days. Not until then did his military secretary, Colonel Chaim Ben-David, communicate the news to Ben-Gurion, who was celebrating the holiday on his kibbutz in the Negev:

"The Little One caught Pifka with his hand in the till."

The "Old Man" was furious: "I'm surrounded by lies," he screamed.

There is no question but that Beer could have engaged in his espionage activities for some time to come, had not his latest control, the press attaché Vladimir N. Sokolov, made a mistake, even though he too had been in Israel for more than seven years without attracting attention—as had his predecessor.

On Friday, March 24, Beer had set up a rendezvous with him by telephone for Sunday, the 26, in a small, quiet café near Dizengoff Circle. Informed of this, Isser Harel decided not to tell Ben-Gurion before capturing Beer "with his hand in the till,"—he had been waiting so long for such an opportunity.

Taking precautions, Sokolov did not show up at the meeting. He arrived on the following evening, probably according to a prearranged signal. Intrigued by his number-one agent's analysis of the current Israeli political situation, Sokolov asked to see Beer again on the following evening, with documents. The Shin Bet agents were able to witness this second, unexpected meeting. Isser Harel had been on his way to the theater when the head of counterespionage telephoned to tell him, "The man is at the meeting." After hesitating a few seconds, Harel passed the order to arrest him at all costs.

On this occasion, however, although the Beer-Sokolov meeting had lasted for only three minutes, the counterespionage agents had managed to see the Israeli hand over a black briefcase to the Soviet agent.

Forgoing the theater, Harel then went to Aharon Chelouche, chief of the police special branch, to request a search-and-arrest warrant for Beer. Informed by Chelouche, Manor was against this, feeling it was a hasty step to take when there was no formal evidence. Isser insisted. Chelouche was concerned about a possible judicial error.

Then fate smiled on the Mossad chief. The Shin Bet agents had continued to follow Beer and Sokolov since their first meeting, and to their surprise, the two men met again around midnight: Sokolov had come to return Beer's black briefcase.

At 2:30 A.M., Chelouche knocked on Beer's door, a search warrant in his hand. Beer answered in his pajamas. After two hours of interrogation, Beer had lost none of his confidence. He calmly continued to deny any contacts with the Soviets—in the light of all the evidence—for more than forty-eight hours. This gave Sokolov time to leave the country. Not until he at last began to cooperate, did Isser Harel call Ben-Gurion's military aide. He realized that his deed would precipitate the government crisis that had been building up ever since the Ben-Gurion-Lavon struggle during the 1954 affair.

A Committee of Seven, presided over by Levi Eshkol, had, in fact, just reinstated the former defense minister who had been the victim of the affair. Ben-Gurion had resigned. To appease the angry lion, the Labor party had then voted, on February 5, 1961, to expel Lavon and remove him from his post as secretary-general of the Histadrut. The other parties in the coalition in power refused to participate in a Ben-Gurion government. The Knesset was dissolved in March, after a mere two years in power: new elections were set for August. The press, both left-wing and right-wing, criticized Ben-Gurion's "tyranny," and he spent most of the time shut away in Sde Boker, like a wounded lion in his den.

It was also during this period that the world press was publishing the news of the construction of the Dimona nuclear center in the Negev, under cover of a textile factory. On January 3, 1957, the American ambassador, Ogden Reid, met with Foreign Minister Golda Meir to ask her five questions, requesting her response before midnight. The United States wanted the right to oversee this center, and its pressure continued even after President Kennedy entered the White House.

After Beer's arrest, the attacks against the Old Lion, who had made Beer his adviser, increased, since the election campaign was at its height. Henceforth, Ben-Gurion was to regard Isser Harel, "the little devil," whose entire career was due to him, as having been responsible for the press campaign against him. It was the beginning of a painful rupture between the two.

At Ben-Gurion's request, the newspaper editors had nevertheless agreed to delay the news of the arrest until April 16, in order not to distract the attention of world public opinion from the opening of the Eichmann trial in Jerusalem a week earlier. But at the time the Beer affair came out, there were several hundred foreign correspondents in Israel to cover the Eichmann trial, and to give it international coverage . . .

We will never know all that Moscow's number-one agent in Tel Aviv had managed to transmit to his headquarters. At the trial, witnesses came forward to tell of the indiscreet questions Beer had asked them on all sorts of subjects unrelated to his official duties. It is possible, however, to evaluate some of the damage done by his activity, not only in Israel, but in the Western democracies as well.

Aside from information concerning preparations for the October 1956 Sinai campaign, Beer must have kept the Soviets aware of Ben-Gurion's reactions, and those of his colleagues, to their threats of intervention. Two years previously, the head of the Israeli network in Egypt, Avri Elad, had—on Peres's advice—given Beer a report on the formation, activity, and destruction of the network at the origin of the Lavon affair. According to Elad, a Russian spy apprehended in Israel who had shared his cell during his imprisonment had been perfectly aware of the whole history of his network. The transmission of Elad's report to Moscow, and possibly to Cairo, had effectively informed Israel's enemy on the operating methods of its special services. Of course, at the time Beer had no official function; but he did not lack for friends among the Palmach veterans, among whom were men in charge of Unit 131, used for anti-American provocation in Egypt.

Beer had also passed the Soviets precious information on Tsahal weaponry, on the composition of its general staff, on the French shipments, and on the status of the NATO forces he had been invited to inspect.

The French general, Marcel Carpentier, who had had occasion to meet Beer, called him the "best military specialist in the Middle East."

During the Sinai campaign, particularly, Beer had spent hours in Shimon Peres's office listening in on discussions and tendering his advice. Alain Guiney, the *France-Soir* correspondent in Israel, had even come across him on the last day of the war chatting with Pierre-Etienne Gilbert, the French ambassador, who was in the process of revealing his government's position in detail.

In addition, on several occasions Peres had asked Beer for special studies on a large number of top-secret plans. Part of the documents found during the search of his home were connected with these plans.

On the other hand, we will never know the value of the information he may have turned over to the Soviets gleaned from his four conversations on strategic questions with the German general, Gehlen. Apparently his controls had put an even higher price on these than they did on his espionage work in Israel itself.

When Isser Harel had learned that the Beer-Gehlen contact might lead to some real cooperation in clandestine action against what Gehlen must have thought was a common Soviet threat, Harel had almost literally choked. Harel had called Beer in upon his return from Germany in July 1960 and had forbidden him to return there. Beer had appealed to Ben-Gurion, who had sided with him against the Mossad chief.

Harel then decided to put the "dear professor" under surveillance. Beer, however, succeeded in eluding him for a while longer, enough time, in any case, to meet with Sokolov, the Soviet diplomat, in mid-December 1960, without his knowing, a few days before the world press began printing headlines about the contruction of the Dimona nuclear center.

On that day, Sokolov had waited for Beer at the entrance to Beer's apartment building in order to fix a meeting in a place still unknown for that same evening. The aim of this meeting dealt with Israel's nuclear secrets.

There had probably been several dozen clandestine meetings between Beer and Sokolov between 1957 and 1961. Following the basic manuals that teach the ABCs of the spy trade, they had simple codes and agreed-upon chalk markings to set up meetings in predetermined places, with provisions to meet elsewhere should the first site prove impossible.

Probably the most intriguing document Beer passed to his control in Tel Aviv, however, was a copy of the file of military operational plans dealing with hypothetic situations, which had been created in 1957 by Colonel Yuval Neeman, the assistant chief of Aman, the Israeli military intelligence services. This copy disappeared mysteriously and has never been found. At the time, it was thought to have been discarded accidentally in the trash.

Israeli investigators snapped to attention a few years later, however, when articles began to appear in foreign newspapers close to Soviet sources, criticizing Israel's "expansionist aims," and accompanied by facts clearly taken from the Neeman file. Most importantly, the Soviets used this document to prepare a forgery that the KGB chief showed to Sadat on May 14, 1967, when Sadat was sent to Moscow by Nasser, purporting to prove Israel's aggressive plans against Syria.

Based on an authentic ten-year-old document, this forgery played a part similar to that played in the Franco-Prussian War of 1870 by the Ems dispatch: it set off the Six-Day War.

Three years before bringing Beer's career to a halt, Isser Harel's instincts had helped him neutralize the Soviet's number-two agent in Tel Aviv: Ze'ev Goldstein, a veteran of the Rado network.

One day in 1957, one of his informers within the Mapam leadership, with whom he had kept in touch when he moved from the Shin Bet to the Mossad, telephoned Harel at his home. They agreed on a meeting place, following the rules governing clandestine activity.

"The Soviets are trying to penetrate the Mossad," his informer told him. "They are trying to infiltrate an agent close to you."

For a year, Isser tried in vain to pick out a suspect in his immediate entourage. In May 1958 he received a visit from a well-known Israeli official, Ze'ev Goldstein, at that time assigned to the Israeli embassy in Belgrade, who had already rendered some services to his organization. Goldstein suggested setting up a Yugoslav intelligence network for the Mossad.

"Out of the question!" Isser interrupted. "We have no interests to pursue in Yugoslavia."

Then he fell silent for a second and stared at his guest, reflecting on his odd proposal. "The Soviets are the only ones who have any real interest in that country," he thought to himself. All at once, the information his Mapam informer had passed on to him leaped into his mind. "The Soviets are trying to slip someone in close to you."

He broke the silence: "You are a Soviet agent!"

Stupefied, Goldstein felt as though he had been slapped in the face; he broke down at once. Harel summoned Amos Manor, his Shin Bet colleague, and turned Goldstein over to him.

In the afternoon, Manor called to confirm Goldstein's spontaneous confessions, which had quickly been verified upon cursory investigation. That same evening, Harel invited a group of his service's high officials to his home for the Sabbath:

"Hold tight," he said. "Goldstein is a Soviet spy."

Goldstein was a typical sleeper agent, planted in the government apparatus long before. Born Wolf Goldstein in 1920, the son of a Russian family that had emigrated to Switzerland before the October Revolution, the future Ze'ev's childhood had been impregnated with socialist ideals, despite the financially comfortable status of his family. Lenin had been a frequent visitor in their home. At age twenty-two, Goldstein had participated in the struggle against Nazism by working for the Soviet espionage network set up in Switzerland by Professor Rado. He had arrived in Israel in 1948, upon proclamation of the Jewish State, already covered with university degrees and with a knowledge of foreign languages that made it easy for him to find a job at the Ministry for Foreign Affairs. He found himself in line for a fine career; he went to dinners, attended official functions, and never missed a reception or other opportunity to cement cordial relations with high officials in the ministry, in which he soon passed for a model diplomat.

In 1952, with a small group of officials, he volunteered to assist newly arrived immigrants in temporary camps. After marrying a girl from Jerusalem, he was appointed commercial attaché at the Brussels embassy in 1955. At that point, the Soviet sleeper became an active spy.

As obliging as he was sociable, Goldstein willingly agreed to take on minor missions entrusted to him by the Mossad, which was profiting—as is the case in intelligence services all over the world—from his diplomatic cover. In the summer of 1956, he participated in the secret meetings at the Paris embassy in which the details of the clandestine arms shipments to Israel were worked out. His superiors had obviously requested he keep them informed of preparations for the tripartite intervention, which was rumored as early as September.

Goldstein's increasingly frequent presence in the French capital could have been explained by all kinds of confidential missions. As if by chance, he seemed always to be there when Lou Kedar, the Israeli chargé d'affaires in Budapest, was in town on a short vacation. They had mutual friends in Jerusalem, where they had met when Goldstein had become engaged. Happy to meet in Paris, Goldstein questioned her about her work in Budapest. Although her stay in a peoples' republic had made her wary of even the most innocuous questions, she saw nothing suspicious in Goldstein's interest in her.

In 1957 Goldstein was transferred to the Belgrade embassy as commercial attaché. From there, he was to be in a position to make his final move: penetration of the Mossad leadership. He asked Isser Harel for an interview to present a proposal he hoped would interest him. Called back to Israel, he told his friends he was on a quick trip home to celebrate his daughter's birthday.

At noon one Friday, when workers were leaving their offices to prepare for the Sabbath, Goldstein arrived at Isser Harel's office in Mossad headquarters and threw himself into the wolf's jaws.

After Goldstein's arrest, which was kept quiet, a veil of mystery was drawn over his fate. His colleagues in the ministry were somewhat surprised by his total and unexplained disappearance. Aryeh Levavi, the Israeli ambassador in Belgrade, awaited his return in vain; he had asked Goldstein to buy a piece of jewelry for him to give to the wife of his British counterpart on her birthday. To his increasingly worried telegrams, the ministry director finally replied: "Find another courier for your present."

Goldstein's spontaneous confession enabled the Israeli services to arrive at a better understanding of the Soviet services' *modus operandi*. The agent actually never had any contact with his controls in Israel itself. Everything happened in Europe, in Switzerland, Belgium, France, or Yugoslavia. And it was perhaps in one of these countries—Yugoslavia—that Goldstein had made the misstep that had led to his downfall. Isser Harel was never willing to reveal the source that had enabled him to exercise his instinct.

Sentenced to twelve years in prison, Goldstein chose to remain in the country after his liberation and to begin life anew in a quiet village. His son is now an officer in Tsahal.

Sentenced to ten years in prison by the district court—a sentence which, when appealed, was changed to fifteen years by the supreme court—Beer died there in 1966, maintaining in his autobiography—the sole testimony to his largely invented past—that his actions had arisen from fear of the catastrophe of an Israeli-Soviet confrontation. He had been trying to protect Israel.

The Suez crisis could have been interpreted as the first step in such a confrontation. The Soviets profited by it to deploy their pawns throughout the eastern Mediterranean and to recruit spies within the Arab world. During this important year of 1956, the most highly placed of their agents had been at the very center of the presidential circles in the Egyptian republic in the person of Nasser's future *chef de cabinet:* Sami Sharaf.

During the time that preparations for the Suez intervention were taking place, Moscow had not lifted a finger to warn Egypt, its new client through the Czech arms agreement. The reasons for this were twofold: on the one hand, the three-power military intervention would enable Moscow to intensify its control of the Egyptian Army's supplies, and to set itself up as the protector of the Arab world in the face of Western aggression. On the other hand, the outbreak of hostilities in the Middle East would be a useful ploy to divert world indignation away from its own decision to intervene militarily in Hungary against the popular uprising in that country.

The CIA's role in the Hungarian revolt is not yet entirely clear. James Angleton, chief of special operations at the time, would later admit having trained thousands of Hungarian fighters who then went into action too early. Was his boss, Allen Dulles, whose brother John Foster was in charge of the State Department, then trying to force President Eisenhower's hand? In any case, the Kremlin must have wondered whether the United States would stand by without reacting to the crushing of the Hungarian revolt. The U.S. reaction of surprise and anger at the tripartite Suez intervention quickly reassured the Soviets. And thanks to the team of superspies it had deployed in the Middle East, the Kremlin was able to win a dual victory by waging one of the most successful deception campaigns since the end of World War II.

On November 4, 1956, Soviet tanks were in Budapest. On the following day, November 5, Premier Bulganin sent ultimatums to Tel Aviv, London, and Paris. His threat to Israel included the Jewish State's very existence if it did not withdraw its troops without delay from the Sinai Peninsula. On November 6 and 7, the KGB played its trump card. Relying on the fears of a Soviet military response to any attack on Egyptian sovereignty that Israel Beer had been instilling in Ben-Gurion since March, the Kremlin set off a series of rumors like a trail of gunpowder: there was a request for a right of way for Soviet warships through the Dardanelles; for the creation of an airlift between Moscow and Damascus; for the stationing of submarines and frogmen in Alexandria; for enlisting volunteers for Egypt; there was a state of alert in all Soviet air bases, etc.

On November 6 the Israeli ambassador in Moscow, Joseph Avidar, who was on vacation in Tel Aviv, sought out Ben-Gurion: he regarded it all as a colossal bluff on the Russians' part, and they must not be deceived by it. However, on the afternoon of the next day, Isser Harel came, in his turn, to tell Ben-Gurion of his fears: according to Mossad sources, Soviet pilots had actually landed in Damascus and were preparing for bombing missions. Part of this intelligence had been garnered in Beirut, where the honorable British correspondent, Kim Philby, was stationed.

The CIA made its contribution to the success of the Soviet propaganda by instigating a move made by the United States ambassador in Paris, Charles Bohlen, vis-à-vis the French authorities: Bohlen was instructed to inform them of the imminence of a Soviet attack upon Israeli territory. And the French passed this information on to the Israelis. To top it all off, President Eisenhower, furious at the behavior of his two principal Western allies, and by the CIA's blunders in Central Europe and the Middle East, joined Marshal Bulganin's appeal for the immediate evacuation of Port Said and the Sinai.

Unable to take seriously the Soviet penetration which had, nevertheless, been on the increase over the past two years in the Middle East, McCarthy's America had reacted weakly to Nasser's—the former agent in the pay of the CIA—nationalization of the Suez Canal, and had been unable to offer any alternative to the Franco-British resolution. While trying to maintain good relations with Nasser, the United States had refused him the favors the Russians were all too ready to provide.

Indicted at the conference of nonaligned countries in Bandung—which had given Nasser a triumphant reception—America, in its present state, was unable to turn the wave of indignation at the Soviet intervention in Hungary—at least throughout Western Europe—to its own advantage.

Caught unaware by the Suez campaign, the CIA representatives in Cairo had kept Nasser informed of the pressure President Eisenhower was exerting on Israel, France, and Great Britain. And it was in part such CIA reports from Cairo, all proclaiming the solidity of Nasser's popular support, that influenced the United States to throw all its strength against the tripartite intervention, thereby enabling the Russians to win on all fronts—and this in the very year that the Khrushchev speech had shaken the Communist world to its foundations.

9
THE WEST RETALIATES

It was dubbed the "Coca-Cola Landing." On July 17, 1958, U.S. marines from the Mediterranean-based Sixth Fleet leaped onto the Beirut beaches and became masters of the Lebanese capital, thus ending the first civil war which since the beginning of that year had been ravaging the peaceable country of cedars. Actually, they had come to replace the Israelis whose aid, in the form of arms deliveries, up to that moment had enabled President Camille Chamoun's beleaguered Christian forces to resist the thrust of the country's pro-Nasser elements. Twenty years later, history was to confirm the permanent character of Israel's attitude toward this minority threatened by the Arab revolution. At that time it was Isser Harel, head of the Mossad, the office of intelligence and special missions, who exerted sustained pressure in Washington, where he had gone to convince the Pentagon brass and high-level officials of the American intelligence apparatus not to abandon the Lebanese Christians to their fate.

The armed intervention of the United States was decided upon on July 15 by President Eisenhower, in accordance with the doctrine that bore his name, the aim of which was to prevent any attempt to weaken those governments situated on the edges of the Soviet sphere of influence.

On the following day, the United States encouraged Great Britain to immediately respond to the appeal for help from King Hussein of Jordan, who, faced with a workers' riot, had barricaded himself in his palace in Amman with his loyal Bedouins, by dispatching a detachment of paratroopers to the area. On July 17 the Cyprus-based British airborne troops received Tel Aviv's eager authorization to use Israeli air space to land in Jordan and rescue, in the nick of time, the Hashemite sovereign who had been deprived for four days of the support of the Iraqi army owing to a putsch in Bagdad.

This time the West reacted instantly to the sudden flame that had again ignited the Near East. The move marked its first counteroffensive to contain Soviet penetration into this region of the world.

On the same day of the joint Anglo-American military intervention, Ben-Gurion, aware of the vanguard role that now devolved upon Israel in this gigantic operation designed to salvage the Western presence, wrote in his personal diary: "Our aim now is to obtain arms from the United States, our participation in the military and political talks concerning the Middle East, and the rapprochement of all the countries in the region opposed to Nasser's will to power and to Soviet expansion."

For Ben-Gurion, this retaliation on the part of the West was also a personal retaliation. Since the great disillusionment that had descended upon the country on November 8, 1956, it had taken Israel almost two years to surmount the humiliating political checkmate of the Suez operation.

On that day, in the early afternoon, Eisenhower had directly informed Ben-Gurion that he would not allow Israel to take advantage of her victorious Sinai campaign in order to get around the UN resolution ordering the withdrawal of foreign armies from Egypt's territory. The day before, Great Britain and France had already complied with the Soviet ultimatum and had begun to evacuate Port Said under American pressure.

Barely recovered from a serious bout with the flu, which had forced him to entrust the conduct of affairs of state during this blitzkrieg to his faithful assistant, Nehemiah Argov, the "Old Man" had yielded to the ephemeral intoxication of the moment.

"The armistice agreement [of 1949] with Egypt is dead and buried," he had proclaimed on November 7 from the rostrum of the Knesset. Then he proposed the opening of direct negotiations so that the "frontiers of peace" could now be defined on the basis of the territorial pawns that had been conquered by Tsahal, the Israeli Defense Forces.

The "Old Man" had not yet fully realized that this military campaign, willed, conceived, and brilliantly won by General Dayan, could yield naught but bitter fruit. Ben-Gurion's obsessive fear of isolation had led him to tie Israel's fate to the fortunes of a hasty and unpopular coalition of the last two remaining colonial powers. And in June 1967, on the eve of the Israeli offensive in the Six-Day War, he communicated this pathological fear to General Itzhak Rabin, prophesying disaster—which produced a temporary depression in the chief of staff.

Much later, on May 11, 1978, on the occasion of Israel's thirtieth anniversary, Rabin again indirectly criticized Ben-Gurion's option when he wrote:

Israel has been able to show convincingly that the Six-Day War was a war of defense, thanks to the political conditions created during the waiting period [between May 15 and June 5, 1967] and because she fought alone, without the cooperation of France and of Great Britain, as was the case in 1956. Thus, in contrast to the results of the Suez campaign, the decision to order a cease-fire was independent of a decision concerning the withdrawal of Israeli troops. For the first time [since 1948] the 1967 war had given Israel some trumps in the political struggle for peace.

The cards held by Israel's armed forces on November 7, 1956, however, had no chance of being transformed into trumps in view of the international conjuncture of events at that particular time.

On November 8, matching Eisenhower's message to Ben-Gurion, American Undersecretary of State Edward Hoover wrote to Golda Meir, Israel's Minister of Foreign Affairs, threatening to impose economic sanctions and to initiate proceedings for the expulsion of Israel from the United Nations. On that same day, half an hour after midnight, the "Old Man" read the text of his reply to the American ultimatum over the radio in a cracked voice. It was no longer a question of annexing the Sinai Peninsula: "We will voluntarily withdraw our forces as soon as an accord is reached at the United Nations for the entry of an international force in the Suez Canal zone . . ."

For four months, Ben-Gurion worked without letup to salvage at least some of the fruits of Dayan's victory: the coastline of the Red Sea and the Gaza Strip, while evacuating the rest of the Sinai, step by step. At the end of January 1957, after dismantling all the Egyptian installations, Ben-Gurion clung even more desperately to Sharm el-Sheikh and to Gaza, despite the riot acts that were repeatedly being read to Israel by the UN. The Americans, however, had already begun to apply their sanctions by blocking a loan that had been promised long before to Israel, by threatening to prevent fundraising campaigns for Israel in the United States, and by interrupting the payment of German reparations. Even the French government, the last loyal member of the October alliance, recommended stationing United Nations garrisons in Gaza and in the disputed territory. To be sure, this was not the view held by General de Gaulle who, at that time, had not yet regained power. When de Gaulle received Menachem Begin, the leader of the Israeli opposition, in his Paris office on rue de Solferino in February 1957, he told him over and over again, emphasizing his words:

"Above all, don't give up Gaza!"

And, as a passing note, he also expressed to Begin his regret that the October tripartite offensive had not thrust forward as far as Cairo. But international necessity is the mother of law.

The Israeli armed forces were given the order to carry out a total evacuation on March 1, 1957, forcing them to give back the territory—to the last inch—that had been conquered four months earlier.

Events were also to compel the Americans to rapidly review their position vis-à-vis the real objectives being pursued by the Soviets and the double game being played by Nasser, who was becoming the champion of revolutionary Pan-Arabism.

A cordon of United Nations troops on Egyptian territory, at the sensitive points of the Straits and of Gaza, would have been a vain undertaking, at best. Nasser's popularity had been consolidated and his army and administration could easily reestablish themselves there in force. Further, Israel had not been really assured of any guarantee about the immediate future while the Suez Canal remained absolutely closed to her ships.

Above all, however, Moscow's penetration into the eastern Mediterranean was so spectacular that it aroused the responsible occupants of the White House even though they had just been freed from the McCarthyite hysteria. Syria had just entered the Soviet orbit, and massive deliveries of Soviet arms were arriving in the Syrian port of Latakia. The CIA was forced to reassess the situation in that area.

Suddenly Ben-Gurion, trying to draw maximum advantage from the Cold War and to exploit American self-criticism, decided to play the card of the Red Menace to the hilt. It was the best means for healing the rift that had been created between Israel and the United States by the tripartite operation in the Suez and for obtaining Washington's blessing for the creation of a kind of Holy Alliance of which he would be the champion in the Near East.

Of course, Ben-Gurion feared the presence of the Russians, and Chief of Secret Services Isser Harel was doing everything possible to keep him under the spell of this obsession; he had been pushing Ben-Gurion along this path, leading to a close rapprochement with the West, for a long time. From the beginning of the 1950s, Harel had been painting a lurid picture of the danger to which the country was being exposed as a result of the activity of the party of the

Socialist Left, the Mapam, to which more than half of the Israeli generals belonged at that time. Ben-Gurion repeatedly catechized himself on the real intentions of the Soviets toward Israel: did the Russians really want the destruction of the State of Israel which they had been among the first, in 1948, to bring to the baptismal font of the United Nations and equip with Czech arms to boot? Apparently, he was never able to clearly answer his questions.

Nevertheless, for Moscow, Israel had become a priority intelligence target. The activity of its secret services, KGB and GRU, had been constantly increasing since 1954; in the next four years, more than one hundred diplomats of the Eastern bloc converged on Israel. Certainly, Ben-Gurion's entire foreign policy during 1957 was essentially centered on the quest for a military guarantee in exchange for Israel's integration into the Western defense system. He was determined to move heaven and earth in order to arrive at such a pact. But, at the same time, he also tried to set up new alliances with a view to encircling and neutralizing Nasser's expansionism.

The political awakening of Black Africa in the process of decolonialization, on the one hand, and the fear of the behind-the-scene Arab intrigues in the non-Arab Islamic states bordering on the Soviet Union—Iran and Turkey— on the other, could furnish the bases of Israel's new political strategy: the solidarity of Russia's adversaries and of Nasser's enemies located at the hinge or on the periphery of the three continents.

In 1957 Ben-Gurion named Ehud Avriel, former right-hand man of Shaul Avigur, who headed the Mossad (Office of Intelligence and Special Missions) in the illegal immigration (Aliyah Bet), ambassador to Ghana. Avriel was the first to occupy the post of Israeli ambassador to this newly independent country, and he was to open the path for Israeli penetration into western and equatorial Africa. Several months later, he was joined by Shimon Peres, the "Old Man" 's special envoy, who had been charged with the task of studying, together with President Kwame Nkrumah, the possibility of forging a tripartite pact of assistance (Ghana, Ethiopia, and Israel) directed against the danger of Nasserism. Christian Ethiopia had been one of the first African states to establish privileged relations with the Jewish state, from which the Negus (ruler of Ethiopia), in the face of Nasser's southern designs, had accepted military aid.

The philosophy of the "African circle," as formulated by Nasser, had already deeply disquieted the Sudanese leaders whose country borders Egypt to the south. One of them, representing the National party had even journeyed secretly to Israel in 1955 to discuss areas of mutual cooperation.

Peres officially became the Adviser in Charge of Special Relations with Africa, an area which was removed from the competence of the Ministry of Foreign Affairs.

In January 1958 Ben-Gurion addressed a letter to the Shah in which he recalled the special relations that had united the Persian and Jewish nations since the time of King Cyrus the Great. His purpose was to strengthen the unobtrusive relations of cooperation that had already been established between the two countries. He likewise sounded out Turkey, which maintained normal relations with Israel, but which for the time being exhibited a hesitancy to proceed further, since she considered that her security was sufficiently guaranteed by her dual membership in NATO and the Bagdad Pact.

This time Ben-Gurion was prudent enough not to take any initiative without the consent and guarantee of the United States. The lesson of Suez had been a very bitter one. Later, American Secretary of State John Foster Dulles himself was to acknowledge that Washington would not have committed the mistake of siding with Moscow if France, Great Britain, and Israel had consulted with the United States and had not, instead, tried to manipulate Washington. The best proof of American goodwill lay in the fact that since June 1956, even before the nationalization of the Suez Canal, State Department functionaries had contacted Reuven Shiloakh, Israel's plenipotentiary, to discuss the matter of neutralizing Nasser. And, on the morning of the nationalization, Allen Dulles, head of the CIA, told Isser Harel, his Israeli counterpart who had been sent to Washington by Ben-Gurion, that he was ready to consider Israel's plans to overthrow Nasser.

After the arrival of the first deliveries of Russian arms to Syria, in August 1957, a high-level CIA functionary kept Tel Aviv intelligence circles constantly informed regarding the American plan for subversion in Syria with the aid of Turkey and Iraq. A group of Syrian leaders living in exile in Bagdad had been assigned the job of fomenting a military coup in Damascus, but it had not been possible to achieve it.

At the beginning of May, Moshe Dayan asked British Field Marshal Montgomery to explain Ben-Gurion's plans of regional alliances to Eisenhower, whom he was scheduled to meet soon in Washington.

In June this secret diplomatic activity was intensified with the precipitous onrush of events that began to tear the Near East apart. The civil war unleashed in Lebanon threatened to transform this pro-Western country into a base for extremist groups. In Jordan, King Hussein's pro-British government vacillated under the blow of anti-British demonstrations led by several officers of the Arab Legion. In addition, the Americans' client regime in Iraq suddenly collapsed in the immediate wake of a bloodbath.

On July 13 by virtue of the agreements linking Iraq to Jordan, the armored brigade of Colonel Abd El Karim Kassem received orders to set out for the rescue of the tottering Hashemite monarch. En route, the brigade suddenly made an about-face: instead of crossing the Jordanian frontier, it marched on Bagdad.

On July 14, at 7:00 A.M., the world learned of the massacre of the young King Faisal of Iraq, of the kingdom's regent, and of Prime Minister Nouri Sayid, the Americans' strongman. In their place, Kassem proclaimed the establishment of a "people's republic." In Washington, as in Tel Aviv, the arrow of the pressure gauge shot up precipitously to the red danger line.

Ben-Gurion wrote in his personal diary: "At seven this morning a thunderclap over the radio: revolution in Iraq." On that very same evening, he summoned his aides and military advisers. Colonel Harkabi, Chief of Aman, the military intelligence service, suggested the possibility of a pro-Nasser revolution in Jordan after the fall of the Iraqi monarchy. The new Chief of Staff, Chaim Laskov, who had just succeeded Moshe Dayan, proposed that Israeli armed forces penetrate the West Bank and preemptively occupy the line of hills between Nablus and Hebron.

After being informed of Israel's intentions, the CIA presented a report to President Eisenhower who, disquieted by its contents, decided to take the initiative by dispatching the marines to Beirut. They were numerous enough to stop the ongoing destabilization process in the region, while at the same time assuring Israel of the West's determination to defend itself. The political landscape changed in a matter of a few days.

On July 16 while England, for her part, decided to intervene in Jordan, Rustu Fatin Zurlu, Turkey's Minister of Foreign Affairs, expressing his government's fears in the face of the new situation created by the recent Arab putsch, invited Israel to send an emissary. The secret meeting took place on July 18 in Ankara where the Israeli representative presented Zurlu with the plan of a "peripheral pact," Ben-Gurion's pet project, between Turkey, Iran, Ethiopia, and Israel: the only non-Arab and pro-Western countries between the Mediterranean and the Horn of Africa. Zurlu accepted the idea of organizing a secret meeting in the Turkish capital between the two heads of state.

Encouraged by the new Turkish attitude, Ben-Gurion gathered a group of experts together in the offices of Golda Meir, in the Ministry of Foreign Affairs, to study the possibility of creating such a pact. In the face of Soviet penetration in the region, the danger current events posed to the Western presence gave Israel a considerable trump card for breaking out of an isolation that ceaselessly haunted the "Old Man" and for turning the tables to Israel's advantage.

On June 20 Ben-Gurion sent Eisenhower an urgent message asking for moral and financial support of his plan for an "unobtrusive" alliance among the four powers. "Our aim," he wrote Eisenhower, "is to create an organization capable of opposing the Soviet expansion which is being actualized through Nasser. This organization would be able to safeguard the independent future of Lebanon and, perhaps, even that of Syria."

But all Moscow had to do was to raise its little finger, and a terrified Ben-Gurion retreated just as he had retreated in November 1956 before Marshal Bulganin's threats to send "volunteers" to the Sinai. When, on August 1, Soviet Deputy Minister of Foreign Affairs Valerian Zorine vehemently protested to the Israeli authorities against the utilization of Israeli airspace by British paratroopers who were being flown to Hussein's assistance, the "Old Man" promptly asked the British to suspend their flights. He authorized them again only at the express request of John Foster Dulles who, on August 4, informed him of Eisenhower's approval of the plan for a peripheral pact.

Preparations moved into high gear. On August 28 at 10:00 P.M., Ben Gurion secretly left Israel for Ankara aboard a military plane, in the company of Golda Meir and Reuven Shiloakh. In the course of the day-long sojourn in the Turkish capital, Ben-Gurion had a confidential conversation with Prime Minister Adnan Menderes. The two delegations discussed questions of economic, scientific, and diplomatic cooperation between the two countries, but the essential item of discussion at this summit conference centered on a program of common defense against their Mutual Enemy No. 1: Gamal Abdel Nasser.

Upon his return, Ben-Gurion believed that from then on it would be both proper and opportune to encourage all and any opposition groups to Nasser, regardless of their source. And there was no lack of opposition groups, even in the bosom of the Arab world.

In Iraq, the new head of state had had the unfortunate idea of pardoning and recalling Rashid Ali Keylani, the mastermind of the May 1941 pro-Nazi coup d'état against the English and who subsequently had found refuge in Germany with the Grand Mufti of Jerusalem. In October, several weeks after his return to Bagdad, Rashid Ali headed a new putsch, directed this time against Kassem. He was in contact with Nasser who had, in part, financed the plot. But the attempt was abortive, and Rashid Ali was sentenced to death. The Egyptians accused Kassem of having accepted the aid of the Israeli secret services in order to save his skin. Cairo Radio identified Michael Wright, the British ambassador to Bagdad, as Kassem's informant, in consequence of which Wright had to leave Iraq in December so as not to exacerbate the situation.

To a great extent, the new policy of alliances, all of which were directed against Nasser's ambitions, depended on intelligence activities. In the majority of cases, it was a matter of establishing or maintaining clandestine contacts with intelligence services, personalities, or governments interested in or concerned about Soviet activity in the Middle East. But the initial stage of this new policy entailed a consolidation of the privileged relations with the Americans and a redoubling of vigilance in order to expose the Soviet agents who had infiltrated the Middle East and who were close to official circles where high-level decisions were made.

Since the spring of 1956 when the United States was still gambling on Nasser and on the policy of détente with the Middle East, the Israeli intelligence services had rendered an enormous service to the West by getting their hands on the first copy of Nikita Khrushchev's secret report on Stalin's crimes to the Twentieth Congress of the Communist party of the USSR. The Americans, who up to then had possessed only an "edited" version of the famous speech pronounced behind closed doors by the new master of the Kremlin, subsequently recognized that the complete and unexpurgated text obtained by the Israeli intelligence services enabled them to better understand the extent, the limits, and the direction of de-Stalinization undertaken by those who, six months later, were to drown the Budapest uprising in blood.

From 1958 on, the Soviet intelligence services exerted themselves to strengthen their apparatus in the Middle East. In Israel they began to count more than ever before on Israel Beer, their agent who had infiltrated Ben-Gurion's inner circle and who, consequently, was able to brief them on the plan of the peripheral alliances which had been put in concrete form following the "Old Man"'s secret journey to Ankara.

1

3

4

FAMILY ALBUM OF THE JEWISH NATIONAL HOME

1. The wedding of Sarah Aaronsohn (center), the future heroine of the Nili network, and Zichron Yaakov in 1915.

2. Head of the Jewish Agency's political department, Chaim Arlosoroff (wearing glasses) and President Chaim Weizmann (with goatee) with Palestinian Arab sheikhs.

3. Itzhak Sadeh, the first head of the Palmach, with his two protégés, Yigal Allon (left) and Moshe Dayan (right) in the spring of 1941.

4. Coast Guard cutter *Sea Lion,* which disappeared in Lebanese waters on May 18, 1941 with twenty-three of Palmach's best members.

A/AMAN (ARMY INTELLIGENCE)

5. Colonel Benjamin Gibli, second head of Army Intelligence (Aman), dismissed in February 1955.

6. Colonel Yehoshafat Harkabi, third head of Aman, dismissed in May 1959, a victim of psychological warfare.

7. Colonel Chaim Herzog, fourth head of Aman, discharged in November 1961 (left) and General Meir Amit, fifth head of Aman, and one of the rare men who had no problems on the job (right).

8. General Aharon Yariv, sixth head of Aman (1963–1972).

9. General Eli Zeira, seventh head of Aman, fired in April 1974 for miscalculating the Yom Kippur War.

10. General Shlomo Gazit, eighth head of Aman, brother of the Israeli ambassador to France.

B/THE MOSSAD (CENTRAL INTELLIGENCE)

11. Isser Harel, second head of the Mossad (1953–1963).

12. General Meir Amit, third head of the Mossad (1963–1968).

13. General Zvi Zamir, fourth head of the Mossad (1968–1974).

14. Israel Galili, former commander in chief of the Haganah, and mystery man in all the Labor party governments.

15. Ehud Avriel, No. 2 man of the Mossad Aliyah Bet, ambassador for special missions.

16. Shaul Meyerov-Avigur, head of the Mossad Aliyah Bet, became the government's mystery man.

17

18

19

AFFAIRS WITH A CAPITAL "A"
AND TOP-SECRET DOSSIERS

17. The Soviet Mig 21 spirited away from Iraq in August 1966 and delivered by the Mossad to General Motti Hod, head of the Israeli Air Force.

18. Defense Minister Pinchas Lavon and Chief of the General Staff Moshe Dayan in 1954, before the Lavon Affair.

19. In 1977 Lavon's man Ephraim Evron (center) switched to Dayan (shaking the hand of American Secretary of State Cyrus Vance).

20. Black September (1970) in Jordan: a terrorist surrenders to an Israeli soldier to escape capture by Hussein's Bedouins.

21. Soviet radar fallen into the hands of Tsahal in 1973.

23

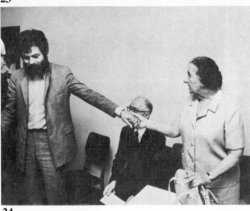

24

CLOSE ENCOUNTERS OF ANOTHER KIND

22. A young Lieutenant-Colonel Itzha Rabin (right) with Egyptian General Said Tah Bey, who surrendered the encircled Egyptia Army on February 27, 1949 at Faluja, in th Negev. This is where General Yigal Allo met Egypt's future president, Gamal Abd Nasser.

23. Archaeological General Yigael Yadi (center) before his abortive meeting of Febru ary 1954 with Colonel Nasser.

24. Painter Marek Halter gets the green lig from Golda Meir for Operation Eliav (Jun 1970).

25. Sadat greets General Motta Gur, Chief the General Staff of Tsahal (smiling in th center between Rabin and Golda Meir) at Lo Airport, November 19, 1977.

26. Egyptian Deputy Premier Hassan T hami, who had secret contacts with Dayan.

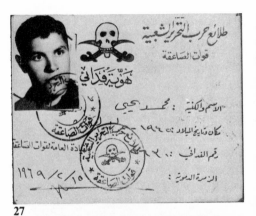

27

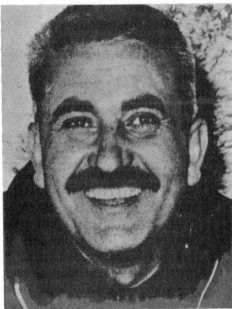

29

28

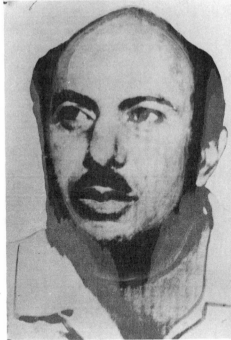

30

ESCALATION OF TERRORISM

27. Identity card of a terrorist belonging to El Saika, a Syrian-controlled Palestinian group.

28. Lieutenant-Colonel Yonatan "Yoni" Netanyahu, hero of the Beirut commando raid on April 9, 1973 and leader of the commando raid on Entebbe, killed July 4, 1976.

29. George Habash, founder and head of the PFLP.

30. Waddia Haddad, head of military operations of the PFLP.

In 1959 the KGB introduced one of its best spies into the region: British diplomat William Blake, who had been recruited seven years earlier in South Korea, where he had served as the British vice consul in Seoul. Four years later, Blake had become the bureau chief of the MI 6 intelligence unit in Berlin. Following the instructions of his Moscow manipulators, he requested and obtained his transfer to the Middle East, where he arrived toward the end of 1959. Meanwhile, he had spent some months in the central office in London where he was placed in charge, as though by chance, of the Israeli desk. Through him, important intelligence on Israel's clandestine relations with the countries of the peripheral pact in the making found their way to Moscow, and eventually to Cairo. (Blake was exposed in May 1960, following the arrest of a double agent who had been one of his deputies in Berlin.)

At this point, interservice rivalries and personal wrangling over the direction they were taking were to affect Ben-Gurion's "peripheral" policy. Internecine squabbling also affected other projects and plans.

The February 1958 appointment of General Chaim Laskov as Chief of Staff of the Israeli armed forces, replacing Moshe Dayan, had been welcomed as a blessing by Mossad chief Isser Harel, who was responsible to Ben-Gurion for the whole intelligence community. The new army chief, whose plans for reforms had displeased a whole group of generals, had been wrangling with Colonel Yehoshafat Harkabi, the chief of his army intelligence service (Aman), since October. Hence Laskov was eager to seize the first opportunity to rid Harel of this competitor who inevitably had become a potential rival.

The opportunity presented itself on the evening of April 5, 1959, when the radio, (Kol Israel), broadcast the code names of military units in nine languages, in accordance with a technique being tried for the first time on the nation's air waves. The simulated call-up of reservists provoked a veritable panic in the population and, by rebound, a military alert in Egypt and in Syria, whose governments began mobilization procedures.

When he heard the first call-up on the radio, Ben-Gurion, who was alone in his Tel Aviv apartment, wanted to telephone Kol Israel and demand the immediate cessation of the broadcast; but, in the absence of his wife and of his secretary, he did not know how to use the telephone.

UN observers and American diplomats immediately intervened to reduce the tension on the frontiers. Later, an Israeli Army commission of inquiry found the two persons responsible for the false alert—General Zorea, the No. 2 man of the Israeli armed forces, chief of military operations in the general staff, and Colonel Harkabi, the chief of Aman—guilty of imprudence. General Itzhak Rabin was designated to succeed Zorea: doubtless he owed his rise to the post of Chief of Staff of the Israeli armed forces and, later, his brief political career at the head of the government to this incident. Colonel Harkabi put away his uniform to devote himself to a university career, and ceded his place to Colonel Chaim Herzog.

Herzog, who was born in Belfast in 1918, is descended from a family of Irish rabbis. At the time of the 1939 mobilization, he had already obtained his doctorate in law at Cambridge and had studied at the Officers' School of the British Army at Sandhurst. He participated in the Normandy landing of 1944 and left the army three years later, with the rank of lieutenant colonel. Upon his return to Israel in 1948, he became the first director of the intelligence department of the Military Operations branch of the Israeli Armed Forces (Tsahal). For several years he was military attaché in Washington. In May 1959 he was appointed head of Aman, the military intelligence branch (formerly the intelligence department of the Military Operations branch).

The "dry-run" mobilization drill that had led to Herzog's appointment was by no means an act of imprudence on the part of his predecessor: actually, it was a psychological warfare operation carefully prepared by Aman's experts in emotional manipulation. The alert unleashed by the simulated call-up of the reservists was designed to give Aman the opportunity to study the reactive capacities of the Arab countries. But this operation had not been submitted to the prime minister or to the chief of staff for approval.

Herzog, the new chief of Aman—the fourth in eleven years!—lost no time in clashing, in turn, with Little Isser and his bosom friend Laskov. From the following spring on, Laskov kept complaining to Ben-Gurion about Herzog's affectations of mystery. He criticized Herzog for not having kept him informed of a movement of Egyptian troops in the Sinai, disclosed by Aman in February. Herzog had not deemed these maneuvers disquieting enough to alert his superior. After being informed of them by some subordinate officers of his service, the chief of staff demanded, with Isser Harel's support, a general mobilization of reservists to parry the danger. But the chief of Aman (whose brother, Yaakov Herzog, was at that time a much-appreciated personal adviser to Ben-Gurion) managed to get the ear of the "Old Man," and he won him over to his point of view: there was no danger in delay. Consequently, the prime minister agreed only to a partial call-up of reservists while, at the same time, suggesting to Laskov that he tone down his ardor. And Ben-Gurion left for an official visit to the United States to show that he did not take the Egyptian military threat seriously.

Nevertheless, the partial call-up, code-named "Rotem," would be revealed, in the course of a commission of inquiry set up by Laskov, as an exemplary combination of armed vigilance and verbal moderation designed to avoid escalation. The Egyptian brigades retreated progressively from their positions in Sinai, and calm prevailed. But not among the Israeli general staff.

In September 1960 a second crisis erupted between Laskov and Herzog on the subject of a meeting of the Mixed Israeli-Jordanian Armistice Commission. This time Isser Harel managed to convince Ben-Gurion to replace Herzog. One year later, and before the normal end of his period of service, the brilliant colonel had to step aside to make way for the fifth chief of Aman, General Meir Amit.

Herzog left the army in 1962 to open a law office in Tel Aviv. Recalled as a military radio commentator in May 1967, he was able to reassure the population in the period of anxiety that preceded the Six-Day War. After his appointment as military commander of the West Bank, he was dismissed by Dayan because of his favorable attitude toward a Palestinian entity. As ambassador to the UN in 1975, Herzog was called to account in Israel by a deputy of the Likud party, Ygal Horowitz, who demanded that Minister of Foreign Affairs Yigal Allon, recall him on the grounds of his insubordination in 1960! Actually, it was a vulgar settlement of scores: Horowitz is Dayan's cousin whom Herzog had severely criticized in a remarkable book on the Yom Kippur War.

General Meir Amit's arrival opened a new chapter in the intelligence services. In contrast to his four predecessors, he enjoyed personal prestige due to his military career: he was General Dayan's No. 2 man during the Sinai campaign, and would have become chief of staff if a parachute accident had not immobilized him for more than two years.

Upon taking his post in the winter of 1961, Amit reinforced the special stature of army intelligence. Aman became one of the two most important bureaus of the Israeli armed forces. As a new rival of Harel, Amit ended up by succeeding him as the head of Mossad, in 1963.

Meanwhile, Little Isser had attained the summit of glory. He had modestly rendered a service to a head of state: General de

Gaulle, and had probably saved his life. There are several versions of how Israel intervened to foil an attempted assassination of the French president shortly before the abortive coup in Algiers in April 1961. The following version is that of de Gaulle's son-in-law, General Alain de Boissieu, Lord Chancellor of the Legion of Honor.

At the time when, as a colonel, de Boissieu was head of the general staff's inspectorship of armored units, he received a visit on March 29, 1961, from one of his former Military Academy classmates, Israeli General Uzi Narkiss (the future conqueror of the Old City of Jerusalem in June 1967). Narkiss had come to ask him to pass on an oral message from Ben-Gurion to his father-in-law. The "Old Man" was bent on informing him personally—but outside diplomatic channels—of the arrest in Israel of a Palestinian Arab: a member of a terrorist team trained in Cairo and commanded by an extremist, who had been charged with the mission to assassinate de Gaulle. The man had been apprehended during a visit with his family in Israel, just before his terrorist team had set out for France.

In his biography of Isser Harel, Israeli historian Michael Bar-Zohar was to provide more exact details. He relates that in the middle of March, an Israeli stationed in Paris received a visit from a Frenchman, a fervent Catholic friend of Israel. He had come to see him for possible assistance in connection with an assassination plot against de Gaulle—branded as the "peddler" of French Algeria—a plot which had been developed over three months in certain army circles. A Palestinian Arab would be trained to execute this mission. Upon his arrival in France, he would pass himself off as an Algerian extremist, which would make it possible to saddle the blame for de Gaulle's assassination on the FLN (the Algerian National Liberation Front) and which would turn public opinion against the proponents of a negotiated peace to the advantage of the *"ultras."* If their attempt succeeded and they managed to gain power, the authors of the plot promised to commit themselves to furnishing Israel with all the arms she would require for her defense.

In a tone of amusement, the Israeli reported this conversation to his ambassador, Walter Eytan, who immediately addressed a confidential letter to Minister of Foreign Affairs Golda Meir. In turn, she summoned her advisers and colleagues to a meeting at which they discussed the possibility of a trap designed to test Israel's loyalty to the French government. She then brought the matter to the attention of Ben-Gurion, in the presence of Isser Harel, among others. Supported by the look on the face of his intelligence chief, the "Old Man" flew into a rage: not only could there be no question of lending a hand to any plot whatsoever against de Gaulle, but it was imperative to alert the head of the French state without losing a minute's time. An ultrasecret telegram, worded on the spot, gave firm and detailed instructions to the Israeli embassy in Paris. On the following day, Colonel de Boissieu received the visit of an Israeli official, after which he gave an account of it to Georges Galichon, director of the departmental staff of the President of the Republic.

We are in a position to add two additional items to this incomplete story. On the one hand, the Israeli who was the source of the intelligence report was supposedly given an inkling of the plan on March 25 by an old war-horse of the intelligence services, Claude Arnoult, who, after having worked for the British intelligence service under the Occupation, maintained close relations with the Vatican Secretariat.

On the other hand, during the March 28 meeting held in Ben-Gurion's office, Isser Harel reportedly clashed once more with Shimon Peres, who was not in favor of apprising de Gaulle of the alleged plot in any form whatsoever. But the head of intelligence knew that he was the adviser to whom Ben-Gurion was most likely to lend an ear. After all, he was the one who, the year before and at the peak of his career, had accomplished one of the most spectacular exploits of Israel's secret history: the capture of Adolf Eichmann, hangman of the Jewish people.

10

ADOLF EICHMANN, ALIAS RICARDO KLEMENT

On May 23, 1960, at 4:00 P.M., the customary opening hour of the sessions of the Parliament in Jerusalem, David Ben-Gurion mounted the rostrum to read a brief declaration. The corridors and the galleries of the Knesset had been buzzing with the rumor that the prime minister was to announce an important event. For the first time, a short, bald, big-eared man with a look as hard as steel, was sitting in a special bay behind the table reserved for the members of the government. There was an especially radiant look about Isser Harel, head of the Mossad, whom few people seated in the benches for the public knew by sight.

"I have to inform the Knesset," said Ben-Gurion in a voice tinged with solemnity, "that a short while ago, the Israeli security services captured one of the biggest Nazi criminals—Adolf Eichmann, who together with the Nazi leaders, was responsible for what was termed 'the final solution of the Jewish problem': the destruction of six million European Jews. Eichmann is already in detention in Israel and will soon be put on trial here under the 1950 law relating to the Nazis and their collaborators."

In the closing paragraphs of the only book which the Israeli government authorized the former head of the intelligence services to publish fifteen years later, *The House on Garibaldi Street,** Harel wrote:

> The Prime Minister's announcement came as a complete surprise to the Knesset members. It had appeared that the government was reacting apathetically to the recurrent reports that Eichmann was alive; no one in the Knesset had known that volunteers from Israel were in action, with the intention of bringing him to justice.
>
> The news flashed from the Knesset to the entire nation of Israel, to the tortured who had survived the murder factory, to the bereaved who had lost so many dear ones. This reconfirmation of the rule of law heartened them and renewed their faith in justice.
>
> And the news reached the far corners of the earth, imbuing all decent people with a feeling of respect, and it carried with it a clear warning to the murderers of the Jewish people hiding in their holes,

* Viking Press, New York.

who thought that the years would whiten their sins and silence the cry of the blood they had shed, and that none would come any more to make them face judgment for the millions that they had slain in their criminal frenzy.

The trial of Eichmann, which opened on April 11, 1961, in the main hall, fitted out like a tribunal, of the House of the Nation, in the process of completion at the entry to Jerusalem, marked a turning point in Jewish history and in the collective consciousness of the Israelis. For the native-born sabras and for the Eastern Jews—natives of the Mediterranean and Arab countries—it was this trial that was to make them understand what had transpired twenty years before in distant Europe. At that time, the unimaginable entered into the inner consciousness of the whole people: the Jews had been exterminated simply because they were Jews.

On that day, the prosecutor, Attorney General Gideon Hausner, began to pronounce a moving *"J'accuse"*:

As I stand before you, judges of Israel, to lead the prosecution against Adolf Eichmann, I do not stand alone. With me, in this place and at this hour, stand six million accusers. But they cannot rise to their feet and point an accusing finger toward the man who sits in the glass dock and cry: "I accuse." For their ashes were piled up in the hills of Auschwitz and in the fields of Treblinka, or washed away by the rivers of Poland. Their graves are scattered over the length and breadth of Europe. Their blood cries out, but their voices are stilled.

Sentenced to death on December 15, 1961, the scrupulous pieceworker of the final solution was hanged on May 31 of the following year and his ashes scattered over the sea, far from the territorial waters so that no portion of the Jewish state could be defiled by them.

Today more than half of the Israelis are sabras, but the memory of the Holocaust, an ineradicable trauma, remains at the base of the national character. The six million victims of Eichmann and of the madness of his bosses, live again without end on this earth of Palestine haunted by so many phantoms. And in large measure it explains Israel's fears and prejudices, her obsessive mistrust, her prideful reactions, her permanent feeling of solitude in a world in which such things are possible. At the same time that it justifies the existence of the State of Israel, the Holocaust prevents her from living in a normal fashion in peace with herself.

Before the departure of Isser Harel for Argentina where he was personally to direct the abduction of Eichmann, who had been formally identified by a team of Mossad operatives, Ben-Gurion had told him: "Bring him back dead or alive." Then he had added pensively: "Preferably alive. It would be very important, morally, for the young generations."

Although the exploit of the Eichmann operation, carried out 18,000 kilometers from Tel Aviv, in the best tradition of spy novels, undeniably was and will remain his title to fame, Harel's role in the long hunt for Eichmann in Argentina was not altogether that which he attributes to himself in his book, and even less that which has been haloed by legend.

The discovery of Eichmann in Argentina was the result of chance, and his identification was due to the tenacity of one man: Dr. Fritz Bauer, the general prosecutor of the State of Hesse in West Germany, a German Jew who had suffered the Nazi persecutions. Without his insistence, his repeated interventions, his pressing solicitations to Chaim Cohen, the legal adviser of the Israeli government, to force the hand of the Mossad chief, the tracking down of the war criminal would have been abandoned. And it took two years of utter persistence on Bauer's part for the hunt to find its quarry. Without his determination, the Mossad would have given up the pursuit. Before the confirmation of Eichmann's presence in Argentina, there was no section, no responsible head, in the Israeli Central Agency for Intelligence charged to follow through on the Eichmann file. This explains why the investigation took so long and the scant zeal with which it had been conducted at the start.

The first intelligence item on Eichmann reached Isser Harel toward the end of the autumn of 1957. It had been transmitted to him by Dr. Pinhas Shinar, head of the Israeli-German reparations mission in Bonn. In the course of a discreet meeting on September 19, Bauer told Dr. Shinar that he had received a communication from Argentina which had made it possible to pick up Eichmann's traces again and to track him to Olivos, a suburb of Buenos Aires. Bauer hesitated giving his government the address which he had just obtained.

"I don't know whether I can wholly count on our administration of justice here, much less on our embassy there," he confided. "That is why I see no other alternative except to turn to you, on the condition that it remain strictly secret between us."

In January 1958 Harel sent one of his agents to Argentina to the indicated address. On the basis of the shabby impression that the premises made on him—a modest house in a lower-class suburb— the Mossad operative concluded that Eichmann could not possibly be living there. He was convinced that if Eichmann were still alive, he would be living in the lap of luxury.

Harel then asked Dr. Bauer, who had such a self-assured air, about the possibility of verifying his source. Several days later, a skilled investigator left to interview Bauer's correspondent in Argentina: Lothar Hermann, a former internee who had lost his sight in concentration camps. The blind man's daughter had kept company with a boy named Nicholas Eichmann, whose father she had once glimpsed in this house, and who might very well be Adolf Eichmann. Hermann offered to pursue the case himself, and the investigator asked him to obtain the necessary elements for Eichmann's identification: his present identity, his photograph, his place of work, and, if possible, his fingerprints. The investigator returned to Tel Aviv in mid-March.

Two months later, Hermann wrote him that the house had been built in 1947 by an Austrian emigrant, Francisco Schmidt, and rented to two tenants named Dagoto and Klement. For him there was no doubt: "This Schmidt is the man we are looking for. The two other names merely serve him as cover."

Harel ordered his agents to verify Hermann's statements. A whole series of tedious steps proved to them that Eichmann could not be the owner. Moreover, he himself had never lived in this house. In the light of these results, the Mossad head concluded that Hermann's information was unreliable. In August 1958 Harel ordered his operatives to break off their contact with the blind man. Investigation was abandoned without taking even one photo of the possible tenants of the house! Toward the end of 1958, the search for Eichmann looked more problematic than ever.

It required prosecutor Bauer's visit to Israel toward the end of the following year to start the investigation again. Bauer told Cohen, the legal adviser of the Israeli government, that he had a new clue in his possession, from an altogether different source, which led once more to Buenos Aires. On December 6, 1959, Cohen and Harel told Ben-Gurion that this time Bauer planned to ask the Argentine authorities for Eichmann's extradition to Germany. The "Old Man" recorded his reply to them in his private journal at the end of the day: "I told them to prevent Bauer from taking this step. That he was to say nothing to anybody, that he merely give us the means to find Eichmann and, if he is there, we will capture him in order to bring him here. Isser will be in charge of the matter."

Then the Hesse prosecutor brought Chaim Cohen an intelligence item of capital importance: his new source, a former Nazi who wanted to even scores with Eichmann, had furnished him with details on the SS chief's escape from Germany. After the war, Eichmann had hidden in a monastery run by Croatian priests who had provided him with false documents under the name of Ricardo Klement. After arriving in Buenos Aires at the beginning of 1950, Eichmann procured himself an identity card with the same name. This name was found in the 1952 telephone directory listed together with a laundry in the Olivos quarter, but the laundry had closed down for lack of business. In 1958 Eichmann worked for an electric company near the city of Tucuman.

Actually, since May 1958, the name Klement had cropped up in Harel's dossier. The first informant, Hermann, had believed that it referred to a fictitious tenant in the house in Olivos where his daughter had spotted the parents of the boy who was courting her. Chaim Cohen phoned the head of the Mossad and asked him to verify the new intelligence.

"Send someone to Buenos Aires," Bauer had to insist. "Let him question the shopkeepers of the neighborhood—the butcher, the owner of the delicatessen—to find out whether he still lives there or what became of him afterward."

It was only at the end of February 1960 that one of Israel's crack investigators was available to go to Argentina. He stopped off in two other Latin American countries to recruit a task force of volunteers who could help him in his mission. On March 4 he sent a bellboy from the Hotel of Buenos Aires to the Schmidt house with a present for "Nicky" Klement from the blind man's daughter; it was, in fact, the young Eichmann's birthday. The Klement family had just moved only three weeks before, leaving no forwarding address. But by persistent questions, the lad managed to find the youngest son, who worked in the neighborhood, and he delivered the parcel to him. He also had the presence of mind to note the license number of the boy's scooter. On March 10 the thread led the Mossad team to a brick house on Garibaldi Street in the San Fernando quarter, which was even shabbier than the Olivos suburb.

From mid-March on, a self-styled representative of a sewing machine company began to call on the houses on Garibaldi Street. He carried a small briefcase inside of which was a concealed camera that could be set in action by pressing a simple button. He unobtrusively photographed Señora Klement and her children. But Ricardo Klement himself was away in Tucuman.

The final proof arrived on March 21 in the form of a modest bouquet of hollyhocks. On that day, at twilight, the sewing-machine representative saw a bald, thin man wearing glasses and sporting a moustache under his large nose, descend from a bus holding these flowers. He pressed the button when he saw him head toward the brick house. He knew that this date was the silver wedding anniversary of Adolf and Vera Eichmann.

Operation Eichmann could begin. Isser Harel landed in Buenos Aires on May 1 at the head of a hand-picked commando force. Ricardo Klement was kidnapped on May 11 as he was entering his house, sequestered for nine days in the same locality, drugged, and, disguised as a steward, placed aboard El Al Special Flight 601 on May 20, during the ceremonies celebrating the 150th anniversary of Argentine independence. For this planning, credit was due to Isser Harel.

"My capture unfolded in an absolutely correct manner," the prisoner had to acknowledge. "The operation had been organized and prepared in an exemplary fashion. My kidnappers took particular care not to injure me physically. I permit myself to express my opinion on the subject because I have a certain experience in the spheres of police administration and of the secret services."

News of the abduction had been transmitted on May 13 to Golda Meir and to General Chaim Laskov by one of Harel's deputies. The "Old Man" was taking a rest in his kibbutz in the Negev and a messenger was sent to him only two days later. Ben-Gurion thought silently for several minutes and then asked the messenger, "When is Isser coming back? I need him."

On May 5 in fact, the prime minister had had his first stormy meeting with the Secretary-General of the Histadrut, Pinchas Lavon, his former substitute at the Ministry of Defense. Lavon had made it obvious to Ben-Gurion that he now possessed proof of the wrongs committed in 1954 by his young aids to drive him from power and that he was determined to put up a fight to become Ben-Gurion's successor. On May 10 the "Old Man" had received confirmation from his military secretary, Chaim Ben-David, of the falsification of the Aman documents relating to this affair. He had then left for Sde Boker in a bad mood. When Harel's deputy asked to see Ben-Gurion on May 13 to tell him of the news from Buenos Aires, Ben-David suggested that he wait for two days if it was not an "urgent" matter.

On May 15 Ben-Gurion wrote in his diary: "Eichmann has been identified and arrested. He will be brought to Israel next week. If there has been no error in identification, it is a beautiful and important operation."

Isser Harel's prestige reached its peak at that time. But it was from that moment of his glory, rather rare for a head of secret services, that his career was to experience a decline parallel to that of his mentor. Nevertheless, he was still ready to render him an eminent personal service when, in March 1962, he responded to a pressing summons from the "Old Man."

A private family drama that went back more than two years had split the country in two and threatened the fragile balance of the government's coalition: the disappearance of nine-year-old Yossef Schumacher. The boy had been abducted from his parents by an ultra-Orthodox Jewish sect in Jerusalem. Secular militants and religious fanatics engaged in a violent confrontation, the authority of the law was scoffed at, the police ridiculed, and the whole life of the nation seemed to be polarized around the question which upset public opinion and plagued the responsible authorities: "Where is Yossele?" Their powerlessness to answer the question struck the majority of the population simultaneously as a disquieting sign of weakness and as one more concession to the religious parties that were opposed to any separation between synagogue and state.

"Where is Yossele?" Ben-Gurion, in turn, asked the intelligence chief. "After all, you tracked down Eichmann, unmasked Beer. Now find me Yossele. The prestige of the state is at stake here, too."

Isser Harel would have been in a position to bow out of the affair. He had accumulated enough recognition and had made enough allies within the government, principally Minister of Foreign Affairs Golda Meir, to decline so exorbitant an order. But he accepted because he wanted to prove once more to the "Old Man" who had fostered his career that he was the most powerful, the most capable, the most worthy of his esteem. He could not know that by taking this assignment he was going to come up against one of the most difficult and ungrateful of missions, because it would lead him to neglect other more essential matters.

So the head of the intelligence service asked to see police dossier 720-60, which summarized the futile investigations to find little Yossele.

The child had been entrusted to his paternal grandfather, Nahman Shtarkes, an ultra-Orthodox religious Jew from Jerusalem, while his parents, who had recently emigrated from Poland, found jobs and decent housing in Tel Aviv. When, in December 1959, his mother, Ida Schumacher, wanted to take the boy back, the old man voiced his fears that she would raise his grandson outside the strict rules of life as laid down by the Torah, and as they are practiced in Mea Shearim, the ultra-Orthodox quarter of Jerusalem, where the religious Jews spend their days in prayer, studying the Talmud, and observing all the rites. Worse still, he had persuaded himself that the boy's parents were preparing to take their son to Russia. He refused to surrender little Yossele.

Yossele's mother took the matter to court. On January 15, 1960, the High Court of Appeals ordered the old man to restore the child to his parents. But Yossele was no longer to be found at his grandfather's house. He had disappeared. The police ran into an order of silence issued by the ultra-Orthodox sect of Neturei Karta (Guardians of the Walls of the City), who had never acknowledged even the principle of the State of Israel. At the end of two months of an impossible search, the police gave up. The Supreme Court reprimanded the police, and ordered Shtarkes's arrest. The press flared up in May 1960 and the affair was placed on the agenda of the Knesset. The strictest religious political party vainly tried to use its good offices with the ultras.

For a whole year, the polemics degenerated into a "war of culture" which imperceptibly pushed the country to the brink of civil war. Old Shtarkes was released from jail even though he had not uttered a word about the boy's whereabouts. And, on the eve of the elections of August 1961, the parties of the Left formed a National Committee for the Liberation of Yossele, while the Supreme Court described the kidnapping as a "repugnant crime." Ben-Gurion was obsessed by the political turn that the affair was taking which threatened to shatter his parliamentary majority, founded from the beginning on a coalition of laborites, liberals, and religious factions. The tension was rising to a new peak when, at the beginning of March 1962, he appealed for help from his faithful secret agent No. 1.

After closing dossier 720-60, Isser Harel mobilized his best task forces of the Mossad and the Shin Bet (internal security) and provided them with an operational file on the cover of which he himself had inscribed a code name: "Operation Tiger."

Harel's agents systematically infiltrated all the communities of Orthodox Jews in Israel, but suffered failure upon failure. They were dealing with people used to persecution who strictly observed the rules of conspiracy. The world of the fanatics appeared to the agents as an alien, closed, hostile world, a kind of *terra incognita* where they felt lost. In this world of long black caftans, round hats and fur caps, long beards, earlocks, and shaved womens' heads, the secret agents of both sexes were betrayed by their outer appearance or their ignorance of rites.

"I had the impression of having landed on Mars with the mission of mixing with the crowd of little green creatures without their perceiving my presence," one of them wrote later.

Convinced that, in the absence of any clue, the boy could no longer be in Israel, Harel personally took charge of the search in all the centers of Jewish fanaticism scattered throughout the Diaspora. He entrusted the dispatch of current business of the intelligence bureau to one of his deputies and flew to Paris on a hunch. He set up an improvised general staff to launch a series of simultaneous operations in France, Italy, Switzerland, Belgium, Great Britain, and as far afield as South Africa and the United States. For weeks, community centers, Talmudic schools, and orphanages were passed through with a fine-toothed comb.

At the beginning of May, the interception of a letter written by an Israeli on army service in a camp in the Negev, and addressed to a woman with a post-office box in Brussels, drew his attention. One sentence in the letter had been crossed out by the censor because it had no connection with the content: "And how's the boy?"

"Find this woman!" ordered Harel.

At the same time, Harel learned that Madeleine Féraille, a French-Catholic woman converted to Judaism, had close relations with the most fanatical Orthodox milieus, whom she had known and aided in the Resistance at the time of the German occupation. He put more than forty agents, mobilized full-time for "Operation Tiger," on her heels. They discovered that this beautiful convert had hebraized her name to Ruth Ben-David and that she corresponded often with the London representative of the Satmar sect, one of the most fanatic of New York.

On June 21 Isser Harel lured the young woman into a trap and sequestered her in the house of a lawyer—a villa on the outskirts of Paris. The Frenchwoman was in no way cowed by the piercing blue eyes of her Israeli jailer. After hours and days of intensive interrogations, the Mossad chief realized that he would not succeed in breaking this woman's iron will by being alternately tough and gentle in manner.

But Harel had another weapon. Threats and the outstretched hand were followed by blackmail: the complete list of all her past adventures, of her tumultuous love affairs that had preceded her conversion. A little publicity would suffice to tarnish her reputation in the eyes of her new friends.

The beautiful Madeleine-Ruth cracked. She confessed that she had taken Yossele from Israel, disguised as a girl, with the aid of a forged passport "like in the time of the Resistance" to a family of the Satmar sect in Brooklyn, where he had been living for two years under the name of Yankele.

The moment she divulged the address, Harel had the Israeli ambassador in Washington telephone Attorney General Robert Kennedy in the middle of the night to demand that a detachment of FBI men be sent immediately to this family in Brooklyn. After Yossele was found, Harel freed the young woman and encouraged her to settle down in Israel, where she ended up marrying an old rabbi from Mea Shearim.

Yossele, restored to his parents on July 4, 1962, later was to become an artillery officer, a student at Hebrew University, employed by the Town Hall of Holon, a suburb south of Tel Aviv, for the reeducation of underprivileged youth, and finally joined the campaign committee of Begin's candidate for the office of mayor of Holon in 1978.

But the price Isser Harel paid for Operation Tiger turned out to be all too high. The immobilization of the whole apparatus of the civil secret services for four months was disproportionate to its object: it engulfed almost the entire annual budget of the Mossad. And, above all, it made Harel miss getting his hands on Josef Mengele, the criminal doctor of Auschwitz, who had fled Buenos Aires on the morning of Eichmann's abduction.

Even more serious was the fact that the mad escapade of Operation Tiger had prevented the Mossad from promptly learning about the activities being carried out by former Nazi scientists who had taken refuge in Egypt.

11

THE TWILIGHT OF THE OLD MEN

Less than three weeks earlier, the plane carrying little Yossele home from New York had been welcomed at Lod Airport in an atmosphere resembling that of a country fair. His return ended an incredible saga that had split the country, widening the gulf between strict religionist and freethinker. Israel was on the way to becoming the only state in the world whose secret services stood for the unity of the entire nation and enjoyed universal admiration. The press went into ecstasies over the devotion of the intelligence community, which was equaled only by its efficiency.

Isser Harel was given a stuffed tiger by his colleagues as a souvenir of Operation Tiger, so successfully concluded on that July 4, 1962.

On July 21 came the rude awakening. Before a horde of journalists, with a triumphant Nasser looking on, the Egyptian Army launched four black-and-white missiles, two large and two small, which made a perfect lift-off in a cloud of flames and reached their target. The news took the world by surprise and shocked Israel, whose leaders were apparently taken completely off guard. The next day, twenty of these missiles were paraded through the streets of Cairo wrapped in the Egyptian flag, the main attraction in the huge military parade commemorating the tenth anniversary of the revolution. An official communiqué noted that of the four successfully tested ground-to-ground missiles, the Al Zafer (Victor) type had a range of 280 kilometers, and that the other two, of the Al Kaher (Conqueror) type, had reached 560 kilometers. To the delirious crowd, the Egyptian president announced that the second pair were capable of "reaching any target south of Beirut."

In the region south of Beirut, a storm of criticism was unleashed against the Israeli secret services. Not only had they been incapable of predicting these resounding explosions in the Egyptian sky, but for months they had been expending all their resources in a family quarrel.

"Instead of paying attention to threats to the country's security," said Little Isser's enemies, "he's been spending his time looking for Yossele and pursuing the Frenchwoman."

Taken by surprise, the chief of the Mossad determined to regain the advantage and to get the job done in double-quick time. He told Ben-Gurion: "I promise that in a few months I will have gathered all the details on Egypt's ballistics program and on the manufacturing of these missiles."

On August 4 Wolfgang Lotz, the Mossad's "mole" in Cairo, who had been planted there a year before, posing as a wealthy German horse breeder who dispensed lavish hospitality to dignitaries of both the former and the present regimes, as well as to his many compatriots in Egypt's German colony, was urgently summoned by his superiors in Paris.

"Cairo society rides in your stables, and champagne flows like water at your parties. That's all well and good, but you weren't able to keep us informed of the essentials. Nasser's missiles were perfected by the German scientists he has hired and who attend your lavish receptions. And you didn't know anything about it! You will have to make up for this failure by getting a foothold in their circles and radically focusing your investigations in that direction."

Not in a few months, as Harel had promised Ben-Gurion, but in just a few weeks, the Mossad agents managed to get all the necessary intelligence: they now knew all about the work of the German scientists who had settled in Egypt.

On August 16 Isser Harel reported to Ben-Gurion's office with a thick file under his arm. Less than a month after the test launches, he gave the "Old Man" detailed information on the German-Egyptian missiles.

Around the middle of 1959, Nasser had decided to begin recruiting German technicians, engineers, and scientists who were still available—the Allies had skimmed off the cream—to man the secret section he had just set up within his army: an office of special military programs entrusted with perfecting secret weapons and operational rockets. The former head of the Egyptian Air Force intelligence service, General Mahmoud Khalil, was appointed to head this secret section, and he left for Germany during the hunting season. His own hunting season—for brains—took him to a villa in Munich where, on November 29, 1959, he signed a contract with the well-known aircraft manufacturer, Willy Messerschmitt, for the construction of an airplane factory in Egypt. Then he stopped in Stuttgart, where he found a hotbed of disgruntled and frustrated scientists in the Institute for the Study of Jet Propulsion, some of whom had already sought asylum in Egypt after the collapse of the Hitler regime for which they had worked. Khalil offered fabulous contracts to the institute's head, Professor Eugen Sanger, to the director of the engine section, Wolfgang Pilz, a former engineer at Peenemunde where the V2 rocket had been created, to the director of the electronics section, Paul Goerke, to the director of the chemical section, Ermin Dadieu, and to the administrative director, Heinz Krug, as well as to Hans Kleinwachter, the director of an electronics laboratory in Lörrach, near Basel. Kleinwachter had worked in France with Pilz and Goerke on the Veronica rocket project.

Nasser's headhunter asked them to secretly develop ground-to-ground ballistic weapons, and also recruited Ferdinand Brandner, an engineer in the Daimler-Benz firm, to build a jet-engine plant.

A few months later, an Egyptian millionaire living in Switzerland, in conjunction with Messerschmitt and Brandner, formed two dummy corporations to purchase raw materials and precision parts. Krug headed another business firm, Intra-Händel, with orders to purchase patents and to forward parts. This company was located in the German offices of United Arab Airlines, the Egyptian airline company.

All of these teams arrived on the banks of the Nile in 1960. In their baggage the Germans carried plans for several types of missiles—modified versions of the Veronica and the V2—and early in 1961 they began building secret installations for manufacturing their missiles. Toward the end of that year, however, the authorities in West Germany discovered the links between the Stuttgart Institute and Intra-Händel, and ordered Sanger to resign. He was succeeded as head of the Egyptian missile program by Pilz.

The secrets of the Special Bureau were filed under three code numbers: 36, 135 and 333.

36 was the white factory building near Cairo where Messerschmitt was building fuselages for the future supersonic jet fighters.

135 was the code for the engine factory set up by Brandner.

333 was the code for the "forbidden city" of Helwan, near Heliopolis, where Pilz was in charge of the missile factory, with the assistance of Walter Shuran for jet propulsion and of Goerke for teleguidance. Goerke was to perfect the system that would aim the rockets at targets situated "south of Beirut."

As the final item in his report, Isser Harel produced a document that revealed the extent of this weapons program: a letter dated March 24, 1962, from Pilz to the Egyptian in charge of the factory requesting 3.7 million Swiss francs for the purchase of the spare parts needed to construct 500 Type 2 rockets and 400 Type 5 rockets.

"Making a total," Harel concluded, "of 900 operational rockets!"

Stunned by these surprising revelations, the Israeli Army took these figures seriously. "Too seriously," as General Zvi Tsur, then chief of staff, was later to admit.

Armed with this file, Harel urged Ben-Gurion to make an immediate appeal to German Chancellor Konrad Adenauer, requesting him to put a stop to this intolerable situation, and to provide him with proof that German citizens in Egypt were producing weapons prohibited in their own country. The "Old Man" refused, since such an approach would upset the process of rapprochement with the "New Germany," which was one of the vital elements of his foreign policy. However, he went along with the suggestion that his deputy Defense Minister, Shimon Peres, write to his friend Franz Josef Strauss, the Defense Minister in the Bonn government, to apprise him of the situation.

On August 17 Peres sent a lengthy message describing the intelligence data provided by Harel and expressing his conviction that the German leaders would certainly be shocked at the idea that the Federal Republic should, directly or indirectly, play a part in Egyptian and Soviet attempts to annihilate the Jewish State. And he let it be understood that in any event this matter of German scientists working for Nasser—which he thought strange that the German embassy in Cairo had apparently not viewed with the slightest alarm—threatened to reopen the deep wound that had been inflicted by the "Other Germany" on the Jewish people in the past. He hoped that as a result Bonn would do everything possible to recall its nationals.

On August 20 Golda Meir asked President Kennedy to exert his influence with the Federal Republic to put a stop to the scandal. Isser Harel decided to implement a plan of action involving the gathering of further intelligence and the carrying out of prompt deterrent actions.

Since the beginning of autumn, Wolfgang Lotz, the Mossad agent in Cairo, had been furnishing a complete list of the forty-four Germans employed in the three factories under the secret Egyptian program. Its overseer, General Mahmoud Khalil, known as "Herr Doktor" Mahmoud, a man who enjoyed close ties to General Gehlen's West German spy network—whose top man in Cairo was Gerhard Bauch—was one of his frequent guests. The list contained the home addresses of the German scientists, their precise duties, and the addresses of their families in Germany. Lotz also provided his superiors with some of the blueprints from Plant

333. His microfilm led to the discovery that the two types of rockets being tested on July 21 had been far from operational, as Harel had claimed. In fact, they were unguided missiles, without any electronic navigation system for teleguidance.

The reprisals and deterrent actions began on September 11. On that day, Dr. Krug, the director of Intra-Händel, disappeared from his Munich offices. Two days later, his car was found in the country, caked with mud. An anonymous telephone call announced his death.

On November 27 a registered parcel purportedly sent by a well-known Hamburg attorney arrived at Professor Pilz's home in Cairo. It exploded in the face of his secretary, who had opened it in his absence.

The next day, a huge package labeled "Scientific Books" sent by sea from Hamburg was deposited at the administrative offices of Plant 333 in Helwan. When an Egyptian employee tore off the wrapping paper, a fire broke out that caused five deaths. Two packages of similarly booby-trapped books were defused in time.

On February 23, 1963, Kleinwachter, who was spending a few weeks in Europe, was attacked at the steering wheel of his car as he was leaving his laboratory in Lörrach, near the Swiss border. A bullet fired by a revolver equipped with a silencer shattered his windshield and lodged in his scarf. However, since he was also armed, the scientist managed to drive his assailants off. The police were unable to find the perpetrators of these attacks, which were kept quiet.

Meanwhile, having been informed of Egypt's purchase of radioactive cobalt, which was delivered by United Arab Airlines to a Cairo gynecologist who was none other than "Herr Doktor" Mahmoud's sister, Golda Meir met with President Kennedy on December 27 to give him a complete picture of the gravity of the situation: the German missiles in Egypt were going to be equipped with nuclear or radioactive warheads—at any rate, with nonconventional ones. She demanded that he intervene forcefully with both Bonn and Cairo.

Golda Meir was convinced that she was not mistaken about Egypt's intentions because two months earlier an Israeli ambassador posted in Europe had received a visit from Otto Joklik, an Austrian who had just arrived from Cairo with the proof that German scientists there were preparing a "poor man's atom bomb" out of the wastes of cobalt 60 and strontium 90. Joklik reported that he himself had been commissioned to provide considerable amounts of radioactive waste materials to Pilz's team. Steps had to be taken to prevent the perfection of missiles carrying such deadly warheads, beginning with the guidance system.

Joklik further volunteered to convince his "colleagues" to stop their evil activities. Around mid-February 1963 he paid a call on Goerke's daughter Heidi, who was a lawyer in Freiburg. He told her that her father had assumed an awful responsibility by accepting the job of perfecting a guidance system for Egyptian missiles intended for the destruction of Israel. He asked her to persuade her father to abandon his criminal work. Otherwise, he could not answer for what would inevitably happen to him.

"If you are fond of your father, be at the Hôtel des Trois Rois in Basel at four o'clock on March second; I'll be waiting there for you with a friend."

Heidi Goerke alerted the Freiburg police, who contacted the cantonal authorities in Basel. The cantonal police packed the hotel with agents and microphones. It had been Theodor Herzl's favorite hotel when he was organizing the first Zionist congresses in that Swiss city.

Heidi Goerke arrived at the meeting, and Joklik introduced her to his friend, an Israeli named Joseph Ben-Gal. Their conversation lasted an hour. The two men told her flatly that her father was running serious risks. They offered to give her an airplane ticket for Cairo, so that she might convince him to return to Germany.

"In that case," they promised, "no harm will come to him."

Both men then caught the train for Zurich, where the carnival season was in full swing. In the costumed throng, they did not notice the dozen masked police officers who were following them. When they separated, Joklik to catch another train and Ben-Gal to the Israeli consulate, the police pounced. The men underwent an official interrogation on their conversation with Heidi Goerke, which the police had recorded.

On the same evening, the Federal Republic police asked for their extradition: both men were accused by Heidi Goerke of having used threats and force against her; they were also suspected of having carried out the abortive attack on Dr. Kleinwachter two weeks earlier, just across the border in Lörrach. However, this double arrest was not made public—nor was the series of attacks that had been going on against the German scientists working for Egypt over the past six months.

As soon as they heard of it through diplomatic channels, the Israelis attempted to persuade the Swiss authorities to free Ben-Gal and Joklik quietly. But the Swiss refused; they had already been served with the German legal papers. Isser Harel rushed to

Golda Meir at the Ministry for Foreign Affairs to inform her of the failure of the mission so far. Now learning of the affair for the first time, Golda thought that Adenauer should be asked to withdraw the extradition request for the "brave young men." Thus encouraged, Harel went to Tiberias, where Ben-Gurion was taking a few days' rest. He suggested that he might send an emissary to Bonn. The "Old Man" categorically refused.

"But if Ben-Gal's and Joklik's arrest becomes public," the Mossad chief objected, "it will be impossible for us to remain silent and keep their motives secret. Everyone will know about the German scientists in Egypt and their commercial arrangements to purchase in Germany the very equipment they need for their death-dealing missiles. The whole thing will come out into the open."

Ben-Gurion shrugged. "We shall see."

For the first time, voices were raised between the head of the government and his chief of intelligence. The difference between their two viewpoints in this affair suddenly revealed to them how far apart they had grown in a short time.

The "Old Man" had been careful to avoid the least reference to Nasser's German scientists in his regular correspondence with his friend Adenauer, believing as he did that the New Germany was determined to expiate the crimes of the other—Hitler's—Germany. Under the terms of a secret agreement they had reached during their 1960 meeting at the Waldorf-Astoria Hotel in New York, Adenauer had set up a half-billion-dollar loan to Israel over and above the German reparations payments to the Jewish victims of Nazism. Bonn had secretly delivered quantities of free weapons to Tel Aviv and had paid for the Uzi submachine guns for its police. Why run the risk of compromising this tacit cooperation by forcing Adenauer to take steps against German citizens who were cooperating with Egypt in a private capacity?

Isser Harel was still profoundly anti-German. He was continually denouncing the presence of ex-Nazis in high positions in the Federal Republic. Ever since studying the Eichmann file, his obsession had grown. He told Golda Meir, who was also deeply opposed to any holdovers from the days of Germany's barbarism.

On the other hand, where this political and emotional issue was concerned, the Mossad chief was in conflict with the deputy Defense Minister, Shimon Peres, who shared the "Old Man" 's views completely, and who was beginning to look more and more like his successor.

Furious that Harel had not kept him informed about his plans to put pressure on the families of the German scientists, as in the unfortunate Heidi Goerke matter, Ben-Gurion went so far as to draft a letter henceforth forbidding Harel from organizing special operations abroad without his agreement. However, following their stormy meeting, in the end he decided not to send it.

The real storm broke on March 15, 1963, when an American news agency announced the double arrest in Zurich, which had occurred two weeks earlier, and the Swiss authorities made public the indictment against the Israeli Ben-Gal and the Austrian Joklik. After having consulted again with Golda Meir, Harel returned to Tiberias to see Ben-Gurion. The "Old Man" was still unwilling to listen. However, some explanation had to be given for the actions of the two accused men.

With the leak as a pretext, the Mossad chief started a newspaper campaign that rapidly became a worldwide propaganda campaign that put Israel into a panic. A flood of more-or-less substantiated revelations engulfed the media:

"Former Nazis are making atomic, chemical and bacteriological weapons in Egypt. They are providing Nasser with the ultimate weapon: the Death Ray. The [German] Federal government has done nothing to prevent this crime . . ."

The storm raged on all sides. The nationalist far right and the Communist far left joined once more in an inviolable union to denounce the specter of a vengeful Germany behind the scandal of the German scientists. On March 20 still in Ben-Gurion's absence, Golda Meir spoke in the Knesset:

"If the criminal activity of the German scientists and experts in Egypt continues, the German people cannot disclaim responsibility. The Federal government has the duty to put an immediate stop to the evil activities of its nationals and to take the necessary steps to bring their cooperation with the Egyptian government to an end."

During the tumultuous debate that followed, Menachem Begin, the leader of the opposition, sharply attacked Ben-Gurion's own policy: "We have been selling machine guns to the Germans, and the Germans are delivering germs to our enemies."

Finally, the Knesset members adopted a strong and unanimous resolution, but it was too late to halt the avalanche. The press was pursuing and widening its campaign in which fantasy vied with the imaginary. The initial panic caused by apocalyptic stories about Nasser's secret weapons was succeeded by an unprecedented wave of Germanophobia.

Ben-Gurion, who had played a passive role up until this point, left his Tiberias retreat to take control and to try to bring things back on an even keel. Late in the evening of March 24, he summoned the chief of the Mossad to his office to tell him of his indignation at the way the press, led by certain factions, was now treating the German question. He demanded explanations and gave Harel an appointment for the next day.

Before seeing Harel again, Ben-Gurion consulted the chief of Aman, General Meir Amit, who gave him an altogether different evaluation of the threat posed by the German plants in Cairo and Helwan. What did this group of scientists really represent? Misfits in the worldwide race for ballistic weapons, a few second-rate experts. Their ground-to-ground missiles lacked a guidance system to make them operational and would for some time to come; by that time, they would be obsolescent. The prevailing state of mind in the country where the German past was concerned had of course served to increase the extent of the Egyptian military plans out of all proportion. The widespread panic of the Israeli leaders was completely out of line with the actual danger. And the world was rightly astonished at their apparent horror over the arrest of one of their agents in Switzerland. At the most, this affair might merit a warning to the Bonn government, but never such a scandal, and even less the intemperate offensive being directed against the Federal Republic of Germany, which was being accused of shutting its eyes to Egyptian plans to wipe out Israel, when it had been firing scientists in the Stuttgart Institute who were cooperating with Egypt ever since the end of 1961.

Armed with these arguments, Ben-Gurion informed Harel that he would disavow all the steps he had taken in the matter, both with regard to overt actions and with regard to intelligence, since they had only served to set Israel against its secret European ally and had been a total waste. He also informed Harel of his intention to call an immediate meeting of the parliamentary Defense and Foreign Affairs Committee and to prove to its members that the fears expressed in the Knesset were without foundation—or at least excessive. In vain the Mossad boss attempted to dissuade him. Then he lost his temper and flew off the handle upon being confronted with the Aman chief's evaluation; he, who had eliminated that organization's five previous directors one after the other.

But Harel's famous flair was not working on this occasion. He was unable to control the chain reaction he had begun by starting up the affair of the German scientists. One of the "Old Man" 's intimates was later to say that, where strategy was concerned, "Little Isser was nothing but a corporal." However, Harel was unwilling to admit his mistakes.

Although Harel wanted to slam the door behind him, he nevertheless had to plan his exit. Upon returning to his office, he dictated a short letter to Ben-Gurion: "Owing to the fundamental differences of opinion between us on the question of the German scientists working for the Egyptian war effort, with all that that implies, I feel it my duty to resign my functions as head of the Central Agency for Intelligence [Mossad] and as head [Memouneh] of the security services."

He then shut himself up in his villa in Zahala and refused to answer the telephone. Late in the evening of March 25, a dispatch courier brought a handwritten letter from Ben-Gurion:

"I cannot accept your resignation. You must remain on the job at least until the government and the Knesset have decided on the policy to be followed on the question we have discussed. It may be that your opinion will prevail in the government or the Knesset, in which case you will be able to continue with your duty as you see it under the orders of a new chief of government."

The next day, Isser Harel returned to his office as if nothing had happened. There he received another letter from the "Old Man," demanding that his intelligence sources on Egyptian military preparations with regard to nonconventional weapons be turned over that very day. In answer, he picked up the telephone and called Ben-Gurion's personal assistant at the Ministry of Defense. He was fairly fuming.

"You tell your boss that if he wants answers to his questions, he has only to address himself to my successor. If human lives weren't at stake, and if our men weren't being held in Switzerland, I wouldn't stay here a second longer. Send over someone to take over the operations and the keys!"

"Fine, but whom shall I send?" Ben-Gurion asked when his assistant told him about Little Isser's anger. "Find Amos Manor for me."

The Shin Bet (internal security) chief was somewhere in the Jordan valley. There was no way to get in touch with him.

"Then call Meir Amit!" ordered Ben-Gurion.

The Aman chief was on an inspection tour in the Negev, but he was contacted by radio and told to return immediately to Tel Aviv. There a letter awaited him: Ben-Gurion was asking him to take over the Mossad until a new head could be appointed, since Harel had done nothing about providing for a transfer of power.

Thus, when on April 1, 1963, the press announced the surprising departure of the seemingly indestructible head of the intelligence services, the man whose name and face were still unknown to the general public, those who knew Isser regarded his resignation as an act of bad temper. It seemed to them to have been impulsive and reminded them of his sudden departure from the kibbutz twenty-five years before.

Isser had come to Palestine in 1930 at the age of seventeen, taking care to conceal a revolver from the rigorous search of British customs. His parents—well-to-do middle-class White Russian Jews—had lost everything in the October Revolution that had seen the Jewish painter Marc Chagall made the first political commissar of their native Vitebsk. The family had then emigrated to Latvia. There the young Isser had learned to fight to protect himself against the fascist gangs, and there he had become a Zionist and a socialist.

He joined a kibbutz near Herzliya, where he took his work so seriously that he was given the nickname "Stakhanovitch" ("hard worker"). To his comrades' astonishment, he married a high-spirited Jewish girl from Poland named Rivka, and for a long time they kept house in a military tent pitched on the sands next to the kibbutz's tower and fence. He had an ironclad belief in egalitarian society, but after thirteen years of a totally communal life, he lost his temper one evening over something someone said about him, and impulsively left the kibbutz with his entire family, carrying no baggage other than the khaki shirt on his back.

Harel became an independent farm laborer. He picked oranges with his family during the day. At night he joined the ranks of the Haganah, where he quickly made a name for himself in intelligence missions. He became part of a coast guard unit, but he had to leave the base after a fight with a British captain whom he had caught operating on the black market. To protect him from trouble, the Haganah leaders offered him a shelter in the Shay, their clandestine intelligence service, which began his career in espionage and counterespionage.

Harel came to Ben-Gurion's attention when one of his Arab agents in Jordan returned from a mission that had enabled him to predict that the Arab Legion would go to war in May 1948. From that time, he rose rapidly through the ranks as the organization of state secret services grew, gaining Ben-Gurion's confidence and setting aside any possible rivals who were members of the establishment: Isser Beeri, Reuven Shiloakh, Shaul Avigur, Ehud Avriel, Benjamin Gibli, Chaim Herzog, and others. In February 1953 he was at the top of the heap.

Harel acted with such discretion that his neighbors had no idea what he did. He often shopped for his wife, who was known as "The Amazon" by the shopkeepers in the neighborhood, since she seemed to wear the pants in the family. When Harel took over the Shin Bet, established in June 1948, and when his barber saw him suddenly wearing a lieutenant colonel's uniform, the man was unable to suppress his astonishment: "A quiet little customer like you! How did you get to be such an important officer!"

In his office, the gentle, shy Little Isser became a giant. His agents, whose lives were constantly in danger and who, without playing James Bond, were nevertheless a fearless lot, respected and feared him. He always protected them when the going was rough.

They would say, "His look seems to penetrate your innermost thoughts. He never takes his eyes off you. With him, you always feel guilty of something."

Very puritanical, Little Isser neither drank nor smoked and was never involved in even the slightest scandal regarding sex or money. His only concession to social life was the weekly receptions held in his villa for high-ranking government dignitaries. Politicians feared him. They quite rightly regarded him as Ben-Gurion's eyes and ears and suspected him of spying on them on the "Old Man" 's behalf.

Nor did Little Isser have the slightest sense of humor. In his rare moments of lightheartedness, he had one humorous remark, which he always used: "The only things that aren't afraid of me and my blue eyes are dogs and children."

His working methods consisted in compartmentalizing everything so that he was the only person with an overall knowledge of any area, of an affair in all its details. His agents knew only the bare minimum they needed for their task. Indeed, he frequently set up "volunteer" commando units drawn from services other than his own, often bypassing their superiors.

Above all, however, Little Isser was driven by an ambition that extended far beyond his functions as a state civil servant. He intervened in many political intrigues and plots, in ministerial appointments, in governmental alliances. Moshe Sharett called him the "little devil" because during the eighteen months he spent as prime minister, Isser had advised against the choice of this or that person (Dayan, Peres, Lavon) or about the person he deemed most suitable to become defense minister. His powers, his influence, and his opinions outweighed those of cabinet members. In fact, the position he held was that of a superminister. Ben-Gurion's door was always open for Little Isser's laconic expression of his views. Aside from their short stature and enormous prudery, both men shared the fact that they were not bound by respect for a long democratic tradition.

Since he was not merely the head of his country's internal and foreign security, as were his counterparts in the other democracies, Isser Harel's resignation was therefore unlike that of some high official, but rather like that of a political leader. Contrary to other people's first impressions, it was not an impulse, a decision arrived at in a fit of rage or humiliation. Quite the opposite: it was the result of a carefully-thought-out plan.

Harel foresaw the "Old Man"'s approaching departure, which had been made inevitable by the belated repercussions of the Lavon affair and other more recent developments. By resigning before this could occur, he thought to make himself ready so that he would more certainly be reappointed by Ben-Gurion's successor. Although he was correct on the first point, he was mistaken about the second, in thinking he was as indispensable to any future government as he had been for preceding ones.

Not only had General Meir Amit, who had taken over his job, dared contradict him in front of Ben-Gurion, but from the first weeks it became clear that Amit was going to prove himself in the administration of the Mossad as he had in that of the Aman, and that once settled in his new post, he would not be leaving it for a long time to come.

Isser Harel was not to resurface until September 14, 1965, when Levi Eshkol, the new prime minister, appointed him adviser for intelligence problems. However, in constant difficulties with the service chiefs, Little Isser held the job for less than a year.

Although the affair of the German scientists was to continue to stir public opinion for a while, the press suddenly put a damper on its revelations and its Germanophobic campaigns. In June 1963 the trial of Joseph Ben-Gal and Otto Joklik opened in Switzerland, which had finally refused to extradite them to Germany. In their defense, the accused produced the notorious purchase order of March 24, 1962, signed by Wolfgang Pilz: 900 different devices and pieces of equipment, 2,700 gyroscopes and other materiel necessary in the production of 900 missiles before 1970. This prospect alone explained their approach to Dr. Goerke's daughter, since he was in charge of teleguidance for the missiles. "A rightful basis for concern," the court concluded, handing down a suspended sentence of two months in prison. It was a moral victory for Israel, which immediately got back its two agents.

In the field, however, the action undertaken to intimidate the German scientists in Cairo continued. On April 2, 1963, the day after Isser Harel's departure, Wolfgang Lotz, the Mossad agent whose elegant receptions, organized by his wife Waltraud, were becoming more and more popular with the top drawer of the German colony and the new Egyptian upper class, received an order from his superiors to go to Paris to collect a shipment of booby-trapped cakes of soap. He was never to use them. However, on July 18 of the following year, Lotz was given an altogether different mission: six letters to mail on September 20 in various post offices in Cairo, addressed to Germans who had not yet been persuaded to leave Egypt by Meir Amit's moderate and quiet tactics—as some of them, such as Paul Goerke and Walter Shuran, had begun to do. Discreet talks with Bonn and Paris had already borne some fruit and had reduced the number of German scientists engaged in Nasser's military projects.

All the letters Lotz mailed on September 20, 1964, upon receipt of the agreed-upon signal, bore the same mysterious signature: The Gideons. The addressees were easily able to make the connection with the name of the biblical judge who had, twelve centuries before, met and defeated the Midianites, the Hebrews' hereditary foes. One of the letters exploded, wounding a post-office employee. The others were followed up by a second wave of mined packages, all mailed from Cairo, but they did not have the hoped-for deterrent effect. At the same time, however, American Assistant Secretary of State Averell Harriman flatly stated that "the departure of German scientists from Egypt could lead to their replacement by teams of Soviet scientists able to accomplish the same tasks, and would not alter in any way the situation in the Middle East, other than to increase Egypt's dependence on the USSR."

An important diplomatic shift was now to bring a halt to the Germans' activity in Cairo and, by a strange coincidence, to the activity of "our man in Cairo" as well.

Nasser's invitation to East German President Walter Ulbricht to visit him on February 24, 1965, sent under pressure from Moscow, aroused the ire of West Germany. The spokesman for the Bonn government gave Egypt official warning that such a visit, tantamount to Cairo's recognizing the East German government, would lead to breaking off diplomatic relations with the Federal Republic and cutting off economic assistance. It would also lead directly to the establishment of normal diplomatic relations between Bonn and Tel Aviv, which had not hitherto existed. Nasser, however, increasingly under Soviet sway, was unable to retreat. This same influence forced him to curtail the activities of agents of the Gehlen network, for whom Egypt was the central point for the Middle East. Their presence was thus declared to be subversive, overnight.

On February 22 two days before Ulbricht's arrival, the Egyptian secret police carried out a preventive roundup and arrested some thirty members of the German colony. Among them were Gerhard Bauch, thirty-nine-year-old radioman in the Gehlen network, Wolfgang Lotz, forty-four, the well-known horse breeder in Cairo society, and his wife Waltraud. In fact, the Egyptians had just killed two birds with one stone, as evidenced by an article published in *Al Ahram* ten days later:

> Several individuals belonging to a terrorist German spy network were arrested at their homes by the counterespionage services. From the confessions of the suspects themselves, it has been discovered that the network in question was directed by the Israeli secret services, which made use of German citizens. Israel obviously considered it more convenient to carry out terrorist acts against German citizens residing in Egypt with the help of other Germans.

Lotz judged it preferable to play the game and admit everything, while continuing to pass for a former Afrika Korps member recruited by the Israelis at a high salary. This attitude won him a verdict of clemency from the Supreme Court for State Security, which did not know that it was dealing with a German Jew who had emigrated to Israel and had been working for the Mossad from the beginning. Lotz thereby regained his freedom less than three years later.

For a long time it was believed that Lotz's arrest had been due to chance, to a combination of circumstances tied to Ulbricht's visit. The man who was known as the "Champagne Spy" because of the luxury of his parties had actually been the second victim of the technical cooperation between Soviet and Arab secret services. A month before his arrest, the famous Israeli spy, Eli Cohen, had been arrested in Damascus following the discovery of his radio transmitter by Soviet detection equipment. Circumstances were infinitely more favorable to Lotz, since they enabled him to escape the hangman.

Walter Ulbricht's visit to Cairo was also to deliver the death blow to plans for combined German-Egyptian missile and airplane manufacturing.

At the beginning of 1965, Ben-Gurion was not present to preside over the historic turning point in the relations between Bonn and Tel Aviv, nor to enjoy the fruits of his patient work toward rapprochement with Adenauer's Germany which had been temporarily threatened by the crisis of the German scientists. At that date, almost three years had elapsed since the "Old Man" had relinquished the reins of power. His authority, already weakened by the aftermath of the Lavon affair, had not lasted for three months in the wake of Isser Harel's departure and the blackmail of Golda's threatened resignation as a result of that crisis.

On March 26, 1963, Ben-Gurion had still been able to impose his views regarding Nasser's missiles on the Knesset's Defense and Foreign Affairs Committee, as he had said he would during his last interview with Isser Harel. But the public announcement of the departure of his secret service chief on April 1 left him at a loss. At almost the same moment, fate dealt him another blow in the death of his old comrade from pioneer days, President Itzhak Ben-Zvi. An additional crisis precipitated Ben-Gurion's decision: the double failure of an attempt to meet with Nasser to initiate a procedure toward peace before leaving the political scene, and of a parallel diplomatic offensive against the treaty creating an Arab federation among Egypt, Syria, and Iraq.

Ben-Gurion's first initiative dated back to December. Taking advantage of Nasser's diminishing influence in the Arab world, Ben-Gurion sent a messenger on a secret mission to Belgrade to sound out Tito. The messenger, Shaike Dan, was a Palmach veteran who had parachuted into Yugoslavia during World War II. Dan met with Tito on the island of Brioni, but the Yugoslav leader refused to act as an intermediary.

In January the editor-in-chief of the London *Sunday Times,* Charles D. Hamilton, met with Nasser, who told him, in the course of a long and rambling conversation, "If Ben-Gurion and I were locked up together in a room for three hours, I believe we could reach a peaceful solution to the Jewish-Arab conflict."

Upon his return to London, Hamilton reported the statement to Baron Edmond de Rothschild, who quickly passed it on to Ben-Gurion. The "Old Man" jumped at the opportunity and invited the journalist to visit him in Jerusalem. The go-between shuttled between the two capitals, via Europe.

"Ben-Gurion is ready to meet you anywhere, even in Cairo," Hamilton told Nasser.

"There are some things—even Israel—one must learn to live with," Nasser replied, avoiding the question of the meeting.

Nasser would certainly not go to war—even for Jerusalem, he

added—but for the moment he was too busy cementing together the Arab world, which was on the point of breaking apart, to think of anything else before September—other than taking command of the federation he had just formed with Iraq and Syria.

At the end of May, Hamilton brought Ben-Gurion Nasser's negative reply that crushed the "Old Man" 's last hope of making a triumphal exit. His final decision was made after both Kennedy and de Gaulle refused to take seriously the threats he discerned in the treaty of the Arab Federation, and also refused to sign a pact of mutual assistance with Israel.

On June 15 Ben-Gurion was preparing to host the weekly meeting of the Bible Circle in Jerusalem when Golda Meir appeared unexpectedly at his home, looking like a Fury and bearing a Telex: the German wire service had announced that Israeli soldiers were being trained in Germany. That was too much! She demanded that the news story be quashed by the military censor.

"I don't have the right to do that," the "Old Man" growled, more peevish than ever.

Golda called Teddy Kollek, the director of the prime minister's office, for help. The discussion in Ben-Gurion's kitchen went on until midnight, but in vain.

On the following day, Sunday, June 16, the "Old Man" arrived at his office and told his substitute secretary—Itzhak Navon was away on his honeymoon—who brought in some documents awaiting his signature: "It's not necessary. I'm not going to the Knesset tomorrow. I'm resigning."

Ben-Gurion caught everyone by surprise, beginning with his appointed successor, Shimon Peres, who was on a mission in Paris, by issuing a one-sentence resignation "for personal reasons."

"It's not the right time," the ministers of his party protested.

"There's never a right time," the "Old Man" interrupted. He had long ago informed Galili of his intentions during the independence celebrations: fifteen years is enough. He had led the Histadrut from 1920 to 1935; the Jewish Agency from 1933 to 1948, the government from 1948 to 1963—save for the eighteen-month Sharett interval.

At the end of his final cabinet meeting, he attended the inaugural luncheon for the new president, Zalman Shazar. And he handed him his letter of resignation during the dessert course. In the evening, he received a visit from General Rabin, deputy chief of staff, and General Amit, head of the Mossad. He was moved to tears.

"The army has no right to engage in politics," Rabin said, "but

I can tell you that the next three years will put the country to the test."

That evening, Ben-Gurion confided his true reasons for leaving to his personal diary:

> In fact, I decided to do it more than two years ago, when the Coyote [Lavon] managed to set everybody in my party against me. But I was afraid for the party . . . The new government coalition in 1961 didn't make for either an advanced social policy or a bold foreign and military policy . . . One would have to be blind not to see that the German scientists affair is the beginning of a power takeover by the Führer [Begin]. The liberals and Mapam will help him to denounce the Federal Republic of Germany as Israel's Enemy Number One. And at the core of this new coalition, which threatens to involve Golda, is, of course, the Memouneh [Isser Harel], who has been playing the same role the Coyote played two years ago. There's nothing like that kind of craziness for bringing fascism to Israel.

Was it a premature departure, as Teddy Kollek still maintains? Was it too late, as Michael Bar-Zohar, Ben-Gurion's biographer, intimates? It was the departure of a wounded man, but a man determined to take revenge on the "Coyotes" even at the cost of sacrificing the hopes of his protégés in the coming generation. Beaten by the old guard at the Mapai congress in 1965 under Levi Eshkol's direction, Ben-Gurion was to involve Peres and Dayan in the Rafi schism (the Labor Party split) and return to the Knesset at the head of a tiny group of ten deputies. Peres was forced to champ at the bit for fourteen more years before leading the Labor party with the consequent loss of its power in the May 1977 elections. Dayan then joined Begin's camp.

Isser Harel's and David Ben-Gurion's almost simultaneous departure in the spring of 1963—the two old companions in power since the creation of the State of Israel—could not have been a more symbolic end to a period of totalitarian democracy.

Levi Eshkol's ascension as prime minister, in fact, opened a new era of democratization in both public life and in the secret services. Meir Amit in the Mossad and Aharon Yariv in Aman restored priority to the military aspect of intelligence with a modernization of techniques and a liberal approach to security matters.

The victorious outcome of the war which was to loom on the horizon four years later would depend a great deal on the preparedness of these services, reputed to be the world's best.

12

SIX DAYS THAT SHOOK THE KREMLIN

A conversation between two Israeli generals in January 1965 was one of the secrets of the victory in June 1967. It took place in the modest office of General Meir Amit, the head of the Mossad. Ezer Weizmann, Commander of the Israeli Air Force, had come to talk about the intelligence needs of his branch.

"What are you most interested in?" Amit asked.

"I want to have a MIG 21," Weizmann replied without hesitation.

A few hours later, Amit spoke with one of his department heads.

"Do you know where we could get a MIG 21?"

The question dumbfounded his colleague. The MIG 21 was the very latest Soviet fighter jet, and its use was restricted to the elite of the Soviet Union's own air force. The air forces of the other Warsaw Pact countries had not yet been considered worthy of it. Nevertheless, in its efforts to gain a foothold in the Near East, Moscow had delivered a few of these jets to Egypt, Syria, and Iraq, under the permanent surveillance of advisers and KGB agents, to be flown only by pilots trained in the Soviet Union.

Within the Mossad, a top-secret special group studied the possibility of obtaining one of these planes. After preliminary inquiries, the director of the group decided that Iraq would be the most vulnerable target of such an enterprise. Agents were sent out on a reconnaissance mission, among them a Jewish woman from New York with an American passport. It took them a year to finally select the Iraqi pilot who was most likely to defect: group commander Munir Rufa, one of the highest-ranking pilots in his country, initially trained by the U.S. Air Force, then sent to the Soviet Union to perfect his skills. Having been carefully screened by both the Russian and the Iraqi security services, Rufa had been given permission to pilot a MIG 21, and was thus promoted to a privileged rank in the hierarchy.

The beautiful Mossad agent concentrated her attentions on Rufa during an upper-crust reception in Bagdad. He, in turn, found it easy to succumb to her charms—the more so since he, a member of the small Christian minority of Iraqi Arabs, was reluctant to participate in the genocide of the Kurdish population that the Iraqi Air Force was practicing in the northern part of the country. He soon confessed his scruples to the young woman when she invited him to dinner. They became intimate and decided to take a short vacation in Europe, and she confided that she had reliable friends in Tel Aviv who could get him out of his quandary. He could travel with her to Israel incognito. She happened to have two plane tickets made out to a fictitious name and a virgin passport in her suitcase.

Munir Rufa took the bait. From the Lod airport, Rufa was taken directly to a secret base in the Negev and given a VIP reception. He gladly accepted the bargain he was offered: in exchange for his MIG 21, he would receive Israeli citizenship for himself and his entire family, who were to be brought to safety before the flight to protect them from any reprisals and a guaranteed income for the rest of his life.

General "Motti" Hod, Weizmann's successor as the Israeli Air Force's commander-in-chief, personally visited him to discuss the details and the itinerary of his defection at the controls of his MIG. The beautiful American traveled back to Bagdad with him, via the European capital of their amorous escapade.

The last weeks of the operation were the longest and most involved: first, it was necessary to convince all the members of the pilot's family to travel abroad, one by one, under various pretexts and at different dates, in order to avoid suspicion. Then Rufa had to wait for a routine flight. The Soviet advisers carefully rationed jet fuel to the strict minimum necessary for the proposed exercises. To be able to avoid the radar scans and air bases of Iraq and Jordan by pursuing a zigzag, hedge-hopping course, Rufa would need a full tank—even a supplementary one. He would also have to observe a precise time schedule for his arrival in Israeli airspace so as to find himself under escort, and not under attack.

On an August morning in 1966, while the Russian advisers at the base were having breakfast together, Rufa calmly walked to his plane and told the Iraqi mechanics to fill all the tanks. He first headed toward Bagdad along his routine patrol course, then took a sharp turn south, and disappeared, headed west. Flying a predetermined course, keeping low to the ground, he negotiated the 900 kilometers. As soon as his MIG appeared at the agreed-on point on the Israeli radar screens, an escort of Mirage fighters met him above Jordan, blithely violating the airspace of the Hashemite kingdom that still straddles both sides of the river, and accompanied him to the landing on the Negev airfield where "Motti" Hod was already awaiting him.

At the moment of landing, General Amit was at Lod airport, saying good-bye to a member of his family who was flying to the United States. Hod called him there.

"The jewel is in its box."

"Jewel" was the code word chosen by Amit for this unprecedented operation of plane theft.

"You may go to any expense," Amit had told the group formed to accomplish it. Ultimately, the operation's cost would prove to have been quite minor in regard to the results obtained from it. The MIG 21, repainted to sport the numerals 007 and the Star of David, would pay for itself many times over. It was the first Soviet-built supersonic plane to fall into Western hands. While teaching him how to fly it, the Iraqi defector provided Israeli commander Danny Shapira with all the training secrets of his Russian instructors and with their aerial combat techniques. A great number of simulated maneuvers made it possible to analyze the craft's qualities and defects. At the beginning of the Six-Day War, the Israeli pilots were able to systematically exploit the MIG's main weakness: the extreme vulnerability of the fuel tanks at the junction of the wings and the fuselage. They also benefited from two other defects in the MIG 21's design: blind spots, in contrast to the 360-degree visibility of their Mirages, and the inferior timing of its guns.

The James Bond-style exploit of "Operation Jewel" merely completed one of the most extraordinary dossiers in the history of military intelligence: that prepared by the Mossad on the Arab air forces. That dossier enabled the Israeli Air Force to gain absolute control and emerge victorious in less than six hours, between 8 A.M. and 2 P.M. on June 5, 1967. "Motti" Hod's planes took the Egyptian Air Force by surprise, destroying its planes on the ground and in the air, and enabled Tsahal's armored units to penetrate the defense lines of the northern Sinai.

The plan of attack had already been conceived in 1963 by Hod's predecessor, General Weizmann, who had gone on to become Chief of Military Operations at the General Staff of the Israeli armed forces, thus joint commander with Chief of Staff Itzhak Rabin. When Weizmann first explained his idea of a preventive attack to his colleagues, they merely considered it to be another crazy brainstorm, typical of the nonconformist general. It took him almost two years of intense discussions to convince them that control of the airspace had to be the prime requirement of all Israeli military strategy.

Six Days that Shook the Kremlin · 205

Scores of agents of the army's intelligence service (Aman) then proceeded to collect and transmit to the study group hundreds and thousands of bits of information on the Arab air forces' composition and condition, while the Mossad gathered an impressive amount of personal data on their officers. Reports, biographies, archive data, plans of air bases indicating the exact locations of planes and installations, detailed accounts of every Arab fighter pilot—his training, his life-style, his social standing—all these flowed in to swell the "top secret" memories of the computers.

The chief of Air Force Intelligence, a very enthusiastic young colonel, knew practically by heart the most trivial details in the life of every Arab pilot known by name. Nothing pleased him more than the information contained in a Mossad agent's report that the shirts of Egyptian Air Force Commander General Sidki Mammoud, were frequently stained with olive oil.

"An officer who neglects his outward appearance this way can't be a stickler for discipline," the colonel told his colleagues. "In an emergency, his attention will probably be just as sloppy as his habits of dress."

Those olive-oil stains on the shirts of the Egyptian Air Force leader played a part in the evolution of the Israeli plan of attack.

Between the first and fifth day of June, the Mossad spies located in the Arab countries were putting the finishing touches on this dossier on the enemy air force. Information kept coming in up to the very last minute. In at least one case, the Israeli pilots received last-minute orders to change course in order to find their assigned targets. On their way to destroy a squadron of Ilyushins stationed on the ground, close to Cairo, they received orders to proceed to another target area at some distance from the Egyptian capital: at the last moment, the agents had discovered that the Egyptians had transferred this unit of heavy bombers, regarded as the most formidable in the Middle East, only the day before.

A few days before D-day, H-hour had been fixed in the greatest secrecy by the heads of Israeli Air Force Intelligence: only about twenty superior officers knew it. It was not a conventional choice in terms of military history. The general staff had two classical options: 5:00 A.M., at sunrise, and 2:00 P.M., i.e. four hours before sunset, which would permit it to act and to escape retaliation under cover of oncoming darkness. It was this latter H-hour that the Egyptians and Syrians later chose to surprise the Israeli Army at Yom Kippur in October 1973.

In early June 1967 the organizers of the Israeli air attack had been presented with a third option by the air force intelligence chiefs, an apparently frivolous time—8:00 A.M.—to achieve surprise where no strategic surprise was possible, since the ground armies already were face to face, ready for immediate confrontation. A state of alert was maintained in the Egyptian armed forces all night long, up to 7:30 A.M., when the officers and the pilots had breakfast. It was this breakfast hour that the intelligence chiefs of Israeli aviation decided on.

The secret was so well kept that it gave rise to an incident at the meeting of the interministerial coordination committee formed early in June under the aegis of Deputy Minister of Defense Zvi Tsur: the representative of the Israeli Air Force refused to divulge the time of H-hour to the representative of the Ministry of Foreign Affairs.

In order to keep this secret to the very end, the Israeli Air Force even engaged in routine maneuvers on June 5 between 6:00 and 7:30 A.M., thus perfectly camouflaging an attack whose only precedent had been the Japanese raid on Pearl Harbor in 1941.

The crisis had begun unexpectedly, one month before the explosion of June 1967. In response to a reprisal strike in Syria during which Israeli Mirages had shot down six MIGs, Nasser embarked on a spectacular course of decisions: he massed his troops at the borders of the Negev, expelled the UN forces from the Gaza Strip and from Sharm-el-Sheikh, closed the Straits of Tiran, thus blocking the Gulf of Aqaba, Israel's second maritime outlet. On May 24 he visited Bir-Gafgafa—later, Refidim—where his pilots told him they were certain that the cities of Israel were at their mercy. A photograph of Nasser at Bir-Gafgafa was reproduced all over the world, and it became obvious that war could not be avoided.

The Egyptian leader's decision to escalate took the world by surprise; not least the Egyptians themselves, to whom he had declared only a few weeks earlier that the time for revenge had not yet come: his army was not ready, and he regarded the development of his country as a priority. Why, then, had he now decided to embark on this adventure? "Because he was only a man": that was the only answer anyone was able to elicit, after his death in 1970, from his Foreign Minister, Mahmoud Riad.

The Arab world greeted the decision with great approbation. "Let's throw the Jews into the sea, to the last man," shouted Ahmed Shukeiry who at the time claimed to represent the Palestinian Arabs. After deciding to rally to the cause, Jordan's Hussein exhorted: "Anywhere you find Jews, kill them, with your weapons, with your fingernails, with your teeth."

"We'll fight to the last drop of blood," the Syrian allies promised, in their turn.

"Cut their throats! Cut their throats!" chanted popular singer Oum Kalsoum. Within a few days, Iraq, Saudi Arabia, Libya, Algeria, and Sudan joined the chorus. Israel felt surrounded and menaced once again, as in the worst days of her history. Nasser did not know what demons he had unleashed in the wounded memory of the Jewish people, nor did he know the price he would have to pay. This time the ghetto-state had soldiers and arms.

But no one knew at the time that the slow fuse that had ignited Israeli-Arab passions had been lit within the Kremlin, during a merciless internal power struggle among the successors of Nikita Khrushchev.

Between 1965 and 1967 the Middle East had become a dominant factor in the course of that rivalry among the new Soviet leaders, manifested by takeovers in Arab countries—as in Syria in 1966—and, in global terms, by a considerable strengthening of Soviet influence in the region, all the way down to the Arabian desert, to Yemen, where Soviet agents gained nearly total control over politics. The crisis of May 1967 marked a culmination of this power struggle within the Kremlin and was a formidable gamble taken by Brezhnev against his rivals. The protagonists of the ensuing war were merely pawns, manipulated by the Soviet master gambler. To bring it about, Brezhnev had only to convince Nasser, who was still hesitant and uncertain about the abilities of his army. Former Egyptian Minister of Defense General Mohammed Gamasy said early in 1978 that at first he had opposed Nasser's decision to blockade the Gulf of Eilat. Nasser himself had tried to resist Moscow's pressure to set the war machine in motion. Thus it had been necessary for the Soviet secret services to mount one of the most fantastic misinformation operations ever.

After Krushchev's removal on October 14, 1964, a triumvirate consisting of the Secretary-General of the Communist party, Leonid Brezhnev, Prime Minister Aleksei Kosygin, and Defense Minister Marshal Rodion Malinovsky had established itself in the Kremlin. Kosygin and Malinovsky joined forces to exercise predominant influence on foreign policy. From the beginning of 1965, Malinovsky had been convinced that China had become the primary threat to the Soviet Union and that it was necessary to concentrate defense efforts in its direction. Therefore, he wanted to avoid all unnecessary confrontations with the West—in Europe as well as in the Middle East. Following the same principle, Kosygin offered his services as mediator to resolve the armed conflict between India and Pakistan and organized a successful peace conference in Tashkent in January 1966. Its satisfactory conclusion seemed to herald a new policy of détente with the West.

To counteract this policy and to assert his own supremacy, Brezhnev had begun to work against the policy by introducing his own men into the Soviet game plan for the Middle East. On October 16, 1964, only two days after Khrushchev's removal, a Syrian delegation arrived in Moscow to request military aid. Marshal Malinovsky, responsible for Egypt's armaments, generously granted the request in order to gain more influence in Syria, which he considered a troublemaker. Brezhnev profited from the Syrian visit by introducing agents of the Soviet Army's counterespionage organization into Syria under the pretext that they were needed there to protect the secrets of Syria's Soviet armaments from the curiosity of Western agents. That selfsame service took its orders from the army's political commissar, General Ipishev, who answered to the general secretariat of the Communist party headed by Brezhnev.

A few weeks later, Ipishev's agents who arrived with the arms promised by Malinovsky successfully blew the cover of a Syrian army colonel recruited by the CIA: it had been this man's task to divert one of the Russian patrol boats delivered to the port of Latakia to American agents stationed in Cyprus. The traitor was court-martialed and hanged in Damascus in February 1965.

In January the counterespionage service led by Brezhnev's man had expanded its activities and had become the Russian leader's favorite instrument in Syria, the main target of his Mideast policy until May 1967.

To begin with, the service introduced radiogoniometry trucks to detect clandestine radio transmitters used by foreign intelligence agents in Syria. A computer-equipped, late-model vehicle of this type enabled the Syrian security services to intercept code messages and to discover the transmitter used by Israel's famous man in Damascus, Eli Cohen. Having adopted the persona of a rich Arab merchant who had emigrated to Argentina and then returned to his homeland, calling himself Kamal Amin Taabes, this Mossad agent had gained access to the most influential sectors of Damascus society. Among the dignitaries he befriended were high-ranking army officers such as the head of intelligence, Colonel Ahmed Suweidani, and Syrian President Amin el-Hafez.

Cohen was hanged in Damascus in May 1965. His dossier served the purposes of Soviet counterintelligence admirably in its vigorous participation, a few months later, in the coup d'état mounted by the left wing of the Ba'ath party. At the same moment that the Malinovsky-Kosygin team successfully demonstrated the spirit of Tashkent in January 1966 by finding a peaceful resolution to the conflict between India and Pakistan, Brezhnev prepared the fuse for the Middle Eastern powderkeg, with the assistance of Marshal A. A. Grechko, deputy minister of defense and Brezhnev's man in the army.

On February 23, 1966, General Salah Jedid, chief of staff of the Syrian Army, and Colonel Suweidani, chief of army intelligence, overthrew President Amin el-Hafez, with the assistance of their friends in the Russian counterintelligence service. General Jedid became prime minister, General Hafez Assad, minister of defense, and Colonel Suweidani, chief of staff. For the first time, there was a Communist minister in an Arab government. A few weeks later, on March 29, a delegation of the Syrian Communist party attended the Twenty-third Congress of the Communist party in Moscow. Its leader made an enthusiastic speech on the eve of the closing session in which he eulogized the close relationship now established between the new regime in Damascus and the Communists. His speech was the Syrian contribution to the hard line of the Brezhnev-Grechko faction and a negation of the politics of détente practiced by the Kosygin-Malinovsky faction which had gained the support of President of the Supreme Soviet Nikolai Podgorny.

When the new rulers of Damascus, Jedid and Assad, arrived in Moscow on April 18, at the head of a Syrian delegation, Minister of Defense Malinovsky remained conspicuously absent from all official receptions organized in its honor.

Toward the middle of that year, Malinovsky was taken ill. His physicians diagnosed terminal cancer and told him that he had only a few months to live. The two rival factions immediately began an intense struggle to determine his successor as the political head of defense. Brezhnev knew that if he could get his candidate—Grechko—installed in that position, his domination of the Kremlin would be assured.

In October the ailing Malinovsky relinquished his post, but not officially, as yet. De facto, Marshal Grechko took over some of the functions that the dying Malinovsky was no longer able to perform and took the opportunity for a series of initiatives.

On November 4 Syria signed a defense agreement with Egypt. In the next few days, the Syrians provoked a number of incidents along the Israeli border, continuing through December and January. On January 3, 1967, the Syrian Ba'ath party's newspaper, *A*

Thaura, announced a shift from the army's defensive strategy to an offensive one.

While manipulating the Syrians, Brezhnev and Grechko exerted themselves to reactivate their contacts with Egypt, which up to that point had proceeded by means of direct consultations between Nasser and Kosygin. On November 24, 1966, Marshal Abd el-Hakim Amer, Vice-President of the Republic of Egypt and supreme commander of its army, paid an official visit to Moscow for a series of negotiations with the Soviet leaders. Marshal Grechko became his primary contact. During one of their tête-à-têtes, Grechko encouraged Amer to take the initiative of expelling the UN forces from the Sinai. Grechko went so far as to promise him, if war broke out, the active support of the Soviet Union that Malinovsky and Kosygin had never wanted to grant Nasser.

A week later, Amer gave Nasser a plan which involved the evacuation of the UN forces that had guarded the borders of the Sinai ever since the Israeli retreat in 1957. Nasser rejected the proposal: he did not think the time was ripe for it.

To indicate his displeasure, Brezhnev canceled his official state visit to Cairo projected for December. Meanwhile, incidents continued to multiply along the border of Israel and Syria.

On January 15, 1967, the Politburo met in Moscow in great secrecy. It disapproved of the new tensions provoked by the Syrian leaders' offensive strategy and did not regard the time propitious for the fomenting of unrest in the Middle East. Syrian Prime Minister Jedid was called to Moscow, and on his return to Damascus on January 25, he reluctantly ordered a resumption of the sessions of the mixed Israeli-Syrian commission established in 1949 to reduce tension along the border.

Jedid reported to the Ba'ath party's central committee, that he had encountered two radically divergent points of view among the Russian leaders. Syrians and Egyptians thus became aware of the power struggle within the Kremlin and how it affected the Middle Eastern policies advocated by the opposing factions.

In March 1967 Marshal Malinovsky was little more than barely alive. When he died at the end of the month, Brezhnev and Grechko had already made their moves regarding his successor. They knew that the majority of the Supreme Soviet favored a civilian: Kosygin's candidate, Armament Minister D. P. Ustinov. In order to change the members' minds and to get his military candidate—Grechko—nominated, Brezhnev had to create an external threat that would justify the presence of an army representative in the government. What better threat than an aggravation of the

Mideastern situation? Thus it became necessary to rekindle the tension on Israel's borders.

An emissary from Grechko arrived in Cairo in mid-March for a secret meeting with Marshal Amer. After his visit, the Egyptian Army chief once again proposed the evacuation of the UN forces to Nasser. Nasser hesitated and decided to test the water with a message to his friend Kosygin. Alarmed, Kosygin sent Foreign Minister Andrei Gromyko to Cairo to dissuade Nasser from this course of action. Gromyko arrived in Egypt on March 29, two days before Malinovsky's death, and remained there until April 1. He informed Nasser of the Supreme Soviet's decision to appoint the civilian Ustinov Minister of Defense.

The decision was made public on April 3. The following day, a delegation of Red Army marshals informed the Supreme Soviet of its misgivings in the face of the deteriorating exterior situation and the unfortunate choice of a nonmilitary man during such a tense period. But Kosygin and Podgorny stood their ground: the Supreme Soviet did not give in.

On April 6 the Syrian delegation to the funeral services for Marshal Malinovsky prepared for the trip back to Damascus. Air Force General Batuv was among the Russian military men who escorted the Syrians to the airport.

On April 7 for the first time in a long while, Syrian Air Force planes went into action on the Israeli frontier. Israeli fighters intercepted them and downed six of the Syrian MIGs. That confrontation seemed to be sufficient explanation for General Batuv's presence at the airport.

On April 8 a group of Soviet Army officers paid another visit to the Supreme Soviet. They cited the seriousness of the aerial incident between Syria and Israel as cause for renewing their objection to the appointment of Ustinov and for demanding the appointment of Marshal Grechko. Their effort became something of a military coup. After three days, the Supreme Soviet capitulated, and on April 11 it ratified the decree appointing Marshal Grechko Minister of Defense of the Soviet Union.

That success, achieved on the eve of the meeting of the European Communist parties at Karlovy Vary in Czechoslovakia, was only the first step in Brezhnev's takeover of total power in Soviet politics. On the day of his candidate's appointment to the key position of defense minister, Brezhnev sent a special envoy to Cairo—Moscow Communist party secretary N. G. Yagoritsev—to confer with the leaders of the one existing party in Egypt—the Arab Socialist Union—Ali Sabri and Sharawi Gomea. They assured him of their support for Marshal Amer's military plan. Later, Nasser's confidant, Hassanein Heykal, was to consider that mission, and one private meeting on April 21 in particular, between Gomea and Yagoritsev, as the crucial turning point in the campaign that would end in the war of June 1967.

Today we also know that the majority of Egypt's military leaders reacted with reserve when, a few weeks after the Yagoritsev visit, Nasser announced his decision to close the Straits of Tiran, at the entrance to the Gulf of Eilat, with specific reference to consultations within the Arab Socialist Union's Central Committee. Returning from an inspection trip to the Israeli-Syrian border, on May 15, chief of staff General Mohammed Fawzi expressed his opinion that the rumors regarding Israeli troop concentrations on the northern front were mere figments of the Soviets' imagination. During his trial in Cairo in 1968, Defense Minister Shams Badran claimed that he found out about the decision to close the Straits only in the newspapers! One of his successors, General Mohammed Gamasy, later said that he had opposed the dangerous adventure upon which President Nasser embarked; he had been encouraged by Amer, Sabri, and Gomea, who had been persuaded to do so by Brezhnev's and Grechko's representative. The day after the Arab defeat, Yagoritsev was relieved from his post as the Moscow Communist party secretary, thus paying for Brezhnev's sins.

Egyptian Sami Sharaf, one of the best spies employed by Moscow in the Arab world, was to play an important role in the campaign devised by Brezhnev and Grechko to stir up emotions to the point of convincing Nasser to go to war. One of the young Egyptian officers at the time, Sharaf had attracted the KGB's attention during a visit to Moscow in 1955, as a member of one of the first delegations after the arms agreement was signed between Egypt and Czechoslovakia. Not long after, and as if by coincidence, Sharaf became the director of the office of Egypt's Prime Minister, Soviet sympathizer Ali Sabri. In that capacity, he attracted the attention of Nasser, who, in 1959, appointed Sharaf his presidential adviser in matters of information. Under this superficially neutral designation, Sharaf proceeded to organize Nasser's personal intelligence service.

According to Vladimir Nikolaievitch Sakharov, a Soviet diplomat who defected to the West in 1971 after having served in Egypt from 1968 to 1970, the KGB recruited Sharaf in 1958, during a visit he made to the UN headquarters in New York. There he had two clandestine meetings with Vladimir Suslev, a member of the Soviet delegation and an agent of the KGB. Suslev gave him instructions on how to contact KGB agents in Egypt. From that time on, KGB documents made actual references to Sharaf under his code name, "Assad" ("lion," in Arabic). In the spring of 1967, Sharaf played a major role in the development of Brezhnev's and Grechko's campaign.

The final phase of their plan began on April 22. On his way to the European Communist Party Congress at Karlovy Vary, Brezhnev stopped off in East Berlin to consult with the leaders of the German Democratic Republic, the closest supporters of his line. According to the testimony of Erwin Weit, Wladyslaw Gomulka's personal interpreter, Brezhnev said to Walter Ulbricht in the presence of the leader of the Polish Communist party: "Even our adversaries will have to admit the success of our Middle East policy. We have partly succeeded in ousting the Americans from the region, and we are about to inflict another blow on them—a serious one—in the very near future. Faced with President Johnson's global strategy, we are going to set in motion our own common strategy, and we shall soon see its effects."

Weit also reported that Brezhnev, in the same conversation and in his presence, said apropos of Nasser: "He has proven that we can trust him to take a chance."

Two days later, in front of the other Communist party leaders, Brezhnev struck an even more belligerent note: "By what right does the American Sixth Fleet patrol the Mediterranean and establish bases in countries adjoining it? The moment has come to demand the withdrawal of the Sixth Fleet from the Mediterranean."

On April 27 the still-undecided Nasser sent Anwar Sadat to the Soviet Union to gauge the consensus prevailing in the Kremlin leadership. Two days later, Sadat met with Aleksei Kosygin and gained the impression that Moscow neither sought nor wished for armed confrontations in the Middle East.

On May 4 Sadat traveled to North Korea. When he returned to Moscow on May 12, he found the political climate totally changed. In a series of secret meetings in the Kremlin during the first week of May, Brezhnev and Grechko, together with the head of the GRU (the military intelligence service), had concocted a forgery designed to convince Nasser of an imminent attack to be launched by Israel against Syria. The document was quite simply based on an authentic document that was ten years old: the Neeman brief.

This working document was prepared in 1957 by Yuval Neeman, the assistant director of Israeli Army Intelligence, to cover all possible situations of confrontation against Israel.

Remember that one copy of that document had disappeared, undoubtedly through the good offices of Israel Beer who hastened to pass it on to his Soviet masters. The Russians merely had to update the document in order to turn it into one that would convince Nasser and make him move. Now they had to make sure of the effect it would produce. The best person to do this was Sharaf, who had become Nasser's closest collaborator and the head of Egypt's secret service. The only problem was that Sharaf-Assad's superior was the head of the KGB, Smichestani, a confidant of Kosygin: he could not be let in on this operational secret. On May 10 Brezhnev executed his masterstroke: by unknown means, he succeeded in engineering the removal of Smichestani and effecting his replacement by one of Brezhnev's own men, Yuri Andropov; a change in the KGB's leadership that was not made public until May 19. Andropov's first task consisted of passing an order to "Assad," who had to convince Nasser of the authenticity of the Neeman document.

(The falsification of authentic texts is the most common KGB propaganda tactic. Thus, in February 1968, the Bombay daily *Free Press Journal* published a letter purportedly addressed to its editor by Gordon Goldstein, a member of the U.S. Office of Naval Research, affirming that the Americans did not have any evil intentions in regard to their stockpiles of bacteriological warfare material in Vietnam and Thailand (the United States never had any such stockpiles there). On March 7 Radio Moscow quoted this letter as proof for its accusation that the United States had launched an epidemic of contagious diseases in Vietnam. On March 9 the Indian weekly *Blitz* published the fabricated letter all over again, as an American admission of facts. Actually, the signature and letterhead of that missive came from an invitation sent out by Gordon Goldstein, a year prior to that time, to members of an international scientists' symposium of which he was cochairman.

The Israeli intelligence services noticed, no doubt, that that same weekly *Blitz* denounced the aggressive intentions of Israel toward its neighbors using quotes from the same Neeman dossier employed by Soviet intelligence to encourage Nasser to go to war.)

Sharaf had also received a document from his Russian supeiors—this one authentic—offering an evaluation of the comparative military capabilities of Israel and her neighbors, as established by Soviet experts. Based on reports from the Soviet embassy in Tel Aviv on social and economic conditions in Israel, the study concluded that Syria and Egypt could advance and vanquish Tsahal in a short time. Soviet Ambassador Chubakhin no doubt alluded to this evaluation made by military experts of his regime when, on June 2, 1967, he told the leader of the Israeli (pro-Soviet) Communist party, Moshe Sneh, "Israel will be defeated in twenty-four hours." In his report to Moscow, the ambassador had added: "Morale in Israel is at its lowest point. All that's left in this country is the espresso generation and a bunch of pimps."

This optimism proved so contagious that at a meeting of the general staff of the Warsaw Pact on June 5, 1967, the first day of the Six-Day War, the Russian generals still predicted a rapid and crushing victory by the Arabs.

Brezhnev finally surmounted the opposition voiced by his rivals Kosygin and Podgorny by confronting them with the Neeman document forged by the GRU. On May 13 Podgorny showed Sadat, who had just returned from Korea, a copy of the forgery.

Arriving in Cairo on the afternoon of May 14, Sadat informed Nasser of the conclusion he had drawn from his trip: far from being hostile to a military initiative on Egypt's part, the Kremlin seemed to desire it. That same evening, Sami Sharaf pulled the noose tighter by insisting on the credibility of the document that Podgorny had given to Sadat.

It may well be that Sharaf also had recourse to another, very special method in order to convince Nasser: a séance. Sharaf had hired a professor from the University of Cairo who claimed to possess the ability to communicate with the spirits of the departed and to receive premonitions useful to his patron. Sharaf used similar subterfuge in his attempt, four years later, in May 1971, to concoct a plot against Sadat in collusion with the leaders of the Socialist left and with Soviet support. That plot failed and put an end to his career as chief of the secret services. After Sharaf's arrest, dozens of tapes were found in his desk, containing, among others, private conversations between Nasser and Sadat. The tapes had been obtained by bugging the offices and homes of most of the Egyptian leaders. Among them was one containing the entire April 20, 1967, conversation between Gomea and Yagoritsev that was so decisive in the commencement of hostilities.

From that point on, events took their inexorable course. On May 15, 1967, in uncertain times, Israel celebrated the nineteenth anniversary of her independence. From a dais erected in West Jerusalem, Prime Minister Levi Eshkol and Chief of Staff Itzhak

Rabin saluted a modest military parade. It was the very day Nasser chose to send his troops into the Sinai and to demand the withdrawal of UN forces. When Rabin asked the head of army intelligence to report on the situation that evening, General Yariv replied, "Nothing to worry about. They're just bluffing."

This was the first time that the Israeli military intelligence service had been taken by surprise and had become a victim of its own conceptual error. But the entry of Egyptian forces into the Sinai and the hasty departure of the UN soldiers caused Israel to call up part of her reserves.

On May 22 Nasser made the fateful decision to blockade the Gulf of Eilat. Israel had no choice: she launched a preventive air strike to break her adversary's wings.

Meanwhile, the Mossad had gotten wind of things: it had discerned the hand of Moscow behind Nasser's latest rodomontades. At the end of May, Israeli diplomats in Moscow became aware of echoes of the factional struggle that had been going on with increasing intensity within the Kremlin. Mossad headquarters was already analyzing the links between the crisis brewing in the Sinai and the events in the Kremlin. Given the turn Soviet infiltration into the Middle East had taken, it seemed vital to ensure American support; but Foreign Minister Abba Eban's discussions with State Department officials in Washington did not seem to indicate that Israel could count on anything—not even a merely benevolent attitude.

On May 31 General Meir Amit made a top-secret trip to Washington. No one knew about it—not at the Ministry of Foreign Affairs nor at the Israeli embassy in Washington. The chief of the Mossad avoided all contact with Israeli representatives and went directly to Richard Helms, the head of the CIA, and one of the American officials most likely to understand Israel's problems. Helms had just presented President Johnson with an analysis of Soviet policy after the Karlovy Vary party conference, concluding that the Kremlin's line had hardened toward the West and that it was preparing for a new conflict in the Middle East. Initially, Helms saw this as a Russian attempt to reduce the pressure the United States was exerting in Vietnam, where, in the course of a few months, military intervention had escalated to the dimensions of full-scale modern warfare. In Helms's opinion, it was unlikely that the Kremlin heavies would risk a confrontation with the United States. "If we show them our teeth, the Soviets will withdraw," he claimed.

General Amit spent six hours with Helms at the national CIA

headquarters in Langley, Virginia. He explained exactly when the situation would become untenable for his country: Israel could not afford to guard her complicated borders with a hastily-drummed-up army of reservists, nor could she go on suffering from a state of progressive asphyxiation. Helms agreed that an Israeli defeat would deliver the entire Middle East into Soviet hands.

The next day—June 1—Helms introduced Amit to Secretary of Defense Robert McNamara, who listened impassively to the analysis given by the chief of the Mossad. Toward the end of the meeting, when Amit already felt as if he had lost this desperate struggle, McNamara dropped a brief phrase:

"I read you loud and clear. I have just heard of General Dayan's nomination for the post of minister of defense. I conferred with him extensively after his visit to Vietnam in 1965. He's a man who knows how to analyze complex situations. Tell him that I hope for the success of his mission."

That same evening, Amit returned to Tel Aviv and told Eshkol and Dayan of the positive results of this trip:

"The Americans will look the other way."

On the evening of June 3, Eshkol called for a special cabinet meeting to determine the final arrangements for a preemptive strike. The ministers approved Dayan's proposal and fixed D-day for June 5.

The Eastern bloc diplomats posted in Tel Aviv did their best to find out what was happening. Members of the Soviet embassy even tried to shadow officers of the Israeli General Staff. An Israeli Air Force commander became aware of an automobile that had been following him all day and remained parked in front of his home all night: it belonged to a Czech diplomat. Yet it was not recourse to these somewhat simplistic methods that provided the Soviets with their knowledge of the date set for the Israeli attack: the diplomat Sakharov, who served in Cairo between 1968 and 1970 before defecting to the West because his contacts with the CIA were on the point of being discovered, later claimed that the Russians were indeed well informed of the intention of an Israeli attack on June 5, 1967. Once again, as in 1956, they did not advise their Arab friends of the coming events, but this time for a different reason.

Brezhnev and Grechko had worked for this war in order to gain the upper hand in the internal Soviet power struggle— but not for the defeat of the Arabs, whom they had armed to the teeth. Despite all the pressure applied to Nasser, Brezhnev still could not be entirely sure that the Egyptian president would really take the giant step; thus the Israeli initiative seemed to fit into Brezhnev's game plan. And it was absolutely necessary to keep the Egyptian leader ignorant of Israeli intentions, to prevent his backing out by announcing, for instance, the retreat of his troops from the Sinai, or the reopening of the Straits of Tiran.

By means of a Mossad contact, Israel had actually transmitted a message to Nasser on May 20 that proposed a demobilization of the forces massed on both sides of the border, to avoid the possibility of a clash. Aware of that message, Brezhnev and Grechko had reason to fear that Nasser might grasp at this straw in order to extricate himself from the precarious situation. Their agent Sami Sharaf enabled them to follow the development of Nasser's most private trains of thought, his scruples and hesitations. Until the last moment, they had pressured, believing that he would, with the help of Syria and perhaps Jordan, be able to counter an Israeli attack and to emerge victorious in the second round.

That was the point at which the Soviet secret services were to experience one of their most severe setbacks. Despite all their efforts, they had not been able to procure Tsahal's plan of operations: thus they could not imagine that the outcome of the war would be determined within the first six hours by a formidable preemptive strike executed by the Israeli Air Force. The GRU erred in its evaluation of Israel's potential and morale. The greatest error in judgment committed by the Soviet services related to their analysis of American reactions.

The KGB's failure was particularly great: it had remained ignorant of Meir Amit's trip to the United States and of the Pentagon's decision to let the Israelis act while opposing an overly direct Soviet intervention.

Nevertheless, the knowledge the Soviets did have of the Tel Aviv decision caused some perplexity among the Israeli services. Was it possible that the Russians had yet another spy placed in a high governmental or cabinet position? The question quite understandably troubled the Shin Bet: after the arrest of Beer in 1961, it had not been able to discover another Moscow agent of equal importance. Yet the presence of an impressive number of KGB and GRU representatives in the Tel Aviv embassies of the Eastern countries testified to a lively interest on the part of those services for this key target in the Middle East.

From the sixties on, the Soviet services had modified their methods of information-gathering in Israel. While still pursuing their effort to recruit as large a number of informants as possible, they had perfected their system of electronic surveillance by means of three special vessels cruising at the perimeters of Israel's territorial waters disguised as fishing boats.

Equipped with antennas, radar, and telecommunications gear, these boats, which patrolled the length of the coast on a twenty-four-hour schedule, carried not only computers, but dozens of Russians with a perfect command of Hebrew who were making a permanent record of all communications they were able to intercept. Not a single conversation conducted over radio waves or telephone lines escaped these enormous ears. The intercepted communications would be processed immediately and retransmitted to a large computer in the Soviet Union which dealt with masses of political, economic, and military information.

The three vessels, named *Caucasus, Crimea,* and *Yuri Gagarin,* were assisted by a flotilla of helicopters based on the *Leningrad* and the *Moscow.* The *Yuri Gagarin* also had the ability to communicate with Soviet satellites and to spy on the American satellites that had, at that time, been circling the skies of the Middle East for some years.

Electronic surveillance from one of these spy ships had enabled the Russians to obtain their information on the date of D-day. In the first half of 1967, the Soviet Navy had tripled its strength in the Mediterranean. At the beginning of June, it had over 80 vessels and 15,000 sailors in those waters, half of whom had arrived after April 30—after Marshal Grechko's appointment as minister of defense, and after Brezhnev's demand for an immediate withdrawal of the Sixth Fleet, expressed at the Karlovy Vary congress.

Nevertheless, during the first six hours of the Six-Day War, the Soviets were not aware of the total demolition of the Egyptian air force.

At 7:59 A.M. New York time (1:59 P.M. Tel Aviv time), on June 5, the hotline between Moscow and Washington was used for the first time since its installation in 1963 after the Cuban missile crisis. Kosygin transmitted a message to President Johnson, informing him that the Soviet Union did not intend to intervene directly in the Middle East conflict.

An hour later, after conferring with his advisers in the White House and CIA chief Richard Helms, Johnson informed Kosygin that the United States did not wish to become embroiled in that conflict either. The next morning, after the full of extent of the military disaster that had befallen the Kremlin's protégés had become better known, the Russians reactivated the hotline to try to obtain American support for a demand for a cease-fire to be agreed upon as soon as possible.

During a secret session of the Politburo, the moderates had carried the day, aided by Johnson's firm opposition to any intervention on the part of the superpowers.

After the second day of the war, the Mossad was aware that the United States had neutralized any possibility of direct military aid from the Soviets to Egypt and Syria. However, the Americans had deliberately refrained from precisely defining the *carte blanche* they had given Israel in dealing with its belligerent neighbors.

Contrary to the predictions of the Mossad and Tsahal's general staff, which were convinced that the Russians would not make a move, Moshe Dayan expressed the fear that the Soviets might have established a limit: a "red line" that could not be crossed without provoking Soviet intervention. He had some personal cause to be afraid of the Soviet Union: he had been chief of staff in 1956 when Marshal Nikolai Bulganin had threatened Israel with Soviet rockets, implying he would use them if Tsahal did not effect a complete and rapid retreat from the Sinai after its victorious Suez campaign.

Dayan's recent visit to Vietnam at the invitation of the Americans had also convinced him that the Soviets never deserted an ally. He had returned impressed by the Vietcong's commando tactics and by the importance of Soviet assistance in the face of the extraordinary firepower employed by the Americans. Under those circumstances, an American military victory seemed unlikely to him. Fearing that the Soviets might render similar assistance to the Arabs in order to save them from total disaster, on June 7 Dayan ordered the general staff to halt the progression of Israeli forces in the Sinai at a distance of 20 kilometers from the Suez Canal. In the evening of the following day, Dayan found himself presented with a *fait accompli:* not meeting with any resistance after the Mitla and Giddi Passes, the spearhead units of Tsahal had arrived at the east bank of the Canal. The order to stop them short had arrived too late.

On June 7 Deputy Premier Yigal Allon demanded that the offensive against Syria be launched at midday in order not to miss the opportunity to gain the Golan Heights and to reach the enclave of the Druze minority oppressed by the Arabs. To his mind, the operation would realize the old dream for which the Druzes of Syria and Lebanon had been fighting during the years of the French mandate: the creation of a Druze state in the Golan and the Djebel (a territory of southern Syria). While permitting the independence of the Druze minority, Israel could thus modify the political structure to her advantage by the creation of a non-Arab state on her northern border.

In a military sense, Tsahal would have been capable of launching an offensive against the Syrians entrenched in the Golan. But Dayan, apprehensive of direct intervention by the Soviet Army whose officers were advising the Syrians, opposed the idea. Nevertheless, as he admitted in his memoirs, he knew that Washington would not have been in the least hostile toward an action against Syria.

While exchanging evaluations with Israeli representatives on June 7, American intelligence estimated that the Russians would not make a move unless Tsahal crossed the Suez Canal. They would not intervene in the Golan. The Israelis would have been able to move on in the north, but Dayan waited two days.

At 9:00 A.M. Washington time, on June 10, the hotline became active again. This time Kosygin's message to Johnson was aggressive. He threatened to intervene unless Israel ordered an immediate cease-fire in the Golan. Johnson calmly replied that he was no more able to control Israel than Kosygin was able to dictate to the Egyptians and the Syrians. Johnson then ordered certain units of the Sixth Fleet to move into position off the Syrian coast in order to discourage any Soviet whim to modify the rules of the game.

Tsahal had been attacking the Golan fortifications since 7:00 A.M. the preceding morning. Surprised by Egypt's acceptance of a cease-fire during the night, Dayan, who had believed that Egypt, sheltered by the Canal, would continue the war indefinitely, agreed to order the occupation of the first Syrian line of defense in the Golan—but of the first line only. However, at 6:30 P.M. on June 10, when the UN cease-fire took effect on the Syrian front, all of the Golan had fallen into Israeli hands. Once again, Dayan deferred to the military *faits accomplis* of his army.

As the Americans had predicted, the Red Army did not hasten to the aid of its Syrian ally. The Soviet Union reacted only on the diplomatic front, by breaking off its, and its satellites'—with the exception of Rumania—relations with Israel.

The day after the crushing Israeli victory, the Soviet Union seemed to have lost on Brezhnev's gamble: its encroachments in the Middle East had been wiped out in less than six days. Both public opinion and political leaders in Egypt and Syria were bitterly critical of the Soviet role.

But at the beginning of July, all such criticism ended. The Politburo had decided to give the Arab states massive aid to enable them to rebuild their military potential as quickly as possible. Brezhnev and his two rivals had arrived at an understanding which put an end to the power struggle, and neither Brezhnev nor Grechko were held responsible for the failure of their politics of tension in the Middle East.

At the end of 1967, it even seemed that the defeat of Egypt and Syria had made them more dependent than ever on their Soviet protector. Enormous quantities of modern armaments arrived in Cairo and Damascus, accompanied by an astounding number of Soviet experts and advisers. Until 1970, when a series of events reversed the trend, the Soviets were implanted more firmly than ever between the Mediterranean and the Red Sea. At the beginning of 1968, they achieved what Egypt had refused to grant them until then: naval bases on its shores.

In great secrecy, the Russians proceeded to construct what was, in effect, their first naval base in the Mediterranean: at Marsa-Matrouh, close to the Libyan border. That enterprise was no doubt connected with the mysterious disappearance of an Israeli submarine, the *Dakar,* between Cyprus and the Egyptian coast on January 25, 1968.

The vessel, en route from Portsmouth to Haifa with a crew of 64, vanished without a trace. There are certain indications that lead one to believe that the *Dakar* succumbed to an attack as she cruised by Marsa-Matrouh. In any case, that mystery of the sea demonstrates that less than a year after losing their shirts on the battlefield, the Kremlin activists were back in action, generating tension in the Middle East. They were going to encourage the Arabs to continue the war by other means: the Egyptian war of attrition in the Canal Zone that would force the Israelis to entrench themselves behind the illusory Bar-Lev Line; the reactivation of the Palestinian organizations that would open up a new battlefront: terrorism.

Book Three
SINCE

The only thing that
changes in Israel
is the past.
——Ezer Weizmann

13
ESCALATION OF TERRORISM

"Kill Ben-Gurion!" With this order to a nationally mixed commando team, Dr. Waddia Haddad, operational chief of the Popular Front for the Liberation of Palestine (PFLP), began his sinister career as the "Dr. No" of international terrorism in the summer of 1969. Within the clandestine community, he was still known as Abu Hani.

In April he had learned of the former Israeli Prime Minister's intention to tour Jewish communities in Latin America. At the time, the "Old Man" was merely an ordinary citizen, and his trip would therefore be unofficial. The private citizen, however, had retained his image as the symbolic incarnation of the Jewish State. His enormous popularity in Israel had returned with his final abandonment of politics to devote himself to his memoirs. His splinter party, Rafi, had rejoined the Labor Party, and Golda Meir had just succeeded Levi Eshkol, who had died in March.

On the third floor of the Kataraji Building in Beirut, Haddad had set up a limited general staff in the apartment that he had been using as a headquarters for the past year: two young assistants and a young woman, Leila Khaled. He decided to send two assassins to Argentina: a Palestinian named Ishmael Souhail and a Swedish mercenary who had been recruited by the PFLP representative in Europe. He had met with the Front's Latin-American representative, Jael el-Ardja, to plan for their trip and accommodations. A native of Beit Jallah, near Bethlehem, el-Ardja had emigrated to Peru—after having studied law in Cairo—where he had joined the Palestinian colony established by people from his village who had come to Lima since the beginning of the century. As cofounder of a fedayeen organization called The Heroes of the Return, which had merged with three others in August 1968 to form the PFLP, he was in contact with various other South American terrorist movements and had recruited—from Montevideo to Caracas—mercenaries such as Ilitch Ramirez-Sanchez, a Venezuelan student who was the son of a wealthy Communist doctor and who had studied in Cuba before attending Patrice Lumumba University in Moscow, where the KGB trained its Third-World agents. Ilitch was to gain fame a few years later in Europe as Carlos. However, he was to play only a minor logistical role in the plot hatched in 1969 to assassinate Ben-Gurion.

In the early summer of 1969, the two killers were to meet in Copenhagen, where one of Haddad's mistresses, a young Arab painter named Muna Soudi, who was enrolled in the school of fine arts, had established one of the first networks supporting the PFLP in the Danish universities. Twenty-four hours before they were to leave for Buenos Aires, however, the police caught them in the midst of their preparations, and the trio's arrest put an end to the plan.

The Israeli-Arab conflict entered its terrorist stage after the Six-Day War. Small units of Al Fatah, which was the earliest and by far the most important group of Palestinian fighters (who had played no part in that war), then began to infiltrate across the Jordan into the occupied territories and to attack vehicles and Israeli civilian targets. Formed in Gaza in 1957, when the Egyptians returned, Al Fatah had already carried out some 60 terrorist incursions into Israel between 1965 and 1967, under the leadership of a 36-year-old engineer stationed in Kuwait, a certain Abu Amar, alias Yasser Arafat. At the time, he was particularly interested in the Jordan River pumping stations. The Palestine Liberation Organization (PLO) had been founded on May 28, 1964, in East Jerusalem (Jordan), and Ahmed Shukeiry, one of Nasser's henchmen and a former Saudi Arabian delegate to the United Nations, had been appointed to head it. The rout of the Arab armies in June 1967, however, had led to the downfall of this demagogue, whose ambition had been "to throw the Jews into the sea."

In order to carry on with its activities, Al Fatah relied on the networks it had set up in the West Bank, which was under Hashemite control, but the Jordanian security files had fallen into the hands of the Shin Bet: the information they contained had enabled the Israelis to take quick action against the first attacks of the clandestine "resistance" organization in Samaria and Judea.

Israel had also countered the infiltrations across the Jordan by installing a double electrified barbed-wire fence equipped with an electronic detection system all along the West Bank. The small fedayeen units that managed to cross were immediately tracked by helicopter-borne paratroops.

On March 20, 1968, Tsahal had stepped up its response to terrorist activities by sending a tank brigade to assault the village of Karameh on the other side of the Jordan. At the time, this settlement harbored Al Fatah's operational headquarters. Yasser Arafat had managed to leap onto a motorcycle minutes before the arrival of the three helicopters carrying a special force of Israeli paratroops and had reached a Jordanian army base. But documents captured in the raid had enabled the Aman officers who accompanied the troops to arrive at a better understanding of the organization of the new Public Enemy Number One. And later on, these documents would play a part in the success of numerous preventive operations.

Chance also frequently played its part. For example, a group of fedayeen was "marked" as they attempted to cross the Jordan by some fluorescent paint used to paint road signs, which had accidentally spilled into the river. The Palestinians turned back into Jordan with terrifying accounts of their escapade. They were convinced that "the Jews had poisoned the Jordan with a powder that affected virility." For two months, the infiltrations ceased.

Although the secret services and paratroopers seemed to be winning the battle of the Jordan, on a more difficult and complicated front another battle was preparing: Europe.

After ratifying the covenant of the VIth Palestine National Council in Cairo in July 1968, four representatives of small autonomous fedayeen groups had met in the restaurant of the luxurious Phoenica Intercontinental Hotel in Beirut to set up the PFLP, a Marxist-oriented organization that supported more radical activities than Al Fatah—above all, an internationalization of terrorism. At its head were two medical doctors who had begun their careers in Amman in the late 1950s: George Habash and Waddia Haddad. Habash had founded the Komeyoun el Arab ("Arab Nationalists"), a political movement founded on the theses that Nasser had expounded in his book, *Philosophy of Revolution,* and which Jordanian communists at the time had seen as a right-wing movement. Habash was primarily a theoretician and ideologist.

Haddad regarded himself as a man of action as well as an intellectual. Born in Safed in Upper Galilee in 1930, he had attended the Scottish school in which his father had taught; one of his pupils had been Zvi Berenson, the future Israeli Supreme Court judge. His family had taken refuge in Jordan during the 1948 war, and he had left Jordan to study medicine in Beirut. Upon returning to Amman, he had met his colleague, Dr. Habash.

Together they opened a clinic in 1963 as a cover for their clandestine political activities (pamphlets, flyers, plots against the Hashemite regime); their movement was prohibited by the Jordanian authorities, and its militants sought by King Hussein's police.

Both doctors were arrested and tried on several occasions. In 1967 upon their release from prison, they left Jordan and went to Lebanon. This was the period when the Arab Nationalists moved to the left, first joining with several terrorist groups and independent figures, and finally becoming the PFLP. To further his Marxist beliefs, Habash assumed its political and ideological leadership, and Haddad took charge of special operations, in which role he remained for some time in the shadows.

"The road to Tel Aviv leads through Amman." With this as its motto, the PFLP was to forge the most formidable of terrorist weapons. In the name of permanent revolution, it turned to operations "off the field of battle," and contacted terrorist movements in Europe and in Asia, going as far afield as Korea and Japan. In fact, the "field of battle" was widened to include the entire non-communist world: airplane skyjackings, the taking of hostages, the kidnapping of prominent figures, attacks on airports, on embassies, and even the poisoning of oranges with mercury.

While still an unknown figure, Waddia Haddad had chalked up his first success on July 23, 1968, when he forced an El Al Boeing on the Rome-Tel Aviv route to land in Algiers. It was a masterful trial run which gave enormous publicity to the PFLP's debut. For the first—and last—time, Israel was forced to give in and agree to free 20 fedayeen in return for the passengers and crew.

The following day, the chiefs of the five Israeli intelligence services met in the office of the head of the Mossad, General Meir Amit, chairman of the coordinating committee. On the agenda: a reorganization of priorities in response to this new menace. They reached a unanimous opinion: it was not enough merely to intensify intelligence efforts; it would be extremely difficult to combat terrorism without striking at its leaders. Although the army, the police, ministerial security services, and transport security would have to be mobilized to combat terrorism, the job fell primarily on the Shin Bet, inside the country, and on the Mossad, overseas, to attempt to reach the leaders of the organizations employing terrorism. The struggle would have to assume different forms, preventive and punitive: military reprisals, like the one at Karameh, commando operations, the penetration of terrorist organizations by hundreds of agents and informers, a permanent file on all the leaders and memberships of such organizations, and "headhunting" expeditions against their leaders.

In 1969 Haddad was spinning his web, drawing in the Japanese Red Army terrorists, German anarchists in the Baader-Meinhof gang, and Latin-American revolutionary groups. In the following year, the Israeli services set up an intelligence information center in conjunction with most of the European police services, with an international file to enable them to obtain an instantaneous read-out of the activities and plans of the Terrorist International.

Heading the list of targets for the liquidation teams was Arafat. The PLO chief had been fortunate in escaping death on many occasions. In December 1967 he had managed to save himself by jumping out of the window of a villa in Ramallah as Israeli soldiers who had been advised of his presence were preparing to close in. On March 20, 1968, he had similarly escaped the Tsahal raid on Karameh. In 1971 however, his car exploded just before he was to enter it. And he had barely left his headquarters building in Lebanon in 1973 when it was strafed by the Israeli Air Force.

George Habash and Waddia Haddad were also high up on the Israeli "Wanted List."

On July 11, 1970, Haddad had miraculously escaped a mysterious barrage at 2:00 A.M. from six Soviet-made Katyusha rockets, three of which destroyed the living room and bedroom of his apartment on Beirut's rue Mukhi Eldin Alkhayat. He had been in his study with Leila Khaled. His wife, Samiah, and his son Hani, aged eight, had escaped with minor injuries.

Haddad soon transferred his headquarters to Bagdad, where he moved constantly, never sleeping more than two nights in the same bed. He was also beginning to free himself from George Habash's control, breaking with the PFLP political leadership on March 7, 1972, to seek financial and logistical assistance from the Iraqi, Libyan, and Algerian intelligence services and also, by means of blackmail, from some wealthy Lebanese. He then set up the PFLP's foreign terrorist group using a war chest he had amassed by skyjacking a Lufthansa jumbo jet to Aden in 1972, for which he was paid a $5 million ransom! Two months later, he concluded a cooperation and mutual assistance agreement with representatives from all of the international terrorist organizations, who met in a top-secret session in the refugee camp of El Badawi, near Tripoli in Lebanon. This indeed became a real stock exchange for terrorist attacks, whose rate he was able to set on the international terrorist market. He was thus behind 90 percent of the political crimes committed throughout the world. His secret weapon was the recruiting of willing females, naïve tourists, and foreign revolutionary elements. He was always on the move, changing his identity; often in disguise, his features were never publicized and he evaded the Israeli liquidation teams up until his death from cancer in 1978.

Although Habash, too, was to be spared, other heads would fall. The vast effort the Israeli intelligence services had begun in 1970 had enabled them to keep the results of the unprecedented terrorist offensive to a minimum. Several hundred Al Fatah and PFLP cells were uncovered in the West Bank, and their members were arrested and tried. Despite the open bridges that allowed for free circulation by Arabs across the Jordan—there were some 100,000 crossings annually—and despite the very sparse military presence in the area, the Shin Bet was able to uncover most of the new networks established in the territories: in 1977 barely 200 young Palestinians remained in the groups in the West Bank and the Gaza Strip; the ten groups identified early in 1978 would not be able to intensify terrorist activity to such a level as to become a factor in the process of negotiation between Egypt and Israel.

The Israeli services were also able to penetrate the European networks, 90 percent of whose emissaries were taken into custody upon their arrival in Israel. These successes were inevitably counterbalanced, however, by a relatively small number of disappointments, failures, and setbacks.

In August 1973 Israeli pursuit planes forced a Lebanese aircraft to land at Lod. The evening before, Aman had received intelligence, collected from various sources, according to which Habash was to have been on the Middle East Airlines plane from Beirut to Bagdad. Alerted by the army intelligence chief, General Eli Zeira, Dayan approved the interception and rerouting of the plane. However, the operation had been planned too hastily. No further attempt had been made to ascertain whether the PFLP leader had actually boarded the plane. Habash had planned to be on the flight, but when the plane set down at Lod, he was not on it. A cursory investigation would have revealed that the plane had arrived in Beirut from Vienna four hours late, and that because of the delay, Habash had simply taken another flight.

Several weeks earlier, there had been another important intelligence failure.

On July 21 of this fateful year, the special teams that had been created to avenge the victims of the massacre at the Olympic Games in Munich had made a serious mistake in their pursuit of the man responsible for those killings: Ali Hassan Salameh, the chief of operations in the Black September organization, the special operations arm of the Rassad, which was Al Fatah's secret agency entrusted with intelligence. Since Salameh would be the most difficult man to find, "Aleph" and "Bet" teams had begun the "Revenge for Munich" operation with names a bit lower down on their Wanted List. When, however, on July 14, word came through a Mossad liaison agent of Salameh's presence in Scandinavia, the Mossad ordered three of its men in Stockholm to find him and follow him. Two teams went to Oslo, where the Mossad's man there, a Danish Jew named Dan Arbel, was waiting for them; Arbel was a successful businessman with dual nationality. The trail led them to Lillehammer, a little town deep in the Norwegian countryside. The Israelis found their prey and shot him down in the street. Unfortunately, their victim was not the man known in their code as the Red Prince, but only a Moroccan waiter named Ahmed Bouchiki who was married to a Norwegian woman. Dan Arbel and five of his companions were arrested. There was a trial and a scandal. (Six years later, in Beirut, a booby-trapped car exploded when Salameh was passing by, killing the man whom the Israelis considered to be the mastermind behind the Munich massacre.)

Up until then, however, the liquidation teams had carried out their missions flawlessly. The first teams had been recruited upon the emergence of Black September, organized by Al Fatah intelligence services after the destruction of the Palestinian bases in Jordan by King Hussein's army in September 1970. Black September was headed by Mohamed Youssef Najjar, known as Abu Youssef, Yasser Arafat's right-hand man for intelligence in the Palestine Liberation Organization. The number-two man was the wily Salameh, who was in charge of operational planning. In the eyes of the new terrorist organization, the murder of a Jew in Europe, or of a Jewish sympathizer, had greater publicity value than the killing of a hundred Jews in Israel. Europe thus became the main arena.

But it was in Egypt that Black September really went into action with its first attack: the assassination of Jordanian Prime Minister Wasfi Tell on November 28, 1971, at the entrance to the Sheraton Hotel in Cairo. Tell was accused of having ordered Hussein's Bedouins to liquidate the last fedayeen outpost in Jordan following the massacre of 7,000 refugees and the exodus of the remainder to Lebanon, and of having been personally responsible for having Al Fatah military leader, Abu Ali Iyad, tortured to death.

After the failure of the taking of hostages operation aboard the Sabena airliner on May 8, 1972, at Lod, the PFLP had hired three killers from the Japanese Red Army who had attended the secret terrorist conference called by Dr. Haddad at the Badawi refugee camp. On May 31 it sent them to Lod Airport, where they emptied their guns into a crowd of passengers, most of whom happened to be Puerto Rican pilgrims. The toll: 27 dead, 78 wounded.

Now international terrorism was clearly on the move. Golda Meir, who had hitherto opposed retaliatory action based on the implacable biblical precept, "An eye for an eye, a tooth for a tooth," gave the nod for escalation by saying, "Crush the heads of the terrorist hydra."

On July 8 Israeli frogmen slipped into Beirut and concealed a radio-controlled bomb beneath the car of the PFLP spokesman, Palestinian poet Hassan Kanafani, who was blown up along with his young niece, whose presence the Mossad had unfortunately been unable to foresee.

The massacre carried out by Abu Daoud and Hassan Salameh, Arafat's lieutenants, under the aegis of the Black September organization, of eleven athletes on the Israeli Olympic team—one weightlifter was an American national—on September 5 at the Munich Games, led Golda to agree to the plan drawn up by Zvi Zamir, the Mossad chief, to form killer-commando groups "Aleph" and "Bet." "Send your men," she ordered, and appointed former Aman chief Aharon Yariv as her special adviser in the fight against terrorism.

A pitiless secret international war began to rage. Ready for action at the beginning of October, the special teams pinpointed thirteen targets: twelve would be hit in the next six months. The thirteenth was missed in Oslo through the tragic error at Lillehammer.

On October 16, 1972, another Palestinian intellectual, Wada Abdel Zwaiter, the man responsible for the El Al skyjacking to Algiers and for a failed bomb attack on another El Al plane, and who was now the Black September chief in Italy, was shot down on his doorstep in Rome by "Aleph" team members led by General Zamir in person. His killers had spent less than five hours in Italy.

The "Aleph" and "Bet" teams' second target was Dr. Mahmoud Hamshari, the official PLO representative in Paris, who was implicated in the abortive plot against Ben-Gurion in the summer of 1969 and had been involved in the sabotage of a Swissair jet on the Zurich–Tel Aviv run, which had resulted in 47 victims. A man posing as an Italian journalist had managed to get him to leave his home on December 7 so that the Mossad specialists could boobytrap his telephone without being disturbed. On the following day, the "journalist" called him and set off the electronic signal that detonated the bomb, mortally wounding the man believed to be head of Black September in France.

On January 24, 1973, a radio-controlled explosive device in his hotel room in Nicosia (Cyprus) killed a Palestinian agent of the

Soviet KGB, Abad al-Chir, charged with providing the Black September with Soviet AK-47 assault weapons. His successor, Zaiad Muchasi, met with the same fate only ten weeks later, on April 9. Three days earlier, the man in charge of weapons supply, Basil al-Kubaissi, a professor at the American University in Beirut, was killed in Paris on the steps of the Madeleine.

Meanwhile, the assassination of two American diplomats who had been taken hostage at the Saudi Arabian embassy in Khartoum (Sudan) on March 1, 1973, by a Black September commando team led by Hassan Gassan, of the PLO, had prompted Zamir to mount a large-scale operation directed by "Dado" Elazar, the chief of staff. This was to be a raid on the Black September central command post in the very heart of Beirut, an action combining military units—paratroopers, naval commandos, sailors and pilots—with Mossad special teams and Aman agents.

At the beginning of April, five European businessmen landed separately at Beirut airport: a Belgian, Gilbert Rimbert, arriving from Frankfurt with his beautiful secretary, Monique Brun; a German, Dieter von Altnoder, from Rome; two Englishmen, George Elder of Birmingham and Andrew Macy, via Frankfurt; and a carefree Frenchman, Charles Boussart, from Paris. Each man rented a luxury car—Buick, Plymouth, or Mercedes—and, after having attended to their business during the day, they would meet in the evening for nocturnal strolls, most often along the coast at Ramlat el-Beida, where steep cliffs overlooked narrow sandy beaches. They paid special attention to two large apartment buildings at the corner of 68th Street and rue Khaled-Ben-Al-Walid, to which their romantic wanderings often led them.

On April 9, at 12:47 A.M., two Israeli torpedo boats which had left Haifa at dusk and had made for the high seas, were cruising off the Beirut coast, opposite where the six rented cars were parked. On board these ships was a mixed team of frogmen, paratroopers, and commandos in civilian clothes. At a signal from the cars' headlights, they disembarked in Zodiac rubber boats, were towed to the beach by the frogmen, and silently met the "businessmen" and the "secretary." Armed with grenades, Beretta revolvers, and submachine guns, they piled into the cars, driving off in three separate directions. They then converged on the two apartment buildings, whose detailed plans the "businessmen" had been able to procure. Splitting into three groups, they knocked out the three guards they encountered and headed straight for the floors on which they knew they would find the apartments belonging to the seventh, eighth, and ninth targets on their Wanted List. They had been provided complete details of the residences of the Black September and Al Fatah leaders and of their organizations' headquarters, with maps, photographs, the positioning of guards, the location of the alarm system, and even a careful survey of nighttime traffic in the Beirut streets in order to facilitate their getaway.

Upon arriving at the door to each apartment designated by Monique Brun, the "secretary," they shot off the locks and hinges with their submachine guns and made directly for the bedrooms. In one, they surprised the Black September leader, Abu Youssef, lying naked in bed in the arms of a woman, killing them both, as well as a neighbor who unwisely ran to see what the noise was all about. In another, they cut down Kemal Adwan, Youssef's right-hand man, in the doorway, and in another they gunned down PLO spokesman Kamal Nasser, whom they found working late at his desk.

Two other groups simultaneously blew up the headquarters of the Democratic Popular Front near a refugee camp in the southern suburbs of Beirut, and the Black September arsenal in the north of the city. One of the two buildings attacked by the first group was destroyed by explosives placed around its foundations, and dozens of fedayeen were crushed under the rubble.

As a confused battle raged outside, members of the first team carefully searched the apartments of the assassinated leaders. One of the men who had killed Kemal Adwan took his time collecting documents. His name was Yonathan Nethanyahu, known as Yoni; he was twenty-seven years old, a student of philosophy and mathematics at Harvard University and at Hebrew University in Jerusalem, and leader of one of the commando teams. He had volunteered to join the raid. When the El Al plane had been skyjacked in 1968, he had written to his family from America: "This act has convinced me I should return to Israel as soon as possible. If the men of Al Fatah are coming to fight there, I owe it to myself. I'm a better soldier than any of them, and my national awareness is stronger than theirs. If they want war, we have no choice but to fight for our existence."

Yoni had asked to join the Beirut raid as an ordinary soldier, since he was not needed as an officer, and joined the special unit under the command of his own adjutant. This officer would be his adjutant at a later date when Lieutenant Colonel Yoni would lead the Israeli commando raid on Entebbe on July 4, 1976, where he would be the only Israeli combatant killed.

The items Yoni lingered behind to collect in his victim's apartment were to be a real treasure for the Israeli intelligence services:

all the operational plans for the PLO networks in the West Bank and within Israel herself.

Yoni was the last to leave the building, tossing his pack into the last car, which pulled away just as two Lebanese police jeeps arrived. He jumped from the running board to stop the two jeeps, but his driver sped off toward the shore without noticing that he had been left behind. When his companions realized he was missing, they turned back to look for him. The future hero of Entebbe had almost been forgotten that night in Beirut.

Israeli Air Force helicopters were hovering over the Lebanese capital ready to assist the fighters dressed as civilians. One set down in the center of the city to collect a wounded officer—and some of the files that had been discovered in the apartments of the three executed terrorist leaders. As the convoy reached the shore, other helicopters dropped nails on the road to puncture the tires of anyone pursuing them. But surprise had been so complete that no attempt was made to intercept the commando unit on its return to the beach. The soldiers put to sea, along with the "businessmen" and their efficient "secretary," leaving the rented cars parked on the waterfront. Two helicopters took off with the two dead and the four wounded soldiers of the commando unit. The operation had taken no more than an hour and a half.

The torpedo boats dropped their passengers in Haifa. The documents Yoni had found confirmed Shin Bet suspicions concerning the Arabs in the West Bank and Galilee who were connected with the terrorist networks. One document revealed that a villager in Galilee, paid by Al Fatah for each item of information he gathered, had created a phony network consisting of his small brothers, aged two and four, and of other people who were either dead or imaginary. Other data collected in the Beirut raid provided proof of Soviet assistance to terrorism. The KGB, with the help of Cuban diplomats, had recruited hundreds of purported students who were later to join terrorist organizations in Ireland, Germany, France, Spain, and Turkey, as well as the ranks of Palestinian organizations.

The Beirut commando team had missed only one of its targets: Yasser Arafat. Once again he had escaped. After this incident, he never again returned to his luxurious apartment in the rue de Verdun, but preferred to stay briefly in one refugee camp or another, surrounded by well-armed guards. From then on he would change his residence frequently to escape the fate of the Algerian Mohammed Boudia, whom the documents captured in Beirut revealed to be Black September's foreign minister: Boudia was to be assassinated on June 28, 1973, when he slid behind the steering wheel of his booby-trapped car in the Latin Quarter in Paris.

Five days after the Beirut raid, the *Queen Elizabeth II,* the Cunard Line's most luxurious ship, left Portsmouth with 580 English and American Jews on board. Its destination: the Israeli port of Ashdod. The purpose of its voyage: the twenty-fifth anniversary celebrations of Israeli independence.

Before its departure, the huge ship had been thoroughly searched by Scotland Yard teams and by Royal Navy experts. Security measures had been extremely tight. Every piece of luggage had been X-rayed. Passengers from the United States had been escorted from Heathrow Airport by police cars and motorcycle police. Some thirty British security agents were traveling on board, along with a dozen frogmen and a dozen special agents of Burns International Security Services Agency, an American company. The crew and its captain, Mortimer Hyer, had been given special instruction and training to ensure the safety of their important passengers. Each of the 580 passengers had been provided with special badges similar to those given employees in United States military installations.

At the stopover in Lisbon, frogmen had surrounded the ship. From Gibraltar on, ships of the Home Fleet in the Mediterranean had been stationed along the route the *QE II* would take. All the way to Cyprus, Lightning reconnaissance planes, able to detect submarines, flew over the ship. And from Cyprus to Ashdod, she was given an honor escort by the Israeli Navy.

Why all these honors and precautions, unique in the history of commercial ocean travel in peacetime? Because the peace was a "phony peace." In April 1973 terrorist activity by the PFLP and Black September (Al Fatah's action arm) had escalated to an even bloodier degree. They had struck at a dozen Israeli and foreign targets. The state of alert in the Mediterranean, however, had been caused by a specific threat.

Around the end of March, Colonel Muammar Qaddafi, the Libyan chief of state, had summoned Black September representatives to his capital and had made them an unusual offer: the sum of $10 million to blow up an Israeli plane with everyone on board. He wanted to take revenge for the tragic loss of one of his own planes that had strayed off course over the Sinai and had been shot down by Israeli fighter planes on February 21, because its pilot—a Frenchman—had neither realized his navigational error nor had been able to understand the orders of the Israeli pilots to set down at the Refidim air base. At the time, Israel had been on the alert for a kamikaze raid over one of its cities; a raid the intelligence services had got wind of through a reliable source.

During the Tripoli meeting, the *Queen Elizabeth II* had also been mentioned as a possible target for future action.

On April 4 two Black September terrorists were arrested in Rome, armed with revolvers and grenades. Members of the Qaddafi "mission," they had been preparing to attack an El Al plane as it stood on the runway. The day after their arrest, two Black September commandos had arrived in England with an order from their clandestine headquarters: "Sabotage the *Queen Elizabeth!*" Scotland Yard had got wind of their mission.

The British and Israelis feared more than a symbolic strike by Palestinian terrorists under these orders. They knew of the Tripoli meeting and of the targets that had been mentioned there. British intelligence feared some irrational act by Qaddafi himself; such as an order to some Arab submarine stationed in the Mediterranean: "Sink the *Queen Elizabeth!*" As a result, Captain Hyer had received orders to keep as far from the North African coast as possible, and the Lightning aircraft increased their surveillance of the sea depths.

In his book, *The Road to Ramadan,* Hassanein Heykal, a former intimate of Nasser, was to relate in detail Qaddafi's attempt to use an Egyptian submarine to sink the *Queen Elizabeth II.* According to his story, on April 17 Colonel Qaddafi issued an order to the captain of a submarine which was stationed in Libyan waters under the accord between the two countries. The Egyptian captain reported the order to his superiors in Alexandria, who awakened President Sadat at 1:00 A.M. Sadat had immediately canceled the order to the submarine captain.

The facts were somewhat different. The submarine captain had been given the definite impression that he was acting on orders from his own president when he started for Malta on the mission transmitted by Qaddafi. The British planes had detected the submarine's movements and had informed the Admiralty. Prime Minister Edward Heath had been alerted and had requested the British ambassador in Cairo to awaken Sadat. At around 1:30 A.M. on April 18, Sadat's personal secretary had been informed of the British request.

President Sadat, who was then preparing his surprise military strike against Israel, had just changed the date of attack in light of the partial mobilization that had been ordered by "Dado" Elazar, the Tsahal chief of staff, and was anxious to avoid making any premature move that might precipitate a crisis that would thrust him into a disadvantageous position. Under these circumstances, he decided to recall his submarine and to stop it from going into action too hastily.

Upon arriving in Ashdod on April 21, the ship was met by Israeli Minister of Transportation Shimon Peres, whose wife Sonia was among the passengers aboard. To the journalists who besieged him with questions, Ben-Gurion's faithful adjutant replied:

"All this publicity about the security measures for Israel's twenty-fifth anniversary is, as usual, an exaggeration by the press. You can see that the *Queen* has arrived without the slightest incident."

While the *Queen Elizabeth II,* safe and sound, was dropping anchor at Ashdod, the *France,* on one of its last voyages, was stationed in Haifa Bay not far from the glittering lights of a small flotilla deployed in the middle of the port: the Cherbourg gunboats.

14

THE UMBRELLAS
OF CHERBOURG

Night had fallen early on this Christmas Eve. Standing before the window of room 214 of the Sofitel in Cherbourg, a tall man puffed on his pipe as he observed the stormy gray sea through the curtain of rain. He was nervous. He had wanted the five gunboats to make their stealthy departure in daylight, precisely at 4:00 P.M.

He had just arrived from Paris, on the stroke of noon, in his black Jaguar, bearing the license plate 59 CD 59. He had asked for a room and filled out his registration form without concealing his identity: "Name: Limon. First name: Mordechai. Age: 46. Nationality: Israeli. Profession: Diplomat." Once in his room, he summoned Colonel Ezra Koshinsky, a strapping, quiet-looking man, a ready smile under his thick moustache and known in Eilat by his nickname Karish ("The Shark").

Karish was categorical: the sea was rough and, above all, the weather report from the meteorological station at Southampton, with which he was in contact, had forecast a wind from the south-southeast positively horrendous for crossing the Gulf of Gascony. He didn't want to risk being held up off the French coast.

Admiral Limon, head of the Israeli purchasing mission and a delegate of the Ministry of Defense in Paris, stared glumly at his interlocutor. The sea was the sea, period. He knew what the sea was like. Let the sailors face the squall; after all, that was their trade! He hadn't come all the way to Cherbourg driving an embassy car at the risk of compromising the diplomatic relations between France and Israel to meditate on the splendors of the ocean. His job was to get five boats secretly off to Haifa.

At 5:00 P.M. he decided to force events. He ordered responsible heads of the operation to round up the ninety or so Israeli sailors scattered in the port and to be ready to set sail in less than an hour. The sailors were still in the dark about the whole affair. All they knew was that, one day or another, the five gunboats which they had been maintaining for six months would certainly wind up in Israel. And they had made no secret of this fact to anyone who cared to listen—including the informants of the French political police.

A first, unobtrusive familiarization run began in rain-soaked Cherbourg. The Israeli officers categorically refused to put to sea. They were becoming increasingly concerned about sailing conditions. Limon gave in. He asked only that the men in command of the operation remain on alert and specifically ordered that, lull or not, the boats would have to be gone by dawn.

As if none of this were happening, the Israeli sailors prepared to participate in the Christmas Eve midnight supper of the "goyim," making reservations for eighty-eight men at the Café du Théâtre and ordered bottles of champagne to be kept on ice. Cherbourg is not so droll under its umbrellas.

At 7:30 P.M. the Southampton station announced a possible lull. Admiral Limon rushed into the meteorological breach and ordered the boats to clear the decks and steer out of the harbor. The ensuing din and glare of lights did not worry him. The export permit, bearing a favorable recommendation from the Board of Directors of Customs, had arrived from Paris on December 18. The official forwarding agent of the shipyards owned by the Constructions Mécaniques de Normandie, that had been building these boats under German license for five years, had received customs clearance several days later. And he had notified customs of the imminent sailing date. Everything was in order—except that the consignee was not supposed to be Israel.

At the beginning, in 1965, the Israeli Ministry of Defense had indeed placed an order with the Cherbourg shipyards for the construction of twelve missile-launcher vedette boats, for the needs of its navy, based on designs drawn up and patented by the Lursen firm in Bremen. At that time, the German government had political reasons for not allowing the boats to be built in the Hamburg shipyards. The chairman of the board of the Normandy firm was delighted to profit from the windfall.

The first boat, equipped with a 14000 HP diesel engine hitting speeds in excess of 40 knots, was launched on April 11, 1967 as a "patrol boat." The Israelis transformed it into a gunboat by equipping it themselves with sea-to-sea missiles of their own design, with a range of 11 nautical miles and baptized "Gabriel."

The embargo on arms deliveries to Israel, imposed by General de Gaulle on the eve of the Six-Day War, was partially lifted, and the Amiot shipyards were able to deliver five more boats in 1968. But on January 2, 1969, de Gaulle decided to revert to a total embargo against Israel. Several days earlier, a helicopter-borne Israeli commando unit had seized the Beirut airport in retaliation for an attack on an El Al plane in Athens by PFLP terrorists who had come from Lebanon. While the commando unit destroyed thirteen planes of the Arab airlines without firing a shot, its chief, General "Raful," calmly sipped a cup of coffee at the bar in the airport lounge.

On the day following the new embargo, a seventh gunboat, whose paint job had not been finished and whose engines were not properly run in, set out from the Cherbourg dockyard for a trial run and never returned. Its arrival in Haifa provoked the wrath of the French government, which demanded sanctions. The port authority refused thenceforth to accept, within the enclosure of the military port, new ships built by the Amiot shipyards because they involved foreign ships for which the French Navy did not wish to be held responsible. (Because they were without military armaments, they could not be held to be warships.) Thus arose an admirable ambiguity: nobody—neither the Maritime Administration nor the harbormaster—knew to what authority, civil or military, the gunboats were answerable upon leaving the shipyards!

In September 1969 Rear Admiral Benny Telem, deputy chief of staff of the Israeli Navy, arrived in France, ostensibly to accompany a member of his family to Lyon to undergo an operation for cataracts. He took advantage of the occasion to unobtrusively slip over to Cherbourg to verify the intelligence received from his services that the gunboats were in fact berthed alongside the commercial port which was not subject to the surveillance of the naval yard. The launching of the last of the five gunboats awaiting completion was set for December 14.

The bold subterfuge was ready to be carried out at the beginning of November. Admiral Limon wrote to M. Amiot that his government, against reimbursement of the partial advance payment, was willing to relinquish its rights to the gunboats, whose delivery had been blocked by the French embargo. Coincidentally, on October 13 the chairman of the board of the Cherbourg shipyards had received a most fortuitous offer from a prospective buyer who was willing to pay cash: a Norwegian businessman of impeccable reputation. Ole Martin Siem, chairman of the Aker Company, well known in shipping circles, had suddenly manifested a keen interest in these boats which the Israelis no longer wanted. He wanted to acquire them on behalf of Starboat, a Panamanian company involved in offshore oil explorations near the coast of Alaska. Moreover, he had met with Admiral Limon to discuss the matter and had disclosed that he was prepared to pay $55 million for the boats which would allow M. Amiot to reimburse the Israelis for the $22 million they had advanced.

The only task that remained was obtaining the authorization from the interministerial commission that controlled the exportation of armaments. It met in Paris on November 18, under the chairmanship of General Bernard Cazelles, Secretary-General of National Defense. Inspector-General Louis Bonte briefed him on the report he had received from his deputy, General de Montplanet, to whom M. Amiot had submitted the contract. After ascertaining that the boats relinquished by the Israeli clients were "warships without military armaments" and that they were anchored off a civilian dock, the commission authorized their resale to the third-party company which agreed to pay with two checks drawn up in dollars: one of them on the Discount Bank of Geneva.

Perhaps this last detail should have aroused the suspicions of the French authorities, but they seemed unaware that behind Mr. Siem stood his close friend, Mila Brenner, an Israeli citrus exporter and the principal stockholder of the *Arias Fabrega y Fabrega* of Panama, whose three attorneys conveniently established the Starboat Company which had been entered in the maritime register on November 5, 1969. Since Panama, the fiscal paradise for ships flying flags of convenience, is not very particular in such matters, it had sufficed to give this phantom company a slightly Norwegian appearance, with the complicity of Siem, who provided it with a simple postal address in that country: No. 25078, Soli-Oslo 2.

The preparations to spirit away the boats continued, smoothly, but in strict accordance with the rules, for it was still necessary to wait for the launching of the fifth gunboat on December 16. On that day the boats were officially transferred to the Starboat Company. Nameplates, "Starboat 1," "Starboat 2," etc., were hastily prepared. A seamstress from Equeurdreville was commissioned to make some Norwegian flags, but there wouldn't be time for them to be of any use. On December 18, 1969, everything was finally shipshape for the castoff.

And on Christmas Eve, while the prefectural, harbor, customs, and police administrations, whose personnel had been reduced to a minimum by the four-day holiday, dozed peacefully, twenty diesel engines boomed loudly in the Atlantic harbor. Ten power plants cast a garish light on the boats and on the quays. Couriers rounded up the sailors in their rooming houses, in the bars, and at the Hotel Tourville and the Hotel Atlantic (owned by M. Amiot). It was no mystery to them: they were setting out for Haifa. They knew it and they said so openly. They packed their kits and dashed off in the rain to the illuminated quay. At 9:00 P.M. all was ready, except for the stormy sea. The girlfriends of the Israeli sailors, who had accompanied them to the quay under their delicate umbrellas, grew weary of waiting.

At 2:00 A.M. the wind veered north. Admiral Limon gave the final order. All of their lights switched on, and, flying no flags, the gunboats put to sea. In exactly seventeen minutes they had cleared port through the western exit past the Homet watchtower. Nobody noticed them—even more surprising was the fact that, officially, not a single soul signaled the departure of the fugitive flotilla.

Admiral Limon calmly returned to the Sofitel, woke up the dozing receptionist, and paid his bill. An odd customer, as the clerk was to comment later, unable to fathom why one should take a room in order not to sleep in it. The Jaguar with the diplomat's plate set out on the road to Paris, where it arrived on Christmas morning.

What high French military authorities two days later were to call "The Cherbourg Cover-Up" had been successfully accomplished. For Admiral Limon, this kind of escapade, carried out with the requisite bravura, had become almost an old routine.

A sabra (native-born Israeli) from Tel Aviv, Limon had studied at the Palmach's clandestine naval school before toiling in the British merchant marine during the war. In 1946 he arrived in Marseille, where he captained illegal transports smuggling European Jews to Palestine. Each time his ship had been stopped and inspected, Limon managed to elude his captors by jumping overboard. In 1948 he conveyed the first transport of Czech arms for the War of Independence. In August of the same year, at the helm of a warship equipped with old French cannons, nicknamed "Napoleonchiks" because of their decrepitude, he had diverted a transport of arms, also of Czech manufacture, destined for Syria, making use of a fictitious steamship company set up in Rome by the Jewish Special Services.

When the news of the escape of the gunboats from Cherbourg was revealed three days later, the French Ministry of Defense issued a clumsy denial: "They were civilian vessels which were the object of a legitimate transfer to a Norwegian company." The Norwegian embassy made it known that the Starboat Company was not listed in the commercial register and that the gunboats, spotted off the coast of Portugal, had no right to hoist the Norwegian flag—which Colonel "Karish" had carefully avoided doing. These boats were as suitable for offshore oil drilling as a Porsche for hauling a plow.

"We have exposed ourselves to ridicule because of the incredible levity and the intellectual complicity of our functionaries!" thundered Georges Pompidou during a meeting of the Council of Ministers on December 31, where it was decided to dismiss Inspector-General Bonte, to suspend General Cazelles, and to demand that Israel recall Admiral Limon. At the same hour, Moshe Dayan was giving a heroes' welcome to the "Shark"'s five gunboats in Haifa. They had been refueled twice on the high seas by a Norwegian oil tanker chartered by Mossad agent Dan Arbel, who, three years later, was to be involved in the Lillehammer mishap.

A collective complicity was discovered in France which went quite beyond the old interpenetration of the French and Israeli secret services, denounced in the Council by Georges Pompidou, and called in question the embargo policy applied to Israel. But the questioning was so general that it did not prompt the responsible authorities to examine the files.

The "Cherbourg Cover-Up" and Admiral Limon's Norwegian umbrella effectively underscored the commandolike aspect of a diplomacy that did not unduly trouble itself with the rules of the traditional game when Israel's vital interests were at stake. And those interests were threatened at the beginning of the 1970s in the face of the Komar and Ossa missile-launcher warships which the Russians had delivered to Egypt and to Syria.

Equipped with Israeli Gabriel missiles, self-guided by electronic radar and superior to the Soviet Styx missiles, the gunboats constituted a tactical answer to the presence of the Russian fleet in the Mediterranean. In the first hours of the Yom Kippur War, in the first missile duel in history, they were to give a decisive advantage to Israel's navy, which had hitherto been considered the poor relation of the Israeli armed forces. And they gave Israel total mastery of the seas with no losses whatsoever. Contrastingly, on the ground, as in the sky, Israel took three days to reassert her supremacy.

As the tiny flotilla that had escaped from Cherbourg was still sailing somewhere in the Atlantic in the direction of Gibraltar, another operation à la James Bond was unfolding on the Egyptian coast of the Gulf of Suez, 200 kilometers south of the Canal. On the evening of December 26, 1969, a commando unit organized in the Sinai by the new chief of staff, General Chaim Bar-Lev, succeeded in completely dismantling a giant Soviet radar unit, after neutralizing its guards and crew. The radar unit, unknown in the West, was capable of detecting low-flying planes, and it was linked to a SAM 2 surface-to-air missile installation set up several kilometers distant from the site. Two helicopters were able to transport the seven tons of components of the radar installation to Israel, where it was reassembled and functioned perfectly.

This was the first major blow in the escalation of the war of attrition which was to pit the Russians and Israelis against each other for the first time.

15

BLACK SEPTEMBER FOR MOSCOW

"Give 'em hell!" Kissinger said to Israeli Ambassador Rabin. And hell broke out several days later over the Suez Canal. On July 30, 1970, two Israeli Mirage jets took off in the direction of the Canal.

It was not a routine patrol. Here, on the Suez Canal, for almost eighteen months, firing had continued without letup. The Israeli planes had become part of the landscape, but they were no longer the unchallenged masters of the skies.

On July 25, 1970, several Soviet-piloted MIG-21s which had made their appearance five days earlier in the Canal Zone, had suddenly loomed on the horizon and swooped down on two Israeli Skyhawk jet fighters above the Gulf of Suez. One of the Israeli planes had been hit but it managed to return to its base, as did the other Skyhawk. This was the first armed confrontation pitting Russians against Israelis.

Five days later, the two Mirage jets took off in the direction of the Canal, seemingly on a routine reconnaissance mission over Egyptian artillery positions which had once more opened fire on the Israeli lines. The two Mirage jets were flying slowly at low altitude. Above the Gulf of Suez, they suddenly banked in the direction of the exact spot where the two Skyhawks had been intercepted by the Soviet MIGs on July 25. Their pilots sighted twelve MIG-21s rushing headlong at them. At that precise moment, the trap set by the young Israeli colonel—one of the country's best pilots to whom the operation had been entrusted—closed in according to plan. Eight Phantom jet fighters suddenly nosedived into the fray. Cannons, missiles, rockets, nosedives—an intricate geometry traced its design against an imperturbable azure sky at a speed of 1,500 mph. The Israeli pilots were masters in these aerial combats where nothing was left to chance. With training and technical mastery far more important than sophisticated military equipment, four MIGs were downed in less than a minute. A fifth tried to return to its base in the Egyptian interior, but minutes later it, too, was downed. Two of the Russian pilots had managed to activate their ejector seats and open their parachutes. The Israeli radio operators tuned in to the same wavelength were astonished to overhear them swear in Russian, "Those Jewish bastards!" The two Mirages which had served as bait and the young colonel's eight Phantoms returned to their base safely. The Israeli Air Force remained the symbol of a country in which it was very satisfying to think that quality would excel over quantity for a long time.

"Right from the outset of the battle," as one twenty-four-year-old Phantom pilot, a former economics student who later became a squadron commander, tells the story, "the two Mirages and the eight Phantoms that had hovered in the background streaked off in pursuit of the MIGs that had climbed to an altitude of 20,000 feet. On my right I saw an air-to-air missile fired by one of the two Mirages score a hit on the first MIG. It caught fire in seconds. I banked to the right and saw one of the MIGs—about 7,500 feet away—swooping down on me. I swung to the left and it was then that I realized that the Soviet pilot, despite the initial advantage of his position, was totally lacking in experience. He had committed two elementary blunders: first, he tried to avoid combat, and then he nosedived from an altitude of 6,000 feet. Above him, at an altitude of 4,500 feet, I regulated my radar and fired a missile. I hit him with the first try, and I saw him disappear in the cloud of the explosion. The other Russian pilots made the same error. This combat, which engaged a total of twenty-two planes, proved to us that the Soviet teachers were no better than their Arab pupils."

The event was a disaster for the Soviet Air Force. It has been the first aerial combat since the end of World War II in 1945. Several days later, the Mossad reports described the joy expressed by Arab pilots in the Egyptian air bases, commenting on the loss of the five supersonic planes:

"The Russians have always complained about our professional incompetence to explain the superiority of the Israeli Mirage and Phantom jets over their MIGs, which they claim are the best fighter planes in the world. Now that the Israelis are beginning to bring down Soviet-piloted MIGs, it just proves Russian planes are inferior, not Egyptian pilots."

The Soviet aerial defeat of July 30, 1970, was not made public, but joy was undiminished at the White House. When Rabin phoned Kissinger with a detailed account of the results of the confrontation, which Bar-Lev had immediately relayed to him, Kissinger told one of his aides:

"Terrific! The Russians will understand the lesson."

The Israeli intelligence services—the Mossad and Aman—were attentively watching for the Soviet reaction. The very next day,

Marshal Pavel Kutakhov, chief of the Soviet Air Force, landed in Cairo to conduct a personal inquiry into the conditions surrounding this disastrous engagement. He shook his head, repeating over and over again, *"Katastropha! Katastropha!"*

On August 2 Kutakhov ordered the withdrawal of the Russian pilots from the Suez Canal Zone. Obviously, the Russians had no intention of risking the humiliation of a second defeat. In Moscow, meanwhile, the Politburo decided, by a strong majority, to avoid any armed confrontation with the Americans; in fact, the KGB was convinced that the aerial ambush of July 30 had been given the green light by the United States. It was not far wrong.

The Israeli leaders had cause for rejoicing. On the day following the first aerial incident, which had occurred five days after the Russian planes had penetrated the Canal Zone, Golda Meir assembled a group of close aides and ministers in her "kitchen" to discuss the new situation. According to Mossad intelligence reports, the USSR had sent its best pilots to Egypt: men who had hundreds of hours of flight time on supersonic fighters to their credit. They had undergone intensive training to familiarize themselves with European weather conditions and were perfectly adapted to flying in bad weather and to the problems of aerial combat in the clouds. In the altogether different climate of the Mediterranean, however, they used the same strategies and the same maneuvers without the slightest deviation. Commenting on this Mossad study, dubbed "Kosher Salami" because of the way Soviet pilots were nibbling away at the famous "red line," the limit fixed by Dayan on the West Bank of the Canal beyond which the enemy was forbidden to cross, General Motti Hod, chief of the Israeli Air Force, explained to Golda, "The Russian pilots are perfectly orthodox in their maneuvers, but they suffer from a serious handicap in relation to us: none of them has been in a real combat situation since World War II. Therefore we are not afraid of the eventuality of a confrontation."

What was to be done? Was it necessary to wait for the cease-fire proposed by the Americans, and recently accepted by Nasser, to come into effect on the Canal without reacting to the Soviet aerial provocation? Such was the suggestion advanced by Dayan, who was haunted by his fear of the "Reds." Or should the Soviets be taught a bitter lesson, as proposed by General Bar-Lev, whose Yugoslav origins seemed to have immunized him against the fear of Russian power? But more than the desire for revenge on the part of the general staff was to influence Golda's dramatic decision. She received another report citing the dissensions between the

Egyptian president and the Kremlin masters on the eventuality of a cease-fire. Any success on the part of the Soviet Air Force would have the effect of prolonging the war by permitting the Russians to install themselves directly in the Canal Zone.

"They are going to penetrate even more deeply," added the Mossad specialists, "and they will be as bold as we allow them to be."

On the next day, in fact, encouraged by this Russian presence in the region, the Egyptians undertook their biggest aerial attack against the positions of the Bar-Lev Line since the War of Attrition. Convinced, on July 30 Golda Meir gave her approval to the general staff's already prepared operational plan to lure the Russians into a trap.

This decision to shoot down Russian planes constituted one of the more difficult moments of 1970—a year fertile with events of a critical nature—and it marked a turning point in the history of the Middle East: the counterthrust to Soviet penetration.

Due to the costly successes that Israel had scored in the last phase of the War of Attrition, from January to August, and to the special and secret ties that had been established between Rabin and Kissinger, which had influenced Israeli policy and American strategy, the Soviets, who had already suffered a series of setbacks in Cambodia, China, Cuba, and Poland, were also checkmated on the most important square of the Middle Eastern chessboard. And Israel, this time confident of her position as the only and indispensable U.S. ally in the region, was able to afford the luxury of saving King Hussein's throne in Jordan and, after an interval of a few months, the regime of Nasser's successor, Egyptian president Anwar Sadat!

It had all begun with the War of Attrition—Israel's fourth war—triggered in March 1969 by Egyptian artillery shelling against the east bank of the Canal. Egypt had better trumps for playing this kind of trench warfare game than did Israel, whose morale and economy could be adversely affected in the long term by the steadily rising casualty figures and the endless reinforcement of a defensive posture along the entire length of the Canal. This trench warfare would lead Tsahal into disavowing all its traditional strategic concepts by slowly entrenching itself under the artillery bombardments and drawing on its reserves.

Believing that the application of sufficient pressure would oblige Israel to maintain a large enough force of civilian soldiers in active service to unbalance her economy, Nasser ordered continuous bombardment of the east bank. By reinforcing the shelters, little by little, the Israelis had turned them into veritable concrete bunkers, solidly buttressed by the railroad tracks of the old El-Kantara-Gaza line. The construction took months, mobilized thousands of workers, and ended up enriching a number of farsighted entrepreneurs.

It was this line of fortification, 160 kilometers in length, that was to be named the Bar-Lev Line, after the chief of staff on active duty at the time. Its construction was to cost the country between $200 and $400 million, deprive the Israelis of concrete for months, and foster the scandalous speculation of a few opportunists. Once completed, however, the Bar-Lev Line would allow soldiers on sentry duty to relax with a degree of comfort superior to that enjoyed by American troops in Vietnam and would supply the generals of Tsahal with a brand-new doctrine: the use of reinforced concrete. Engineering corps units, subcontracting from commercial companies formed for this specific project, built a formidable sand dike 45 to 75 feet high and 600 feet wide between the small forts of the forward positions and the Canal itself. Countless tons of sand had been piled onto it, but it also contained the fatigue of days of combat and nights of vigil, and it was going to engulf all the illusions of the 1967 victory. It represented a new freedom from anxiety, and perhaps also an excessive contempt for what might be transpiring on the other side of this sand curtain. This geometric dune was to serve as a kind of blind by blocking out the landscape. It clearly signified that under the shade cast by the Bar-Lev Line, Israel was at last to live a time of normalcy by closing her eyes and ears.

Strictly speaking, it was not a defense line: rather, it consisted of outposts of a complex system that included artillery, tanks, aviation, underground hospitals, and other facilities. Hence it had nothing in common with the French Maginot Line, save for the fact that immediately after the harassment of the War of Attrition, which was to cost the lives of more than 400 Israeli soldiers, the Bar-Lev Line would quickly become the symbol of illusory security.

In December 1969 the Tsahal general staff realized that without the massive use of aircraft to carry this war of attrition deep inside Egyptian territory, there would be no chance of bringing about a cease-fire. Defense Minister Dayan opposed the idea for fear of provoking a Soviet response to the bombing of Egypt. Rabin, who was in charge of sounding out the Americans, apprised his government that though a formal guarantee was impossible to obtain, he was familiar with Kissinger's thoughts on the matter, and an aerial penetration deep into Egyptian territory would have his consent.

However, Kissinger was not an expert on the Middle East: before becoming Nixon's adviser in December 1968, he had never set foot in an Arab country and had made only two visits to Israel as a private citizen. Occupied as he was with drawing up a new Vietnam policy, restructuring the National Security Council, and coordinating overall relations with the Soviet Union—including the question of strategic arms limitations— he officially left the Israeli-Arab problem to Secretary of State William Rogers and his deputy for Mideast affairs, Joseph Sisco. But he never concealed his personal sympathy for the Jewish State.

Paradoxically, Rogers and Sisco were then in the process of presenting to the parties to the conflict, as well as to the USSR, a peace plan essentially based on the return of Israeli-occupied territories. Their proposals, agreed to in principle by the Soviets, were still based on a timetable for Israeli withdrawal, the guarantee of Israel's security, the rights of the Palestinians, and the status of Jerusalem. The Rogers Plan had been made public on December 9.

Kissinger deemed its publication inopportune. In his opinion, one could negotiate with the Soviets only from a position of strength. If an accord was to be imposed on Israel, an ally of the United States, and on Egypt, an ally of the USSR, Israel must first be allowed to put an end to the War of Attrition. Far from making the smallest effort to support the Rogers Plan, Kissinger let Rabin understand that the United States would not oppose Israeli bombardments—even at the risk of provoking the Soviets. In fact, Kissinger possessed a CIA report on Brezhnev's aggressive intentions in both the Middle East and in Vietnam.

As a result of its ambassador's report, the government in Jerusalem decided to deal with the White House directly and in secret from then on, bypassing the State Department. It approved Bar-Lev's plan to bomb strategic objectives in the interior of Egypt, far beyond the Canal.

On January 7, 1970, the Israeli Air Force launched its first lightning raid against the Inchas military camp, 30 kilometers north of Cairo. On January 13 the Kauka base, 20 kilometers from the capital, was attacked. On January 22 a Tsahal unit stormed and occupied the island of Shadwan in the Gulf of Suez.

On that day, a panic-stricken Nasser flew secretly to Moscow to demand increased military aid. It was the occasion Brezhnev had been waiting for to hoist himself back in the saddle. The crushing defeat of his Arab clients in the Six-Day War had prevented him from seizing absolute power in the Kremlin, with the aid of Marshal Grechko. Grechko managed to escape criticism by accusing his deceased predecessor in the Defense Ministry, Marshal Malinovsky, of inadequate preparation of the Arab armies; the subordinates paid for the shortcomings of their superiors, and the status quo was preserved in the Politburo in order to keep the Brezhnev-Kosygin tandem on an equal footing. Brezhnev subsequently took advantage of the defeat of the Czech revolution in August 1968 to resume the offensive by exacerbating world tension in Southeast Asia, Korea, and, of course, in the Middle East. He encouraged Nasser to undertake the War of Attrition, while attempting to replace him with a more docile leader, Ali Sabri. More devoted to the cause of socialism than Nasser, Sabri was the head of the Arab Socialist Union. Finally, Brezhnev sabotaged the Rogers Plan, which was favorable to the Arabs, by laying down a series of conditions which the Americans found simply impossible to meet.

With the support of the faithful Grechko, Brezhnev offered Nasser a complete aerial cover: batteries of SAM 2 and SAM 3 surface-to-air missiles manned by Soviet crews, Soviet-piloted MIG 21s, and military advisers to officer his army troops up to the company level. He had convinced his hesitant colleagues in the Politburo that it was necessary to dispatch Russian soldiers to Egypt by skillfully exploiting the incident of the radar installation that had been ingeniously spirited away by Israeli commandos because the Egyptians had failed to guard it properly.

For the price of his assistance, Brezhnev asked Nasser to reinstate Sabri to the post of secretary-general in the Arab Socialist Union and groom him to be his successor. But Nasser would permit only a reinstatement, to take effect in March. Promoting the man who had attempted to usurp his place was hardly in order.

On January 25, 1970, while Nasser was concluding his secret deal with Moscow, Rabin secretly met with Kissinger in the White House, without the knowledge of the State Department, which seethed with indignation over the Israeli raids into Egypt's interior. Kissinger was informed of Nasser's trip by the CIA, and Rabin was informed by the head of Aman, Aharon Yariv. Yariv continued to send him reports from the army's intelligence service, just as General Zvi Zamir continued to keep him abreast of all the operations being conducted by the Mossad—an exceptional privilege enjoyed by no other Israeli ambassador. Doubtless it was this privilege that made the former chief of staff of the Israeli armed forces the much-appreciated interlocutor of both Kissinger and the

Pentagon. Rabin was literally captivated by the loftiness of the views expressed by Nixon's adviser, who was more sensitized than others to the interplay of international events among the world powers.

Kissinger unhesitatingly consented to Rabin's request for the delivery of delayed-action bombs, instead of the additional Phantom jets which had been denied by Nixon.

On February 6 Kissinger persuaded Nixon to reply firmly to a letter from Kosygin asking the United States to use its influence to halt Israeli aggression against Egyptian territory. In fact, it was Kissinger who used his growing influence over Nixon to wrest the monopoly of their Middle East mission from the Rogers-Sisco team and influenced Nixon "to reestablish the credibility of the United States" by ordering the invasions of Cambodia two months later.

In March and April the Russians actually began to assume a direct operational role in the defense of Egypt. They ringed Cairo with their batteries of SAM 2s and SAM 3s, manned by their own crews. Their pilots patrolled the sky above the Egyptian capital.

On April 18 at the hour when Jews traditionally gather in the bosom of their families to celebrate Passover, the miraculous exodus of their ancestors from bondage in Egypt, two Israeli Mirage fighter jets on a reconnaissance mission over Egyptian territory spotted eight MIGs that seemed to be escorting them. The pilots heard the instructions the flight commander openly gave in Russian to the squadron. It was as if the Soviets were deliberately bent upon making their presence known to the Israelis. The message was clear: "Watch out! We are here!"

The two Israeli pilots relayed this message when they returned to their base. Dayan took the Soviet threat seriously and ordered the immediate halt of air raids beyond the Canal Zone. He publicly announced a "red line" 30 kilometers west of the Canal beyond which Israeli planes were not to venture as long as Soviet pilots refrained from crossing it from the other direction. This decision infuriated Kissinger.

"Don't be afraid of those bastards!" he told Rabin. "Why unilaterally give up your penetration raids? You should have let me negotiate an agreement on the matter, and I would have extorted some concessions from the Egyptians in exchange. Dayan doesn't know the Russians!"

Dayan also gave Kissinger the impression that he (Dayan) didn't understand the Americans either. Dayan believed that they were too busy in Vietnam—and, in May, too concerned about

Cambodia—to worry about Soviet intervention in the Middle East. He had realized that the Israeli penetration raids, as was to be expected, had provoked the Russians into installing a network of antiaircraft missiles that subsequently would have opportunities to prove their effectiveness. What Dayan had always feared most came to pass: the direct involvement of the Soviets in the Israeli-Arab conflict.

Kissinger's strategy began to take shape. On April 29 he succeeded in obtaining from Nixon direct control of American policy in the Middle East and was asked to evaluate the situation in the Middle East in the face of the Soviet war effort. Kissinger's reflections concentrated on the balance of power, the strategy of the two superpowers, and the risks of a world war kindled by the sparks of local conflicts.

On June 26 Kissinger delivered his "raw" conclusions to a group of top-flight editors invited to San Clemente. He told his listeners that the geopolitical framework of the Israeli-Arab conflict reminded him of the Balkans at the beginning of the century:

> The nightmare is that no one wanted World War I, except, at one particular moment, Austria and Serbia. All the leaders of major countries went on vacation in July 1914; on their return, they found themselves involved in a widespread conflict. Today the powder keg is no longer in the Balkans, but in the Middle East. . . . An open-ended war of attrition means in essence that Israel will be destroyed. Consequently, the Israelis must aim for tactical superiority. Now the Soviets are injecting their own troops into the region. Their presence, regardless of their intentions, represents a long-term threat to Western Europe and Japan and, therefore, to us.

In Kissinger's view, the threat was that subversion by extremist groups in Jordan and Lebanon, encouraged by the Russians, would endanger Saudi Arabia, ever vulnerable to a coup d'état, and, in particular, her oil reserves as well as those of the emirates of the Persian Gulf, and ultimately those of Iran. The region's wealth and strategic value would ultimately be denied to the West and would inevitably shift the balance of power to the Soviet Union.

"We are trying to expel the Soviet military presence," he concluded—emphasizing the verb *expel*—"not so much the advisers, but the combat pilots and the combat personnel [before they become firmly established]."

Expel! Two days later, the word made the front page of the *Washington Post.* This altogether unorthodox diplomacy had a quality about it that delighted Ambassador Rabin and disquieted Ambassador Dobrynin. But, above all, it sowed panic in the State Department where only a week before, Secretary of State Rogers had proposed to Egypt, Israel, and the USSR, a ninety-day cease-fire on the Suez Canal formulated in two parts: "Stop shooting and start talking." Did Kissinger's verbal bombshell risk sabotaging the initiative? To some extent, this was precisely what Kissinger had in mind: he feared that the Russians would permanently install themselves in Egypt during a cease-fire.

The artillery duels on the ground and the aerial bombardments proceeded at a pace that smacked of a real war. Toward the end of June, in the course of a military operation mounted and controlled by the Soviets, the Egyptians, in the space of one night, managed to install a dozen batteries of SAM 3s along the Canal. Now Brezhnev no longer wanted an immediate cease-fire any more than did Kissinger. Brezhnev was bent on achieving a clear military resolution to the matter at hand.

But such calculations failed to include Nasser, who lived in fear of imminent disaster. On June 14 he declared over American television that he was ready to agee to a ceasefire. On April 29 he flew to Moscow to discuss the new Rogers initiative. Two Kremlin leaders, Kosygin and Podgorny, favored the cease-fire. As the guiding spirits of the moderate camp, they were forever looking for a policy which would permit the USSR, through an opening to the West and through the dissolution of the two antagonistic pacts, Warsaw and NATO, to reduce the burden of military outlay, to increase the production of consumer goods, and to come to terms with the Chinese peril. But the third leader, Brezhnev, saw to it that the talks dragged on. Nasser's stay was extended: nineteen days instead of five. In part, the extension was due to the treatment that he was scheduled to undergo at the Barvikha Clinic near Moscow; in part, it was due to the differences between Brezhnev and Kosygin over the appropriate action to be taken vis-à-vis the Rogers proposal.

On July 18 Nasser finally returned to Cairo after promising his mentors to do everything possible to gain time. But, four days later, he suddenly informed the American ambassador that he agreed to the cease-fire. Surprised, the Soviets were forced to follow suit on July 23.

Brezhnev was furious. He ordered the head of the KGB to find out why the intelligence services had not been aware earlier of Nasser's decision, so diametrically opposed to what had been agreed upon in Moscow. What was Sami Sharaf, Moscow's man and the head of the Egyptian secret services, doing all that time at the presidential palace? And the Russian doctors who had been supervising Nasser's medical treatment? And, finally, what about Ali Sabri's pro-Soviet group, now reinstated in positions close to the seat of power?

Soon afterward, the Soviet Air Force moved into action in the Canal Zone.

Kissinger told the Israelis:

"Give 'em hell! If they advance on the ground, we won't stay idle."

On the day of their aerial victory, the Israelis, in turn, agreed to the cease-fire, which was not to go into effect until August 7, because of another dispute between Sisco and Kissinger over its implementation. One of the clauses provided for the total prohibition of any troop movement or of any military reinforcement in a 50-kilometer zone on either side of the Canal.

On August 8 the Egyptians and the Soviets began to construct new missile sites close to the Canal, openly advancing the already-existing batteries. Rabin provided photographic proof to Kissinger. But four weeks went by before Rogers and Sisco acknowledged the violations. Skeptical about the chances of a further Soviet withdrawal, Kissinger told Rabin, "If you think that these violations are too dangerous for you, all you have to do is bomb those silos and missile bases!"

A temporary estrangement ensued between Israel and the United States, but the family quarrel was brief. The following month, the Russians hurled a new challenge at the West by kindling the fire that suddenly ignited another country of the Middle East "battlefield," the kingdom of Jordan.

The dubious test of strength between Palestinians, Syrians, and Jordanians that began there on September 1 rapidly became the mirror image of the global power play between Brezhnev and Kissinger. A veritable civil war had been smoldering since June when the Hashemite sovereign and his army were drawn into conflict with the fedayeen organizations that controlled a part of the country where they had created independent institutions. New disorders erupted shortly after Hussein approved the Rogers Plan on July 23.

During a secret meeting on the shores of the Red Sea, Hussein had told Deputy Prime Minister Yigal Allon that he could not work toward a peace treaty between the two countries until he put an end to the threat to his kingdom represented by the Palestinian organizations on his territory, populated largely by the refugees of the 1948 and 1967 wars.

Moreover, Hussein was being vigorously pressed toward this confrontation by his Jordanian Legion and his Bedouins. Most of the high officers of the Jordanian Army could no longer endure the arrogance of the Palestinians, who had formed their own military police and controlled traffic at the approaches to the cities. They also feared that terrorist strikes beyond the Jordan River would provoke a new confrontation with Israel. The commandos of the different factions of the PLO—Al Fatah, especially—seemed determined to overthrow Hussein's pro-Western regime so that they could use Jordan as a base for raids against Israel, in addition to bases already established in South Lebanon and on the Syrian Golan Heights. Both the Mossad and Aman anxiously followed the evolution of the situation.

The general staff of Tsahal had presented Golda Meir with an assessment of the possibility of a bloody confrontation between the Jordanian Army and the fedayeen. At least one cabinet meeting, held one Sunday morning in Jerusalem, was devoted to a discussion of the options open to Israel in the event of a Palestinian victory in Amman. Yigal Allon told the gathering that he favored a military intervention to save the little king. Dayan exhibited an indifference to the fate of Hussein, whom he had never considered an ideal negotiating partner, but was hardly in favor of the even greater evil of Arafat's taking Hussein's place.

On the other hand, General Arik Sharon, the commander of the southern region, perceived an advantage in the establishment of a Palestinian government beyond the Jordan River because the Israeli-Palestinian problem would be reduced to a conflict between two states. But Sharon's interesting analysis had no chance of prevailing in midsummer 1970; after the installation of the SAM 2s and 3s on the Canal, a victory for Arafat in Amman would give rise to missile bases all along the Jordan River, an untenable threat to Israel.

In August Israeli Army intelligence reports clearly indicated the imminent clash between the Palestinians and Hussein's army. But the Israeli leaders, preoccupied with the crisis resulting from the presence of missiles in the Canal Zone in violation of the cease-fire accord, had diverted their attention from the eastern border. Meanwhile, Hussein had expressed his desire to rid himself of the Palestinians to the U.S. ambassador and to the CIA representative, who had already financed his "special operations." He told Nasser that he was not out to crush the Palestinian resistance but to uproot the subversive elements; a crackdown would allow him to dissociate the moderate Moslems of Al Fatah from the Christian revolutionaries of George Habash's PFLP and from Nayef Hawatmeh's leftist DPFLP.

Upon being informed of Hussein's intentions, Kissinger gave them his blessings through Richard Helms, the head of the CIA. All that remained to do was to choose the date of the operation. Thanks to the vast network of informants of the Rassad—the intelligence service of Al Fatah—the Palestinian leaders also knew what to expect, and they prepared for the oncoming explosion.

In Beirut, several weeks after the firing of a katyusha, which he miraculously escaped, in the feverish atmosphere of his residence in the fashionable Hamra quarter, Dr. Waddia Haddad, once more plotted Hussein's assassination. The king was his sworn enemy, and his assassination would bring about a seizure of power conforming to PFLP doctrine, which Arafat seemed at last to have endorsed: that the road to Tel Aviv passed through Amman. The operational plan drawn up in August by Haddad provided for two combined actions: one team would be assigned the job of laying an ambush for Hussein, while five other terrorist teams would simultaneously hijack five commercial airliners from different European airports. The assassination of the king and the arrival in the capital of hundreds of passengers of all nationalities, taken hostage aboard these planes, would give the signal for a popular uprising that would bring the PFLP to power.

Since he distrusted Arafat, Haddad did not want to make him a party to the plot. He preferred to entrust its execution to Hawatmeh's men, whose organization prevailed in certain quarters of the Jordanian capital and to his own PFLP commandos, who were to carry out the plane hijackings. But the Jordanian secret services uncovered the first half of the plot.

On September 1 in order to avert the assassination attempt against Hussein, who was scheduled to meet his daughter, Princess Alia, at the airport, the army launched a mopping-up operation against Palestinian concentrations on the periphery of Amman. The fighting raged for four days in the most crowded suburbs. But Hussein, not altogether sure of his chief of staff, General Mashur Hadita, who maintained good personal relations with Arafat, hesitated to go further and ordered a cease-fire.

Calm was barely restored when, on September 6, the PFLP commandos abroad carried out the corresponding phase of Waddia Haddad's plan. Under the direction of his confidante, the beautiful

Leila Khaled, four groups of terrorists seized four planes in flight, all bound for New York: a Pan Am Boeing 747 which had left Amsterdam with 171 passengers, a TWA Boeing 707 after takeoff from Frankfurt with 151 passengers, a Swissair DC 8 which had set out from Zurich with 155 passengers, and an El Al 707 which had taken aboard 145 passengers in London. The El Al plane was the only one not to be forcibly diverted from its course: the hijacking attempt, in which Leila Khaled personally took part, failed after an Israeli security agent managed to subdue the young woman, who had been wounded in the arm, after he had overcome her companion. Immediately handed over to the British authorities, the femme fatale of Palestinian terrorism was not to remain behind bars for long.

The Pan Am jumbo jet only got as far as Cairo, where it was blown up by the terrorists after they had freed the hostages. The Jordanian authorities permitted the two other planes to land at Dawson Airfield, an abandoned, former British airstrip in the middle of the Zarka Desert, 25 kilometers from Amman. They were joined three days later by a BOAC Viscount that had been hijacked between Bombay and London. In all, 477 hostages, most of them American tourists returning from vacations in Europe. The Jordanian military units dispatched to the abandoned airstrip where the hostages were roasting in the heat of the sun, threatened by their captors, stood by helplessly. Faced with this direct challenge to Hashemite sovereignty, King Hussein had been unable to prevent his kingdom from being used as a base by the hijackers. The TV networks of the whole world flashed the dramatic images of this ghastly poker game being played by the PFLP. As an opener, its spokesmen demanded the liberation of all Palestine terrorists jailed in Germany, Switzerland, and Israel. Jerusalem categorically refused to yield to the blackmail.

Thanks to the intervention of the UN, on September 12, the hostages left their sweltering prisons for internment in Palestinian camps in the area. The three planes were blown up immediately after their departure. The terrorists then freed most of the hostages, except for 56 Jewish passengers.

Meanwhile the fedayeen went on the offensive against the royal forces in their areas. On September 13 and 14 they seized the city of Irbid and gained control of nearly all of northern Jordan. Hawatmeh's DPFLP proclaimed the region's independence, the first step toward the total liberation of the country.

In Amman and in Zarka, a group of high-ranking Jordanian Army officers conferred secretly before pressuring Hussein to make a decision. Among them were officers of the Circassian tribes, one of whom had a brother in the Israeli Army. On September 15 at midnight, after the signing of a new cease-fire agreement between Arafat and their chief of staff, General Hadita, they proceeded to the royal palace and presented an ultimatum to Hussein. The little king agreed to declare a state of emergency and to form a military government, at the head of which he placed the highest-ranking Palestinian officer in the Jordanian Army: General Mohammed Daoud. The real powers were concentrated in the hands of Marshal Habbas el-Majali, the former minister of defense, now military governor of the kingdom. Daoud, a native of Silwan, near Jerusalem, had another attribute: he represented Jordan for more than twenty years on the Mixed Armistice Commission with Israel and consequently enjoyed cordial relations with the Jewish military authorities, all the way from Dayan to the general staff officers. It was his idea, in 1955, to establish a "red telephone" between Israeli and Jordanian delegations to this commission, to allow for immediate consultation in the event of serious incidents.

It was after midnight in London when the chief of MI 6 phoned 10 Downing Street to inform Prime Minister Edward Heath of Hussein's decision that night. Heath immediately tried to get Kissinger on the phone. Kissinger was at Airlie House in Virginia, at a black-tie dinner honoring Defense Secretary Melvin Laird, in the company of CIA boss Richard Helms, Admiral Thomas Moorer, head of the Joint Chiefs of Staff, and Joseph Sisco. At 8:30 P.M. Kissinger got a call from the White House from his deputy, General Alexander Haig, passing on Heath's message.

Kissinger ordered a helicopter and, still wearing black-tie, returned to Washington with his three table guests. He immediately called an emergency meeting of the WSAG (Washington Special Action Group), an ad hoc committee set up in April 1969 to deal with sudden international crises. Sketchy intelligence furnished by the CIA on the civil war that had just erupted in Jordan signaled the arrival of Syrian tanks, with Soviet advisers, on the Syrian-Jordanian border. Kissinger asked the members of the committee to study two contingencies if Hussein was overthrown: an American intervention or an Israeli intervention, according to the possibilities.

Meanwhile, Kissinger ordered the reinforcement of the Sixth Fleet. The helicopter-carrier *Guam* set out to join the fleet in the Mediterranean. Two aircraft carriers, the *Saratoga* and the *Independence,* rendezvoused about 160 kilometers off the Lebanese coast. Hercules C 130s prepared to take off for Greece and Turkey, where a state of alert had been declared in all American bases. Then Admiral Moorer drew Kissinger's attention to the limitations of the available American forces. Despite a budget of $75 billion, the sailors of the Sixth Fleet lacked helicopters capable of transporting them to Jordan. The *Guam* would take a week to arrive. The Seventh American Army in Germany, entirely motorized, could not be redeployed by air. The C 130s, with their 4,000-kilometer range, would require an intermediate air base. Impossible to use the British bases in Cyprus. The Italian and Turkish bases could be used only within the framework of NATO, or for a humanitarian action. In short, it was the kind of tactical nightmare which Kissinger never imagined. That same evening, he phoned his friend Rabin, just to exchange some ideas. The Israeli ambassador informed him of his government's fear that the 20,000 Iraqi soldiers stationed permanently in Jordan might intervene in favor of the fedayeen.

On September 16 Marshal el-Majali launched an offensive against the Palestinian positions in Amman and in Ramtha, their supply depot, near the Syrian border. In Israel, the government decided to order a partial mobilization and concentrated tanks in the Jordan Valley in order to occupy the Gilead Heights on the East Bank of the Jordan River in the event of an Iraqi intervention. In Chicago, Kissinger publicly tried to fathom Soviet intentions and the "flagrant" violation of the cease-fire by the Egyptians almost from the first day. It was a way of coddling Golda Meir on the eve of her visit to Washington.

The next day, while Hussein's army pursued its advantage on the ground, Nixon expedited the delivery of eighteen Phantoms to Israel and granted her request for $500 million.

The following day, April 18, while Nixon was busy cajoling Golda, Kissinger received a Soviet note warning against any foreign intervention in the Jordanian-Palestinian conflict. But the same evening, at the time when it seemed that the crisis was drawing to a close in Hussein's favor, Kissinger received two alarming phone calls: the first from Rabin, the second from the young Jordanian ambassador, Abdul Alamid Sharaf. Both informed him that one hundred Syrian T 55 tanks, of Soviet manufacture, had entered Jordan.

"The bastards!" he exclaimed. "They'll pay for that!"

Kissinger immediately convened a new session of the WSAG. Never had the White House bustled so hyperactively as on that Saturday morning, September 19, 1970. as Kissinger prepared to preside over an interrupted meeting of the committee in the Situ-

ation Room. (The "Sit Room" is a soundproof room in the basement of the White House, with tables seating fourteen persons, and
with facilities for direct communication to the CIA, Pentagon, and
Army headquarters.) Kissinger, in contact with the Pentagon and
the National Security Council, devoted himself to the first *Krieg-
spiel* of his career. With Nixon's approval, he placed American
forces on alert—notably the 82nd Airborne Division of Fort Bragg
in California—and ordered the 81st Airborne Division in West
Germany to move units conspicuously along the autobahns in a
manner perceptible to the Soviets. A third aircraft carrier—the *J.
F. Kennedy*—set course for the Mediterranean.

"This was his real baptism of fire in a crisis management situation," one of his aides said later, describing Kissinger, bent over
maps, dispatching toy battleships from one end of the Mediterranean to the other, wrangling with admirals, and phoning the heads
of the Joint Chiefs of Staff to modify the deployment of the Sixth
Fleet.

"The World War II sergeant had suddenly become a general
and an admiral and, during that crisis, a kind of deputy commander-in-chief," Marvin and Bernard Kalb wrote later in their
authoritative biography, *Kissinger.** Rogers, the chief of American
diplomacy, took a dim view of all this commotion.

In Moscow, meanwhile, there was another difference of opinion
between the Brezhnev and Kosygin factions. The two leaders were
in agreement only on postponing the Twenty-fourth Congress of
the Soviet Communist party. Faced with numerous points of disagreement with the United States, Kosygin balked at the prospect
of a new crisis in the Near East. Brezhnev, however, favored revenge for the recent setback suffered in Egypt and believed that
the American military involvement in Cambodia would reduce the
possibility of a U.S. reaction in Jordan. Brezhnev could also count
on the unconditional support of Syrian President Salah Jedid, who
was obligated to him for supporting him in April 1969, when the
central committee of the Ba'ath party tended to favor his rival,
Defense Minister Hafez Assad. For that matter, Soviet aid to the
Palestinian movement passed through Damascus, which had become the center of influence of the PLO. El Saika was now an
integral part of the Syrian Army.

To maintain the defense of the Golan Heights and the support
of his loyal armored division of 300 tanks against the eventuality of
a coup d'état, President Jedid was prudent at first. The first Syrian

* Published by Little, Brown and Company, Boston, 1974.

tanks that invaded Jordan on the morning of September 18 were daubed with the colors of the Palestine Liberation Army. But that evening 100 tanks entered the country without this camouflage. Concerned about the possibility that the tank operation might provoke an Israeli aerial response—the only factor that would permit the Americans to foil the Brezhnev-Jedid plan—Commander of the Syrian Air Force Assad refused to provide them with an aerial cover.

On September 19 Hussein's army succeeded in containing the arrival of new Syrian reinforcements. But the next day, another 100 Syrian tanks pushed forward toward Irbid, raising the number of troops already in northern Jordan to division level.

Hussein opposed this invasion with only the Patton tanks of his 40th Bedouin Brigade and about 30 British planes. The other available armored brigade was defending Amman. His tanks were fast retreating on the road from Irbid to the capital; and Irbid, the second largest city in the kingdom, had already fallen into the hands of the Palestinians. The Jordanian Air Force was powerless to check the Syrian advance. Hussein's position became precarious.

The little king's hysterical voice, relayed from the American embassy in Amman, resounded in the Sit Room in Washington at 5:00 A.M. September 20:

"I'm okay up above, but in bad trouble down below."

It was his way of saying that, although his air force was holding out, his ground forces were being mauled and were sending a desperate SOS.

When Sisco phoned the king's palace, located outside Amman, Hussein himself picked up the receiver. He was alone, his retinue had deserted him, and his palace, completely isolated, was being fired upon by the Palestinians.

"Things must really be going bad for him," Sisco commented as he rejoined Kissinger in the Sit Room, where Nixon dropped in from time to time to supervise his adviser's actions.

The Israeli government, gathered in session in Jerusalem, presided over by Yigal Allon, authorized General Bar-Lev to reinforce the troops on the Golan Heights and to dispatch reconnaissance flights over Jordan. An authoritative report cited the discord that had surfaced between Syrian leaders Jedid and Assad.

Around 6:00 P.M. Washington time, a new appeal arrived directly from Hussein to Kissinger, who was still locked up in the Sit Room of the White House. Hussein entreated the United States to intervene without delay or to let Israel intervene to save him and his throne. Nixon authorized Kissinger to call on the Israelis for help.

In the middle of the most serious international crisis an American president had faced since the Cuban missile crisis in 1962, Kissinger sent for Rabin, who, accompanied by General Yariv, was in New York with Golda Meir, the main attraction at an Israel Bonds gala held in the Grand Ballroom of the New York Hilton. It was past 10:00 P.M. and Golda had been talking for over an hour to an audience of 3,000 invited guests. She had warned them that her speech would be a long one if her swollen feet did not hurt her, and a short one if they did. An aide handed an urgent note to Rabin: "Call the White House immediately." Using a telephone in the lobby, Rabin called Kissinger, who asked tensely whether Israel was ready to provide Jordan with aerial support to counter the Syrian invasion.

Rabin promised a reply in under an hour, on the condition of an American guarantee in the event of an escalation. In a small anteroom, echoing with muffled sounds from the Grand Ballroom, Golda conferred with her assistants: Rabin, who had unobtrusively ushered her into the room, Foreign Minister Abba Eban, Yariv, Simcha Dinits, and Shlomo Argov. A strange scene: a prime minister in an evening gown, a minister and an ambassador in black tie, and a general in full military dress, seated around a small table discussing the fate of a war being waged 10,000 kilometers from this carnival atmosphere! Golda phoned Allon, more than ever in favor of intervention. It was 6:00 A.M. in Tel Aviv when she roused Dayan out of his sleep.

The Defense Minister hesitated: "Syria is Moscow's protégé. If we intervene against her in Jordan, we risk a Russian intervention on the Canal."

When they separated—Golda, for Kennedy Airport where an El Al plane waited to fly her back to Israel, Rabin, for La Guardia Airport, where Kissinger had dispatched a Jetstar for his use—she gave Rabin a twofold reply to deliver to the White House: The Israeli Air Force would intervene if the Syrians pushed beyond Irbid or introduced their air force. The United States would have to intervene militarily if the Soviets reacted militarily.

Upon awakening from a deep sleep during the flight, Golda astonished her entourage by asking whether the Syrians were still in Irbid.

Rabin returned to his residence at 3:00 A.M. on September 21 and held a closed-circuit telephone conversation with Kissinger, who was still in the Sit Room maneuvering his toy ships, and with

Sisco, who was holed up in the State Department's Operations Center. Later in the morning, Nixon commissioned his adviser to negotiate an unprecedented arrangement for a joint military action. The two men set to work in the White House basement, while in a small room nearby, the Jordanian ambassador gulped down cup after cup of coffee. They reviewed the whole spectrum of Israeli military plans.

During this time, Israeli tanks were climbing the Golan Heights along secondary roads, raising clouds of sand in full view of Syrian Army headquarters. Israeli planes demonstratively overflew the Syrian positions while an armored brigade moved inexorably toward Irbid. At 10:00 A.M. an American reconnaissance plane carrying a group of intelligence officers from the aircraft carrier *Saratoga* landed in Tel Aviv. The flight had appeared on the radar of a Soviet spy ship cruising in the proximity of the Sixth Fleet. Kissinger wanted to show the Russians that he meant business. There was a discussion of coordinating the Israeli and Jordanian forces, perhaps even on the bridges of the Jordan River.

The Kremlin began to show signs of distress against any foreign intervention in Jordan, manifested by a protest lodged by the Soviet chargé d'affaires in Washington. The Politburo dispatched an emissary to Damascus to ask the Syrians to halt their advance on the ground. But new tank reinforcements were poised to cross the border. That evening, Hussein flashed another SOS. Rabin informed Kissinger of Israel's readiness to intervene in exchange for the assurance of an "American umbrella." Nixon authorized Kissinger to pass on his guarantee, and Golda agreed that written confirmation could follow later. The Israeli general staff set the H-hour of the Israeli intervention for September 23, at dawn.

Encouraged by the announcement of the American-Israeli accord (Kissinger had apprised him of it at midnight, Amman time) Hussein ordered Marshal el-Majali to unleash a counteroffensive and throw all his forces into the fray. At dawn, el-Majali diverted half of the armored brigade protecting Amman toward the Jordan valley, from where it was again to make the push toward Irbid, to give the impression that it was an Israeli armored column coming from the direction of the Jordan River. The entire Jordanian Air Force swooped down on the Syrian-Palestinian positions, destroying more than 100 tanks. At around 6:00 P.M. the Syrian forces received the order to break off operations and regain the border.

Informed by Rabin of the sudden change in the military situation, Kissinger attended a cocktail party where he was sure to meet the Soviet chargé d'affaires, Yuli Vorontsov, whom he had deliberately snubbed for forty-eight hours.

"Your clients started the circus, it's up to them to put an end to it," Kissinger told him, confident that the Soviets would no longer budge.

On September 23 the Syrians completed their evacuation of Jordanian territory. After a radio exchange of passwords in code, the conciliation committee of the Arab League met Arafat, who had taken refuge in the Egyptian embassy. The PLO leader's precautions were not without basis. His men were utterly exhausted and he himself was being tracked by all sorts of secret agents, some of whom abducted Daoud's wife and daughter, while he was on a mission to Cairo, to force him to resign the Jordanian premiership. Abandoned to their fate, the Palestinians were pounded by 155 mm cannons and phosphorous shells. The refugee camps were leveled by the Patton tanks of the Bedouins. The toll: 7,000 dead. In flight from the savage vengeance of the royal army, scores of fedayeen, preferring prison to certain death, crossed the Jordan to seek asylum in Israel. Later, upon their release, they were authorized to remain on the occupied West Bank. Seven years later, one of the escapees was among the crowds in the great square of the Mosque of Omar in Jerusalem to acclaim Sadat.

Hussein and Arafat signed a cease-fire accord in Cairo on September 27. On September 28 Nasser died suddenly, struck down by an illness that had been taking its toll since his last trip to Moscow in July. The next day the last six hostages of Zarka were released, abandoned by their jailers. There would be no war. Above all, however, the September massacres of the Palestinians constituted a black September for Brezhnev's policy, defeated on all fronts.

Meanwhile, the Americans were still in Cambodia. Their massive May landing had surprised the Soviets. The delivery of arms to Vietnam by the long route around the Cape of Good Hope posed problems to the Kremlin leaders. Above all, considerable changes had taken place in Peking. On September 6 the day on which the planes were hijacked to Zarka, in the course of a secret meeting of the Chinese Communist party's central committee, the moderate policy of Chou En-lai, who was in favor of an opening to the West, prevailed over the hard-line policy of the extremist Lin Piao, and, several months later, Mao Tse-tung was to manifest his desire to establish relations with the Nixon White House by having Kissinger secretly invited to China.

On September 15 CIA negatives of a series of reconnaissance

flights, carried out routinely by U-2 spy planes over Cuba, revealed the installation in progress of a base for nuclear submarines in Cienfuegos, in violation of the Kennedy-Khrushchev accord of 1962. On September 16 in Chicago, Kissinger addressed a discreet public warning to the Soviets regarding this matter. On September 25 he clearly warned that Nixon considered the construction of such a base in Cuba as an act of hostility. American-Soviet tension was to mount steadily until October 22, when the CIA produced photographic evidence of the interrupted construction in the port of Cienfuegos. A crisis of major proportions between the two superpowers was presumably nipped in the bud by Kissinger's preventive diplomacy.

Meanwhile, the prospect of Israeli-American military cooperation had halted the advance of Syrian tanks in Jordan and allowed Hussein to crush the hotbed of Palestinian subversion and expel the terrorists from his kingdom.

Since the beginning of 1970, at the moment when Brezhnev's strategy seemed to be on the verge of triumph, and when Admiral Moorer defined the situation as very critical for the United States before the National Security Council, a whole series of events modified the balance of power between Moscow and Washington. The Soviets were obliged to retreat and, in particular, lose influence in the Middle East.

Brezhnev's setback in Jordan played a determining role in the succession to Nasser in Egypt, which confirmed the decline of Soviet influence in the region. A Syrian-Palestinian victory in Amman would have strengthened the chances of Egyptian Marxist leader Ali Sabri.

Upon his arrival in Cairo to attend Nasser's funeral on September 29, Kosygin expressed to the new president, Anwar Sadat, the USSR's wish to see Vice-President Ali Sabri become prime minister. The November announcement of Mahmoud Fawzi's appointment to this post could only have come as an unwelcome surprise.

In a bid to regain his place at the summit of the pyramid of power, Ali Sabri, who had already resurfaced twice under Nasser's regime, thanks to Russian support, allied himself with head of the presidential office Sami Sharaf, and Minister of the Interior Shu'a-rawi Goma. (Sabri was unaware that Sharaf was Moscow's agent in Cairo.) Sharaf's influence had grown since Nasser's death. Now he controlled not only intelligence, but all the important government appointments as well. This "superminister" had been an ambitious little bureaucrat when, as part of one of the first Egyptian military delegations to Moscow in 1955, he was spotted by the

KGB. He was recruited in New York in 1958 by Vladimir Suslev, who registered him with his agency under the code name "Assad" (Lion). According to the words used to describe him by a *Figaro* correspondent based in Cairo, he was well on the way to becoming "the most powerful man in Egypt."

With his hunched shoulders, his prominent stomach, his somber, globular eyes, and impressive moustache, the six-footer looked rather like an overripe pear. This masterspy, whose official duties allowed him to meet openly with Vadim Kirpichenko, the KGB's resident agent in Cairo, was shrewd enough to part company with Sabri in 1959 and play the role of a supernationalist according to a minutely-thought-out plan conceived by his superiors. It had given him more clout to direct an anti-West campaign and to shape Nasser's policies. For his help, he received regular payments from the KGB deposited in a numbered Swiss bank account.

In November 1970 Sharaf induced Sadat to appoint one of his own men, Ahmed Kamel, as head of the Mukhabarat, the Egyptian Central Intelligence Agency. This assured him almost absolute control of domestic intelligence and enabled him to manipulate the "special services" of the Arab Socialist Union. The group of "plumbers" at his disposal bugged the offices and residences of all the regime's dignitaries. Hidden microphones were even installed in Sadat's bedroom and thus was compiled a voluminous dossier on the private life, the habits, and the conjugal relations of the new president! Most of the anecdotes dating from that time that ridiculed Sadat stemmed directly from this dossier—such as the story picturing the Egyptian president standing before his mirror repeating over and over again the English words over which he tended to stumble. Thanks to the microphones installed by his "plumbers," Sharaf also became privy to the comments and views of Sadat's wife, Jihan, at the breakfast table. Sharaf carefully preserved copies of the original tapes which he regularly had delivered to the KGB.

In December 1970 Ali Sabri headed a delegation of the Arab Socialist Union which went to Moscow to meet the Kremlin leaders. In a private session, he briefed them on the fragility of Sadat's position and on his own intentions to hasten his downfall. Once more, Kosygin and Podgorny objected that the moment seemed ill-chosen to involve the USSR in a new Middle East crisis. But Brezhnev, thinking only of recouping a prestige badly tarnished by the succession of failures inflicted on his policy, promised to support him.

Brezhnev desperately needed a success to consolidate his position in the Politburo. In March he was again obliged to compromise with his two colleagues of the triumvirate for a year's postponement of the Party Congress. The debate, initiated in 1968, before the coup in Prague, between the conservatives, whose spokesman he had become, and the reformers, represented by Kosygin, had still to be settled. But in May Brezhnev had unexpectedly imposed his presence at cabinet meetings; something which no secretary-general of the party had ever dared do before him without at the same time occupying the position of premier. He also reverted to his own personality cult by having an enlarged portrait of himself hung among those of the eleven Politburo members, abandoning the accepted alphabetical order. He demanded to become No. One officially in order to ratify the policy of cooperation with West Germany, successfully practiced by Kosygin. Though born on December 19, he celebrated his birthday on December 31, 1970, so that it coincided with the USSR's traditional holiday, taking advantage of the confluence of events to address a televised speech to "his people."

Two events, however, made Brezhnev suddenly adopt his rivals' moderate and reformist line: the fall of Gomulka in Poland and the helping hand discreetly tendered by Kissinger, past master of the art of alternately wielding the carrot and the stick. The bloody workers' revolt that erupted in the port of Gdansk in December led to the fall of the old Polish leader and forced his successor, Edward Gierek, to meet the demands of the protesting workers whose action risked spreading the contagion of revolt to the other popular democracies of Eastern Europe. And it made Brezhnev realize that, if he did not want to share Gomulka's fate, it would be necessary to decontrol the economy and liberalize the regime. Basing his actions on a CIA report dealing with this vulnerability, Kissinger convinced Nixon to extend a helping hand to Brezhnev: to propose massive economic aid in exchange for a policy of détente. On January 9, 1971, Nixon addressed a secret message along these lines to the secretary-general of the Soviet Communist party, pointing out to Brezhnev that the acid test would be negotiating an agreement on the limitation of strategic armaments (SALT) which were inhibiting the progress of peaceful coexistence. Brezhnev's reaction was immediate. He authorized Soviet ambassador Anatoly Dobrynin to open the negotiations with Kissinger which four months later were to lead to the first agreement. At the twenty-fourth Congress of the CPSU, which opened on March 29, 1971, in

Moscow (for the first time the functionaries were in a 45 percent minority), Brezhnev executed a 180 ° turn in favor of a consumer economy made possible by détente with the West. "More butter and fewer guns, thanks to peace!"

The ornithological mutation of the hawk into the Kremlin's number-one dove did not suit the Egyptian Marxist, Sabri, nor his allies. This time, in February 1971, his friend, Interior Minister Goma, returned empty-handed after a secret journey to Moscow. The KGB even asked Sharaf to keep an eye on the plot being hatched against Sadat by Sabri and Goma. But the all-powerful agent decided to swing into action for himself. At the beginning of April, as part of the Egyptian delegation to the Soviet Communist Party Congress, he kept his bosses informed of his intention to take over the leadership of the plot for which Sabri and Goma had recruited General Fawzi, the Minister of Defense, the Minister of Information, the chief of the Mukhabarat (Central Intelligence Agency), and the secretary-general of the Arab Socialist Union.

On April 25 Sabri pressed the Arab Socialist Union to reject the treaty establishing a federation between Egypt and Libya that Sadat had just signed in Benghazi with Qaddafi. This hostile vote directed toward Sadat had been orchestrated by the "special service" manipulated by Sharaf. Goma ordered his secret police to surround the building housing the national radio station to prevent Sadat from making an appeal to the nation.

On May 1 Sadat condemned the faked elections of the Arab Socialist Union and, on May 3, dismissed Sabri from his post as vice-president of the Republic.

On May 13 Sadat dismissed Goma from his post as the minister of the interior. The night before, a *Mbakhas* (secret police) agent had brought Sadat some recordings of tapped telephone conversations which Goma had ordered. That afternoon head of the presidential office Sami Sharaf, Minister of Defense Fawzi, the Minister of Information, the Minister of Housing, and the Minister of Energy resigned en masse and announced their decision over TV, even before apprising Sadat. But they had not counted on the army officers who were loyal to their president foiling the maneuver by arresting General Fawzi on the spot and by placing all the ministers who had resigned, as well as the chief of the Mukhabarat, under house arrest.

Warned of the plot, Sadat had made a round of visits to the officers' mess halls. Long before May 13, he was thus sure of the support of all the high officers on the military bases. How had he been warned?

In June 1970 CIA agents in Cairo had obtained an astonishing lead from Vladimir Nikolaievich Sakharov, their informant in the Soviet consulate in Alexandria. Sami Sharaf was a Moscow agent! Sakharov himself had picked up this intelligence item from a verbal slipup of a member of the GRU, Viktor Sbirunov, who during a meeting with the consul-general, Shumilov, had let this choice information escape:

"Sharaf is our solid trump in Egypt. We are counting on him."

It took the CIA six months to cross-check Sakharov's story. In April 1971 according to General George Keagan, the former head of the intelligence service of the U.S. Air Force, the Israeli authorities had passed on to the Americans what they themselves had learned of the plot masterminded by Sabri, Goma, and others, and the extent of Sharaf's involvement.

On April 26 Sadat, apprised of this latter intelligence by the CIA, summoned Ahmed Kamel, the head of the Mukhabarat, whom he had not yet seen since his appointment to that post in November on Sharaf's recommendation, and confirmed that Kamel must be involved because he did not betray the conspiracy. On the contrary, he told Sadat of his intention to travel to Moscow on May 15 at the invitation of the Soviets.

"It would amaze me," Sadat replied cryptically, "if you were able to be absent on May fifteenth." He did not dwell on the matter any further.

At the beginning of May, American Secretary of State William Rogers traveled to Cairo to renew his peace efforts. American security agents helping Sadat check his office for electronic devices discovered half a dozen microphones planted there by Sharaf's "plumbers."

The discovery of the bugging marked the end of Sharaf's career. His May 13 resignation did not surprise Sadat. After Sharaf's arrest on May 15, the Egyptian president completely reorganized the secret services by purging all pro-Soviet elements. All the professional links woven by Sharaf over a period of twelve years between the Russian and Egyptian services were broken. Police found a hoard of hundreds of thousands of dollars in Sharaf's residence; its purpose was never discovered. They also found copies of the recordings of the telephone taps—particularly the secret conversation held in Cairo on April 20, 1967, between Goma and the secretary of the Soviet Communist party, Yagoritsev, which played an important role in Nasser's decision to provoke a *casus belli* with Israel.

The tapes also included the recordings of two séances organized by Sharaf on April 20 and May 4, 1971, to reinforce Goma's flagging determination. In the course of the séances, an Ein Shams university assistant, recruited by Sharaf as a medium, invoked the spirit of a sheik named Abdel Rahim. The "ghost" had assured Goma that the plot would meet with success, while at the same time advising against hasty action following Ali Sabri's dismissal. He had also assured General Fawzi of the validity of his battle plan against Israel.

It is probable that Sharaf had already used this method to influence the decisions of other Egyptian leaders. Condemned to death on December 9, 1971, his sentence, like that of Sabri and Goma, was commuted to forced labor for life. But he was the only one not to benefit from any court pardons. No one was ever to hear of him again.

Countered by Israel on the Suez Canal and in Jordan, less than one year later, the Kremlin was to lose its best agent in the Middle East, thanks to an intelligence report relayed by Israel which, after foiling an assassination attempt, was to allow Sadat to rid Egypt of Soviet tutelage.

One year later, in May 1972, Sadat could tranquilly expel the 3,000 Soviet experts and technicians whose presence was a source of humiliation to his army: the memory of Brezhnev's black September served him as umbrella.

Meanwhile, the Russians had increased their capacity for electronic espionage in the region, shifted the focus of their Middle Eastern policy from Suez to the Gate of Tears, Bab el-Mandeb, which commands access to the Red Sea from the south: Bab el-Mandeb and the strategic position of the Horn of Africa, controlling the all-important oil route from the Arabian peninsula and the Persian Gulf.

16

BAB EL-MANDEB
(THE GATE OF TEARS)

"It's unbelievable!" said a French diplomat stationed in Tel Aviv. "The Russians and Israelis are both backing Ethiopia in its continuing conflict with Somalia; the United States and the Arabs are backing Somalia. The world is upside-down!"

This paradoxical inversion of alliances is not the only reason this region of the globe has been in the harsh spotlight of world attention since the beginning of the 1970s. Having freed themselves from age-old colonial masters, the countries of Africa's eastern Horn have assumed a prime strategic importance because they control the entrance to Bab el-Mandeb, the Gate of Tears. This strait not only shuts off the southern outlet to the Red Sea—and hence the Suez Canal—but it also controls access to the Persian Gulf, the oil route to Europe and the United States. It has become an area as essential to Israel's survival as the Straits of Tiran at the entrance to the Gulf of Eilat. It is vital to the flow of Israel's petroleum supply and to its trade with Africa and the Far East.

Israel's relations with Ethiopia, the only non-Arab country in the region, go back to 1956. Tsahal officers equipped and trained the army of Haile Selassie's old empire. The pilots, paratroopers, and officers of the emperor's general staff were all trained in Israel, as were his personal bodyguards.

Indeed, the Arab countries were quick to accuse Ethiopia of serving as a base for Israeli secret service activities in Africa. And it is true that the ties between Ben-Gurion's Israel and Haile Selassie's empire were of a special character. On December 14, 1960, when Selassie was on a state visit to Brazil, a group of Ethiopian officers took power in Addis Ababa in a military putsch.

The emperor started home at once, but during the night he stopped over in Monrovia, where he contacted the Israeli embassy in Liberia to find out whether the province of Eritrea had also fallen to the conspirators. If Eritrea was still loyal to him, he asked Israel to inform the Eritrean governor of his arrival. From there he would attempt the reconquest of his throne.

A senior official in the Israeli government who was in Monrovia at the time took charge of the matter and telegraphed his office in

Tel Aviv. Officials in the Israeli defense ministry, however, were hesitant about taking a position or making a favorable reply to the emperor's request because they were acquainted with most of the officers, whom they considered to be friendly to Israel. The official had to insist that his question be communicated urgently to Ben-Gurion in person.

When he was awakened by his military aide at 4:00 A.M., the "Old Man" had but one remark:

"The emperor is our ally, is he not? So we must help him."

In a few hours, the first Ethiopian military coup d'état was quashed, and Haile Selassie had regained his palace.

In Ben-Gurion's eyes, relations with Addis Ababa had an almost mystical quality. He often referred with passion to the biblical love affair between King Solomon and the Queen of Sheba. He had on more than one occasion dreamed of visiting Ethiopia in great pomp, but his dream was never realized.

Even after the emperor's deposition in 1974, Israeli ties with the new regime continued. Israeli personnel who had had to leave Ethiopia after the 1973 Yom Kippur War returned discreetly three years later during the open conflict with Somalia. Moshe Dayan personally approved Israel's sending military supplies to Addis Ababa to counterbalance the aid Egypt was furnishing to the Somalis, who were already receiving long-term assistance from the Libyans and the Syrians.

This military aid was only one aspect of the battle being waged for control of Bab el-Mandeb. The secret war being waged there by the world's major intelligence services had turned the picturesque area between the former Pirate Coast and Slave Coast into one of the more important crossroads where spies and double agents met. The exotic port of Aden had come to share with Tangier and Hong Kong the dubious honor of being an international city of cosmopolitan mystery. A center of clandestine activities during the days of English colonialism, upon South Yemen's independence, Aden became a paradise for international terrorism. The Peoples' Republic that had been set up in that country was one of the most "activist" in the world, and offered refuge to all types of terrorist movements. As just one example, one of the largest training camps run by Dr. Waddia Haddad, chief of operations of the Popular Front for the Liberation of Palestine, was set up on the outskirts of Aden.

Since the capture of Sharm el-Sheikh in June 1967, Bab el-Mandeb had been a focal point in Tsahal headquarters' map room. It was also one of the target areas of the Israeli secret services.

On June 11, 1971, the red light flashed on in Bab el-Mandeb for the first time. The *Coral Sea,* an oil tanker flying the Liberian flag, was en route to the Israeli port of Eilat with a cargo from the Persian Gulf when it was approached by a motorized launch camouflaged as a fishing boat near Perim Island, in the Red Sea. Aboard the launch were four PFLP terrorists armed with bazookas. Six of the shells fired struck the tanker, which burst into flame. The assailants sped off to avoid the explosion and made for safety in the nearest port—Hodeida, in North Yemen.

With the help of its Greek captain, the crew of the *Coral Sea,* 25 of whose 37-man crew were Israelis, succeeded in bringing the fire under control and in reaching Sharm el-Sheikh.

The captain had sent a radio message to the Eilat station at 12:30—"We are under attack from a fake fishing boat"—and the naval air base at Sharm el-Sheikh had gone on red alert. Prime Minister Golda Meir summoned her colleagues, along with Minister for Foreign Affairs Moshe Dayan; on the same evening, Dayan sent urgent cables to the governments of Britain, Italy, and the United States to express Israel's concern at the opening of this new front south of Suez. In Washington, Itzhak Rabin informed the White House that his government would be forced to respond to this type of aggression.

The Americans then informed the Soviets of their serious concern regarding this act of piracy against international navigation in the Red Sea. At the time there were various indications that Moscow must have quickly intervened with its allies in North and South Yemen, asking that they cease lending support to such operations. Indeed, the Russians were not overeager to advertise their presence in the area, where they were in the process of consolidating their control. A reprisal would only make their process of penetration more complicated. And they recalled that a few years earlier, Israeli Phantom jets had bombed and sunk Egyptian warships in the port of Ras Banas, 600 kilometers south of Suez, in response to an assault by Egyptian frogmen against a freighter in the port of Eilat under the command of the former captain of the *Exodus.*

Saudi Arabia, which at the time was still the main source of funds for the Palestinian organizations, also exerted a moderating influence; according to the June 25, 1971, issue of *Time* magazine, its oil was flowing to Eilat through a 30-million ton per year pipeline which ensured its progress on to the Mediterranean and Europe.

This diplomatic activity was only one aspect of the preventive measures undertaken by Israel. General Zvi Zamir called a special meeting in his Mossad office to consider the new situation created by the outbreak of terrorism in the vital Bab el-Mandeb region. He ordered the chief of operations to intensify his activities there.

A few days later, Captain Baruch Zaki Misrahi, an intelligence agent, was dispatched to the scene to collect as much information as he could get. Through him it was learned that the four attackers of the *Coral Sea* had been given two months of special training in Lebanon before leaving for South Yemen, where a PFLP representative had provided them with the boat, the bazookas, and orders to attack the tanker. In order not to involve the authorities of the new Peoples' Republic, the terrorists were to fall back on the port of Hodeida, where they could further count on the complicity of the leaders of the Republic of North Yemen.

According to stories that later appeared in the Arab press, Misrahi supposedly arrived in Aden under the identity of Ahmad al-Sabag, a Moroccan businessman with commercial interests in various Arab countries, to set up his network and gather information. Misrahi was an Egyptian Jew born in Cairo in 1928, and had taken business courses at the university, so he had no trouble with this cover.

According to these stories, Misrahi had emigrated to Israel in 1956 and had begun his career as a policeman in Ramat Gan, a suburb of Tel Aviv. Promoted in 1965 to the special police section detailed to deal with domestic enemies, he had joined the Shin Bet in 1968, and later the Mossad. One Egyptian newspaper reported that his first mission had been to procure authentic Arab passports for the Mossad, and that he had once managed to purchase the passport of an Arab ambassador in Ethiopia for the price of a case of whiskey.

Caught spying on a cargo of Soviet arms in the port of Hodeida, where the four attackers of the *Coral Sea* had taken refuge, Misrahi was arrested on May 18, 1972.

For almost a month, the Yemenite security agents to whom the Soviets had delivered him were unaware of whom they were dealing with or who his employers were. First they had thought he was a spy from some anti-Soviet Arab country. Later they decided he was an agent of South Yemen, which was then fighting against the northern republic. Although adequate information is unavailable, it would appear that at that juncture Israel let slip an opportunity to save him.

However, once the Yemenite services managed to penetrate his cover, he was subjected to grueling torture. When the minister of the interior of the Republic of Yemen announced on July 12, 1972, that an Israeli spy of Egyptian origin had been captured, Cairo sought and obtained his extradition. Tried before an Egyptian military tribunal, Misrahi was sentenced to solitary confinement.

After the Yom Kippur War, Misrahi was among those Israel requested in the prisoner exchange that was set up during the preliminary military discussions after the cease-fire. During their talks in the tent at Kilometer 101, General Yariv on several occasions asked his counterpart, General Gamasy, to have Misrahi's name included among the Israeli soldiers to be exchanged for Egyptian soldiers. Kissinger had to personally intervene with Sadat in order for Misrahi to be returned to Israel upon the conclusion of the first disengagement agreement between the forces stationed in the Canal Zone, on March 5, 1974. The price: freeing 65 Arab agents who had been detained by the Israelis as Egyptian spies. Repatriated to Israel by the International Red Cross, Misrahi was given a warm welcome by his Mossad comrades, but he soon disappeared from view to begin a new life somewhere in Israel, far from cameras and publicity.

Among the 65 Arab agents exchanged for Misrahi was the most important Egyptian spy of the period, Abd el-Rahim Abd el-Raouf Karaman. He was an Arab with Israeli citizenship; the Cairo weekly *Ahar Saah* reported in 1976 that he had obtained the plans of the Bar-Lev Line for the Mukhabarat, the Egyptian central intelligence agency whose Number-One agent he became in Israel. According to this publication, he had managed to become friends with Israeli Defense Minister Moshe Dayan—whose weakness for antiquities was common knowledge—by presenting him with the gift of a fake Egyptian miniature he had procured from Cairo headquarters for this purpose.

Uncovered, nevertheless, by Israeli counterespionage, Karaman was tried in Haifa in 1970 for the crime of high treason. According to the indictment, he had been recruited in Paris in 1968 by an agent of the Egyptian secret services posted at the Egyptian embassy in France. Karaman came from an Arab family in Upper Galilee which the future chairman of the Defense and Foreign Affairs Committee in the Knesset, David Hacohen, had helped, during the 1948 war, to stay on in its home in Ibtan, an Arab village near Haifa. The young and handsome Karaman, now an Israeli citizen, had learned to speak perfect English, Hebrew, and even Yiddish, and in 1956 he had married a Turkish Jew. After divorcing her because she had not given him a child, he remarried twice—in 1964 and 1967—both Frenchwomen. Still without an heir, he had gone to Paris in 1968 to find a child of Palestinian or Egyptian origin to adopt. It was at this juncture that he met the Egyptian consul in Paris. The consul quickly introduced him to the Mukhabarat agent, who made him a tempting offer: an adoptable child for some information.

The offer was accepted and Karaman—now the proud father of a family—returned to Israel after a stay in a Mukhabarat residence on the Belgian coast, where he had been taught to use hidden cameras, microtransmitters and invisible inks: all the items that make up the modern spy's stock in trade.

He now took advantage of his connections with the authorities to photograph the Golan region from every angle and to cement friendships with Arabs employed by firms engaged in constructing the Bar-Lev Line, through whom he was able to obtain Israeli passports. He was also assigned to infiltrate the far-left Israeli Matzpen political group, which was militantly opposed to territorial occupation.

Sentenced to twelve years in prison at his first trial, Karaman's sentence was increased to sixteen years on appeal. When he, too, was liberated on March 5, 1974, under the disengagement agreement, he left his large family behind in Galilee: his sister, Suat Karaman, was to continue to make Arab broadcasts over the Israeli national radio.

The Egyptian press was to tell of Sadat's personal intervention with Kissinger to obtain Karaman's exchange in return for Israel's man at Bab el-Mandeb.

Misrahi's capture was only part of the normal risk of the job of spying. During the next year, however, the Israeli secret services were to have a series of accidents which had serious consequences: a commercial Libyan plane was shot down by mistake in February over the Sinai when it strayed off course; a Lebanese Airlines plane was intercepted on Dayan's orders because Aman believed that George Habash, the PFLP leader, was on board; a Moroccan barman was killed in July in Lillehammer, Norway, because he had been mistaken by Mossad agents for the man who had organized the massacre of the Israeli Olympic team in Munich.

General Zvi Zamir, their boss, flew to Oslo immediately, and upon his return, he tendered his resignation to Golda Meir, who refused to accept it. She had noticed the popularity he enjoyed with his men when she had met with some of the Mossad's permanent agents in an orange grove on the little farm of Beit Berl.

And at the beginning of the autumn of 1973, the Israeli services' reputation for infallibility was seriously damaged when a last diversionary maneuver distracted their attention from the only-too-evident military preparations then taking place on the country's frontiers. On September 29, 1973, eight days before the surprise Egyptian-Syrian attack on Yom Kippur, a terrorist commando unit from Czechoslovakia commandeered a railroad car on the Chopin Express, a train bringing Russian Jewish immigrants to Vienna. Bruno Kreisky, the Austrian chancellor, was forced to agree to shut down the castle of Schoenau, the Jewish Agency's transit center for refugees en route to Israel. The Israeli leaders brought all their attention to bear on this affair. No one seemed aware that the "Eagles of the Revolution," the commando group responsible for taking the hostages, was really part of El Saika ("Lightning"), a Palestinian organization controlled by the Syrians. Had the Syrians really been trying to divert Israeli attention, they could hardly have done a better job.

17
KIPPUR

"Remote probability." The classic expression so often used in intelligence reports irritated Knesset member Begin. The ex-chief of the Irgun, who had assumed the leadership of the nationalist opposition in the summer of 1970 and continued to choose his words the way pilots place their bombs, would have liked the expression banished.

"Arab logic is not the same as ours," he repeated constantly in the halls of the Knesset. "You can never know why they will suddenly decide to set off a war."

But for General Eli Zeira, Chief of Aman, Israel's military intelligence, "remote probability" was a valid assessment right up to the morning of October 6, 1973, Yom Kippur (Day of Atonement), the most sacred day of the liturgical calendar. As early as April, when authoritative sources called attention to an imminent offensive, including an Egyptian-Syrian battle plan, Zeira, the new chief of army intelligence, allowed only the "remote possibility" of a real threat. Nevertheless, Chief of Staff David Elazar took the alert seriously. He managed to convince the government to mobilize the day before the Twenty-Fifth Anniversary Independence Day Parade. But there had been no war. "Dado" Elazar was rebuked for a mobilization which cost $15 million to an economy whose priorities had become dangerously selective.

When Zeira came up with the same "remote possibility" in September, the second time in six months that an Egyptian-Syrian offensive was reported, nobody dared challenge the intelligence chief's assessment. Despite other sources—such as the CIA, which notified Israeli intelligence on September 25 of the imminence of a simultaneous attack on two fronts, north and south— the opinion of the heads of Aman remained unchanged. On that day the Americans were involved with a UFO which had been photographed over the Middle East by their Skylab. Could it be a Russian spy satellite? The Israelis took pains to reassure them there was no real danger.

On October 1, Lieutenant Benjamin Siman-Tov, an intelligence officer attached to the Southern Command, transmitted a report to his superior: *War Preparations in the Egyptian Army?* His observations contradicted the official evaluation, and Lieutenant Colonel David Guedalia did not forward the report.

And on October 3, weren't the Arab armies amassed and ready for action in plain view of all the press correspondents? The Israeli correspondents were carefully briefed by the spokesman for Tsahal, who saw nothing in the movement of the Egyptian and Syrian troops other than "political maneuvers calculated to keep the area heated up."

And General Aryeh Shalev, Zeira's adjunct (Zeira was ill that day) said to Elazar, "I don't consider this a serious threat for the near future. Aman takes considerable precautions to alert the government at least forty-eight hours before any enemy attack.

Why wasn't Tsahal given maximum alert when information was received that the families of the Soviet advisers in Syria had made a precipitate departure during the night of October 4? General Zeira continued to be convinced that war was not likely. Furthermore, the dossier submitted by Colonel Yonah Bendman, director of military intelligence's Egypt Division, concluded unequivocally: "Notwithstanding the existence of military strength on the Canal front which appears to be ready for action, to the best of our knowledge there has been no significant change in Egyptian evaluation of their military potential versus Tsahal's. Therefore the probability of an Egyptian attack is unlikely." For General Zeira, interrogated by a council of ministers which had been hurriedly assembled in Tel Aviv, the least likely probability was an attempt to cross the Suez Canal; the most likely was a series of raids and artillery action across the borders.

On October 6 at 4:00 A.M. Dayan was awakened by a phone call from the Mossad announcing a combined Egyptian and Syrian attack before sunset. Zeira, who had been summoned at 5:30 A.M. by Dayan, held to the same position as in January and May when warnings of the same nature had proved unfounded. He also pointed out that the Americans, who had thought war possible ten days earlier, had reversed their opinion. According to them, any attempt to cross the Canal was a technical feat well beyond the Egyptians' capacity.

Zeira had overlooked (thus causing a fatal delay in alerting the reserve troops) the possible American intoxication with the Israelis: a predisposition which multiple victories—particularly that of the Six-Day War—had bloated out of proportion in the insular world of intelligence and counterespionage. The Israeli Army intelligence service had put together a well-developed and highly sensitive system of analysis and evaluation. At the level of data compilation—agents, monitoring, observations, cross-checking—most of the major intelligence-collecting agencies are on a par. The differences occur in the subjective (and perhaps irrational) aspects of the individuals who are responsible for interpreting the facts "objectively."

Eli Zeira, a friend of Dayan, had taken over a difficult position from Aharon Yariv only a year earlier. He had not yet had the time to restructure his service in his own way, which was to be very different from his predecessor's. A product of the paratroops and the armored division, Zeira was not known as a man who tolerated any serious questioning of his way of seeing things.

Less than four hours after the green light for a partial mobilization, the wail of sirens tore into the silence of Yom Kippur, interrupting the briefing Zeira was giving at the army spokeman's bureau for the benefit of the group of first-string journalists who were called in for the occasion. In an almost-fatal meeting of the unexpected with the unexpectant, the Israelis were to discover that not only were the Arabs able to hold out longer than six days, but that they also had good reasons to set off a war that they were not sure of winning militarily.

On April 1, 1974, a commission of inquiry presided over by Judge Shimon Agranat made public a 32-page interim report on the preparedness deficiencies at the outbreak of the Yom Kippur War. The report showed that the Israeli Army Intelligence Service had remained blindly attached to its erroneous evaluations. At the same time, the commission exonerated the political heads of state who actually made the decisions: Minister of Defense Moshe Dayan and Prime Minister Golda Meir.

In fact, the commission took care to distinguish between the responsibilities of the military, which it was capable of judging, and that of the political heads, which it deemed itself unqualified to evaluate. Being neither a council of wise men nor a superparliament, the commission did not want to define the elusive ministerial responsibility which, after all, did not exist in the constitutional dispositions of the State of Israel.

However, the commission did recommend that General Eli Zeira and his aides, General Shalev and Lieutenant Colonels Yonah Bendman and David Guedalia, be relieved of their duties. And, of course, General Elazar, in his role as scapegoat, was the first head to roll.

Thus, the name of Eli Zeira was added to the long list of Israeli Intelligence Service heads fired or forced to leave as a result of differences with their superiors. The Aman chiefs predominated easily, with five out of seven who were not able to stay the normal term of their missions. Isser Beeri, the first chief of military intelligence, had been fired by Ben-Gurion because of the Tubiansky affair (see Chapter VI). The second—Benjamin Gibli—because of the Lavon affair. The third—Yehoshafat Harkabi—because of an aborted psychological campaign. The fourth—Chaim Herzog—stayed at his post only two years because of his run-ins with Chief of Staff General Chaim Laskov. Only Meir Amit and Aharon Yariv lasted out the full term of their appointments.

Other branches of intelligence were treated no better, nor were their chiefs less subject to purges. Boris Gourel, the first director of the Mossad, did not last a year. His successor, Reuven Shiloakh, had to step down; but since he was sent to the United States as minister plenipotentiary, he continued to be active in undercover operations. In the course of these operations, he often opposed his successor, Isser Harel, who had had an active role in a number of the dismissals.

The "boss" who established the longevity record—Harel himself—walked out in anger twice: in 1963, over the German scientists incident, and in 1966, when he was in charge of coordinating the intelligence services of the Levi Eshkol cabinet and could not get the cooperation of the heads of the Mossad and Aman. "What a business!" said the director of one of the intelligence services one day. "The Talmud teaches us that since the destruction of the Temple, only fools can be prophets in Israel. And here we are asked to be prophets on a full-time basis!"

The fact that the Middle East is a hornet's nest of secret service agents and activities did not help the Israelis. After Hong Kong, the Middle East harbors more agents per square mile than anywhere else: Aden, Beirut, Jerusalem, Nicosia, Cairo, Riyadh, Teheran, Istanbul, Bahrein, Kuwait—all are objectives in the highly concentrated world map of espionage.

In the thirty years since 1948, the two main central agencies—the CIA and the KGB—have had their dozen or so resounding failures. But the unpreparedness before the Yom Kippur War remains, above all, the most shameful failure of the Israeli secret services, or rather that of Aman—the army's intelligence service which had taken the lead above the others.

It was not only a total miscalculation of the Egyptian-Syrian military plans, it was worse: the breaking down of a defense system which was badly in need of repair after years and years of excellent service which had quietly become routine. In a country which has had to live in a state of preparedness ever since its creation, the rapid turnover in military intelligence heads attests to the difficulties and the ingratitude inherent in the job, and reflects the hazards of politics as well.

The exercise of leadership is a particularly trying business in Israel. Prime ministers themselves are not in the habit of finishing out their terms: Ben-Gurion stepped down from office twice. Moshe Sharett was forced out of office. Levi Eshkol died while in office, no doubt from the strain. Golda Meir was tumbled by the political fallout created by the Yom Kippur War. Rabin tripped over the hitches in the economic-financial imbroglio left by the big-money manipulator, Pinchas Sapir. The conflict of a young country striving for normalcy while in a perpetual state of siege makes the governing of Israel an extremely difficult task.

In an attempt to accommodate half-truths and half-measures in order to realize the wonderful dream of a successful consumer society in the tempting shadow of the Bar-Lev Line, Israel became, on the eve of Yom Kippur, the victim of a triple error in judgment concerning the intentions of the Egyptians, the Soviets, and the Americans. The first cost the highest in human lives and national image. It was not the fault of insufficient information; for fifteen days, information came pouring in from all sides. From a tactical point of view, dozens of military reports from soldiers and officers posted along the Canal (including aerial information) described preparations which went far beyond the usual training maneuvers. In his October 1 report, Lieutenant Siman-Tov ("good omen" in Hebrew) showed that every indication proved that the Egyptian forces were regrouping for an attack. "If these were simple military maneuvers which they would normally undertake, why are they all taking place along the banks of the Canal?"

From a strategic point of view, Aman was informed of the sudden departure from Syria of Russian technicians' families as well as of the coordinating measures taken by the Syrians and Egyptians. Furthermore, the word *war* turned up more and more frequently in the reports from the Mossad's local agents. Their chief, General Zvi Zamir, left the country in utmost secrecy to see for himself how valid those reports were. When his frantic cable arrived at 4:00 A.M. on October 6, "The war will break out today," it was already too late.

"What more could I have done?" he asked later of his critics. "Threaten them with my revolver? Threaten to commit suicide if they didn't pay attention?"

During the course of its investigation, the Agranat Commission of Inquiry found and documented 400 such warnings.

"If their contents had been brought to my attention," protested Chief of Staff General "Dado" Elazar, "I would certainly have taken different measures as soon as Golda returned from Vienna."

Unfortunately, no one had seen nor read this impressive collection of messages before the commission compiled it. This astounding communications gap between the various services and departments was the result of the totally erroneous reading of the situation by the political-military establishment. According to the elaborate theory developed by Dayan who became, in the wake of the euphoria which reigned after June 1967, the superstar of Israel's security, the Arabs would not be able to overcome their disadvantage and start another war for another ten years. *"Aravi ze Aravi"*—which translates pejoratively to mean: "An Arab is always an Arab"—was one of his shibboleths. But Dayan did not draw the same apocalyptic conclusions as Begin: Dayan maintained that all one had to do was beat on tin pans to frighten away the Syrians just as he did in his childhood kibbutz, Degania, to scatter the grasshoppers.

The contradictory messages arrived at the army intelligence department for research and evaluation which was as convinced as Dayan (or by Dayan) that war was impossible. Just to make sure that they were right, they put aside all proof to the contrary. The plans for the joint Egyptian-Syrian attack were known for months. D-day was known a few hours before the attack. But, as incredible as it seems today, right up until the last moment, the Israeli military chiefs could not admit and accept the fact that the Arabs were really going to attack.

After the fact, what appears to be a clear-cut case of aberration was nothing more than the manifestation of a complete mental block: the defense mechanism psychologists call "denial." To accept such a possibility was not only to question a system which had already proven its value, but—more dramatic—it was to put oneself in question as well. Victorious and vainglorious generals are rarely given to that sort of introspection. The facts, evidence, and logic were all trimmed, twisted, and reshaped until they fit into the desired picture like the various pieces of a puzzle; a general picture, which had become on the eve of the general elections (initially scheduled for October 30) a kind of political vote of confidence.

In the middle of the election campaign in September 1973,

Dayan was pushing for a reduction of the military service which was to improve the image of the Labor party coalition! The same superiority complex was also valid for General Ariel Arik Sharon, who posed in front of the Suez Canal for a promotional film for the opposing coalition (Likud).

"What you see here," he said before the camera, "is the most formidable tank obstacle in the world." In order to break the Aman monopoly in the domain of alerts and intelligence evaluations, the Agranat Commission of Inquiry recommended the nomination of a national security council with real powers answering directly to the prime minister. In addition, they asked for the creation of a research center within the Foreign Ministry. But these recommendations were never followed up, and Dayan, having become Begin's Minister for Foreign Affairs, personally saw to their substantive demise.

In October 1973 the military also misread the meaning of the Arab war objectives. On the third day of the conflict, Dayan foresaw "a long war lasting for several months." This error in judgment had two detrimental effects: the cessation of the October 8 counteroffensive on the Canal by Generals "Brenn" Adan and Arik Sharon, and the painful setting up of an airlift that put Israel into an obvious position of dependence on the United States. Actually, Sadat's plan was limited to staying camped on the Sinai bank while holding out for American mediation and the UN cease-fire decision.

Israel was also wrong about the significance of Egypt's 1972 expulsion of Soviet experts: General Yariv, the former chief of army intelligence, was convinced that Sadat had eliminated all military options. In the absence of accurate intelligence-readings concerning the intentions of the Kremlin, despite excellent and copious intelligence-gathering, the Israelis were unable to accurately measure two crucial political factors at the end of the Yom Kippur War: the degree of bluff involved in the October 24 Russian threat of military intervention to protect the Egyptian Third Army which was encircled in the Sinai; and the American threat of nuclear mobilization in order to persuade the Israeli Army to end that encirclement.

Jerusalem actually committed three errors concerning American intentions—errors which to some extent must be attributed to its embassy in Washington. First: Israeli intelligence "enlightened" the CIA (which, unlike the Israelis, accurately announced the danger of war ten days before Yom Kippur). Twenty-four hours before Yom Kippur, Minister for Foreign Affairs Abba Eban, met with Kissinger at the Waldorf-Astoria and showed him Zeira's "remote probability" analysis which had immediate CIA support. The same evening he had received an envelope from Israel which arrived by special courier and was marked: "TOP SECRET. URGENT FOR KISSINGER." Nobody bothered to inform Eban of its contents. Thus Eban had it delivered by messenger to Kissinger's office in the Waldorf-Astoria only the next day. He then took his telephone off the hook and went to bed, where he intended to spend the entire Day of Atonement. He was awakened at 6:00 A.M., New York time, by his personal assistant, who had been hammering at the door for fifteen minutes with a telegram announcing Israel's mobilization. Eban contacted Kissinger, who had not yet received the famous envelope.

"Is this Israel's military initiative?" Kissinger asked.

"I'll find out," Eban replied.

The message in the envelope which Kissinger did not receive until two hours later—that is, two hours after the war started—was a new Aman intelligence analysis of the situation, this time much more pessimistic concerning the Egyptian-Syrian military preparations! If that envelope—which contained precious new information, including aerial photos—had reached Kissinger in time, twenty-four hours earlier, Israel might not have had to move without the major military support of a preventive air strike which Golda Meir and Dayan refused to allow General Elazar because "it would alienate American sympathies."

The second error concerned the misjudgment of American intentions regarding the cease-fire. Eban did not grasp the meaning of Kissinger's phone call the evening of October 19 informing him that "something important is going on." That evening, without even checking what Kissinger meant, Eban left for Israel. During a stopover at Orly the next morning, he learned of "Dear Henry"'s departure for Moscow, accompanied by Soviet ambassador Anatoly Dobrynin. Eban assumed that the head of American diplomacy was making the trip in order to allow Israel to gain time. So did most of Israel's top politicians. On a visit to the Canal front on October 21, Deputy Prime Minister Yigal Allon told General Sharon, who was preparing a major attack on Ismailia:

"Take it easy, Arik, there's no rush."

The third major mistake of Golda Meir's cabinet occurred on the night of October 24. It found itself completely surprised by Kissinger's collusion with the Soviets to deprive Israel of a military victory by playing up the danger of a nuclear clash between the two major powers. But even the trauma of Yom Kippur and the recommendations of the Agranat Commission of Inquiry were not enough to evoke a coherent decision-making process capable of protecting Israel from a political surprise—potentially as dangerous as a military one.

But then, American policy makers were no safer than the Israelis from CIA mistakes in the sinking sands of the Middle East. In less than a quarter of a century, no less than ten serious mistakes and blunders have placed the United States at a disadvantage vis-à-vis the global-strategy players in Moscow.

1. In giving rise to the Bagdad Pact in 1955, Washington pushed Nasser into the arms of the Russians.
2. In the midst of domestic witch-hunts, the Americans minimized the importance of the first armament contract between the Communists and Egypt in 1955. This event, which opened the door to Soviet penetration in the area, passed almost unnoticed by the CIA.
3. The CIA was caught by surprise by the Israeli-Franco-British tripartite Suez operation in 1956. The angry reaction of the United States strengthened the Soviet position.
4. The CIA was equally surprised by the fall of the pro-American regime of Iraq on July 14, 1958.
5. In April 1970 the CIA backed a Pentagon report which insisted that there would be no direct participation of the Russian military in the war of attrition on the Suez Canal. Shortly thereafter, the clash over the Suez Canal of Israeli and Soviet pilots proved the fallacy of that thesis.
6. The CIA was taken in by Israeli overconfidence on the eve of the Yom Kippur War.
7. Former CIA head Richard Helms, compromised in the Watergate affair, and, later, ambassador in Teheran, did nothing to stop Kissinger from sacrificing the Kurds in 1975, after the CIA had encouraged them to revolt against Iraq in 1970. The 1978-79 crisis in Iran proved the terrible mistake of the Irani-Iraqi rapprochement at the expense of Kurdish lives.
8. The CIA did not anticipate the Rabat Arab summit decision in October 1974 to recognize the PLO as the representative of the Palestinians to the detriment of King Hussein of Jordan. This decision surprised the Israelis and the Egyptians as well. It did, however, receive the benediction of the KGB whose agents in Nicosia (Cyprus) met with the emissaries of the PLO and approved a plan created by two of Arafat's lieutenants, Abu Ayad and Farouk el-Kadoumi, which would revenge the Sep-

tember 1970 Palestinian defeat in Jordan. This plan included the assassination of King Hussein while en route to Rabat, the taking over of the conference's information services, and the intimidation of the summit participants.

One week before the opening of the conference, 200 armed Palestinians infiltrated the Moroccan capital of Rabat, occupied the offices of the Moroccan Minister of Information, and censored all the conference publications and bulletins. It took Sadat's threat to Arafat to throw every Palestinian out of Egypt before PLO headquarters would agree to drop the plan to murder Hussein.

9. In May 1977 the CIA was totally taken aback, as were many others, by the victories of Begin and the Likud in the national election.

10. The CIA completely misinterpreted Dayan's sudden visit to Morocco in September 1977 to prepare the Begin-Sadat encounter in November 1977, by assuming that the tension along the Israeli-Egyptian cease-fire line in October 1977 would be an obstacle to such an encounter. The CIA analysis did not allow for the strong reaction of Egypt's president to the American-Soviet joint declaration of October first which reintroduced Moscow to the diplomatic negotiating process in the Middle East.

"What a colossal blunder!" cried out one of Sadat's close collaborators upon learning of the project for the joint communiqués.

A congressional committee, chaired by Congressman Otis Pike, was formed at the end of 1975 to inquire into CIA failures and blunders. It was particularly critical of the CIA's failure to predict the October 1973 crisis: the report of a high-placed agent in an Arab country concerning the hostile intentions of Egypt and Syria had been set aside with no consideration given to it at all; the evacuation of Russian civilians from Syria should have signaled a red alert at once. Kissinger confirmed the CIA's failure: "We asked our intelligence service as well as Israel's three times during the week that preceded the war to give their evaluation. Both U.S. and Israeli intelligence were agreed that the breaking out of hostilities was so unlikely that we could estimate the probability as being zero."

The Pike Report further revealed that two hours after the start of the war, the special security committee which met during crisis periods had concluded, on the basis of information in their possession on October 6, that there was only "a Syrian raid of limited consequence."

The report showed that the CIA had requested only two limited reconnaissance flights on October 13 and 15; the agency preferred to base its evaluations totally on the Israeli analysis of the situation. This decision cost two CIA officers and another at the Pentagon their careers.

The close relations between the American and Israeli intelligence services, which the Pike Report considered dangerously interdependent, has not always been a negative factor for the United States.

"The manufacturers of military materials and the American specialists in problems of defense have received a constant flow of information concerning the performance of American equipment and captured Soviet equipment during the Yom Kippur War. This information allowed for the possibility of important military modifications," explained a former American Air Force intelligence officer in the Israeli daily, *Maariv,* on May 6, 1977. His superior, General George Keagan, told American news correspondents that he was able to examine at length Soviet arms and equipment which he would never have had occasion to do otherwise.

"Israel's contribution has been a major help in improving our own national security," he declared during a seminar in Washington on May 17, 1978. "This immeasurable contribution is worth at least fifty billion dollars. Five CIA's would never have been able to do the same job for us."

On July 15, 1977, when Israeli Prime Minister Menachem Begin inaugurated his first visit to the United States, he presented President Carter with a "top secret" dossier which enumerated in detail every case of an Israeli contribution to the American national defense.

The next day, Carter said to Begin, "It's incredible! I had no idea of any of this."

From the time of the Sinai campaign in 1956 to the antiterrorist expedition in Southern Lebanon in 1978, the Israelis managed to acquire enormous stocks of Soviet weapons: T-34, T-64, and T-65 tanks; MIG-17, MIG-19, and MIG-21 planes; SAM 2, 3, 6, and 7 ground-to-air missiles; radar installations, antitank missiles, and similar materiel. According to American reports, all this war booty (probably mentioned, for the most part, in the Begin report) was made available to the United States.

But it was in the realm of practical experience that the Israeli contribution was by far the most important: the American war effort in Vietnam, with 50,000 men killed in antiguerrilla combat, does not measure up to the experience of large-scale combat chalked up by Tsahal, especially during the Yom Kippur War, when more than 5,000 tanks were engaged in battle—the equivalent of all the front-line armored forces of NATO!

Israel is the only Western country to have battled in the air against the Soviets and to have adopted electronic countermeasures in the missile war. According to a May 1978 *Aviation Week* report, Israeli tanks equipped with a special magnetic-protection system suffered no losses from antitank missiles during the April 1978 military operation in southern Lebanon.

Thus it was not merely a simple act of politeness when General George S. Brown, then U.S. Chairman of the Joint Chiefs of Staff, addressed a congratulatory message to Tsahal's new Chief of Staff, General Rafael (Raful) Eytan. Since the rectification of the failures during the Yom Kippur War, the links uniting the two armies have been extended to include an exchange of strategic analyses and other areas as well.

Significantly, the ex-head of the Mossad, Isser Harel, admitted the existence of joint operations by the CIA and Israeli intelligence in the March 10, 1977, issue of *Yediot Aharonot,* Israel's evening newspaper. According to the testimony of former CIA agent Philip Agee, relations between the two agencies were maintained through a separate department, free from potential leaks, by the head of the counterespionage section, James Jesus Angleton, until his resignation at the end of 1974.

Thanks to his reputation as a champion of anticommunism, this sensitive poet, this devotee of shellfishing, was able to carve out for himself an almost impregnable position as head of special counterespionage operations. From his office in a top-secret wing of CIA headquarters in Langley, Virginia, Angleton directed both the work involved in the detection of double agents and those operatives concerned with drug traffic, as well as anti-Soviet operations in Central Europe and the Near East.

In January 1956 Angleton established his initial links with the Israeli services during the secret mission of Robert Anderson, Eisenhower's special envoy to Jerusalem and Cairo, Though he failed to do so, Anderson's mission had been to arrange a meeting between Ben-Gurion and Nasser before the state of affairs became irreparable. At the time, Angleton was supervising the training of hundreds of Hungarian, Polish, Rumanian, and Czech agents in a secret West German camp directed by a former Yugoslav officer who had himself been trained at the Hapsburg military academy. Its aim: provoking popular uprisings in the Soviet satellites.

In April the Mossad sent Angleton the first complete, unpublished text of Khrushchev's report before February's Twentieth Congress of the Soviet Communist Party. Angleton decided to speed up the formation of these groups and their entry into action. However, in this election year, Eisenhower had decided to reap an immediate political advantage by publishing the report with no regard for the fact that he was compromising the climate of East-West détente by making America look like an instigator of unrest. Angleton, who was in the midst of his preparations, was opposed to this publication. Later on, the chief of the CIA counterespionage service was to attribute the failure of the October uprising in Hungary to the premature publication of the Khrushchev report which did not give him time to put his agents in a position to intervene efficiently. Moreover, this tension between the White House and the CIA was related to Eisenhower's decision to act with Marshal Bulganin against the Israeli-Franco-British Suez Canal operation.

Several weeks after being accused by the American press of contributing to the overthrow of Allende's socialist regime in Chile in September 1973, Angleton was tripped up by the repercussions of a new scandal reported in *The New York Times* on December 22, 1974: the illegal monitoring and indexing of the private correspondence of tens of thousands of American citizens suspected of subversive opinions during Richard Nixon's presidency. The FBI, in permanent rivalry with the CIA's counterespionage section, and the new head of the intelligence agency, William Colby, appointed by President Ford after the Watergate scandal, took advantage of these events to demand Angleton's resignation the very next day.

But the real reason for Angleton's disgrace was his stubborn insistence on establishing a link between the KGB and Lee Harvey Oswald, the official assassin of John F. Kennedy. Angleton had based his conviction on the fact that soon after the killing of Kennedy, and then of Oswald himself, KGB defector Yuri Nosenko, who had been responsible for Oswald during his Moscow stay, had asked for asylum in the United States. For three years Nosenko repeated in vain to his FBI and CIA interrogators that the Soviets had had nothing to do with the Kennedy assassination; Angleton alone refused to believe any part of Nosenko's story. Since Angleton had devoted his entire career to unmasking double agents, he had convinced himself that Nosenko, as well, was a double agent sent to the United States by the KGB precisely in order to wipe out all trace of its role in the affair. He also strongly believed that there was a double agent in a very high position in the United States administration.

"Take a good look around you," he confided to Isser Harel, "and you will surely find a Soviet agent."

Angleton's departure in December 1974 unquestionably affected the relationship between his department and Israel at a moment when the reassessment of American policy in the Middle East, following the results of the Yom Kippur War, the evolution of the Egyptian regime, and the increasing importance of Saudi Arabia, was to cause the CIA to undertake initiatives that were not favorable to Israel.

Since 1975 the CIA has leaked more and more information with the aim of proving Israel's superiority in the balance of power with the Arab countries and Israel's supposed nuclear capability. On several occasions its assessments of the situation in the Middle East helped White House efforts to modify Congress's traditional pro-Israeli position. In mid-May 1978, a secret CIA report concerning Soviet penetration in the Horn of Africa presented to Senate members shortly before the vote, influenced a closed-door Senate decision in favor of the sale of combat planes to Egypt and Saudi Arabia by presenting both countries as most apt to oppose such penetration.

The CIA has never stopped increasing its presence and intelligence operations in the Middle East since the Yom Kippur debacle. Reconnaissance coverage by satellites and planes of the SR 71 type have been stepped up to the point of taking up to one photo every six hours! Aerial photos are regularly developed, blown up, and studied at the CIA's surveillance center, the famous building at 213 M Street in Washington, not far from the Capitol. The photos are so sharp that a viewer can make out the time on a wristwatch worn by a soldier on sentry duty in the Sinai. More than ever, spy ships intercept all radio and telephone communications in the region. And, hardly by chance, the chief of the American Field Mission in the Sinai is a senior staff member of the CIA.

In Egypt, even during the difficult years of the Cairo-Moscow honeymoon, the CIA, using Kermit Roosevelt, its agent in Cairo, maintained a discreet liaison with Nasser (whom it had supported at first) through the intermediary of a close collaborator of the Egyptian president.

"Contacts with the Americans during this whole period were all the more complicated because of the fact that they insisted on keeping two channels of communication," noted Hassanein Heykal, a confidant of the late Nasser, in his book, *The Road to Ramadan.* "Secretary of State Rogers' messages went through diplomatic channels to Egypt's Foreign Minister, Riyad, while Nixon's messages to Nasser were channeled through the CIA and Egypt's secret services."

In a January 1975 interview in *Business Week* Kissinger did not hide the fact that under certain conditions the United States might well overthrow a foreign government through the use of "political pressure." It is not inconceivable to wonder to what extent the CIA might have had a part in the political pressure acting to overthrow the government of Menachem Begin in Jerusalem in 1978. On the morning of the electoral surprise of May 1977, the CIA prepared a dossier concerning the popularity factor of the new government; the probable evolution of popular opinion regarding it; the state of health of the prime minister; and the chances of his successors. Its special report, giving an edge to General Ezer Weizmann in the struggle for succession, was transmitted to Sadat in November, before his departure for Jerusalem. This bit of information might explain why the first question the Egyptian president asked upon landing at Lod Airport, outside Tel Aviv, was: "Where is Ezer?"

If it was out of the question for the CIA to undertake a subversive action against Begin, it was perfectly possible for the Agency to make life difficult, just as it had managed to do when it turned Prime Minister Rabin's visit to the United States in March 1977 into a catastrophe. So much so, in fact, that Rabin lost out in the struggle for the leadership of the Labor party to his Defense Minister, Shimon Peres, and the Labor party itself lost the May 1977 elections.

The CIA had, in fact, never hesitated in the past to infiltrate the Israeli embassy in Washington and to monitor every conversation that went on in it. Apparently, the Agency had even seen fit to record all telephone calls exchanged in September 1970 between Golda Meir and Rabin when Rabin was working with Kissinger on the joint operation intended to save Hussein from the Syrian-Palestinian offensive supported by Moscow. Kissinger wanted to be kept apprised of Israel's activities by any means whatsoever.

Much more recently, in May 1978, a U.S. vice-consul in Israel was surprised inside the Khares military base, near Tulkarem, on the West Bank, in the process of observing the establishment of a new Israeli settlement.

Contrary to appearances, the KGB and the GRU turned out to be better informed than the other intelligence services in the Middle East at the time of the October 1973 crisis. Not only were the

Russians aware of Egyptian-Syrian intentions at least ten days in advance, thanks to their antennae in Damascus, but having learned from their former disappointments, they decided to furnish Sadat with all the material assistance necessary for the realization of his objectives. It is ironic that after having expelled the Soviet experts in July 1972, with the benediction of the Americans, the Egyptian president received the maximum in military equipment from Moscow. Planes, missiles, and tanks were delivered upon demand by the Russians between July 1972 and July 1973. Russian assistance even extended as far as techniques in interception of radio communiqués. When they crossed the Suez Canal the afternoon of October 6, the Egyptians were in possession of the Israeli Army code map of the Sinai, baptized *Sirius,* already translated in Arabic. They were thus capable of immediately tuning into and decoding the conversations and the messages of Israeli tactical units and could thus aim their artillery fire precisely at the headquarters and principal command posts of Tsahal's various divisions, brigades, and battalions.

That is how General Abraham (Albert) Mandler, commander of the front-line armored division in the Sinai, was killed by artillery fire aimed at his vehicle a few seconds after he had given his exact position to the commander of the southern front, General Shmuel Gonen who was overflying the Giddi pass in a helicopter: a little crest bearing the code number 61 on the *Sirius* map. The headquarters of General "Brenn" Adan, commander of a second armored division in the Sinai, were permanently subjected to Egyptian cannon fire and the officers had to keep moving in order to dodge the constant attacks.

In fact, Colonel Dany Matt, the first to cross the Canal on October 15, at 10:00 P.M. at the head of a parachute unit, was soon aware that each of his radio exchanges provoked a storm of shells from mortar and Katyusha rocket launchers.

But the tactical interception of radio communiqués did not yield only positive results for the Egyptians. On October 16 at 6:50 A.M., General Arik Sharon began to transport his tanks on barges to the West Bank of the Suez Canal without waiting for the construction of the first bridge to be completed. His move was contrary to the instruction of General Bar-Lev, who was in command of the southern front. Sharon called Bar-Lev's headquarters in Oum Kheshiba to advise that he had sent only three tanks to the African shore to protect Dany Matt's 200 paratroopers. Indeed, more than 30 tanks had already crossed the Canal. But the Egyptians who intercepted Sharon's message to Bar-Lev decided that the number three indicated that it was merely a diversionary operation on the tactical commando level.

When on that same day, October 16, at 4:00 P.M., Golda Meir announced to the Knesset that "an Israeli force was at this very moment operating on the West Bank of the Canal," Sadat received a phone call from his Minister of Defense, assuring him: "It is nothing more than three tanks which have infiltrated the other side of the Canal.".

Fearing a catastrophe, Soviet Premier Aleksei Kosygin canceled that evening's appointment with the Danish prime minister in order to rush to Cairo. Sadat victoriously waved Communiqué No. 45 from the Egyptian high command announcing the liquidation of an Israeli unit which had infiltrated the West Bank of the Canal. But the next day, KGB agents in Cairo informed Kosygin that satellite camera Cosmos 597, sent into orbit October 3 at an altitude of 300 kilometers, and at an inclination of 65°4″, which was observing the battlefields on the Israeli borders, had taken some disturbing photos: an Israeli operation of huge proportions was developing on the West Bank of the Canal.

The Soviets were the first to comprehend the importance of Sharon's offensive. Kosygin alerted Sadat and met with him three times on October 18 before leaving for Moscow. The very next day Kosygin began using his hot-line connection to the White House.

Its accurate appraisal of the Yom Kippur situation hardly compensated for all the errors committed by the KGB since the inception of its operations in Egypt:

(1) The Soviets were wrong to base an entire Middle East strategy on Nasser's ability to open all doors for them, beginning with Yemen, which an Egyptian expeditionary corps did not succeed in conquering.

(2) They miscalculated the military capacity of their allies, Egypt and Syria, at the outset of the Six-Day War.

(3) They did not believe the Israelis capable of taking the risk of encountering Russian pilots in 1970.

(4) They were surprised by Nasser's decision, at the same time, to accept a cease-fire on the Canal.

(5) They underestimated the American reaction to the Syrian intervention in Jordan in September 1970.

(6) They did not anticipate Sadat's decision to expel Soviet technicians and experts, etc.

In 1974 the Kremlin decided to change the axis of its Middle East policies as the result of a KGB report presented at a secret meeting of the Politburo. The KGB report suggested, on the one hand, that the Soviet Union activate its support to such extremist groups as the PFLP of Waddia Haddad; the international terrorist network headed by Carlos; and the pro-Iraqi front of Abu Nidal; since these groups were capable of fomenting confusion and turmoil in the area. On the other hand, it recommended concentrating penetration efforts in the regions of the Persian Gulf and the Horn of Africa. The Politburo immediately adopted a new emphasis in the Eastern Mediterranean favoring the anticommunist Muammar Qaddafi of Libya, where Kosygin was officially received several months later. The objective was to torpedo all attempts at direct negotiations between Arabs and Israelis, using terrorism if necessary. Thus it is easy to understand the assassinations of British journalist David Holden in Cairo just before the start of the Israeli-Egyptian conference in December 1977; of Sadat's friend, Egyptian journalist, Youssef Sebai, in Nicosia; of Said Hammami, the moderate representative of the PLO in London; and perhaps that of Henri Curiel in May 1978, in Paris.

But, on October 24, 1973, the Kremlin leaders committed their gravest error. Their verbal threat calculated to impose a cease-fire provided Kissinger with the pretext he needed to save the Egyptian Third Army from Israeli encirclement by using the nuclear scare.

Kissinger had set the stage for a switch in American policy in the Middle East from the fourth day of the Yom Kippur War.

"Since you have not kept your part of the bargain to quickly break the Arab military offensive, it's my turn to play," were his words to a prominent Israeli.

Kissinger seized the opportunity to play out the second part of his conquest of Egypt after the expulsion of the Soviet military in 1972. From the end of that crucial year, he set into motion the plans for a meeting with Hafez Ismail, his opposite number in the Egyptian administration. Donald Kendall, the president of Pepsi-Cola, was sent to intercede with Heykal, Nasser's former adviser. Nixon had been Kendall's business lawyer, and he remained an intimate friend.

In February 1973 Ismail arrived on an official visit to Washington. During an audience at the White House, Nixon went on for over an hour on a theme close to Kissinger's heart: the reduction of the Israeli-Arab conflict to the simple equation of a balance between Egyptian sovereignty and Israeli security. Nixon believed this could be accomplished through the pursuit of secret negotiations under the guidance of Kissinger, and unknown to the State Department. On February 24 and 25, 1973, Ismail did, in fact, have three long secret meetings with Kissinger in Donald Kendall's country home in Connecticut. The two negotiators had practically mapped out the entire strategy of future Egyptian-American relations: mutual confidence, no dirty tricks, and secret coordination of policy vis-à-vis Israel. Kissinger offered a *pax americana* in the form of procedures and rules to be negotiated separately and secretly under his aegis with a key phrase thrown into the middle of the conversation:

"The United States cannot impose a solution on Israel, but it has the means to exert a certain amount of pressure based on special moral grounds."

Upon Ismail's return, after hearing this phrase, Sadat decided to launch a war whose objective would be to furnish those "moral grounds." Originally intended for May, the war was postponed until October in order to allow for an "opinion-molding" campaign. Kissinger's new policy orientation led him to maneuver against Israel's interests five times in less than three months: between October and December 1973.

On the fourth day of the Yom Kippur War, Kissinger took advantage of Dayan's bewilderment, induced by a computer error concerning Tsahal's reserve of weapons and munitions in the event of a prolonged conflict, to delay the setting up of the airlift which Israel had requested. Thus the major part of the materiel airlifted to Israel by a chain of giant Galaxies, shortly after the Soviets started their airlift to Syria, never managed to be delivered on time for the fighting.

On October 16 Kissinger informed General Mustafa Barzani, the leader of the Kurdish rebellion in Iraq, who had received CIA support up until that time, that he opposed the Kurds' accepting the Israeli appeal of October 14 to attack the rear of the Iraqi Army. Such a move would have prevented the strengthening of the Iraqi military intervention in the Golan Heights area, which could have forced Israel to delay Sharon's attempt to cross the Canal.

A Kurdish offensive at that time would not only have relieved Tsahal of a menace on its northern front, but would also have given the Kurds an important advantage in safeguarding their national survival, cynically sacrificed by Kissinger two years later.

The Pike Report reveals the Kurdish tragedy in detail. According to this report, in order to respond to Soviet penetration in Iraq, the CIA had Iran deliver the Russian arms that had fallen into Israeli hands during the Six-Day War to the Kurdish rebels. The head of the CIA bureau in Teheran had easily won over the support of the Iranian authorities, who were at that time embroiled in a controversy with Bagdad regarding the control of the Shatt el-Arab region on the Persian Gulf.

But in February 1975 the Iraqis and the Iranians reached a compromise. One of the secret clauses called for a cessation of all help to the Kurds. On March 10 the head of the CIA bureau in Teheran pleaded with Kissinger not to sign the death warrant of the Kurdish people in Iraq by turning them over to their executioners. To no avail. Kissinger allowed the genocide of the Kurds after having prevented them from saving themselves by assisting the Israelis in their counteroffensive.

And yet, as early as 1966, Israel had brought the Kurds humanitarian aid through a medical mission led by the Vice-Minister for Commerce and Industry, Aryeh (Lova) Eliav. He had met the aging Barzani in December in the mountains of Iraqi Kurdistan, transmitting to him, along with the good wishes of Levi Eshkol, his prime minister, an offer to build a field hospital. The rebel chief gave Eliav his sword as a gift for the president of the Knesset. According to Ubidallah, one of Barzani's sons, who defected to the Iraqis in 1971, Israeli assistance to the Kurdish revolt was also to include military equipment, advisers, instructors, and direct radio contact. According to columnist Jack Anderson, "The head of the Mossad visited Barzani in his mountain fortress at least once."

However, on October 16, 1973, this alliance was no longer to Kissinger's liking. Three days later, having understood the scope of the Israeli military reestablishment on the southern front, Kissinger flew discreetly to Moscow. Although he had every possibility to prolong his wheeling and dealing in Moscow, in less than forty-eight hours he had concluded an agreement for a cease-fire without even consulting his former allies in Jerusalem. He blamed this "breakdown in coordination" on the bad electronic transmissions between Moscow and Washington.

In order to force Tsahal to respect the cease-fire, which was set for 6:00 P.M. on October 22, and to loosen the Israeli hold on Suez, where the encirclement of the Egyptian Third Army was threatening to become a military and political catastrophe for Sadat, Kissinger did not hesitate to simulate an international crisis on October 24 by placing the Strategic Air Command (SAC) on a state of third-degree alert. Kissinger professed to have responded to a Russian nuclear threat. However, Secretary of Defense James Schlesinger later revealed that he attempted to oppose this measure, which "was not justified." In fact, Egypt's call for help was limited to a request for a joint team of Soviet and American observers to oversee the cease-fire. And Moscow was quite satisfied to send 70 observers on October 24.

A Telex exchange between Assad and Sadat was the document which, on the night of October 24, Kissinger offered as providing the justification for a nuclear alert. From this document, it was possible to deduce, at most, that the Syrian president had *himself* asked for help from the Russians. And when Brezhnev threatened, in a communication to Nixon—that if a coordinated action could not be agreed upon, Nixon would be held liable—Kissinger was able to prevail over Schlesinger. There was no problem in getting Nixon to agree. He had just fired Attorney General John Mitchell, on October 20, in connection with the Watergate scandal. A world crisis was a welcome diversion.

For Kissinger, the state of alert supplied the "moral grounds" on which to put pressure on Israel. At midnight, on October 26, when Golda Meir asked him by telephone to link the sending of food and supplies to the encircled Egyptian Third Army to an exchange of prisoners, Kissinger's answer was:

"If you would rather have Russian helicopters fly the supplies to them, that's fine, but we want no part of it."

On December 21 a few days before the opening of the Geneva Conference, Kissinger worked against Israel's interests for the fifth time. He was displeased with the rapid progress the Israeli and Egyptian negotiators, Generals Yariv and Gamasy, were making under a tent at Kilometer 101 toward the disengagement of forces on the Israeli-Egyptian cease-fire line. He telephoned Golda Meir:

"If you make those concessions to the Egyptians now, what will there be left to negotiate at Geneva?"

With general elections only a week away—having been postponed from October 31 to December 30 because of the war—the prime minister was interested in a diplomatic coup in Geneva. Yariv was ordered to slow down the negotiations at Kilometer 101.

A few weeks later, during the course of an impressive shuttle between Jerusalem and Aswan, Kissinger obtained the signature on a first agreement for military disengagement. The same agreement had been within reach during the Gamasy-Yariv negotiations.

"That agreement could have been concluded at Kilometer 101—nothing more than that, perhaps, but certainly nothing less," was the bitter comment of the ex-chief of Israeli military intelligence, Yariv.

Thus the opportunity for a first real direct Israeli-Egyptian dialogue following the Yom Kippur War slipped away. It took the Entebbe raid in July 1976 for Israel to get over its trauma and restore confidence in Tsahal.

18

OPERATION THUNDERBOLT

Delirium! All over Israel, the resonant sound of the shofar—the ram's horn blown by the rabbi on high holidays—could be heard. The crowd that had begun to arrive at Ben-Gurion Airport to greet the hundred liberated hostages and to give a triumphal welcome to the commando unit returning from Entebbe, suddenly recognized Menachem Begin, with his impassive face and fixed smile, his austere black suit and habitual polka-dot tie, stiff as a dummy in the Tel Aviv Wax Museum. It lifted him up off the ground and bore him through the air, passing him from shoulder to shoulder amidst cheers, shouts of approval, and showers of red carnations.

The long-time leader of the opposition party had been among the first to arrive at Ben Gurion Airport on this hot morning of July 4, 1976: the ministers and the military chiefs, led by Rabin and Peres, had gone directly to the base in the Negev where the Hercules airplanes used in Operation Thunderbolt had first set down, leaving to him alone the acclaim of the mass of people who had come out to greet the hostages' return. The popular ovation on that day gave Begin a kind of legitimacy; one that he was to later use as a springboard in his rise to power in the coming year. Yet he was unaware of this when he approached the rostrum in the Knesset, which had met in special session at 3:00 P.M. to salute the prime minister of the Labor government with the heartfelt cry of *"Kol Hakavod!"*—"All Honor!"—the age-old formula of congratulations the former Irgun leader had hitherto kept for the army alone.

Common joy drowned out everything else: the dissension, the feeling of isolation and discouragement felt throughout the country, still reeling from the shock of the Yom Kippur War; economic problems, strikes, concern about Arab unrest in the West Bank, and even in Galilee. Israel knew only one thing: she had won, and no one else in the world could have managed such a victory . . .

A reception held ten days later by the French ambassador in the gardens of his residence in Jaffa to celebrate Bastille Day provided an opportunity for all the leaders of Israel to demonstrate their unity: a unity brought about by the fantastic exploit of the lightning raid on Uganda. And at the center of this scene: Begin being hugged by Rabin. Two years earlier, the leader of the hawks had been lashing out sarcastically at Golda Meir's successor: "We haven't seen a dove like him since the days of Noah's Ark!"

On this evening, his shirt collar open wide, Rabin was grinning broadly. He had just learned that his party's propagandists were preparing a film to be used in the forthcoming elections, a high point of which would be this scene of Begin's congratulating him. Some were even beginning to joke that the campaign ought to be called the "Uganda Plan."

Entebbe had suddenly become legend, even before becoming a part of history. Rumor, the newspapers—soon to be followed by books and films—spewed out stories, most often from foreign sources, which Defense Minister Shimon Peres would note had but one thing in common: they were all fantasy. Such was the case with the rumor of the Idi Amin double supposed to have been used by the Israeli commandos to distract the Ugandan soldiers and terrorists guarding the hostages from the Air France Airbus who were being held in the old terminal. Such was the case with the paratroopers supposedly dropped over Lake Victoria by moonlight with their inflatable boats. Such was the case with the fake messages supposedly sent by the first Hercules to the control tower, announcing the arrival of fedayeen who had been liberated in exchange for the hostages. Such was the case, too, with the bombing diversion that was supposed to have occurred before the airborne commando force landed.

"The secret of the operation," Peres would add, "was that it was kept secret up to the end."

In fact, owing to Rabin's decision to have the opposition party share in the most difficult decision of his own military and political career, Begin was one of the few people privileged to have been let in on the secret.

July 1, 1976: only forty minutes remained. The ultimatum of the air pirates who had diverted the French plane on the Tel Aviv–Paris flight on June 27 during its stopover in Athens was to expire at 11:00 Greenwich Mean Time on that day. If they did not obtain the release of 53 detained terrorists, 40 of whom were in Israel, the 206 hostages they still held would be killed. The hostages, half of whom were Israelis, knew the terrorists would carry out their threat. They also knew that, in the past, Israel had never given in.

At 10:20 GMT, Jerusalem informed Paris of its decision to enter into negotiations, using France as an intermediary. Israel *was* giving in! It was unbelievable. But was it true? At that particular moment, it probably was.

"The sands were running out," Rabin was to explain later. "After the captured Airbus had landed at Entebbe during the night of June 27–28, we had hoped to mount a military operation. But we didn't have time before the ultimatum expired."

The war cabinet which had been urgently assembled in Jerusalem was thus, for the first time since July 1968, about to give in to terrorist blackmail. It was unable to figure out an alternative solution in so short a time: the dead of Munich, of Kiryat Shmona, and of Maalot, would all have been for nothing. To bring Israel to her knees, the terrorists had only to take their hostages to a distant, accomplice state.

The alternative would involve a lightning raid that might mean an end to blackmail, but at the cost of the lives of a great many hostages. And time was needed to organize it.

Euphoric with their success, the terrorists made two mistakes. Even before learning of the Israeli reply, they decided to extend their ultimatum by 72 hours—until July 4, at 11:00 A.M.—and to free 100 non-Israeli hostages. In doing so, they underestimated the daring and imagination of their adversary. The freed hostages were able to add to the information gathered by the Israeli secret services from the 48 who had already been freed. The unexpected three-day grace period was to enable Tsahal's general staff to draw up and perfect plans for an unprecedented military expedition to be carried out 4,000 kilometers away, in the most absolute secrecy. General "Motta" Gur, under urgent pressure from Peres, had ordered his chief of operations to come up with complete plans for the action, code-named *"Kadoor Haraam"* (Thunderbolt). It was Rabin, however, who, on July 3, after a dramatic struggle with his conscience, took responsibility for giving it the green light. Meanwhile his government was keeping two irons in the fire: an operational plan being drawn up in great haste by an elite army group, with the assistance of Intelligence; and negotiation, in which it had less and less faith because the terrorists' demands were now complicated by those of Idi Amin Dada.

"The plan is so outlandish that it will probably succeed," Yigal Allon announced to a limited meeting of the cabinet on July 2.

A task force of 150 men from six different army corps and under the command of the chief of the paratroops, General Dan Shomron, took off the next afternoon aboard four Hercules C-130s, which managed to fly over Africa unnoticed. In liaison with the general staff via a Boeing 707 that was serving as advance headquarters, the task force landed during the night on the main air-strip at Entebbe without attracting attention from the control tower. In 45 seconds, one of the units had eliminated the four terrorists guarding the hostages, and in the next minute it had mowed down three more, while the other units took over the airport installations. During the shooting, three hostages were killed, along with Yonatan (Yoni) Netanyahu, the commando leader. Between the landing of the first plane and the evacuation of the 102 hostages aboard the second, barely 42 minutes had passed.

Up until the denouement, however, the blackout was maintained in Israel. Even the Israeli ambassador in Paris, who was telephoned the evening of July 3 by Rabin and Allon for a lengthy discussion of the negotiating process, was kept in the dark. The Hercules planes had taken off for Entebbe more than three hours earlier, and Rabin and Allon were calling from the operations room in Tel Aviv. They knew that their conversation could be overheard and that it would lay a false trail. But they also knew that if for any reason the Hercules had to turn back at the last moment—a landing site had been discreetly arranged for in Nairobi, in friendly Kenya—then the only option left would be negotiation. Even if they felt that they had no chance of success, they had to leave the door open. It was this uncertainty—under the circumstances necessary up to the last minute—that would later give rise to cries of "Deception," and that would, after the raid, cause irritation on the part of a few European chancelleries. And particularly in Paris, which was responsible in principle for the fate of the Air France passengers.

In the absence of President Giscard d'Estaing and Foreign Minister Jean Sauvagnargues, who were in Puerto Rico, the Quai d'Orsay had responded to the skyjacking of the plane on June 27 by sending Marc Bonnefous, a Foreign Office senior official, to Kampala on the following evening, to "supervise" the ambassador in Uganda, Pierre-Henri Renard. In the deserted Élysée Palace, presidential secretary Claude Pierre-Brossolette thought it unnecessary to bother Giscard in Puerto Rico. When he was later informed by the Foreign Office on June 28, Giscard told it not to take any steps before the kidnappers announced their demands. The next day, Idi Amin handed those demands to Bonnefous in the presence of the Somali ambassador, whom the Palestinians had commissioned to act on their behalf. On June 30 Idi Amin delivered 48 hostages over to the French diplomats, who were not allowed to make contact with the 206 who remained. A message from Giscard to Amin, who was being treated with confidence and courtesy, was Telexed to the embassy in Kampala, but the two French diplomats spent most of the night decoding it and translating it into English, and it was not transmitted to Amin until the next afternoon at the airport, where the terrorists freed 100 additional hostages and extended their ultimatum. Bonnefous and Renard informed Amin of the Israeli decision to negotiate; they were surprised at the suddenness of this decision, since they had guessed that the initial time period fixed by the terrorists would be prolonged. Meanwhile, Brossolette had telephoned Giscard at the Angers prefecture to inform him of Jerusalem's surprising decision.

The illusory Israeli acceptance now led the French to believe that things would drag slowly on and to hope that some compromise solution would ultimately be reached.

On July 2 the Israeli delegation at the Quai d'Orsay reproached the French for trusting Idi Amin, and for believing in a happy outcome to a negotiation so difficult to hold together. In Kampala, the Somali ambassador handed Bonnefous a ransom demand that had been spelled out the previous evening by the PFLP to the French embassy in Aden. Bonnefous refused to consider it.

On July 3 he handed the Somali ambassador the fourteen points raised by the Israeli delegation in Paris with regard to the means by which such an exchange might be effected. He had the impression he could obtain a further delay and that he could, in the end, reduce the terrorists' demands.

On July 4 at 1:10 A.M. Brossolette was awakened by a telephone call from Sauvagnargues informing him of the Israeli raid, but he decided not to call Giscard, who was spending the weekend at his family home in Authon. When the Israeli ambassador in turn called him to transmit a message from Rabin to the French president, he told him to drop it off at the entrance to the Élysée Palace, where the official on duty would find it first thing in the morning. At 8:30 Brossolette finally telephoned Château d'Authon, but Giscard was out walking his dogs. He heard about the outcome of the drama over the radio. Shocked that he had not been kept abreast of the operation, he instructed the Élysée to issue a communiqué expressing French satisfaction—but devoid of any word of congratulations for Israel.

Israel couldn't have cared less. The triumphal return on July 4 raised its morale to its highest point. Less than three years after the Yom Kippur disaster, the Israelis were finally able to smile again. But their rejoicing after Operation Thunderbolt was nothing like the wild rejoicing that had followed the 1967 victory in the Six-Day War. This time it was mitigated by the bestial vengeance against Dora Bloch, a seventy-five-year-old passenger on the sky-jacked Airbus, who had been transferred to Mulago Hospital when she fell ill on the eve of the rescue. She had been torn from her bed on the following day by four Ugandan policemen in revenge for the failure of the blackmail attempt. The steps taken on her behalf by a British representative and the French cultural attaché in Kampala, who had been the last persons to see her in the early afternoon, were too feeble to prevent this horrible act of reprisal.

To Israel, Dora Bloch was more than a symbol. She had been born in Jaffa at the turn of the century, the daughter of Joseph Feinberg, one of the fourteen Russian pioneers who had come to Palestine in the vanguard of the first wave of Jewish immigration, and she and her family were part of the Israeli "Mayflower" legend, members of Jerusalem's Jewish elite. In her father's home—he had founded the village of Rishon-le-Zion—a Bohemian poet named Naphtali Herz Imber had composed the hymn of hope, that was to become Israel's national anthem, on her mother's piano. Theodor Herzl had danced with her mother on the terrace of the Kamenitz Hotel in Jaffa during his visit to Palestine with Kaiser Wilhelm II. And her father had been a staunch opponent of Herzl's "treason" when the author of *The Jewish State* had put before the 1903 Zionist Congress Colonial Secretary Joseph Chamberlain's offer after his return from the shores of Lake Victoria: "That might be a good country for Dr. Herzl."

The cruel and tragic irony of history: the old lady from Jerusalem, a cousin of Absalom Feinberg, a friend of the Aaronsohn family, a guiding spirit behind the Nili network, had met death in the country her father had rejected as a national homeland for the Jewish people—the country where her own son, Bertram, had worked as a construction engineer on the Entebbe airport!

However, Entebbe was also to be the graveyard of the bloodthirsty hopes of the "Dr. No" of the PFLP, Waddia Haddad.

At the beginning of May 1976, the Israeli services had alerted their Western counterparts of a new wave of attacks being prepared, particularly airplane skyjackings. Having been crushed by Falangist shelling in Lebanon, having been betrayed by their Syrian "brothers," the Palestinian movements had in fact just given the go-ahead to Dr. Haddad's extremist group.

On June 4 the Lebanese radio laconically announced the signing of a military agreement between the Palestine Liberation Organization and the Rejection Front, which was concerned, in particular, with the escalation of terrorist activities abroad. Haddad picked this moment to begin preparations for an operation whose scope would far surpass the usual skyjacking and taking of hostages. It would include implicating other governments in order to exert diplomatic pressure on Israel, involving states other than Arab states, out of reach of Israeli reprisals, and would achieve a strategic success that would act as a warning to "moderate" regimes and as an example to activist minorities.

In mid-June, Haddad called together his general staff in an Aden apartment. Seven of the twelve leaders of the organization participated in these working meetings—at which Haddad was always the last to arrive—which had been called to plan one spectacular operation. The following elements were discussed: the choice of victims, modus operandi, division of responsibilities, composition of units, logistical preparations, and other important details. Although for the past year their relationship had been marked by love-hate, and by many impulsive acts, Haddad had summoned the infamous Carlos from Tripoli, the man who six months previously had carried out the kidnapping of eleven oil ministers from the OPEC headquarters in Vienna, the symbol of the domination of the "moderate," oil-rich regimes over the rest of the Arab world. A twenty-seven-year-old Venezuelan, Carlos had donned a Che Guevara disguise on that occasion to polish up his image as an international terrorist star. Having been thrown out of Moscow for moral turpitude—a frequent alibi among spies who have come in from the cold—passing via East Berlin and Beirut, the usual path for infiltration into the Palestinian networks, he had succeeded Mohamed Boudia in July 1974 as the leader of a commando unit operating in Paris and controlled by one of Haddad's Lebanese adjutants, Michel Mukarbal. Among his other exploits, Carlos had organized the taking of hostages at the French embassy in The Hague, an attack on the Drugstore Saint-Germain in Paris (2 dead, 34 wounded), and two abortive attacks on El Al aircraft at Orly Airport. On June 27, 1975, he had gunned down Mukarbal along with the three French security police the Arab had been leading to one of his Parisian hideouts.

From Libya, Carlos had come to the secret meeting in Aden with two of his devoted followers: the Ecuadorian Antonio Dagues Bouvier, his acolyte in the London network, and the German Wilfried Boese, a left-wing publisher from Frankfurt who had been associated with the Baader-Meinhof gang, his accomplice in his last Paris attacks. Haddad entrusted Boese and Bouvier each with the command of a successive phase of the projected operation, since he was well aware of Carlos's inability to follow anyone else's orders.

The meetings were also attended by three of the top men in the Haddad group: Jael el-Ardja, who had recruited Carlos and Bouvier and was the second in command of the PFLP's external relations; Abd el-Razak, Haddad's representative in Germany; and Fayez Jaaber, the PFLP's head of military operations. They all took part in carrying out the plan Haddad submitted to them: to skyjack a large jet en route to Israel and divert it to Uganda, in the heart of Africa, where the fedayeen enjoyed official status and had a training center.

The choice fell on Air France, an airline that was considered immune from terrorist activity due to its government's "Mediterranean" policy. And the takeover was to occur in Athens, the ideal stopover because the resurgence of tourism following the return to power of a democratic government had eliminated any serious controls there, particularly in the transit areas. Haddad planned to set up headquarters for the operation in Somalia, from where he could be in close contact with the embassy in Kampala.

On June 20 the PFLP representative in Kuwait got the order to purchase two economy-class tickets to Paris via Bahrain and Athens, taking care to reserve two seats for Sunday, June 27, on Air France flight 139, Athens-Paris. He was to turn the tickets over to two young Palestinians recruited on the spot, Abu Ali and Abu Khaled. On June 25 Haddad had a long interview with a young German girl who he had decided would direct, along with Boese, the activities of the two young men: Ingrid Siepmann was perhaps not very well-balanced sexually, but she was a trained terrorist. Sentenced to twelve years in prison for her part in the murder of an appeals court district attorney in West Berlin, she had been released in April 1975 in exchange for Deputy Peter Lorenz, kidnapped by the Baader-Meinhof gang, and had been put on a plane for Aden. A member of Carlos's commando group in Vienna, she had shot down an Austrian guard in cold blood at OPEC headquarters. On June 26 the two Germans left Aden for Kuwait, where they purchased two first-class tickets to Paris via Bahrain and Athens. At 5:00 P.M. they took off along with the two young Palestinians, who were carrying two large boxes of dates labeled "Produce of Iraq," but which actually contained a supply of hand grenades and explosive charges. The four passengers each had 7.65 mm revolvers. They spent the entire night in the transit lounge of the new Bahrain airport: Flight SQ 763A of Singapore Airways was announced for 3:00 A.M.

During this time, Haddad had taken a Somali Airlines flight to Mogadishu at 12:10, and had arrived there at 4:30 P.M. Bouvier's group, which was to handle the hostages on their arrival in Uganda, had prudently taken the preceding flight.

On the next day, Sunday, June 27, the German couple and the two Palestinians disembarked separately at 7:00 in the transit section of the Athens airport. They were, of course, traveling with forged passports. At 10:45 they mingled with the 56 passengers holding yellow boarding cards who were entering the Airbus. The Air France plane had set down fifteen minutes late. As had been foreseen, there was no check on hand baggage, and no search at the exit from the transit area. From the observation level of the air terminal, another pair of Germans watched the passengers. Rolf Pohle, carrying a Peruvian passport, had been freed from prison in April 1975, in exchange for Deputy Peter Lorenz. Gabriela Tiedemann was the widow of a German terrorist who had been killed when his suitcase exploded on May 25 at Lod Airport. At 11:33 the plane took off. Eight minutes after takeoff, the 4 terrorists took over the Airbus and its 254 passengers. Boese gained control of the radio and directed the proceedings from the cockpit, forcing the captain to change course for Benghazi, in Libya. Ingrid Siepmann controlled the passengers and the cabin crew while the Arabs searched them. The plane refueled in Libya. After five and a half hours of flight, the Airbus landed at Entebbe, where another team of terrorists was waiting, brought in through Somalia from Aden. The hostages were confined in an unused terminal at the old airport.

On Haddad's demands were superimposed those of Carlos: after a round trip to Libya, he had, on his own initiative, demanded a ransom from the French embassy in Aden to make sure that he would get the money he wanted for himself: money that Haddad had refused to pay him. Probably without Haddad's knowledge, Carlos had this demand presented to the Somali ambassador by his friend Bouvier.

In the end, Israel's "Thunderbolt" was to put an end to all the blackmail and to the careers of three of the principal lieutenants in the most formidable of the Palestinian groups. Only Bouvier, who had spent the night of July 3 in Kampala, Carlos, en route alone between Aden and Tripoli, and Haddad, himself, safely out of danger in Mogadishu, were to escape death. But only temporarily. The discredited "mastermind" of Arab terrorism was to die of cancer on March 31, 1978, in an East Berlin hospital.

The mighty lesson of Entebbe served as a warning to governments supporting terrorism. Above all, however, it served as an example to the free world by demonstrating that it could free itself from the nightmare of air piracy, that modern form of barbarism. It contributed to the soul-searching that was to be translated into action for the first time in the United Nations Security Council, when the Arab-Communist bloc was unable to form a majority to condemn "Israel's flagrant aggression against Uganda's sovereignty." And, for the first time, the West reached an agreement on outlawing the perpetrators of international terrorism, over whom Abu Nidal, Arafat's sworn enemy controlled by the Iraqi services, henceforth took control.

Sixteen months after Entebbe, opposition to terrorism had been manifested on several occasions. It was demonstrated on October 18, 1977, in, ironically, Mogadishu itself, where the Somali authorities had assisted a West German commando unit in attacking a Lufthansa plane diverted there by 4 PFLP terrorists, and in freeing the 90 hostages.

In Larnaca, on February 19, 1978, the Cypriot National Guard tragically wiped out an Egyptian commando force that had flown in to free 11 hostages taken by 2 terrorists who had commandeered a plane after having assassinated the editor of the Cairo daily newspaper *Al Ahram,* Yussef Sebai, a close friend of Sadat.

At Orly on May 15, 1978, the French police had shot down 3 armed "Sons of South Lebanon" who had been preparing to massacre El Al passengers en route to Tel Aviv. Back in 1975, the same police had placed an airplane bound for Bagdad at the disposal of 3 of their predecessors in the Carlos network who had just wounded 20 persons in an attempt to destroy an El Al aircraft with rockets from the observation level at the same airport.

The refusal to give in to blackmail even spread to Italy, with the sacrifice of Aldo Moro, the leader of the Christian-Democratic party, kidnapped on March 19, 1978, and assassinated after a fifty-four-day martyrdom.

The Palestinian murderers at Larnaca had a precise political objective: they were attempting to disrupt the negotiating process in the Near East that had begun with Sadat's trip to Jerusalem.

19

ENCOUNTERS OF
ANOTHER KIND

"Allah Akbar!" Dressed in a business suit and surrounded by bodyguards, his face dripping with sweat and his eyes and hands lifted to the vaulted ceiling, the president of the Arab Republic of Egypt, Anwar Sadat, knelt at his devotions in Islam's third most holy place, El-Aqsa mosque in the heart of the Old City of Jerusalem. On their television screens, the entire world watched as the Egyptian president repeated the prayer for Id al-Adha, the Feast of Sacrifice, with an intense fervor.

"At El-Aqsa I prayed for peace!" he was later to say at the rostrum of the Knesset, standing beneath the portrait of Theodor Herzl.

The Jewish television viewer could not believe his eyes. And certainly not those who, on that Sunday, November 20, 1977, could still hear in memory the clash of arms and the words spoken by this same head of state on April 25, 1972, in Cairo's El-Hussein mosque on the occasion of the Prophet's birthday:

> With the help of God, we will wrest Jerusalem from the hands of those of whom the Koran has said: "It is written that they shall be humiliated and poor. . . ." They talk of direct negotiation, but they were the Prophet's neighbors in Medina, they were his neighbors and he negotiated with them, and he reached an agreement with them. And, in the long run, they turned out to be men of deceit and of treason, for they concluded a treaty with his enemies to strike at him in Medina and to attack him from within. The greatest thing the Prophet did was to drive them out of the entire Arabian peninsula. . . . We will never hold direct negotiations with them. We know our history and theirs at the time of the Prophet. They are a nation of liars and traitors, of plotters, a people born for perfidious acts. . . .They will become again what the Koran has said of them: "Condemned to humiliation and poverty." On this, we will not give in. It is not only a question of liberating our country. . . . We will see them returned to their former state.

And, for his part, what did Dayan have to say about Nasser's successor? He made no attempt to conceal his contempt for this ridiculous Nile peasant with his little moustache, his grand speeches, and his threats, which Dayan could not bring himself to take seriously.

"Sadat," he said in his drawling voice during a military exercise, "Sadat isn't worth a single shell."

But in three days all that had changed. It took no more than a gesture from the landing steps of a plane on November 19 to bring about a miracle: the representative of the greatest Arab power had come solemnly to Jerusalem to meet with the representatives of the Jewish nation.

"It's greater than the first man on the moon!" exclaimed Hamdi Fuad, of *Al Ahram's* foreign desk, one of the Egyptian journalists present.

An American news agency paid $2,000 cash for the picture of Sadat's first step onto Israeli soil. A bearded policeman in a skullcap murmured the prayer for the first harvest. Emotion ran so high that witnesses to the scene thought they must be dreaming.

The charm was complete when the Egyptian president was presented to the political, military, and religious leaders of Israel, one by one, and gave the impression that he had known them forever. He had a friendly word for each one. Then, all misgivings finally laid aside, an insane hope gripped the country. For Israelis, it was like a tremendous shock, an earthquake as mighty as the surprise Yom Kippur attack in 1973.

It was an event without historical precedent, totally transcending political rationality. In a conflict basically founded in passions—"seventy percent psychological" as Sadat himself was to say—he had just broken through the wall of hatred built up between the two countries over the past thirty years. Hatred gone, it became possible to talk together. To talk, and to come to know each other.

The psychological wall crumbled like the Bar-Lev Line in October 1973. And an incredible peace offensive replaced the massive offensive of war. This turnabout was not brought about by any special concession; it was a revolution that occurred in men's minds.

"The pyramid is upside-down," said one of Dayan's close advisers. "We had hoped up to now, in our most optimistic dreams, that perhaps one day, after very lengthy negotiations, our efforts would be crowned by Arab recognition, translated into the handshake of a head of state. This gesture would have been the capstone of the structure. And exactly the opposite has occurred. Today everything is based on Sadat's handshake. All else must come later. We do not have the right to allow the pyramid to fall."

Indeed, the approach to the Middle East conflict had been changed by Sadat's double gamble of facing up to Israeli hopes and Arab suspicions. The surprise move had been announced only a few days before. But it was actually the outcome of a series of secret meetings in which, as always, the intelligence services had played their role.

At midnight on November 20, on the sixth floor of the King David Hotel, from where guests could look down on the walled splendor of the Holy City, American journalist Barbara Walters asked him, nervously, in the presence of the Israeli prime minister, "What do you think of Mr. Begin?"

Sadat replied, "Both President Jimmy Carter and Rumanian President Nicolae Ceausescu have told me about him, and yesterday in the car on the way from Lod to Jerusalem, President Ephraim Katzir spoke to me about him."

"You see, Barbara," Begin added, "three heads of state recommended me to President Sadat. And we are getting along very well."

Obviously, things had been more complicated than that: six messages and three secret meetings had paved the way for the Begin-Sadat meeting. And Begin had envisaged an equally secret tête-à-tête. In trumpeting the meeting to the world, Sadat had surprised everyone and had transformed the meeting to his advantage into a pilgrimage for peace.

It is possible, by consulting various European and American sources, including the revelations of former intelligence chief U.S. Air Force General George Keagan, to reconstruct the background to this decision.

It had all begun a year earlier, on October 9, 1976, when Israeli Prime Minister Itzhak Rabin had paid a secret visit to King Hassan II of Morocco. Since succeeding Golda Meir, Rabin had constantly sought an understanding with Egypt, which he saw as the key to any solution in the Middle East. He asked Hassan to lend his good offices to the attempt to arrange a secret meeting with the Egyptian president.

Rabin had addressed himself to the Moroccan sovereign because Hassan had long held that an Arab-Jewish understanding would be "the most successful combination in the world." During the 1960s, Hassan had suggested bringing Israel into the Arab League, and he had later invited various Israeli leaders to Morocco—men like Professor André Chouraqui, the writer Amos Kenan, and Rabbi Abu Hatzirah—in an effort to smooth Israeli-Arab relations.

According to an article in the magazine *Jeune Afrique,* Hassan had transmitted Rabin's proposal to Sadat, but the Egyptian president had given a negative response, feeling as he did that the Israeli government was too weakened by internal divisions after the trauma of the Yom Kippur War to embark on the necessary processes of negotiation. Sadat was still very much under the influence of Kissinger, whose opposition to direct contact between his "clients" was demonstrated by the sabotaging of the Israeli-Egyptian talks at Kilometer 101.

In the spring of 1977, however, two events occurred to alter the political facts: the Egyptian-Libyan conflict, and the Israeli elections.

In April Colonel Qaddafi, who had become the Soviets' new protégé in the region, made a deal with KGB agents stationed in Tripoli: in exchange for the transit facilities the USSR requested for shipping arms and Cuban military personnel to Ethiopia and Angola, he asked the KGB's help in assassinating Sadat, whom he regarded as his Number One Enemy. He had already made several attempts. The main one had entailed his paying Carlos, the terrorist leader, the sum of £10 million to carry out the mission. In vain. In the last attempt, Qaddafi had even sent agents from his own services, but they had all been discovered and arrested by Egyptian security.

The KGB agreed to furnish instructors to train a joint commando group made up of Palestinian terrorists, Libyans, and foreigners, on a secret base to be set up in an oasis 35 kilometers from the Egyptian border. The commando leaders settled on the date of the anniversary of the Egyptian revolution—July 23—as D-Day for the attack plan drawn up at this base.

According to American sources, Israel learned of the Libyan plans at the end of May. Prime Minister Rabin was about to resign; on May 17 his coalition had lost the elections that had for the first time returned a right-wing majority to the Knesset. However, he was still tending to ongoing business because Begin, his designated successor, had not yet completed choices for his new government.

"What would you have done with this kind of intelligence in the past?" Begin asked.

"It is usually transmitted to the CIA for them to act on as they see fit."

"Why not tell Sadat directly what Qaddafi is planning against him and thereby show our goodwill?"

In May 1978 General Keagan admitted that "On two or three occasions, Israel had saved the life of President Sadat."

For the temporary Begin-Rabin team, the problem was now to find some way to get in touch with the Egyptian authorities directly. In the absence of any diplomatic relations between them, it was difficult to entrust an Israeli diplomat to make contact with the Egyptian ambassador in Paris, London, or Washington to inform him of such information.

According to some reports, the approach may have been made through the friendly ties that had developed between the delegates to the Atomic Energy Commission in Vienna, one of the rare privileged places where Israelis and Egyptians could meet. The former Egyptian delegate, who had very good relations with his Israeli colleagues on the Commission, Mohammed Hassan Tohami, had in the interval become the Egyptian deputy premier. In this post, he coordinated the Egyptian intelligence services, and he was also Sadat's special envoy for delicate missions.

At sixty years of age, Mohammed Hassan Tohami was one of the first "Free Officers" under Nasser's leadership who had overturned King Farouk's corrupt regime in July 1952. Once in power, Nasser had appointed him vice-premier, in charge of coordinating the secret services. A pious Moslem from a very wealthy family, Tohami was a member of the right wing of the Nasserian revolution. Around 1960, he had quarreled with Amin Huweidi, the head of the espionage center (the Mukhabarat), and Nasser had settled the dispute by firing both of them. Tohami was then sent to Vienna as delegate to the International Atomic Energy Commission. The episodic contacts he had had there with the Israeli representatives to this international agency now permitted the establishment of a tenuous liaison between the two countries' intelligence services when, in June 1977, the Israelis sought to pass their information concerning the Soviet-Libyan plot directly to Sadat.

In any event, the information arrived at Tohami's office in Cairo. At first the Egyptians had trouble believing in Israel's goodwill, but aerial reconnaissance across the frontier soon confirmed the existence of the secret training base Israel had reported in an oasis in the Libyan desert. On July 21 during Begin's first official visit to the United States, Egyptian General Gamasy ordered his troops across the frontier into Libyan territory. It was outright war and lasted for six days. On July 25 a helicopter-borne commando team took the oasis, 35 kilometers from the border, and wiped out the secret base where the KGB instructors had been training the terrorists. Two days later, the Egyptian forces crossed back over the frontier, their mission accomplished, and ceased firing as suddenly as they had begun. Egypt was later to admit that the purpose of the Six-Day War with Libya had been to destroy this base and to liquidate the terrorists. Meanwhile, having returned from his American trip, Begin had sent Sadat a third goodwill signal. From the rostrum of the Knesset, he publicly assured him that Tsahal would not attempt to take any advantage whatsoever in the Sinai because of the situation caused by the possible transfer of Egyptian forces from the Suez Canal to the Libyan front.

Sadat had received his second signal a few days earlier from President Carter. It was a pressing invitation to a secret summit meeting.

On August 25 the Israeli prime minister arrived in Bucharest on a five-day official visit to Rumania, the only country in the Soviet bloc having diplomatic and commercial relations with the Jewish State. His arrival coincided with the end of a visit by an Egyptian parliamentary delegation. Allowed to meet with the Jewish community, still consisting of some 70,000 Rumanian citizens, Begin then met in private on August 26 with President Nicolae Ceausescu. On the evening before, despite an incident that had occurred at table during the reciprocal toasts between Manea Manescu, the Rumanian prime minister, and his guest, a secret meeting had been set up between Begin and Sayed Merei, the president of the Egyptian Assembly. The two men talked about the possibility of a future secret summit. As a cover-up, however, a communiqué issued at the conclusion of the second interview between Ceausescu and Begin indicated that the Israeli-Rumanian talks had not brought about any change in the positions of Jerusalem or Bucharest on the conditions for reopening the Geneva conference on an overall settlement of the Israeli-Arab conflict.

A few weeks later a new Moroccan initiative made possible the setting up of a preliminary political meeting between Egypt and Israel.

On September 16 the new Israeli Foreign Minister, Moshe Dayan, who was on his way to the United States, stopped in Brussels for a meeting with NATO commander American General Alexander Haig, and to see the leaders of the Jewish community— one of the most active in Western Europe.

In the middle of the afternoon, Dayan's motorcade drew up to the Sabena plane on which he was to proceed to New York. Dayan and his wife Rachel boarded the plane. When the DC 8's jets began to whine, and just as the airport personnel were preparing to remove the landing steps, a man wearing a wide-brimmed hat to hide his face, dark glasses covering his eyes, appeared in the still-open door and hastily descended the steps, followed by two other unknown men. This strange trio got into a black Citroën DS that was still parked on the landing strip. The car sped off, driving a few hundred meters down the deserted runway. It came to a halt alongside a military plane with the insignia of the Moroccan Air Force. The man in the hat and dark glasses quickly got into the aircraft, and the plane took off with its civilian passenger, who was none other than Dayan himself. Destination: Tangier.

There he was met by the Egyptian deputy premier, Hassan Tohami, Sadat's special envoy, who had been invited by King Hassan. Tohami carried a positive reply from Sadat to Begin's proposal for a secret meeting. There was but one condition: an assurance to return all of the Sinai to Egyptian sovereignty. Dayan agreed that this preliminary seemed acceptable, and he promised a quick reply from Begin.

From Tangier, Dayan took off for Paris and landed at Orly, to everyone's surprise. He retired to a room at the airport's Hilton hotel to get some rest while awaiting the first plane for Tel Aviv, where he showed up unexpectedly on September 17. The next day, he actually took off for New York, where his wife Rachel was waiting for him, but he made a stopover in Zurich to give the Egyptians Begin's positive reply regarding the return of the Sinai to Egyptian sovereignty.

The CIA figured out the mystery behind Dayan's disappearance at his Brussels stop, but it thought the one-eyed general had been spirited to Tangier to see King Hassan II. It was unaware of the contact with Tohami, who was the number-two man in the Egyptian government.

The United States, kept totally in the dark about this meeting and the results of Dayan's airborne adventures, intensified its diplomatic efforts toward a reconvening of the Geneva Conference, suspended since its inaugural session in December 1973. On October 1, 1977, it signed with the USSR, its co-chairman at the conference tentatively set to reopen in December, a joint declaration on the bases for an overall settlement which was made public simultaneously in Moscow and in Washington.

The American-Jewish community reacted violently against this American-Soviet *rapprochement* in the Middle East. Senators and congressmen spoke out against the "unbelievable concession" their government was making to the USSR, which the joint statement appeared to restore to its status as arbiter; a status that Kissinger's step-by-step diplomacy had denied it and one that the moderate Arab governments, primarily Egypt and Saudi Arabia, no longer wanted it to have. Now a determined adversary of Soviet presence in the region, Sadat in fact feared that the Geneva Conference would allow Moscow to regain an influential role in the Near East.

Sadat was later to tell how the American-Soviet declaration had precipitated his decision. However, there was another event in October that also made him act urgently: a sudden, inexplicable military tension in the Sinai. On both sides, there were signs indicating that the commanders were expecting some surprise move. Troops were reinforced on both sides of the demilitarized zone in preparation for an initiative from the other side.

Chief of Staff "Motta" Gur was expecting some propaganda effort by Sadat analogous to the one in 1973, designed to lull Israeli vigilance. He was perplexed by the Egyptians' agreeing in principle to a secret meeting with Begin, of which he had been informed by the cabinet. He therefore preferred to take the maximum military precautions. Thus there was an increase in tension: one that went unnoticed by foreign governments and by the media, but one that made both general staffs of the armies massed on the border—one at the Canal, the other in the hills—extremely nervous.

This would explain Sadat's words to General Gur when he met him on November 19 on the tarmac at Ben-Gurion Airport: "You see, it wasn't a bluff . . ."

Another secret meeting, however, had to be called in mid-October between Tohami and one of Begin's envoys in order to resolve this tension, which had almost brought the two countries to the brink of war—and barely a month before their first reconciliation!

The Israeli-Egyptian front was completely calm, however, when Sadat in turn arrived in Bucharest on an official visit on October 29. There, he found another message Begin had secretly sent: the seventh since the formation of his government. Sadat decided that such persistence deserved testing—especially since disquieting news from Lebanon was making him fearful of Syrian provocation south of the Litani River, Israel's "red line." One not to be crossed. An Israeli-Syrian clash would risk involving Egypt in a show of military solidarity—a risk that he wanted to avoid at all costs.

On October 31 in his plane on the way from Bucharest to Teheran on the first leg of a grand tour of the Middle East, Sadat read an open letter from Abie Nathan, an Israeli famous for his spectacular acts and daring courage, and for his independent thinking: Nathan, nicknamed "The Pilot of Peace" for having dared land his small plane at Port Said with a bouquet of flowers for Nasser, ran a pirate radio station at sea called "The Voice of Peace." In his letter, Nathan suggested an exchange between the two countries of professional visits by Egyptian and Israeli journalists.

Sadat was later to tell one of the Egyptian journalists accompanying him to Jerusalem that this proposal had finally tipped the scales.

"Why only journalists?" he had wondered. "Why can't I myself make a spectacular visit there?"

Thus, on the flight from Bucharest to Teheran, Sadat conceived the notion of transforming his secret meeting with Begin, to which he had agreed in principle, into an official visit to Israel.

Upon returning to Cairo on November 9, and without having consulted anyone on his tour of the Arab world, Sadat dropped his bombshell in the Egyptian National Assembly:

"To protect the life of one single soldier, I am ready to go to the ends of the earth—even to Jerusalem!"

Surprised at the twist the Egyptian president had given his plan for a meeting, Begin quickly responded with a public invitation. However, the Israeli security services stepped up their precautions. The unbelievable initiative taken by Sadat was viewed with suspicion right up until the moment when he appeared in the doorway of his plane on November 19, at the close of the Sabbath.

As all of Israel's past and present leaders lined up along the red carpet laid out at the foot of the landing steps, elite sharpshooters discreetly occupied positions on the roofs of buildings at Ben-Gurion Airport. The men responsible for Israel's security were able to breathe freely again only when they saw with their own eyes Sadat standing in the doorway of the Boeing 01 with the Arab Republic of Egypt's colors.

Forty-eight hours later, the Egyptian President stood once again on the stairs leading to his Boeing. Menachem Begin shook his hand firmly. "Believe me, Mister President," he said, "we shall make peace." Sadat nodding his head in agreement, replied, "For sure, for sure."

Nevertheless, it took sixteen months before Begin and Sadat could meet again on the lawn of the White House in Washington to sign the Peace Treaty. "Those sixteen months were the most difficult months of my life," Begin said. One of the Israeli negotiators said, "While most of the time odds were highly in favor of a positive conclusion of the Treaty, there were at least three dangerous moments during the negotiations when we came very close to a total collapse of the talks." Three dangerous moments, but also three missed opportunities to conclude the talks at an earlier date. All resulted from misunderstandings, mistrust, and failure to understand the other party's position and limitations. Above all were the internal and external obstacles which both Sadat and Begin had to face and painstakingly resist. "Sadat replaced three foreign ministers during that period," said an American diplomat, "while Begin had to face three difficult and painful confrontations with people who were his close friends, followers, and comrades of the resistance and the political desert."

The role of the U.S. in the peace process also became the subject of internal conflict in Israel. Moshe Dayan, who played a major role in the clandestine talks with the Egyptians preceding Sadat's visit to Jerusalem, consistently defended an active American involvement in the negotiations, while Cabinet members like Ezer Weizmann, Minister of Defense, and the hawkish Arik Sharon, Minister of Agriculture, supported the idea of direct negotiations with Egypt with a minimal American involvement and presence. After his lengthy night meeting with Carter in Washington in the early part of October 1977, a meeting that the Israeli Minister of Foreign Affairs described as "brutal," Dayan gained the impression that the American President was ready to put all the weight of the presidency behind the effort to reach an agreement between Israel and the Arab countries. Dayan believed that only an active presidential participation in the process could squeeze out of both parties the necessary mutual concessions.

But the U.S., genuinely surprised by the dramatic decision of President Sadat to go to Jerusalem, was slow to react. It took several days before the White House came out with a declaration of support for the Egyptian initiative. It is widely believed that those few but important days of indecision made it difficult and later impossible for Jordan to join in the talks.

In the middle of December 1977, Begin, convinced by Dayan's reasoning, flew unexpectedly to Washington to present President Carter with the Israeli Peace Plan. In Cairo, where the preliminary talks between the Israelis and Egyptians had just started, in the sumptuous dining room of the Mena House overlooking the pyramids, Egyptian officials did not hide their dismay. A few days later, in Ismailia, where Sadat and Begin held their 1977 Christmas meeting, an Egyptian official exploded: "Why conclude things with Israel if we have to confirm everything with the U.S. anyway?"

In the colonial-style buildings of the Suez Canal Authority, where the two leaders met in December 1977, the atmosphere was cordial. In front of several hundred journalists from all over the world, a smiling Sadat took the driver's seat of an elegant black sedan and drove his guest, Menachem Begin, through the red bougainvillaea alleys and along the sleepy esplanade of the Suez Canal. But, in spite of the congenial atmosphere, the meeting did not produce results. The two leaders failed to proclaim a six-point declaration of principles, of which five had been nearly accepted by both presidents. A last-minute effort by Begin and Dayan almost succeeded, but the Egyptian Foreign Office officials finally convinced Sadat to reject the Israeli compromise. Dayan claimed several months later that in Ismailia the Egyptians had insisted on a clear declaration in favor of a Palestinian State. It is also possible that an early Egyptian-Israeli agreement could have been concluded in Ismailia on the basis of a compromise formula accepted by Sadat during his brief January 1978 meeting in Aswan with President Carter. This proposal was almost adopted nine months later in the Camp David agreement. The Aswan formula recognized the "right of the Palestinians to participate in the determination of their future."

The Ismailia deadlock was considered by Sadat to be a personal failure. He also deplored what he considered to be the absence of an appropriate Israeli gesture in response to his trip to Jerusalem. On January 18, 1978 he recalled his delegation from the political talks that opened in Jerusalem under the chairmanship of Cyrus Vance, thereby nearly suspending the negotiating process.

On March 30, 1978, the process seemed to regain some momentum. In the Winter Palace of President Sadat, not far from the Russian-built Aswan Dam, he met with Ezer Weizmann. The two men spent several hours reviewing problems and chatting in a relaxed atmosphere. It was the fifth meeting between the Egyptian President and the "enfant terrible" of Israeli politics. Butrus Butrus Ghalli, Egypt's Minister of State for Foreign Affairs, gave a vivid description of the special relationship that developed between Sadat, several other Egyptian leaders, and Ezer Weizmann. "A positive chemistry developed immediately between President Sadat and Weizmann. He is a very pleasant man, an extrovert. He understands the Arab dimension of Egypt. His star is rising and he might even become Begin's successor. We feel much more at ease with Weizmann than with Dayan or Begin." During the three-hour conversation with Weizmann in Aswan, Sadat made several important concessions that could have made an agreement possible. But the next day, while Weizmann was still reporting on the results of his talks to Prime Minister Begin, a message transmitted through the American ambassador in Tel Aviv containing last-minute amendments asked by Sadat gave several Israeli Cabinet members the opportunity to discredit Weizmann's mission altogether.

A few months later, in mid-July, General Gamasy, Egypt's Minister of Defense, called Weizmann on the "hot line" which linked their two offices. "Ezer, it is the last chance!" Gamasy's voice sounded semi-official. "President Sadat is ready to meet with you in Salzburg." With the Cabinet's consent, Weizmann met with Sadat in the ornate castle of Fuschl in Salzburg, where the Egyptian President, a close friend of Austrian Chancellor Kreisky, was spending a short vacation. The meeting was in fact initiated by an Austrian industrialist, Karl Cahana, a millionaire Socialist and friend of Chancellor Kreisky. Cahana was also on good terms with Weizmann, having conducted business with the Israeli aircraft industry, and with Egypt's Sadat, for whom he had provided contacts with European Socialist leaders.

Weizmann returned from Fuschl Castle with the recommendation that the Israeli Cabinet approve a quick return of Al Arish, the Sinai capital, to Egyptian sovereignty as a special good-will gesture to Sadat. Weizmann's impression, as opposed to Dayan's, was that Egypt was now ready to sign a separate peace treaty with Israel as long as it would not be announced as such. Weizmann's aides were convinced that after the Salzburg meeting it would be possible to sign the peace treaty with Egypt at even better conditions for Israel than those which were obtained eight months later. But the adverse publicity in the press to the required concealment made Begin declare: "There will be no unilateral gestures."

A week later, Ibrahim Kamel, Egypt's Minister of Foreign Affairs, Cyrus Vance, and Moshe Dayan met at the British castle of Leeds. The castle, surrounded by hundreds of soldiers, and protected by unprecedented security measures, resembled a besieged fortress. Nothing leaked out of the conference room but the results were very meager. The Leeds Castle talks dramatically changed the U.S. role for the first time from one of honest broker to that of full partner.

In mid-August, President Carter held a series of meetings in the White House and at Camp David with a small group of close advisers: Secretary Vance, Zbigniew Brzezinski, and political adviser Hamilton Jordan, who played a major role in the shaping of Carter's Middle East strategy. It was Brzezinski's idea not only to convene the Camp David summit meeting but to keep all negotiators locked in until they reached an agreement. Brzezinski was reported to have said: "Put the pressure on Begin very hard, until he cracks." But Hamilton Jordan, who feared the possible damaging consequences of a Camp David summit failure on the President's chances for reelection, pleaded a more flexible approach. Jordan wanted to avoid a repetition of the March 1978 aborted anti-Begin campaign which resulted in an SOS cable from the U.S. Ambassador to Israel, Samuel Lewis: "News of a CIA plot to overthrow Begin only contributes to harden the Israeli position and get the Israelis united behind Begin." American Jewish leaders had also expressed concern over Carter's anti-Begin stand, and became even more disturbed by the news of White House adviser Mark Siegal's resignation on the grounds of what he perceived as a systematic anti-Israeli policy.

This time Jordan did not wish to have a head-on confrontation with the Israelis. The talks at Camp David started on September 5 in a relaxed atmosphere. "Habemus pacem [We bring you peace]," exclaimed a joyous Begin as he climbed out of the helicopter which landed on the small strip of the heavily guarded presidential retreat in the Catoctin Mountains.

The atmosphere of seclusion and the relaxed ambiance inside the camp—the joint meals in the dining room, the tennis, the billiards, the swimming pool, and the informal meetings at the morning jogging sessions—helped to create an intimate relationship between the representatives of the two parties. "A very pleasant prison," exclaimed Egyptian Minister of State for Foreign Affairs Butros Gali. But Gali insisted that, in spite of the inconveniences of a semi-military timetable ("If you weren't at the breakfast table by 9:00—no food"), the success of the Camp David meeting lay in the thirteen days of secrecy and "in the personal involvement of President Carter in the smallest details. Once, when I expressed my surprise at the intimate knowledge that President Carter showed of the Sinai, where he could locate and name all the settlements, the President told me that he had maps of the Sinai in each of his four official residences so that he could follow the events at all times."

In spite of the relaxed atmosphere (including the almost unbelievable—Begin in a stiff, starched but open-necked shirt!), a crisis seemed inevitable on September 5, the morning after the arrival of the two delegations at the Camp. "As soon as we received the document containing the Egyptian proposals," said an Israeli negotiator, "Begin called a meeting of the Israeli delegation and everybody present had the feeling that the conference was doomed to fail." "We nearly packed our suitcases and made ready to leave," recalled another Israeli negotiator, who considered the fifth of September to be, at least from the Israeli point of view, the most difficult and dangerous day of the sixteen months of negotiations.

American observers believed that Israel had made several mistakes during the negotiation process simply because the Israelis misjudged the Egyptian negotiating method. "From the very beginning it became clear that Sadat had definitely abandoned the path of war," said a senior American diplomat, "and that he was negotiating the best terms he could get." Several times during the talks, as on the first day at Camp David, the Egyptians brought up proposals as if they were just starting the negotiations at that moment. This created total confusion on the Israeli side and added weight to the arguments of those Israeli leaders who claimed that Sadat was playing a strategic game of deception on a world-wide scale. The Israeli Chief of Staff, Mordechai ("Motta") Gur, and the Chief of Military Intelligence, General Shlomo Gazit, both held that view. Twenty-four hours before Sadat's arrival in Jerusalem, Gur requested that Yigael Yadin, Deputy Prime Minister, who filled in as Minister of Defense for Ezer Weizmann while he was hospitalized from a car accident, approve a partial mobilization of reserve troops against a possible Egyptian "Kippur-style" surprise. From his sick bed in the hospital, Weizmann succeeded in defusing what would have been a tension-triggering bomb.

Suspicions and mistrust on both sides certainly prevented a more rapid conclusion of the agreement which was, at that time, technically feasible. On at least one occasion a lack of sensitivity on the U.S. side prevented the agreement from being concluded by as early as December 17, 1978. As the Tel Aviv-based U.S. Ambassador Lewis said, "We made a mistake in December when we tried to convey to the parties a sense of urgency that was lacking on both the Israeli and the Egyptian side, because it was interpreted as an unfair pressure."

On September 16, it was Egypt's turn to play the "pack and leave" game. On the evening of the fifteenth, most of the Egyptian delegation members at Camp David were passionately following the televised prize fight between Mohammad Ali and Leon Spinks, directly transmitted from New Orleans. In the middle of the match Sadat convened a small group of close advisers, telling them of his decision to create an atmosphere of crisis. The next morning, Saturday, official rest day for the Israeli delegation, Sadat asked the Camp commander to provide a helicopter for his immediate departure. Soon afterward Carter asked Sadat to change his decision. Meanwhile, the Camp Marines' commander delayed the arrival of the helicopter "on technical grounds." Ezer Weizmann, who was also alerted by the news, called Sadat on the house phone and asked to see him immediately. "Don't make a hasty decision," he said during their meeting at Sadat's cabin, "we'll find a solution." The major stumbling block at that moment was Egypt's request that Israel accept the total evacuation of all Israeli settlements in the Sinai as a condition for the conclusion of a peace treaty. Until then Begin had hoped that Sadat would allow the Israeli settlements to remain in the Sinai under Egyptian sovereignty but with a special status. On Saturday night, after lengthy discussions with several members of the Israeli delegation, Begin accepted the total evacuation of the Sinai, but not before he called General Arik Sharon, his Minister of Agriculture, to get his advice. "If there is no other choice," said Sharon, "it's O.K. with me."

Though the breakthrough was finally achieved, it took another last-minute crisis before the three leaders could meet in the White House to sign the agreement. Three hours before the signing, Vance delivered to Begin the text of a letter from Carter in which the U.S. expressed, after a strong Saudi request, a desire for the return of East Jerusalem to Arab sovereignty. Begin, however, refused to sign the agreement until the letter was withdrawn. A last-minute change left the problem of Jerusalem open and saved the Egyptian-Israeli accord.

After thirteen days of hectic negotiations and twenty-three drafts, the Camp David framework agreements contained important concessions by both parties. Israel accepted the total evacuation of the entire Sinai peninsula, the dismantling of Israeli settlements there, and the evacuation of three important air bases. Israel agreed, for the first time in a written document, to recognize the existence of a Palestinian people and the right of the Palestinians to participate in the determination of their political future. The autonomy plan for the West Bank and Gaza, initially proposed by Begin, had acquired in the Camp David agreement the status of a temporary arrangement pending the overall solution of the Palestinian problem.

The Egyptians accepted a full normalization of their relations with Israel, including open borders and the exchange of ambassadors within less than a year. This was something which nobody had thought possible two years earlier. Moreover, in spite of the connection between the Israeli-Egyptian peace agreement and the problem of autonomy for the West Bank and the Gaza area, it was clearly understood that the Egyptians would accept, at least in the first stage, a separate peace treaty with Israel. Only two months earlier, after the talks with the Egyptians at Leeds Castle, Israeli Foreign Minister Moshe Dayan considered it impossible that Egypt would sign a separate peace treaty.

On the night of September 17, the date of the Camp David agreement, a lunar eclipse was observed in the Middle East, where eclipses are still considered to announce heavenly messages. For President Sadat, who reportedly consults with astrologists, the moon eclipse might have been considered a good omen. It is also interesting that, on March 13, the day that President Carter made the announcement at the Cairo airport of a peace agreement between Israel and Egypt, another lunar eclipse occurred. That same date of March 13 had also been marked several months ahead on the White House calendar as the target date for the signing of an Egyptian-Israeli peace. . . .

On December 17, 1978, the date by which, according to the Camp David agreement, the detailed Peace Treaty between Israel and Egypt should have been signed, the U.S. diplomatic efforts had reached a dead end. In spite of tremendous personal efforts by President Carter, he had failed to close what he called "the disgustingly narrow gap" between the two parties. On the evening of the seventeenth, it suddenly became clear why the White House attached such an urgency to the conclusion of the treaty by that date. In simultaneous declarations in Washington and Peking, the U.S. and the People's Republic of China announced the complete normalization of their relations.

At the end of December, at one of the White House Friday-morning breakfast meetings, Brzezinski asked to let the Middle East "cool off" for a while. The Saudis were pressing hard against the conclusion of an Israeli-Egyptian agreement. In Iran, the position of the Shah had become desperate. Brzezinski also said that in the coming two months two major foreign policy subjects should take priority over the Middle East: U.S. relations with China and the still-evasive SALT agreement. He proposed to wait until the end of February before resuming the talks, which would end according to the plan in a second Camp David-style summit meeting in Washington toward the middle of March. The target date set for the signature of the Egyptian-Israeli Peace Treaty was March 13, a day not only marked for a lunar eclipse, but also a day of great significance in the Jewish calendar. It was the day of Purim, or Pour ("fate" in Hebrew), the Jewish Mardi Gras, a day of carnival in celebration of a 2300-year-old miraculous salvation of Persian Jewry from a threat of physical extermination.

At first it all seemed to move according to the White House

plan. Toward the third week of February 1979, the second Camp David talks started among Secretary of State Cyrus Vance, Moshe Dayan, and Egypt's Prime Minister and newly appointed Minister for Foreign Affairs, Mahmoud Khalil. Toward the end of the month, however, the talks were already in a deadlock. The Americans discovered that Dayan did not enjoy the support of his colleagues in the Israeli Cabinet and that most of his proposals and recommendations were rejected. President Carter decided to move ahead to phase three: the tripartite summit meeting in Washington. Then still another obstacle prevented the scenario from unfolding according to the original script. President Sadat refused to come to Washington and Prime Minister Begin refused to attend the summit with Khalil. On March 3, 1979 Carter met with his top five aides: Vice-President Mondale, Secretary of State Vance, NSC Adviser Brzezinski, political adviser Hamilton Jordan, and White House spokesman Jody Powell. The meetings were also attended by public relations adviser Gerald Rafshoon and Special Adviser for Jewish Affairs, Ed Sanders. The President informed the group of his decision to depart immediately for Cairo and Jerusalem to conclude the negotiations and press the parties into signing the Peace Treaty. Both Mondale and Powell expressed concern, emphasizing the possible negative repercussions of a failure on Carter's image. But Hamilton Jordan supported Carter's decision, insisting that only a major move, like the Presidential trip, could bring the two Middle East leaders to a final compromise. Jordan also believed that the drama of a Presidential visit to the area and the victorious announcement of a peace treaty could provide a badly needed success on the home front where the President's popularity had dropped to an all-time low. In consultation with leaders of Congress prior to the announcement of his Middle East trip, the President received an almost unprecedented blank check to commit the U.S. to financial assistance as well as to military presence in the Middle East. When Carter left for his first stop, Cairo, the only important stumbling block was the question of an Egyptian request for observers in the Israeli-controlled Gaza strip. When Carter arrived in Jerusalem on Saturday night, March 10, he already knew that Sadat would not break the agreement because of that one point. Nevertheless, his first meeting with Begin that same night started on a bad note. Begin insisted on having the Knesset approve the Treaty before he signed it, thereby defeating Carter's hopes to bring the two leaders together for a signing ceremony in Jerusalem on March 13. On Monday, March 12, prospects did not look good. This time it was Carter's turn, acting on

Brzezinski's advice, to play the "pack and leave" game. At 12:00 P.M. as Carter stood at the Knesset rostrum, Dayan quietly left to join Vance in the VIP gallery and suggest another try at a solution. After three hours of deliberations, they arrived at a compromise. The agreement did not mention the special status of Egypt in Gaza, but the Egyptians maintained the right, strengthened by an American commitment, to bring up the subject of Egyptian observers in Gaza when the talks for the implementation of the autonomy plan were to start.

The agreement was now safe. On March 26, the first Peace Treaty between Israel and an Arab state was signed in a media-crowded ceremony on the north lawn of the White House. A week later, when a group of Egyptian dancers performed on the lawn of the Royal Palace of Kobbeh in Cairo, the radiant Begin seated next to Sadat, an Israeli journalist remarked, "Last week on the lawn of the White House a piece of paper was signed. Today, on the lawn of Kobbeh Palace, peace is being made."

*   *   *   *

Over the past thirty years, the Israeli secret services had become used to the unusual role successive governments had obliged them to play in arranging brief encounters of another kind with Arab leaders. Up until now, however, the series of planned clandestine meetings and furtive rendezvouses that had marked the long path paved with hope had resulted in many stillborn dreams and missed opportunities.

Many of these carefully arranged contacts had been canceled at the last minute. In at least two cases, they had been destroyed by some shocking act of Palestinian terrorism. According to its former head, Meir Amit, the Mossad had often assisted in organizing such surprising encounters. Whether in a black Mercedes near the Gulf of Eilat, in some anonymous apartment in London or New York, or in a luxurious Hong Kong restaurant or a palace in Tangier.

A partial list of such attempts gives sufficient evidence of the huge effort devoted to this purpose for over thirty years, from both Golda Meir's and Dayan's secret meetings with Abdullah, in the years 1948-1949,* to the conflicting views exchanged in Paris between left-wing Israelis and moderate PLO Palestinians in 1976-1977.

In August 1952 Ben-Gurion himself had sent a message of congratulations to Neguib after Neguib had seized power in Cairo with Nasser's help. Yigal Allon, who in 1949 had negotiated the

---

* See Chapter VI, "Birth of a Nation."

surrender of the Faluja pocket in the Negev, with a certain Major Gamal Abdel Nasser, later attempted to get in touch with Nasser when he in turn succeeded Naguib. Such attempts did not go beyond a private and indirect correspondence, but in April 1954, Prime Minister Moshe Sharett proposed a high-level meeting through the intermediary of the ambassadors in Paris and Washington, in an effort to control border incidents. Plans were drawn up by Israel's minister plenipotentiary in Washington, Reuven Shiloakh, ex-head of the Mossad; the American chargé d'affaires in Tel Aviv, Francis Russell; and U.S. Ambassador in Cairo, Jefferson Capri, for an "informal meeting" with the Egyptian Mahmoud Riad "over a cup of coffee." The Dulles brothers (John Foster at the State Department and Allen at the CIA) made efforts to avoid a new explosion. Israel's representatives in Paris, Dan Avni and Ziama Divon, maintained a liaison with the Egyptian military attaché in Paris, Colonel Saroit Okasha, who acted as a liaison between Sharett and Nasser in an attempt to prevent a worsening of relations caused by the discovery of the Zionist network in Cairo.*

At the beginning of 1955 a summit meeting was held at the CIA, attended by the new chief of the Israeli desk, Jim Angleton, where it was decided to propose to Nasser via Kermit Roosevelt, the number-one U.S. agent in Cairo, the settlement of two points: the return of a certain number of Palestinian refugees to Israel and indemnification of the others; and the construction of a road linking Egypt and Jordan, overpassing the road to Eilat. The second point did not please Nasser.

"And what if some day an Arab driver pisses off the bridge onto an Israeli car passing below—it would mean war," he said to Kermit Roosevelt.

Thus Nasser rejected the CIA proposal, which he called the "pee-pee plan," but he did agree to meet secretly with the Israeli emissary, General Yigael Yadin, who was pursuing his archaeological studies in London. On January 26, 1955, Mossad chief Isser Harel delivered Sharett's instructions to Yadin via diplomatic pouch. On the following day, however, the death sentence passed on the two leaders of the Cairo Zionist network compromised this initiative.

"If your friends in the CIA can stop their execution, we will continue," Sharett told Harel. "Otherwise, there will be no secret Nasser-Yadin meeting in the shadow of the gallows."

Already under criticism for his moderate views, Sharett was unable to pursue further contacts with Egypt. With the hangings in

* See Chapter VII, "A Dreyfus Affair in Israel."

Cairo, the attempt at an Israeli-Egyptian settlement became the invisible victim of the frivolity of the army's intelligence service when it provoked the scandal of the Lavon affair.

On March 11, 1955, after Ben-Gurion's return to the Defense Ministry—at once evidenced by a massive reprisal raid in Gaza and the death of 55 Egyptian soldiers—there was still a ray of hope in an urgent meeting of the Mixed Armistice Commission held at Nitzana in the Negev: Salah Gohar, the Egyptian delegate, and Joseph Tekoah, the Israeli delegate, agreed to renew contacts. However, a few weeks later, Nasser returned from the world conference of nonaligned countries in Bandung, crowned with glory as the new champion of the Third World, and broke off all contacts with Israel, dismissed as an outpost of Western imperialism. At Bandung, Chou En-lai had promised Nasser that he would intervene with the Soviets on his behalf to ensure the delivery of 200 MIG fighter planes, 28 Ilyushin bombers, 100 Stalin tanks, and 6 submarines, camouflaging these military supplies under the form of an Egyptian-Czech commercial treaty. The signing of this agreement on September 27, 1955, took the American government by surprise; misled, as it was, by CIA reports from Cairo.*

"A single word from the United States would have been enough to make Moscow draw back," Isser Harel was to say when he was sent to Washington by Ben-Gurion. "However, this word was not spoken. On the contrary, the impression was given that the United States was in favor of Soviet penetration. I can see only one explanation: the Americans have a pro-Arab complex. . . . And all this happened during a Republican administration, in the midst of McCarthyism and the witch-hunts, when a hysterical fear of communism was rampant in the United States, when America was determined to stop communist expansion throughout the world. Everywhere but in the Middle East."

Greatly annoyed by Israel's protestations, Eisenhower entrusted a final conciliation mission between Cairo and Tel Aviv to Robert Anderson, a Democratic businessman with influence in oil circles, whom he was later to appoint Undersecretary of Defense and then Secretary of the Treasury. Anderson arrived secretly in Cairo around mid-January 1956, and Kermit Roosevelt brought him together with Nasser. Still relying on U.S. financial support for his large-scale dam project at Aswan, Nasser said he was prepared to negotiate with Israel using Anderson as a go-between. On one condition: absolute secrecy.

---

* See Chapter VIII, "The Russians are Coming!"

Anderson avoided staying in hotels. He went to the presidential palace at Kubbeh only at night. And then he left for Athens, from where he took off for Tel Aviv with equal discretion, accompanied by Jim Angleton, who took him to a villa in Jerusalem that Ben-Gurion's wife, Paula, had borrowed from personal friends, the Rosenblums, for this purpose. Only six people in Israel were aware of Anderson's presence: Ben-Gurion, Moshe Sharett, Harel, Dayan, Herzog, and Teddy Kollek, director of the prime minister's office. Aryeh Dissentchik, the editor-in-chief of *Maariv,* and a friend of the Rosenblums, almost jeopardized the whole setup by dropping by the villa. Intrigued by the presence of security agents instead of the usual occupants, he pursued his investigation and finally uncovered the whole plot. He kept the secret for ten years!

Shortly after this action-packed visit, Isser Harel handed Jim Angleton the unpublished text of Khrushchev's report before the Twentieth Congress of the Soviet Communist party dealing with de-Stalinization.

Through Anderson, whose complicated, clandestine trips back and forth continued for two months, Ben-Gurion informed Nasser that he was prepared to meet him "anytime, anyplace, even in Cairo." However, the Egyptian president was unable to continue the double game he was playing between Moscow and Washington.

"I would have been ready to meet with Ben-Gurion, but I would have been assassinated an hour later," he finally told Anderson. Anderson went back to inform Ben-Gurion that his mission had failed.*

Since America refused to supply the weapons Israel was seeking to re-establish the balance of forces that had been compromised by Soviet-Czech assistance to Egypt, Ben-Gurion then turned to France and to the preventive Sinai campaign in October.

Anderson was to return to Egypt on two further secret missions: one for President Johnson in June 1967, in order to avoid a new outbreak of hostilities, and one for Nixon in April 1970 to arrive at a cease-fire on the Canal and to prevent direct Soviet intervention in the War of Attrition.

Until June 1967 a "hot-line" linked the Israeli and Jordanian delegations to the Mixed Armistice Commission, then separated by a few hundred meters in the heart of Jerusalem. The hot-line was established to limit destruction when frontier incidents occurred and to cut down on negligence among the United Nations observ-

---

* See Chapter VIII, "The Russians Are Coming!"

ers. When a delegate turned the crank on the little black apparatus in its leather case, the bell make a sound like a cricket's chirp. On the Jordanian side, it was often used by Commander Daoud (future prime minister during the Black September of 1970), who had maintained good relations since 1949 with his Israeli counterparts on the Mixed Commission. Meetings between the two delegations continued to take place on the second floor of a small building near the Mandelbaum Gate that then separated the two sectors of Jerusalem. Hung with the United Nations flag, the building had two entrances: one on the Jordanian side, the other in the Israeli sector.

It was over this little black telephone that an officer of the Tsahal general staff transmitted to his Jordanian opposite number, on June 5, 1967, at 8:00 A.M., Israel's recommendation to Jordan that it keep out of the war that had just broken out in the skies of Egypt and the Sinai desert. The recommendation was not heeded, and General Gur's paratroopers arrived in Jerusalem in strength. The following year, after the first massive fedayeen infiltrations across the Jordan and the costly reprisal raids against the Jordanian village of Karameh, where Yasser Arafat had set up his advance command headquarters, Israeli Defense Minister Moshe Dayan took part in three curious attempts to meet with the PLO leader.

On October 12, 1968, Dayan invited a Palestinian poetess from Nablus, Fadwa Tukan, to his villa in Zahala, north of Tel Aviv. The girl, whose fiery patriotism had greatly impressed Dayan, arrived with her uncle, Dr. Kadri Tukan, who was prepared to believe in the possibility of peaceful coexistence by reason of a comment attributed to Ben Gurion: "If we have to choose between the conquered territories and peace, I would prefer having peace to having the territories."

Fadwa turned to her uncle and said, "Kadri, go to see Gamal [Nasser] and urge him to sit down with the Israelis to negotiate for peace!"

Two months later, Dayan again met the poetess at the King David Hotel in Jerusalem. She told him that Nasser had disapproved of the meeting held with her uncle at Zahala. She had come away disillusioned and further convinced that even if the Israelis withdrew from the West Bank, Al Fatah would oppose any peaceful arrangement and would torpedo any agreement.

Dayan then told her that he had recently spoken to a fedayeen in Al Fatah who had been taken prisoner, and that he had offered him his freedom "to go and find Abu Amar [Yasser Arafat] and tell him I'd like to meet him." However, the prisoner had turned down his proposal. He preferred to stay in prison in Israel. According to Dayan's autobiography, Fadwa then told Dayan, "I'm only a woman, but I'm no coward, and I want peace. Nasser doesn't want to make peace with you. When I go to Beirut, I'll see Abu Amar and suggest that he meet with you. We must have peace."

Dayan does not know whether the poetess from Nablus went to see Arafat. He never heard from her again. This attempt would appear to have been less serious than the first. The third failed for other reasons. On this occasion, Dayan knocked on the wrong door: he picked another prisoner, Tayassir Kubeah, president of the Palestinian Student Association, to renew his offer. At the time of his arrest, Kubeah had been sent into Israel not by Al Fatah, but by its rival, the PFLP. And he was not at all eager to be mixed up in a Dayan-Arafat transaction in exchange for his freedom. At the conclusion of his prison term in 1970, he returned to Beirut, where he became a liaison agent between the PFLP and terrorist networks in Europe, before taking over from Dr. Waddia Haddad in March 1978.

Indeed, Dayan seemed less eager to work out some compromise with the Palestinian "resistance" leaders than in putting pressure by this means on King Hussein, in order to make him realize that without an agreement, he might have to deal with a Palestinian alternative.

World Jewish Congress President Nahum Goldmann's attempt to intercede with Nasser in April 1970 seems hardly more realistic. Invited by the Egyptian president, Golda Meir denied this progressive and trinational Zionist permission to speak on behalf of Israel. It may be that Nasser, despite massive Soviet aid, was still attempting to make a secret overture toward the West, and had been manipulated by the CIA to release a trial balloon with the Goldmann affair.

This feeler had been passed on by a Parisian painter, Marek Halter, a Polish Jew who, as a child, had escaped from the Warsaw ghetto and had been educated in the USSR with the youth groups of the Communist party. Along with some friends, he had founded a leftist international committee for a negotiated peace in the Near East in the aftermath of the Six-Day War, and he suggested to an Egyptian diplomat with whom he was acquainted that Nasser should invite some Israeli figure to meet with him. Perhaps Lova Eliav, who was then secretary-general of the Labor party, and who had taken an ultra-dovish stand in his committee's magazine, *Éléments.*

The following month (June 1970), Nasser evinced interest in the proposal, on condition that this time his invitation was kept secret and that his next guest would not be disavowed by the Israelis. Halter dashed off to Jerusalem, forced his way in to see Golda Meir, and in twenty-four hours had been given the green light for "Operation Eliav."

The emissary who had been chosen was no stranger to clandestine missions. A former artillery officer in the British forces in Libya, Eliav had been one of the first clandestine immigration agents sent into Italy by the Mossad at the end of the war. Aryeh (Lova) Eliav had commanded the perilous voyage of a ship that had left Sweden in February 1947 with 646 Jews from the camp at Ravensbruck—among them his future wife. In November 1956 disguised as a French officer, he had secretly disembarked from an Israeli warship off Port Said, then occupied by French paratroops, in order to save Jews assembled there in a synagogue. He planned to load them onto his ship and then to follow the French forces to Cairo, where he would free the prisoners of the Zionist network. When the Anglo-French expedition failed, however, he left with the Port Said Jews. In 1966 Eliav had headed a medical aid mission that had lent humanitarian assistance to the Kurdish rebels in Iraq.

Twice canceled by Nasser, who was caught up in the events of the summer of 1970 which projected him into the American orbit, Lova Eliav's mission never took place. Nasser's sudden death at the end of the Amman Black September brought Marek Halter's first initiative to an end.

The next year was really to be a year of lost opportunities. On February 4, 1971, Sadat announced that he was prepared to sign a peace treaty with Israel. Even if the conditions turned out to be unacceptable, Rabin, the ambassador to the United States, thought he should be taken up on his proposal. However, Sadat probably knew in advance that Golda Meir would veto the plan. The month before his initiative, Nathan Yalin-Mor, the former Lechi leader who had become one of the leaders in the Israeli peace movement, had been invited to an urgent meeting by Henri Curiel, a Communist Jew expelled from Egypt, in Curiel's Paris apartment with the editor-in-chief of the Cairo weekly *Roz el-Youssef*, Ahmad Hamrouche. A former intelligence colonel, Hamrouche was a militant Nasser left-winger.

Hamrouche informed Yalin-Mor, "Sadat suggests that Israel and Egypt quietly appoint middle-level representatives to examine possibilities for a peaceful settlement. If they can find sufficient basis for further discussion, then secret negotiations can follow at a higher level."

Upon his return, Yalin-Mor transmitted this message to Yigal Allon, the deputy prime minister, who brought him together with Zvi Zamir, the head of the Mossad. During a second interview, Zamir gave Yalin-Mor a negative reply. Golda Meir, who was very much on her guard, feared a trap by "leftists." She had never forgiven Hamrouche for having acted as a go-between for Nasser and Goldmann the year before.

Three months after this, according to George Keagan, Israel sent the Americans information on the anti-Sadat plot. Warned by Rogers, Sadat liquidated his left wing and determined to turn solidly toward the West and to rid himself of his Soviet advisers. Israel obviously had missed an opportunity to transmit its intelligence directly to Cairo, as Begin was to do with the Soviet-Libyan plot of June 1977.

And finally, in July 1971, Golda Meir asked the Rumanian Ceausescu to intervene with Sadat to set up a meeting. In October Kosygin was to act as the Rumanian president's envoy to Sadat, in the hopes of following through with the "Sprit of Tashkent," of which he was the creator. He therefore suggested setting up a secret meeting in that city. This time it was Sadat's turn to refuse. He didn't want to owe anything to the Soviets!

In May 1972, when Sadat decided to expel the Russian experts, Marek Halter went to see Dayan to suggest that he make some gesture such as restoring the Suez Canal to Egypt, in order to get the negotiating process under way. Dayan, who had always supported a certain flexibility in this area, encouraged him to speak to Golda. She replied, "As long as a man like Sadat says he is willing to sacrifice a million human lives, I cannot trust him. Can anyone really want peace if he doesn't respect human life?"

However, Golda did authorize Halter to sound out the Egyptians. His new initiative occurred in the midst of talks in Washington and New York arranged by Joseph Sisco between the two parties to arrive at an agreement for disengagement from the Canal. Furthermore, Kissinger had begun his process of mediation in the Middle East by meeting secretly with Sadat's adviser, Hafez Ismail, in the Connecticut home of Donald Kendall, the head of Pepsi-Cola. Nixon's adviser had even suggested to his interlocutor that they meet again later on at the same place when the situation permitted, with some Israeli representative like Minister for Foreign Affairs Abba Eban.

In August 1972 Halter met in Geneva with Murad Ghaleb, the new Egyptian Minister for Foreign Affairs. To back up his proposal, he referred him to the dozens of Sino-American meetings that had preceded the official recognition of the Peoples' Republic.

In this way, some practical methods of Israeli disengagement from the Canal might also be arrived at.

A first meeting in London between Ghaleb and Dayan was fixed for mid-September. However, the terrorist massacre at the Olympic Games in Munich compromised everything. Once again . . .

A year later, in September 1973, Kissinger received an encouraging message from Sadat suggesting an Israeli-Egyptian meeting. However, this positive move was only a part of the Egyptian propaganda campaign, and it was so successful that in the early hours of the Yom Kippur War, Kissinger was still wondering whether it wasn't an Israeli military initiative after all. This marked the end of the time of illusions.

But, according to George Keagan's revelations in June 1978, Israel discovered a second assassination attempt against Sadat, who had by then long since rid himself of his Soviet advisers. The miracle of the Egyptian president's visit to Jerusalem could come to pass.

The signing of the peace treaty between Israel and Egypt on March 26, 1979 was only the first step on the long and crisis-ridden road to an overall peace in the Middle East. President Sadat offered to the other Arab countries the use of El Arish, the Sinai capital with its palm trees and beautiful Mediterranean beaches, as the ideal site for future negotiations between them and Israel. He also added, "If they want secret talks, we can see to that too."

Considering the intense hostility declared by a majority of the Arab countries toward the Peace Treaty with Israel, the era of shadow diplomacy is far from over. Israel's untold history will not end tomorrow.

Kfar Shmaryahu-Neuchâtel-Paros-Washington-Cairo,
August 1976—April 1979

GLOSSARY

Aliyah to "rise up," "to ascend" to the Land of Israel; hence, "immigration."

Aliyah "B" clandestine immigration during the time of the Mandate, mainly of Jewish survivors of the Nazi concentration camps.

Aman the Israeli military intelligence branch.

Betar (*Brit Trumpeldor*) youth movement of Revisionist Zionist Movement founded by Jabotinsky.

Bilu the first settlers from Russia in 1882. The name is an acronym of Isaiah 2:5 "O, house of Jacob, come ye, and let us walk in the light of the Lord."

Biryonim a small group of activists, under the leadership of Achimeir, the theorist of the Revisionists, named after an extremist sect in antiquity.

Hachomer the guard units of the first self-defense militia in the early 20th century.

Haganah The Yishuv's self-defense forces; a semi-official workers' militia.

Herut the most important political group of the Likud, founded by Menachem Begin.

Histadrut the Israeli General Federation of Labor founded in 1921 with David Ben-Gurion as first Secretary General.

Irgun Zvai Leumi (*IZL, "Etsel"*) military cladestine group, headed by Menachem Begin (from 1942) with the aim of fighting the British and establishing an independent Jewish state.

The Jewish Agency the executive organization of the Zionist movement.

Likud the alignment of right-of-center political groups which came to power in 1977.

Mapai the Palestine Jewish Labor Party before it evolved into the present-day Labor Party. Since the early 1940s, the most important political group in Israel until the upset elections in 1977.

Mapam a left-wing Labor party.

Mossad "The Institution." The Israeli Central Agency for Intelligence.

Mukhabarat The Egyptian Central Agency for Intelligence.

Palmach (*Plougot Hamahatz* or shock troops) the striking force of the Haganah headed by Itzhak Sadeh.

Shay the Haganah's intelligence service.

Shin Bet (*Sherut Bitahon*)—the Israeli internal security service (equivalent of FBI).

Tsahal (*Tsva Haganah Le-Israel*)—an acronym for Israel Defense Forces.

Yishuv The Jewish community of Palestine before 1948.

Zionism The Jewish National Liberation Movement. The first Zionist Congress took place in Basel in 1897 under the leadership of Theodor Herzl.

Index